morning glories

volume four

truants

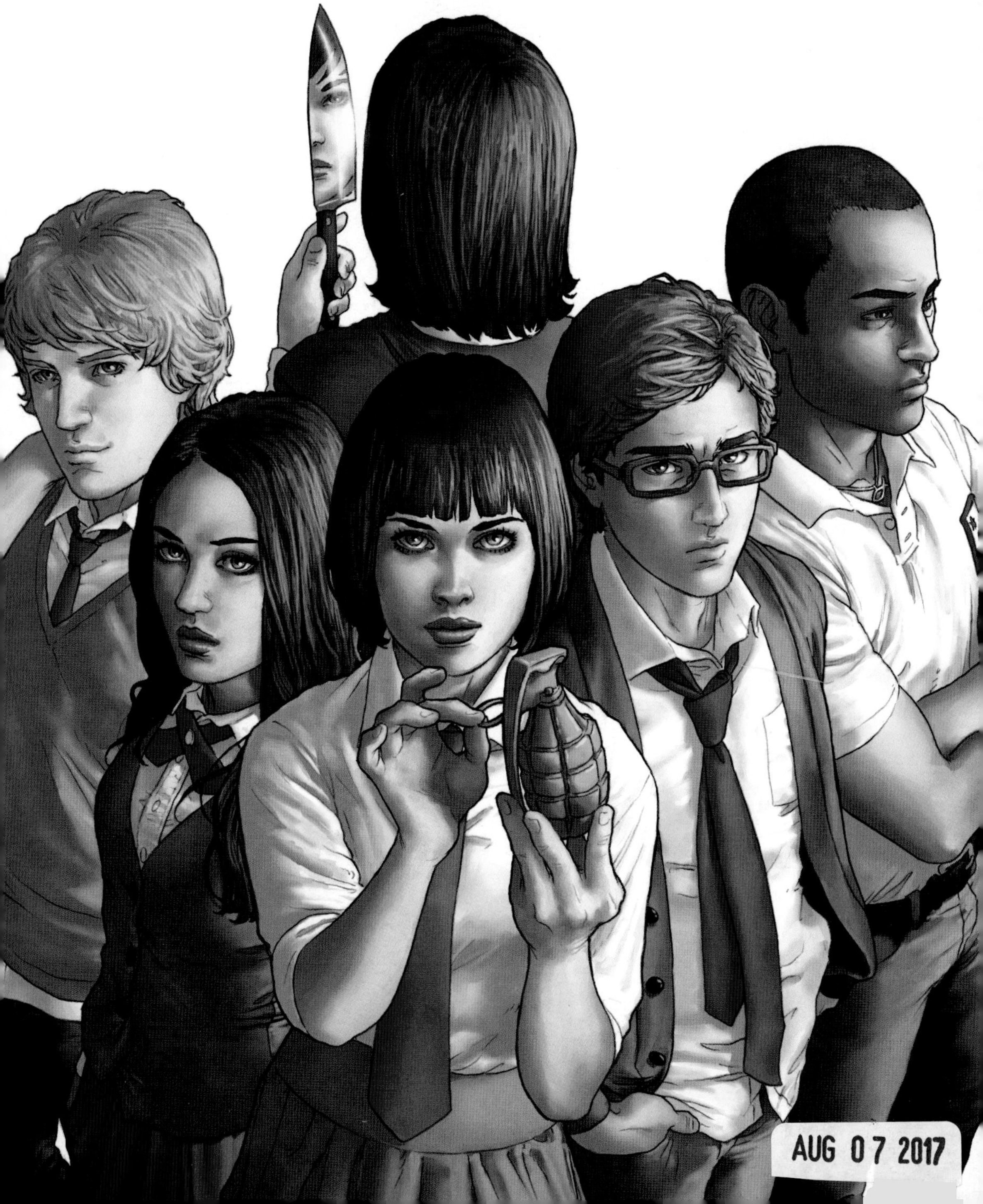

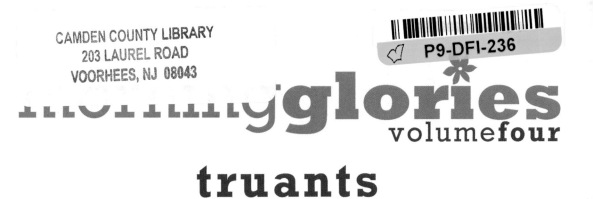

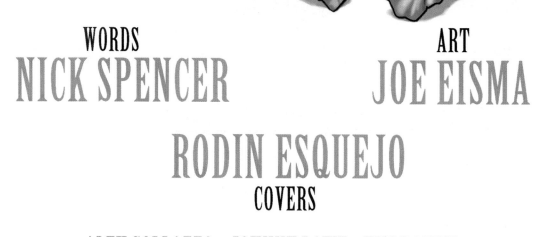

WORDS
NICK SPENCER

ART
JOE EISMA

RODIN ESQUEJO
COVERS

ALEX SOLLAZZO - JOHNNY LOWE - TIM DANIEL
COLORS   LETTERS   DESIGN

IMAGE COMICS, INC.
Robert Kirkman - chief operating officer
Erik Larsen - chief financial officer
Todd McFarlane - president
Marc Silvestri - chief executive officer
Jim Valentino - vice-president

Eric Stephenson - publisher
Ron Richards - director of business development
Jennifer de Guzman - pr & marketing director
Branwyn Bigglestone - accounts manager
Emily Miller - accounting assistant
Jamie Parreno - marketing assistant
Emilio Bautista - sales assistant
Susie Giroux - administrative assistant
Kevin Yuen - digital rights coordinator
Tyler Shainline - events coordinator
David Brothers - content manager
Jonathan Chan - production manager
Drew Gill - art director
Jana Cook - print manager
Monica Garcia - senior production artist
Vincent Kukua - production artist
Jenna Savage - production artist
www.imagecomics.com

twenty

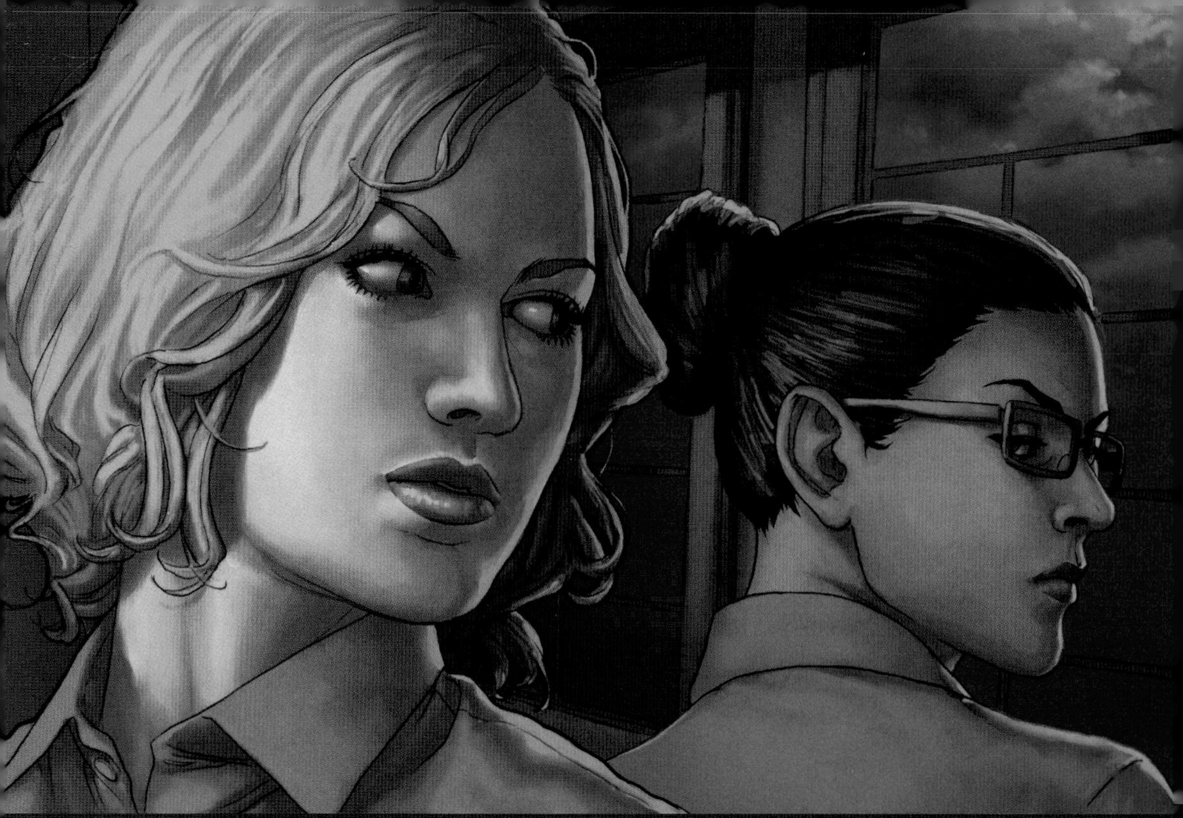

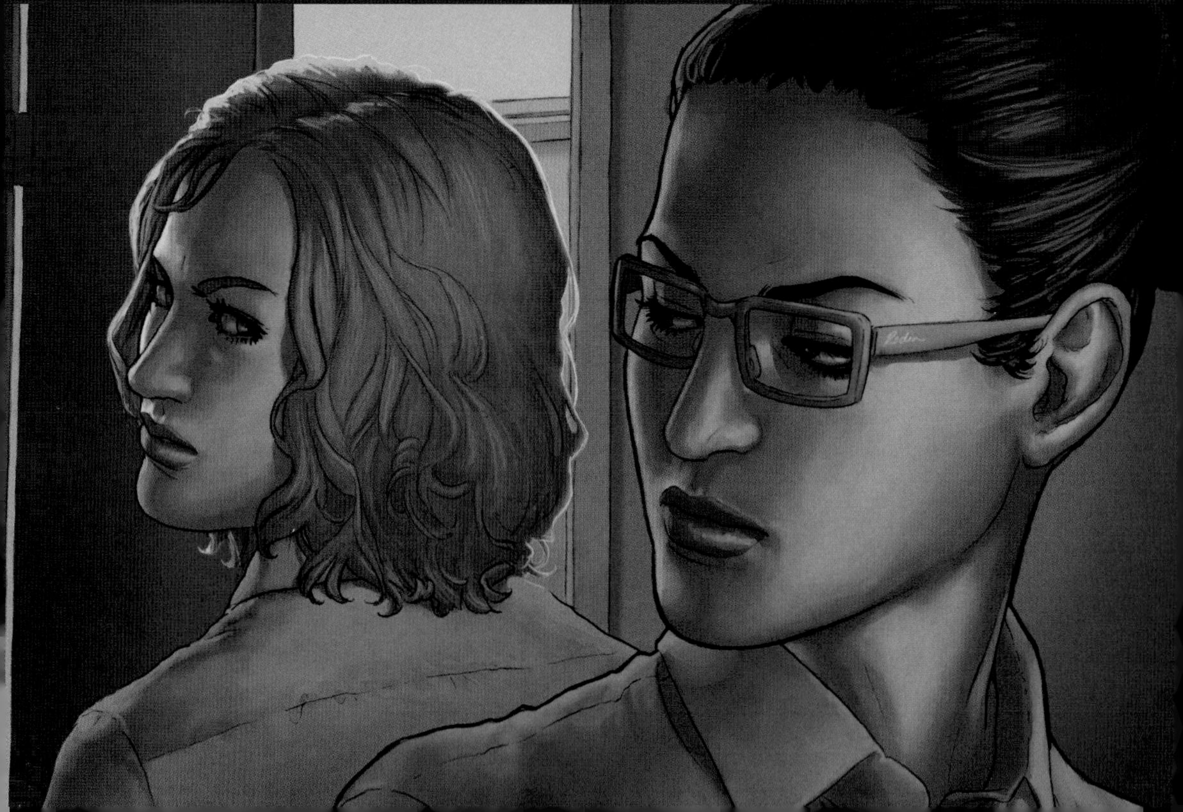

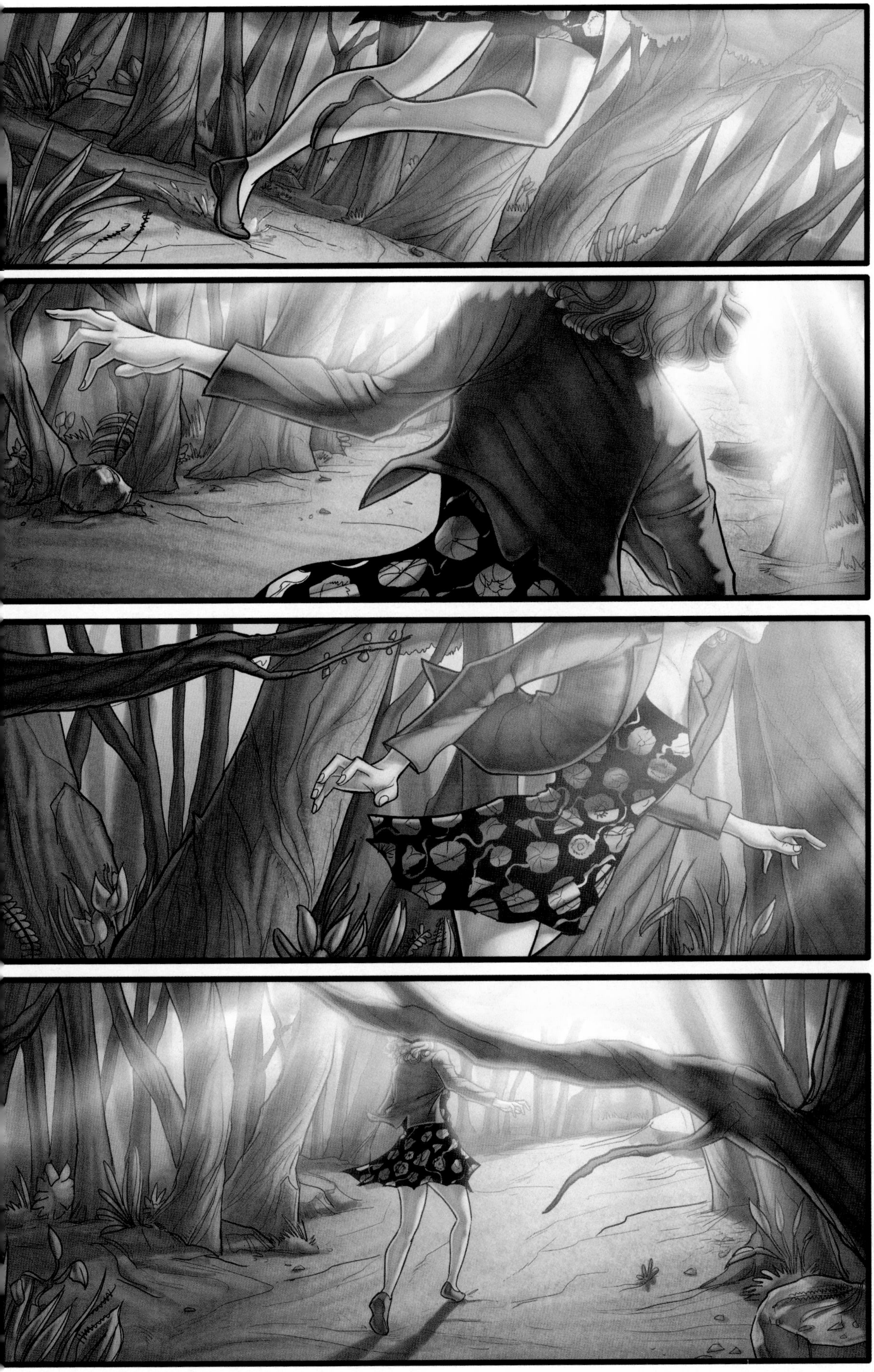

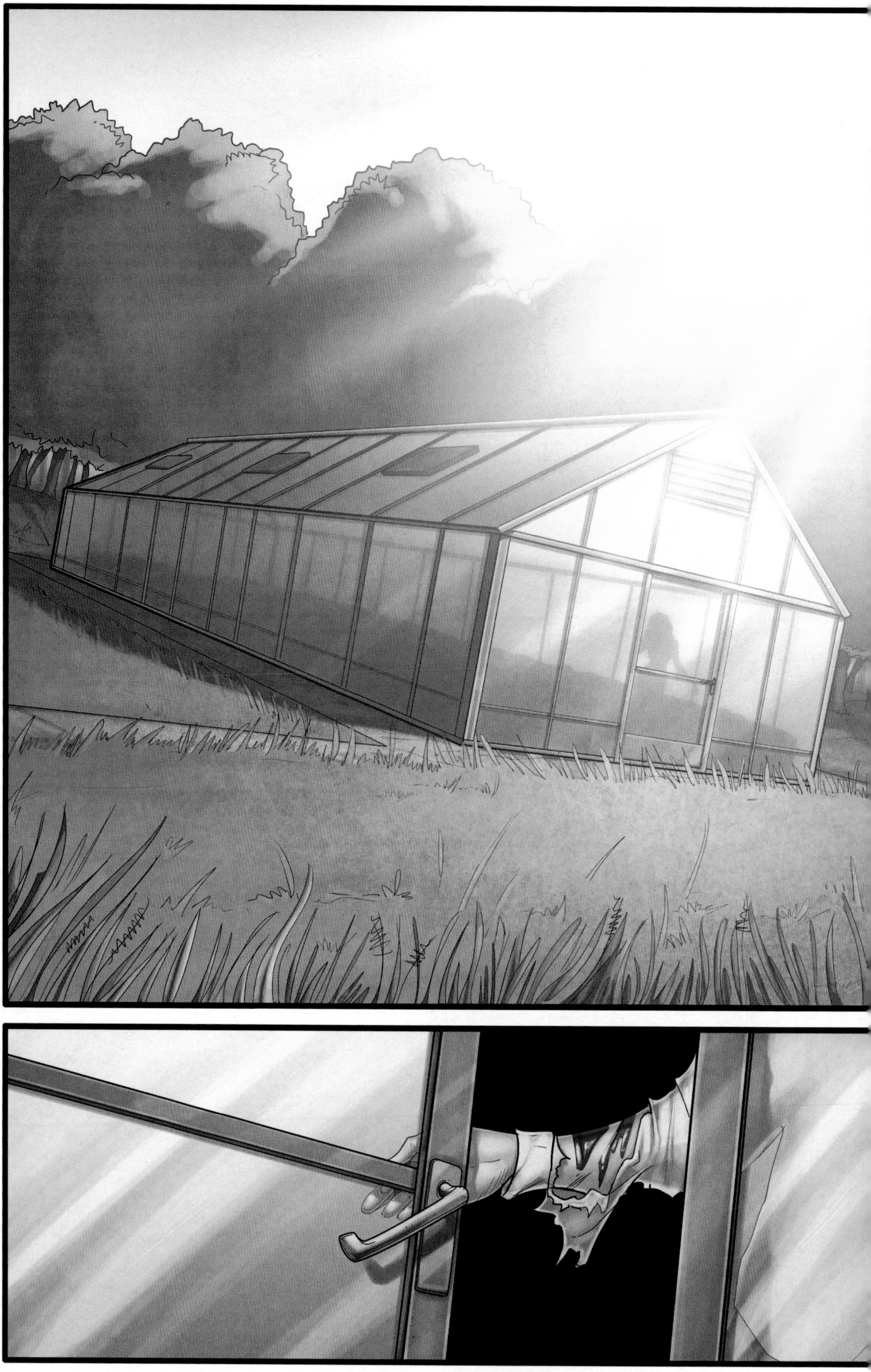

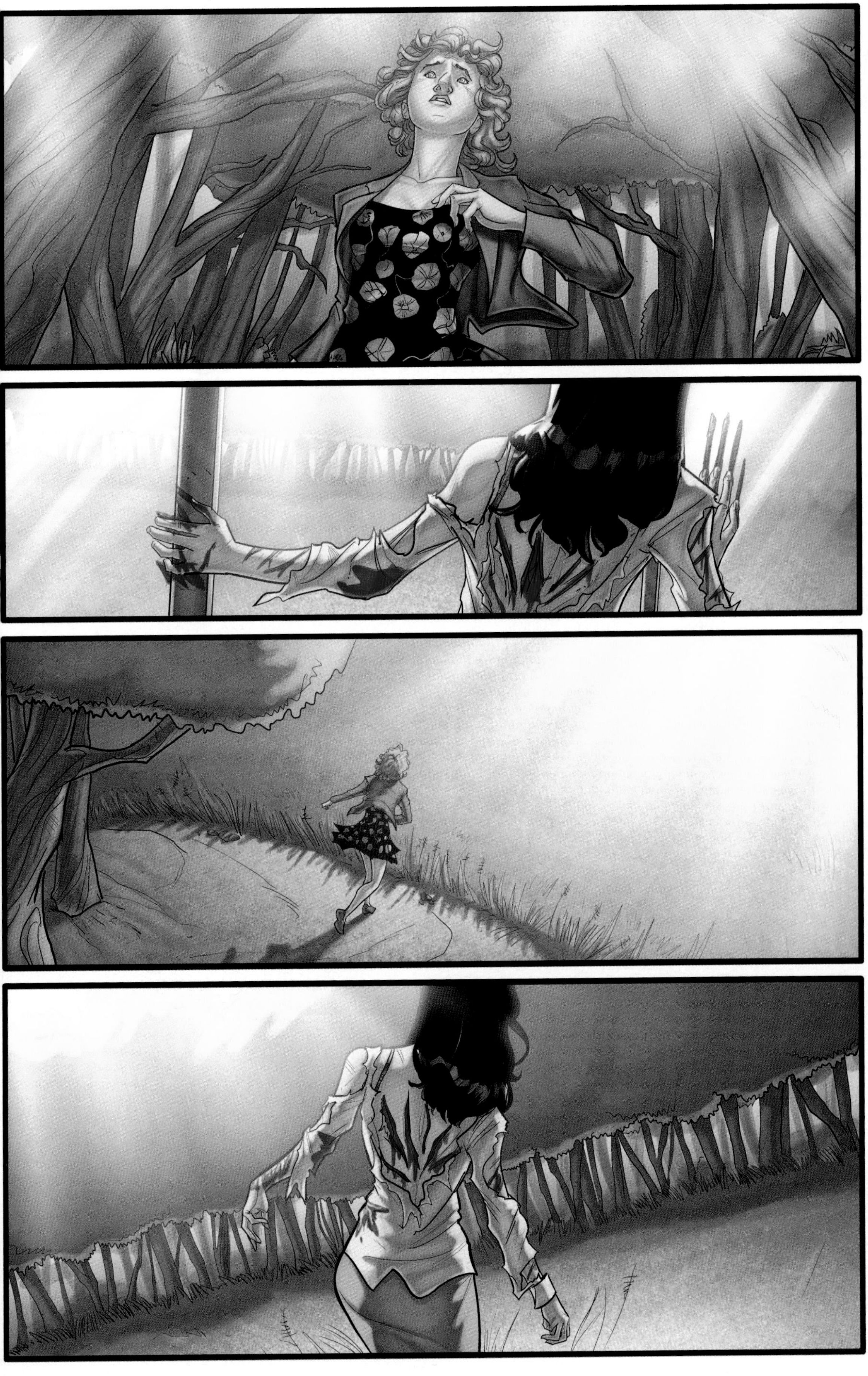

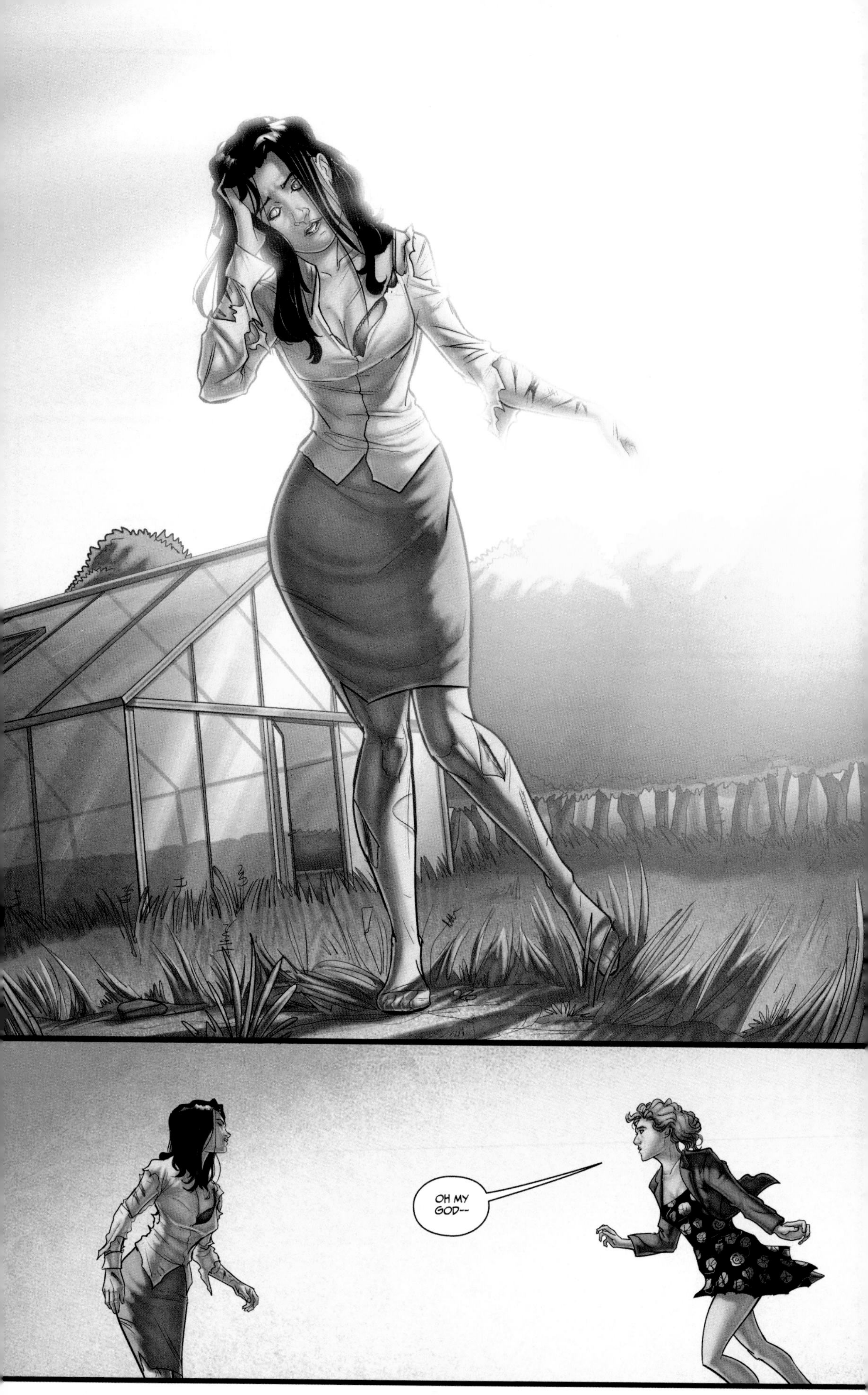
OH MY GOD--

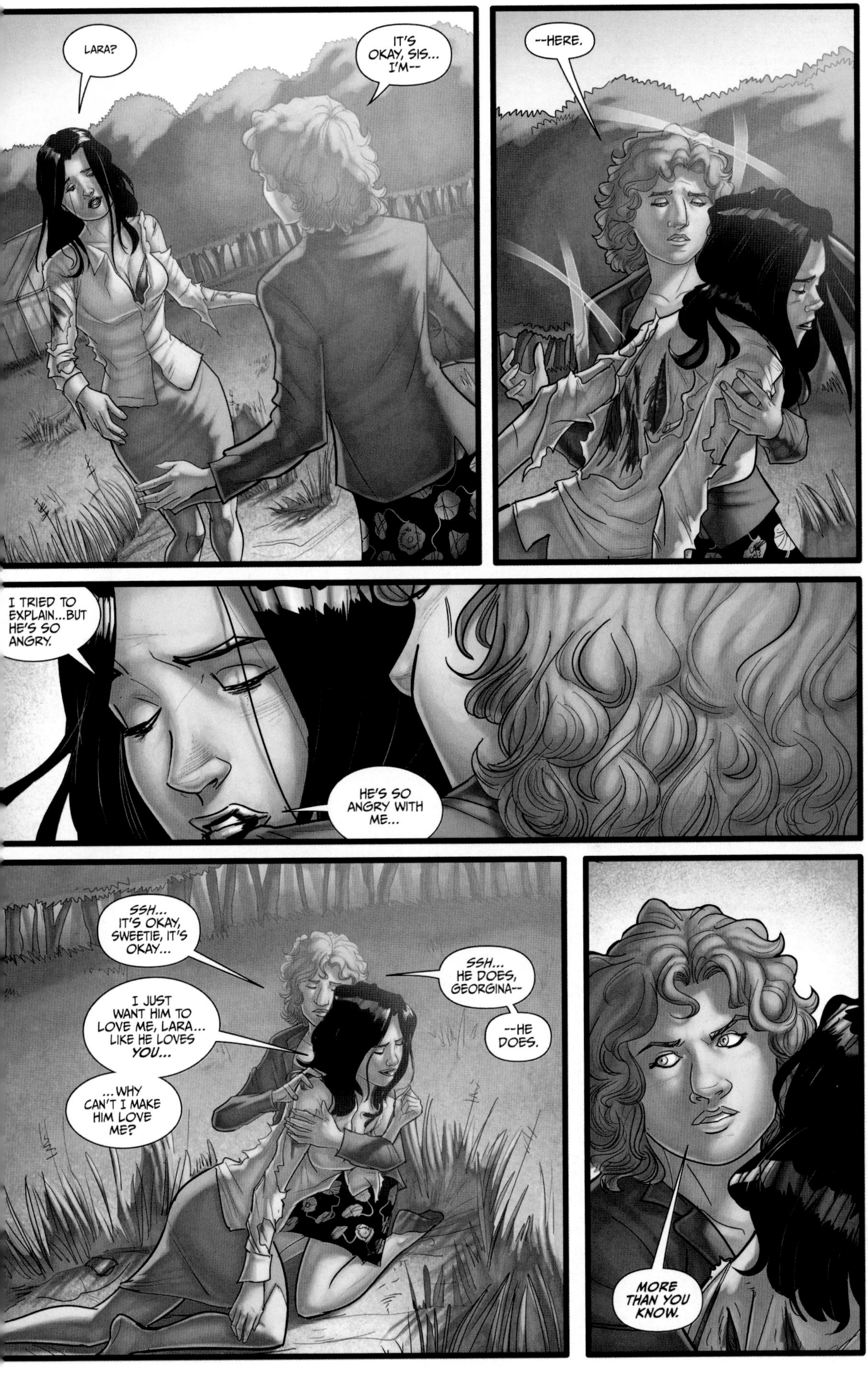
LARA?
IT'S OKAY, SIS... I'M--
--HERE.
I TRIED TO EXPLAIN...BUT HE'S SO ANGRY.
HE'S SO ANGRY WITH ME...
SSH... IT'S OKAY, SWEETIE, IT'S OKAY...
I JUST WANT HIM TO LOVE ME, LARA... LIKE HE LOVES *YOU*...
...WHY CAN'T I MAKE HIM LOVE ME?
SSH... HE DOES, GEORGINA--
--HE DOES.
MORE THAN YOU KNOW.

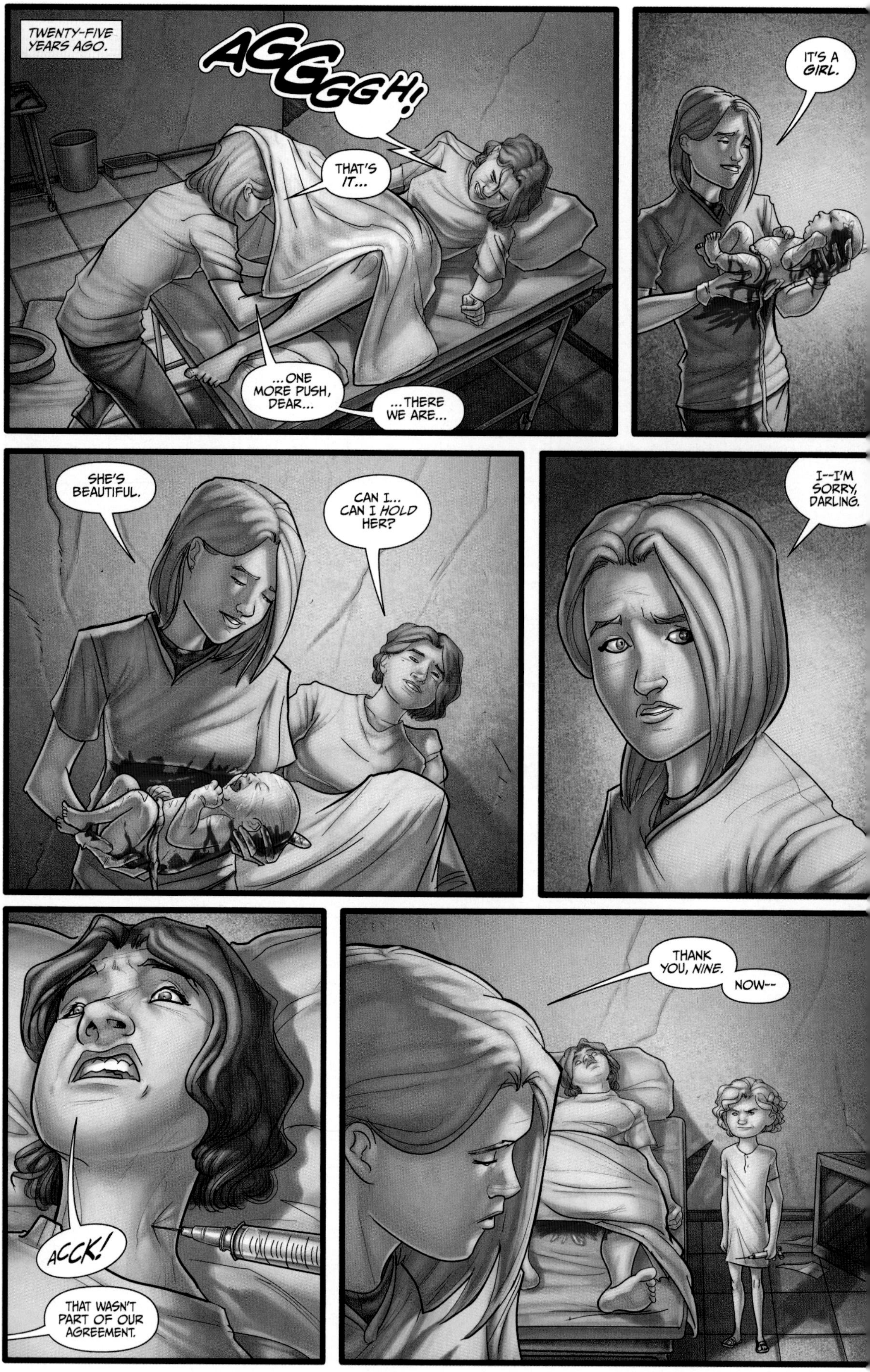
TWENTY-FIVE YEARS AGO.
AGGGGH!
THAT'S IT...
...ONE MORE PUSH, DEAR...
...THERE WE ARE...
IT'S A GIRL.
SHE'S BEAUTIFUL.
CAN I... CAN I HOLD HER?
I--I'M SORRY, DARLING.
ACCK!
THAT WASN'T PART OF OUR AGREEMENT.
THANK YOU, NINE.
NOW--

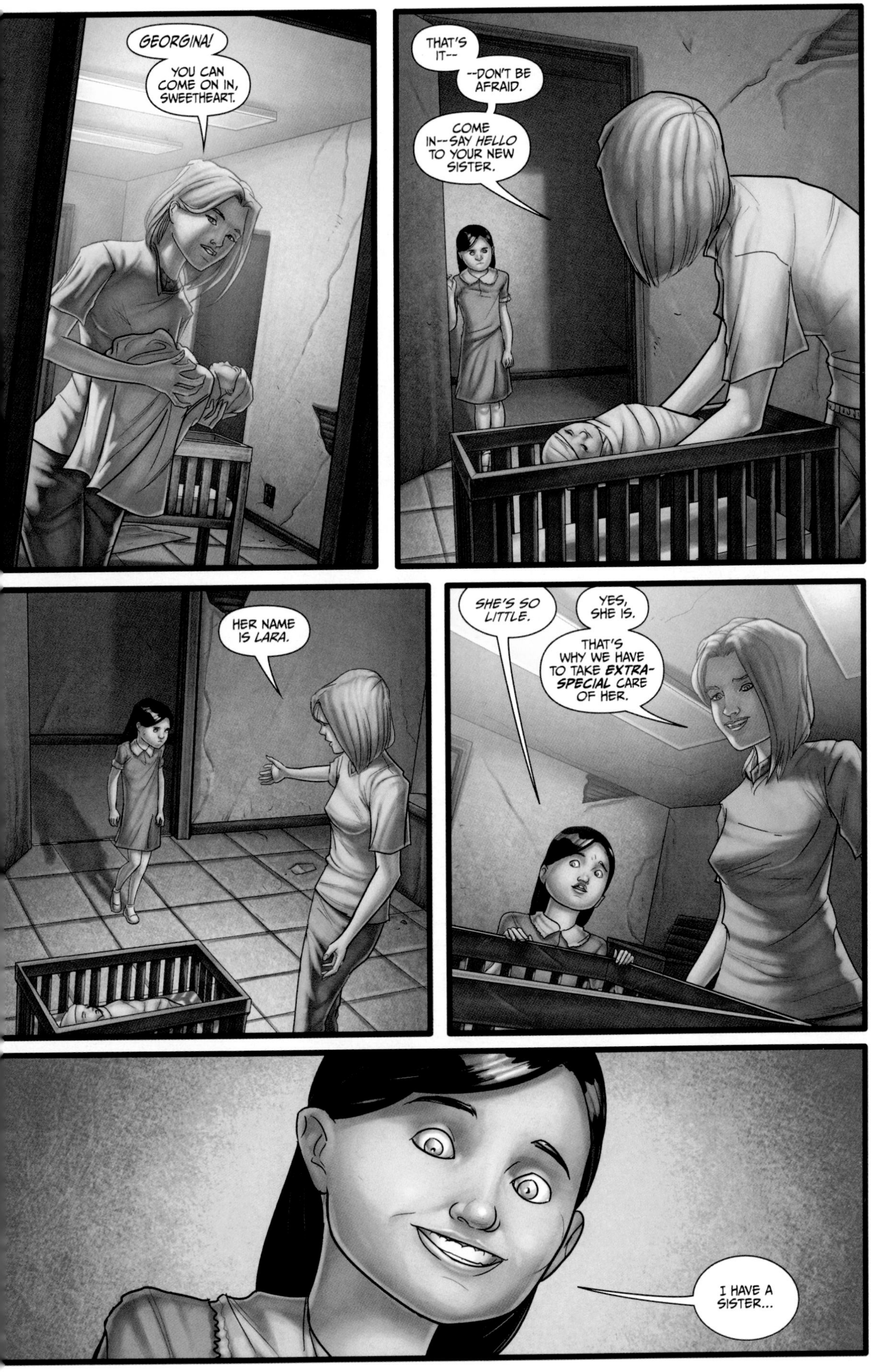
GEORGINA!
YOU CAN COME ON IN, SWEETHEART.
THAT'S IT--
--DON'T BE AFRAID.
COME IN--SAY *HELLO* TO YOUR NEW SISTER.
HER NAME IS *LARA.*
SHE'S SO LITTLE.
YES, SHE IS.
THAT'S WHY WE HAVE TO TAKE ***EXTRA-SPECIAL*** CARE OF HER.
I HAVE A SISTER...

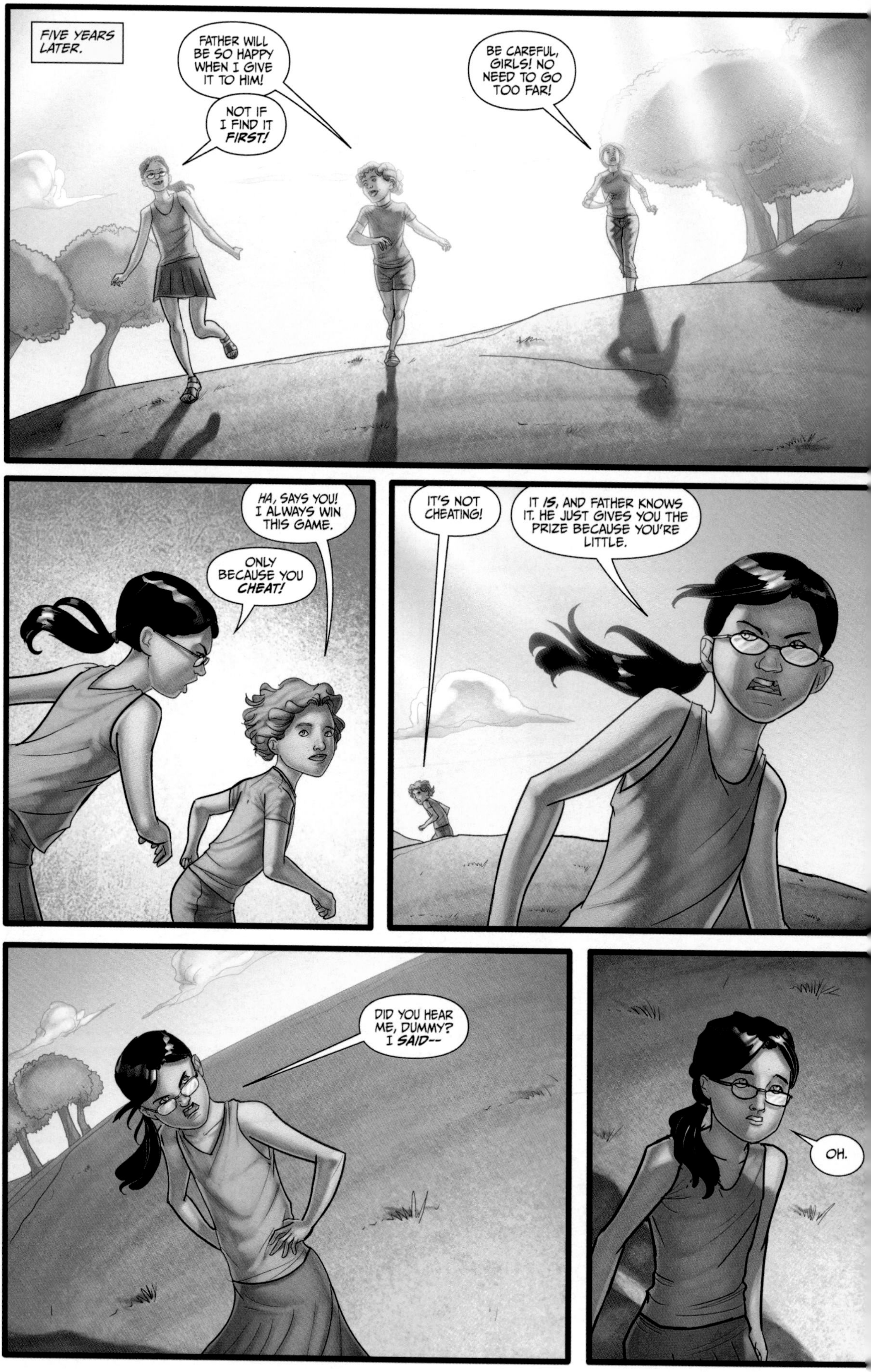
FIVE YEARS LATER.
FATHER WILL BE SO HAPPY WHEN I GIVE IT TO HIM!
NOT IF I FIND IT FIRST!
BE CAREFUL, GIRLS! NO NEED TO GO TOO FAR!
HA, SAYS YOU! I ALWAYS WIN THIS GAME.
ONLY BECAUSE YOU CHEAT!
IT'S NOT CHEATING!
IT IS, AND FATHER KNOWS IT. HE JUST GIVES YOU THE PRIZE BECAUSE YOU'RE LITTLE.
DID YOU HEAR ME, DUMMY? I SAID--
OH.

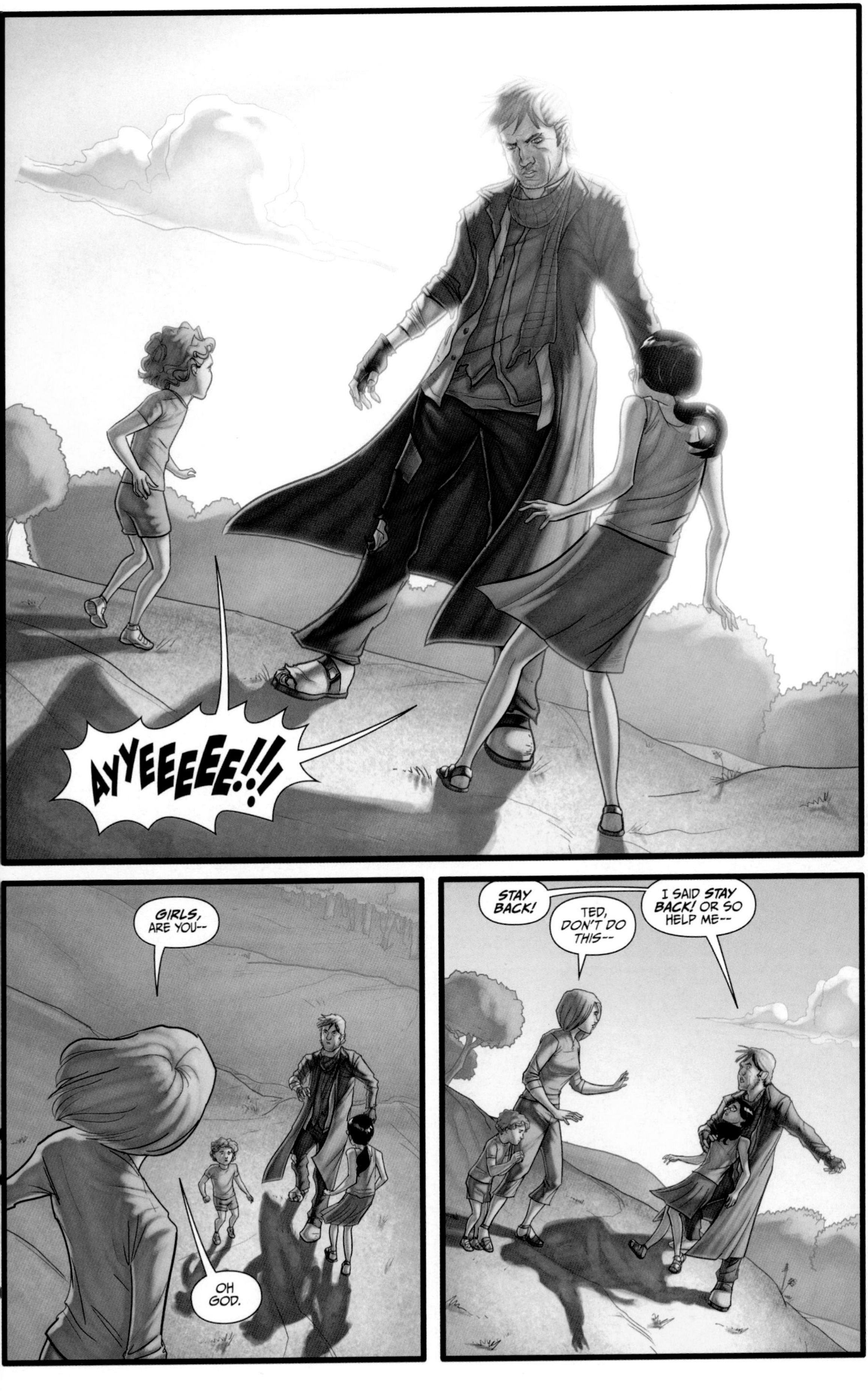
AYYEEEEE!!!
GIRLS, ARE YOU--
OH GOD.
STAY BACK!
TED, DON'T DO THIS--
I SAID STAY BACK! OR SO HELP ME--

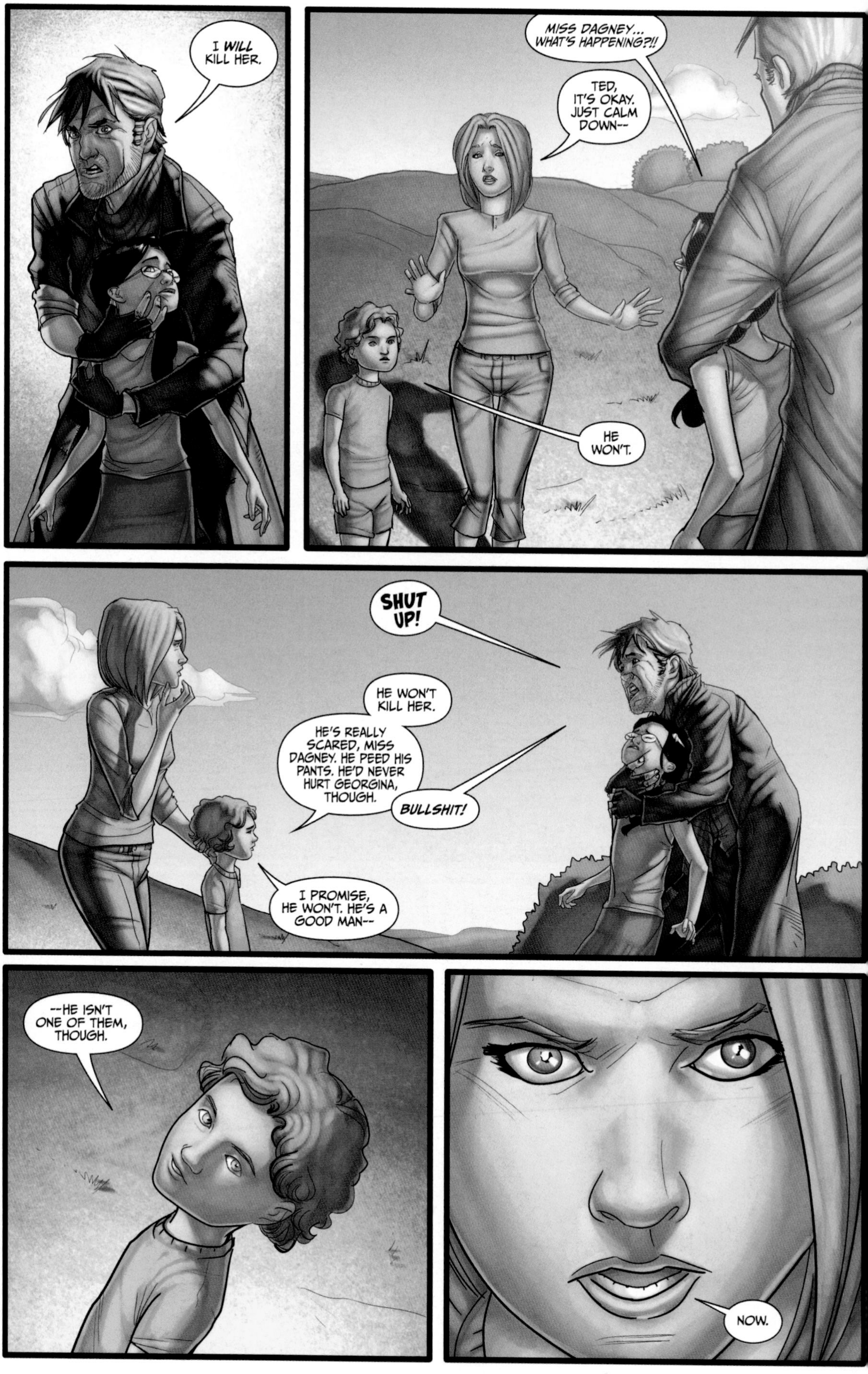
I WILL KILL HER.
MISS DAGNEY... WHAT'S HAPPENING?!!
TED, IT'S OKAY. JUST CALM DOWN--
HE WON'T.
SHUT UP!
HE WON'T KILL HER.
HE'S REALLY SCARED, MISS DAGNEY. HE PEED HIS PANTS. HE'D NEVER HURT GEORGINA, THOUGH.
BULLSHIT!
I PROMISE, HE WON'T. HE'S A GOOD MAN--
--HE ISN'T ONE OF THEM, THOUGH.
NOW.

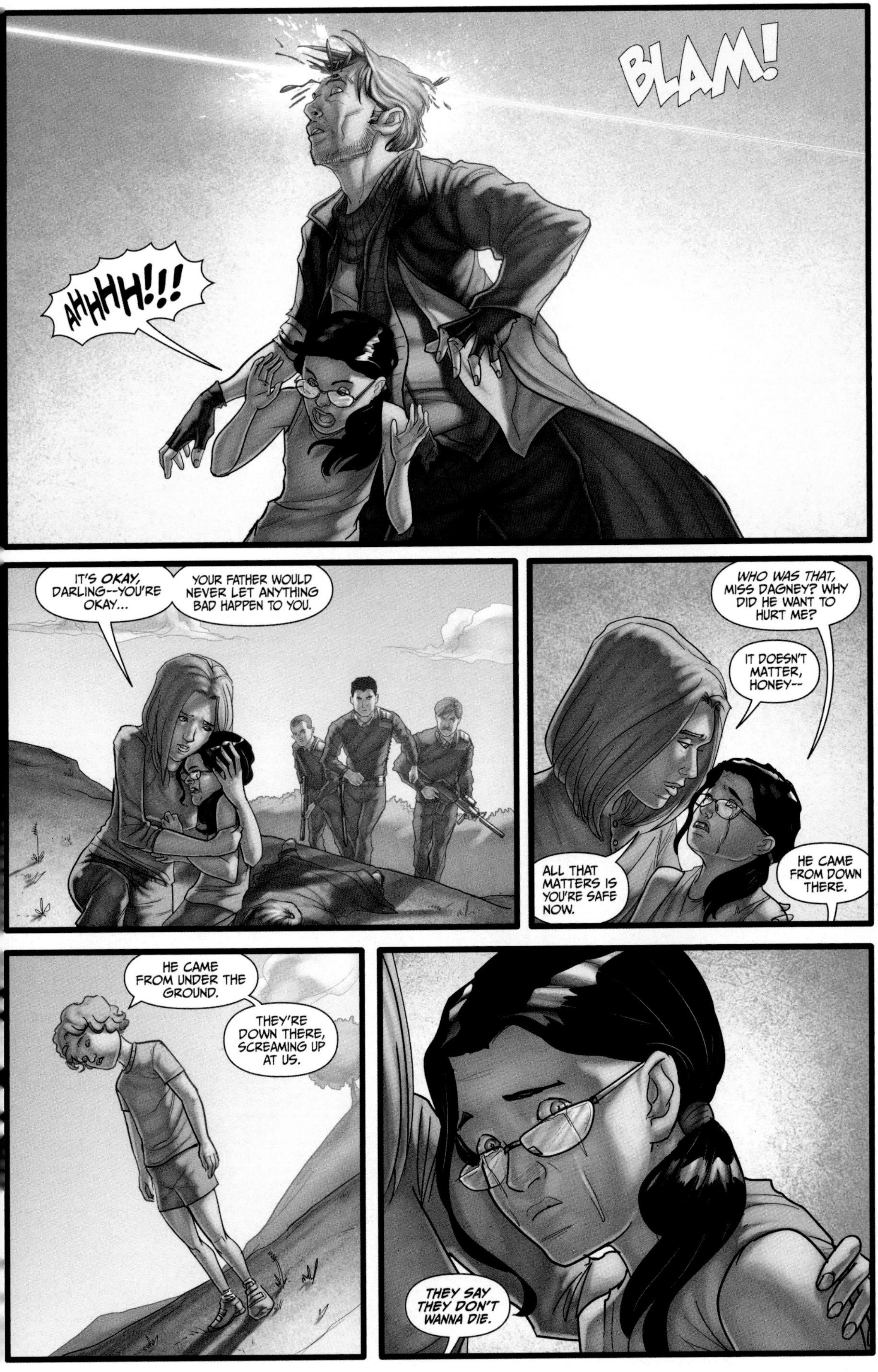
BLAM!
AHHHH!!!
IT'S *OKAY,* DARLING--YOU'RE OKAY...
YOUR FATHER WOULD NEVER LET ANYTHING BAD HAPPEN TO YOU.
WHO WAS THAT, MISS DAGNEY? WHY DID HE WANT TO HURT ME?
IT DOESN'T MATTER, HONEY--
ALL THAT MATTERS IS YOU'RE SAFE NOW.
HE CAME FROM DOWN THERE.
HE CAME FROM UNDER THE GROUND.
THEY'RE DOWN THERE, SCREAMING UP AT US.
THEY SAY THEY DON'T WANNA DIE.

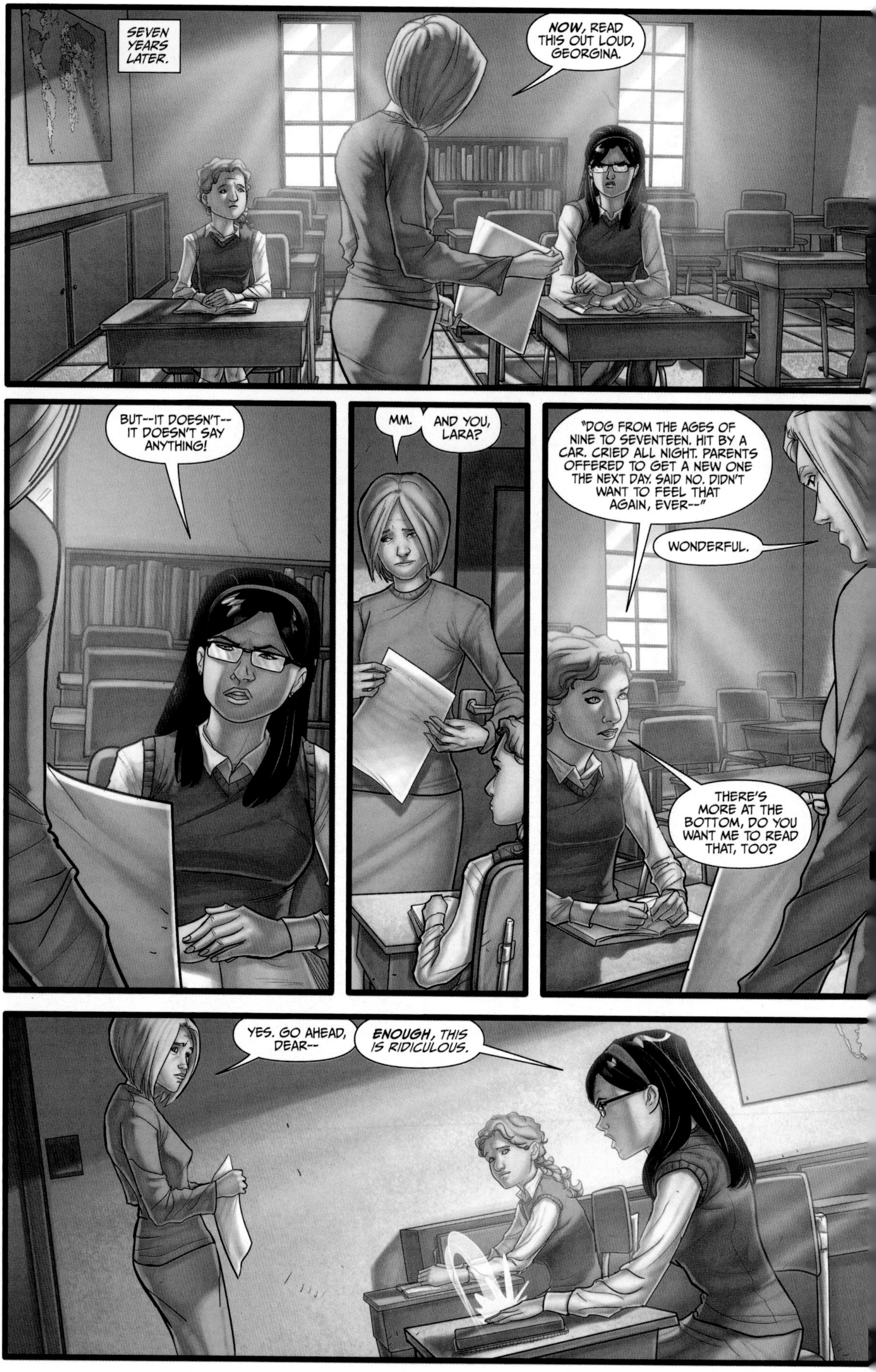
SEVEN YEARS LATER.
NOW, READ THIS OUT LOUD, GEORGINA.
BUT--IT DOESN'T-- IT DOESN'T SAY ANYTHING!
MM.
AND YOU, LARA?
"DOG FROM THE AGES OF NINE TO SEVENTEEN. HIT BY A CAR. CRIED ALL NIGHT. PARENTS OFFERED TO GET A NEW ONE THE NEXT DAY. SAID NO. DIDN'T WANT TO FEEL THAT AGAIN, EVER--"
WONDERFUL.
THERE'S MORE AT THE BOTTOM, DO YOU WANT ME TO READ THAT, TOO?
YES. GO AHEAD, DEAR--
ENOUGH, THIS IS RIDICULOUS.

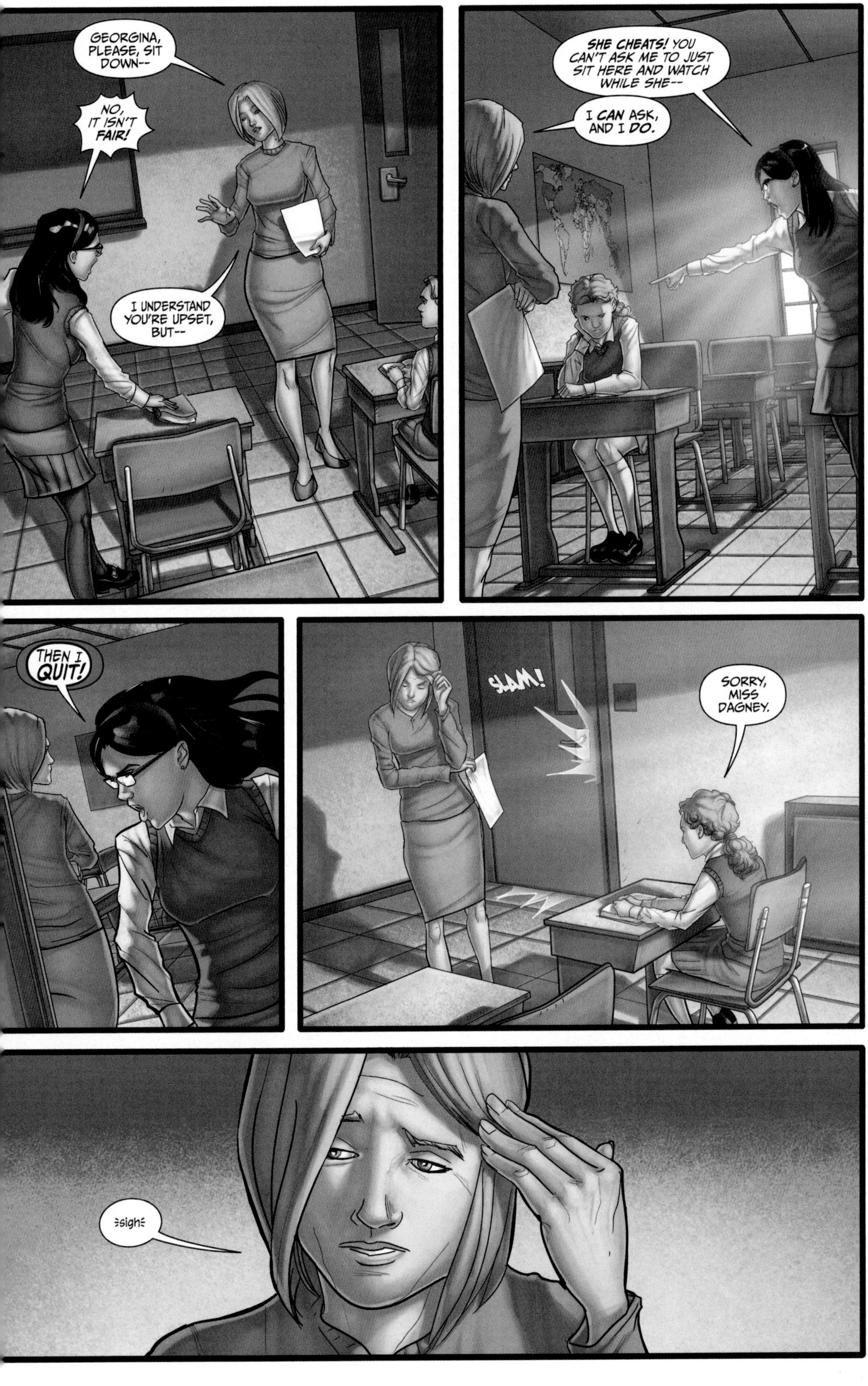
GEORGINA, PLEASE, SIT DOWN--
NO, IT ISN'T FAIR!
I UNDERSTAND YOU'RE UPSET, BUT--
SHE CHEATS! YOU CAN'T ASK ME TO JUST SIT HERE AND WATCH WHILE SHE--
I CAN ASK, AND I DO.
THEN I QUIT!
SLAM!
SORRY, MISS DAGNEY.
sigh

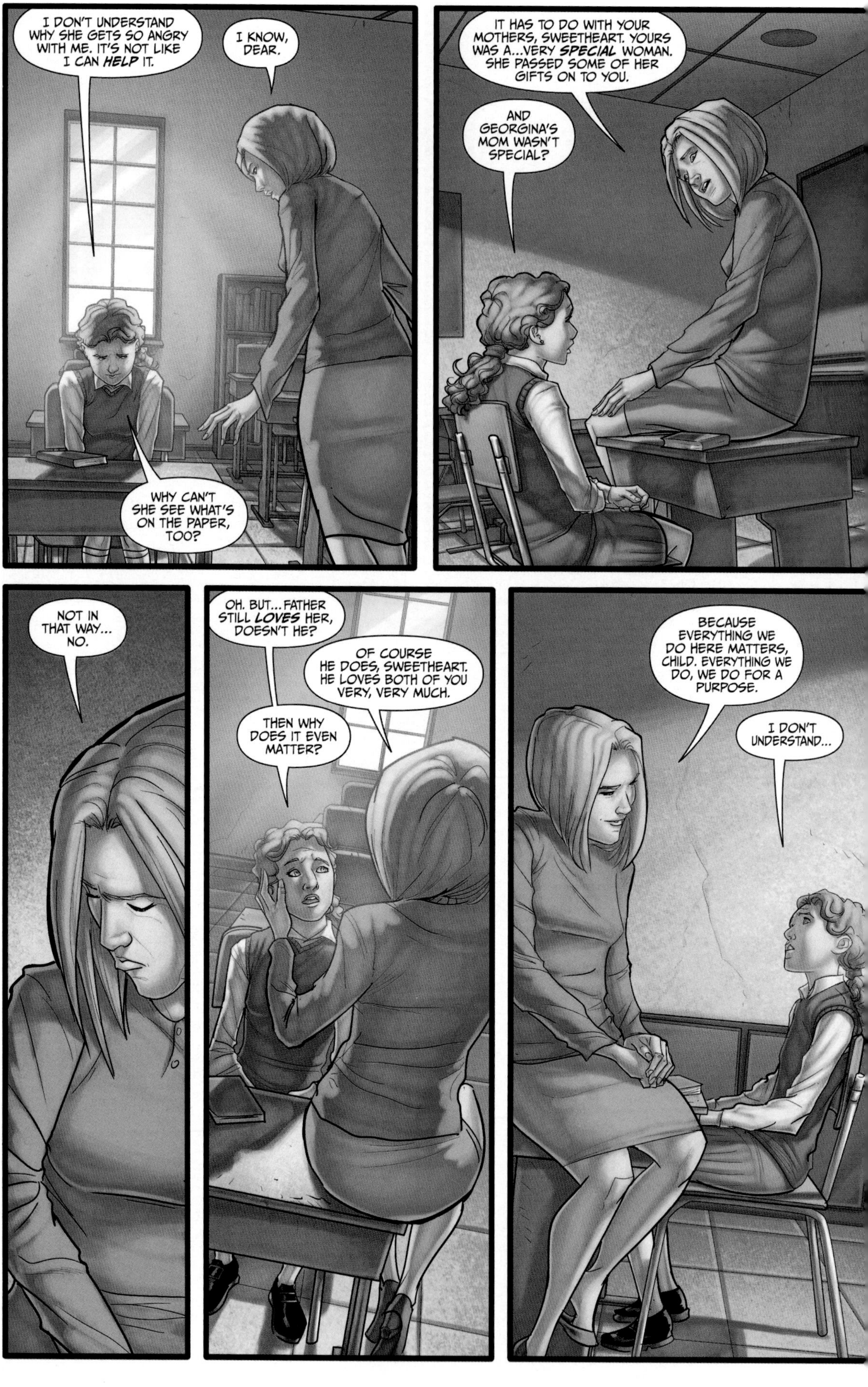

I DON'T UNDERSTAND WHY SHE GETS SO ANGRY WITH ME. IT'S NOT LIKE I CAN *HELP* IT.
I KNOW, DEAR.
WHY CAN'T SHE SEE WHAT'S ON THE PAPER, TOO?
IT HAS TO DO WITH YOUR MOTHERS, SWEETHEART. YOURS WAS A...VERY *SPECIAL* WOMAN. SHE PASSED SOME OF HER GIFTS ON TO YOU.
AND GEORGINA'S MOM WASN'T SPECIAL?
NOT IN THAT WAY... NO.
OH. BUT...FATHER STILL *LOVES* HER, DOESN'T HE?
OF COURSE HE DOES, SWEETHEART. HE LOVES BOTH OF YOU VERY, VERY MUCH.
THEN WHY DOES IT EVEN MATTER?
BECAUSE EVERYTHING WE DO HERE MATTERS, CHILD. EVERYTHING WE DO, WE DO FOR A PURPOSE.
I DON'T UNDERSTAND...

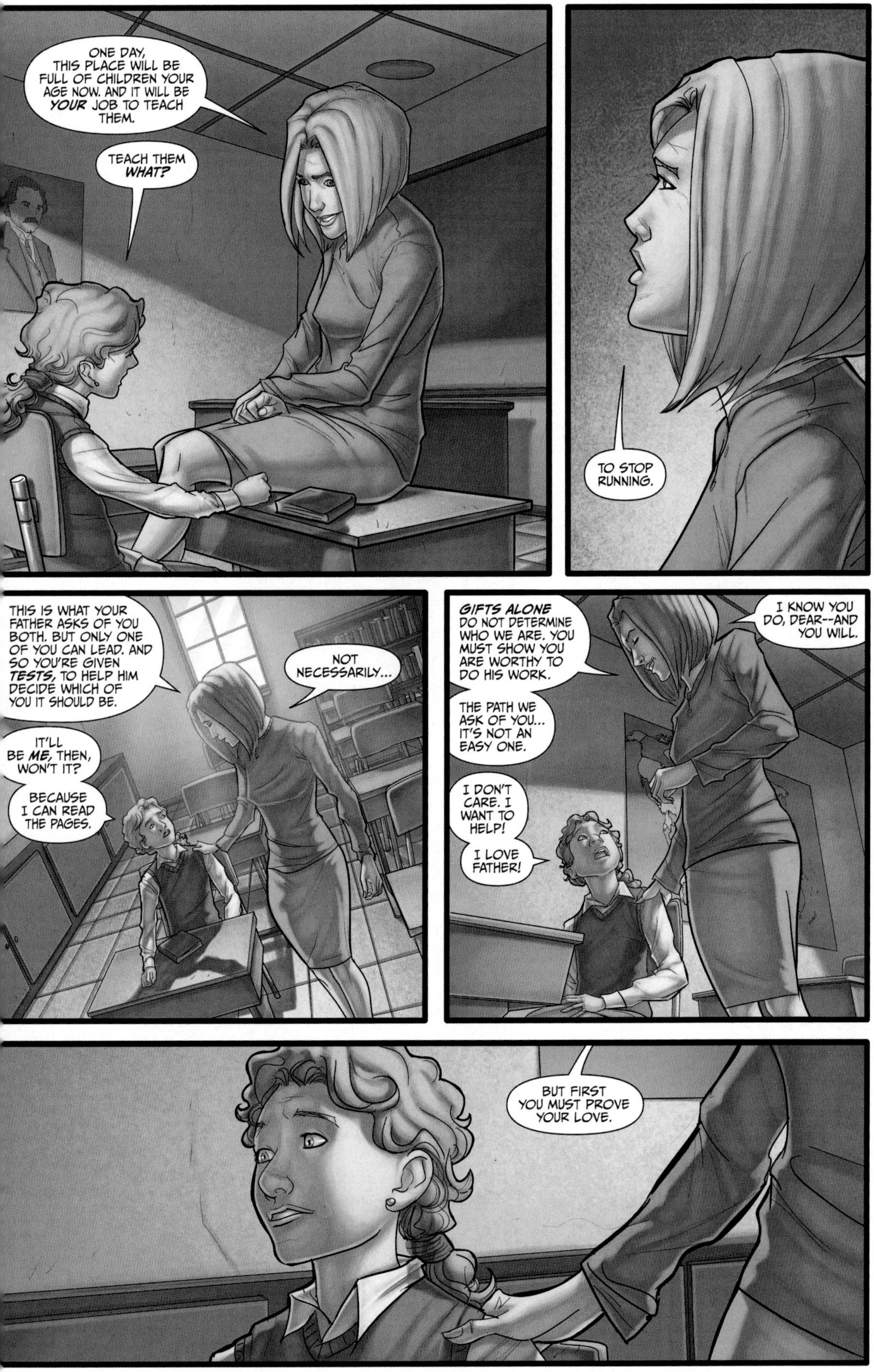
ONE DAY, THIS PLACE WILL BE FULL OF CHILDREN YOUR AGE NOW. AND IT WILL BE *YOUR* JOB TO TEACH THEM.
TEACH THEM *WHAT?*
TO STOP RUNNING.
THIS IS WHAT YOUR FATHER ASKS OF YOU BOTH. BUT ONLY ONE OF YOU CAN LEAD. AND SO YOU'RE GIVEN *TESTS,* TO HELP HIM DECIDE WHICH OF YOU IT SHOULD BE.
IT'LL BE *ME,* THEN, WON'T IT?
BECAUSE I CAN READ THE PAGES.
NOT NECESSARILY...
GIFTS ALONE DO NOT DETERMINE WHO WE ARE. YOU MUST SHOW YOU ARE WORTHY TO DO HIS WORK.
THE PATH WE ASK OF YOU... IT'S NOT AN EASY ONE.
I DON'T CARE. I WANT TO HELP!
I LOVE FATHER!
I KNOW YOU DO, DEAR--AND YOU WILL.
BUT FIRST YOU MUST PROVE YOUR LOVE.

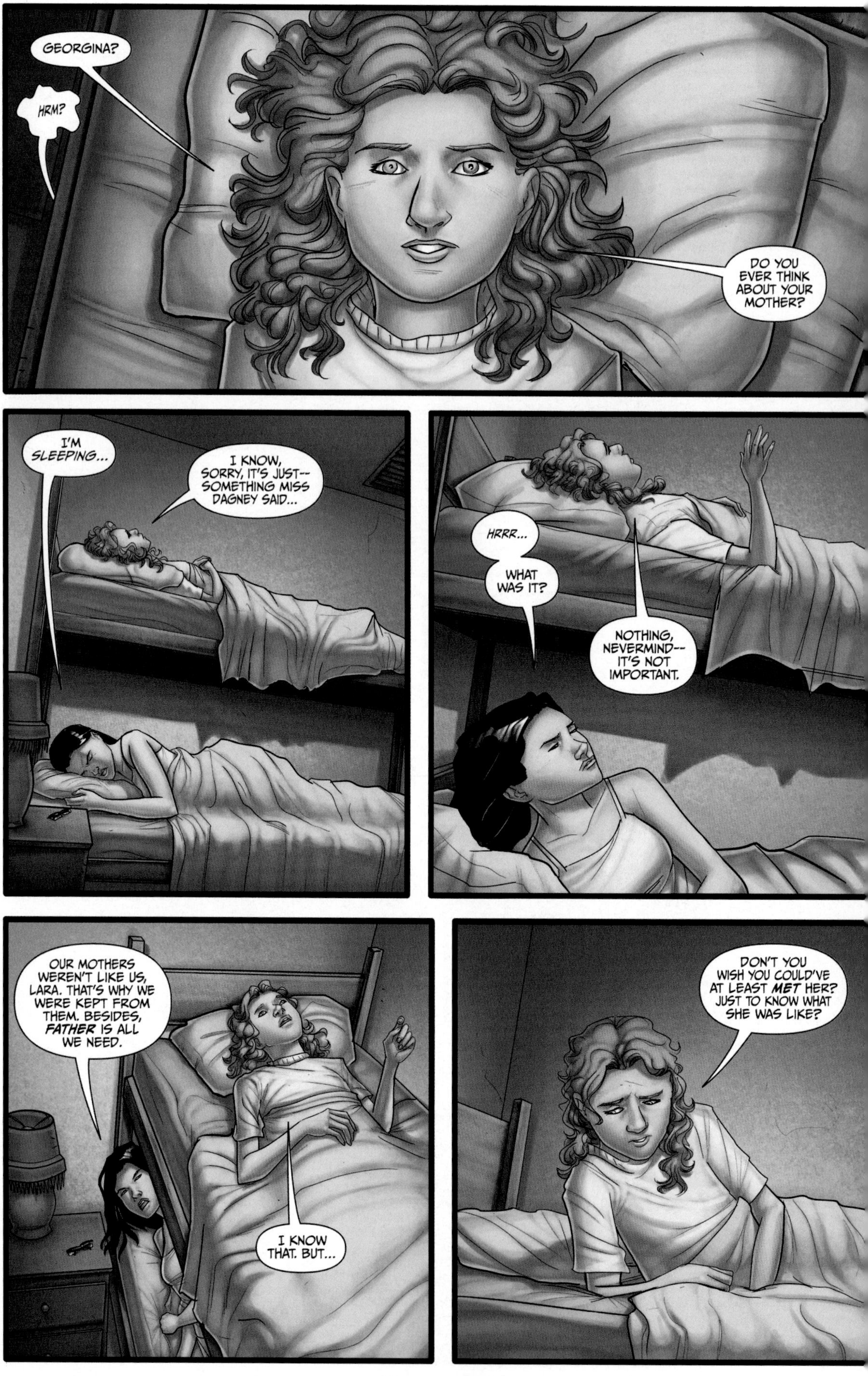
GEORGINA?
HRM?
DO YOU EVER THINK ABOUT YOUR MOTHER?
I'M SLEEPING...
I KNOW, SORRY, IT'S JUST-- SOMETHING MISS DAGNEY SAID...
HRRR...
WHAT WAS IT?
NOTHING, NEVERMIND-- IT'S NOT IMPORTANT.
OUR MOTHERS WEREN'T LIKE US, LARA. THAT'S WHY WE WERE KEPT FROM THEM. BESIDES, FATHER IS ALL WE NEED.
I KNOW THAT. BUT...
DON'T YOU WISH YOU COULD'VE AT LEAST MET HER? JUST TO KNOW WHAT SHE WAS LIKE?

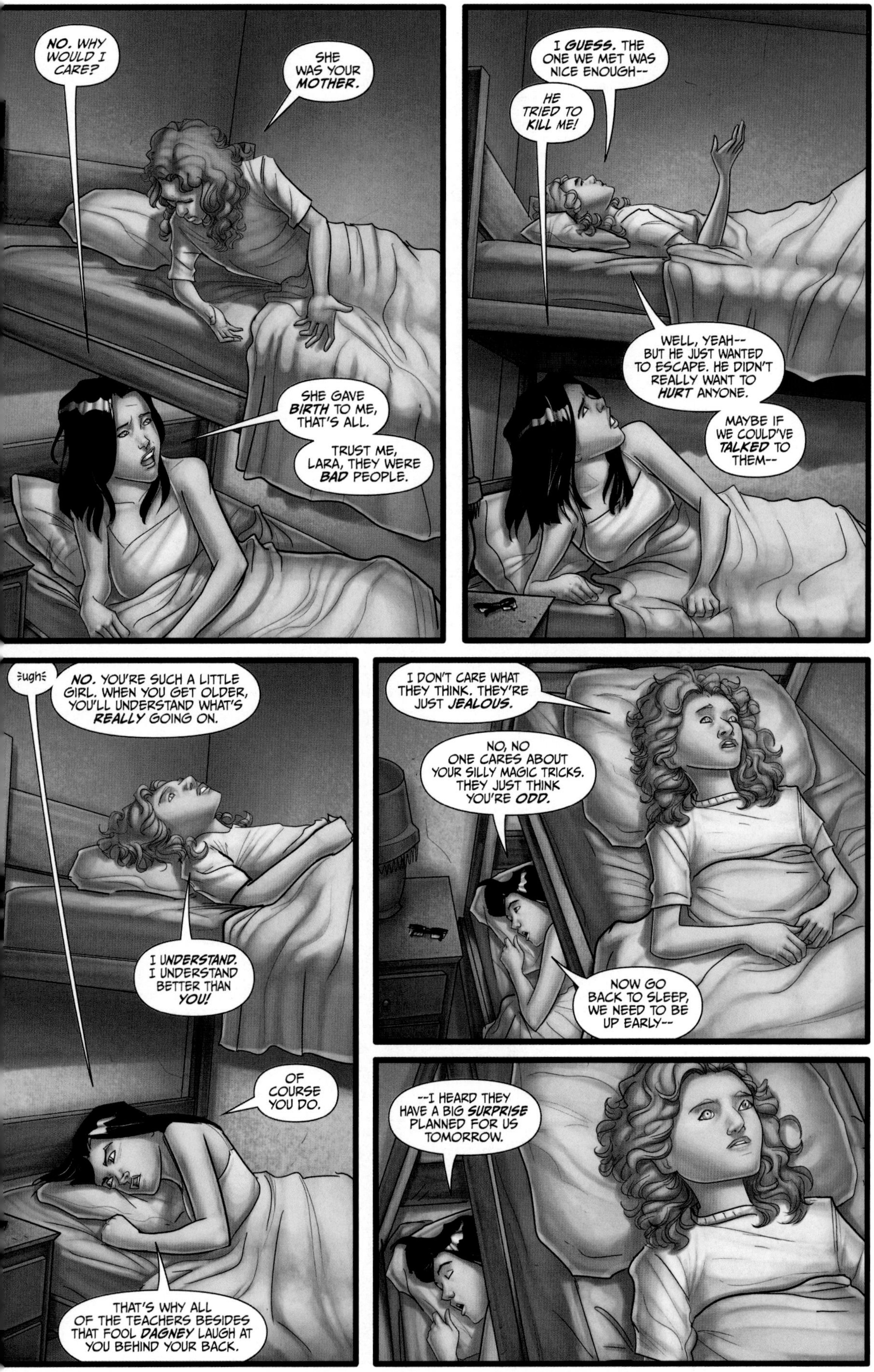
NO. WHY WOULD I CARE?
SHE WAS YOUR MOTHER.
SHE GAVE BIRTH TO ME, THAT'S ALL.
TRUST ME, LARA, THEY WERE BAD PEOPLE.
I GUESS. THE ONE WE MET WAS NICE ENOUGH--
HE TRIED TO KILL ME!
WELL, YEAH-- BUT HE JUST WANTED TO ESCAPE. HE DIDN'T REALLY WANT TO HURT ANYONE.
MAYBE IF WE COULD'VE TALKED TO THEM--
ugh
NO. YOU'RE SUCH A LITTLE GIRL. WHEN YOU GET OLDER, YOU'LL UNDERSTAND WHAT'S REALLY GOING ON.
I UNDERSTAND. I UNDERSTAND BETTER THAN YOU!
OF COURSE YOU DO.
THAT'S WHY ALL OF THE TEACHERS BESIDES THAT FOOL DAGNEY LAUGH AT YOU BEHIND YOUR BACK.
I DON'T CARE WHAT THEY THINK. THEY'RE JUST JEALOUS.
NO, NO ONE CARES ABOUT YOUR SILLY MAGIC TRICKS. THEY JUST THINK YOU'RE ODD.
NOW GO BACK TO SLEEP, WE NEED TO BE UP EARLY--
--I HEARD THEY HAVE A BIG SURPRISE PLANNED FOR US TOMORROW.

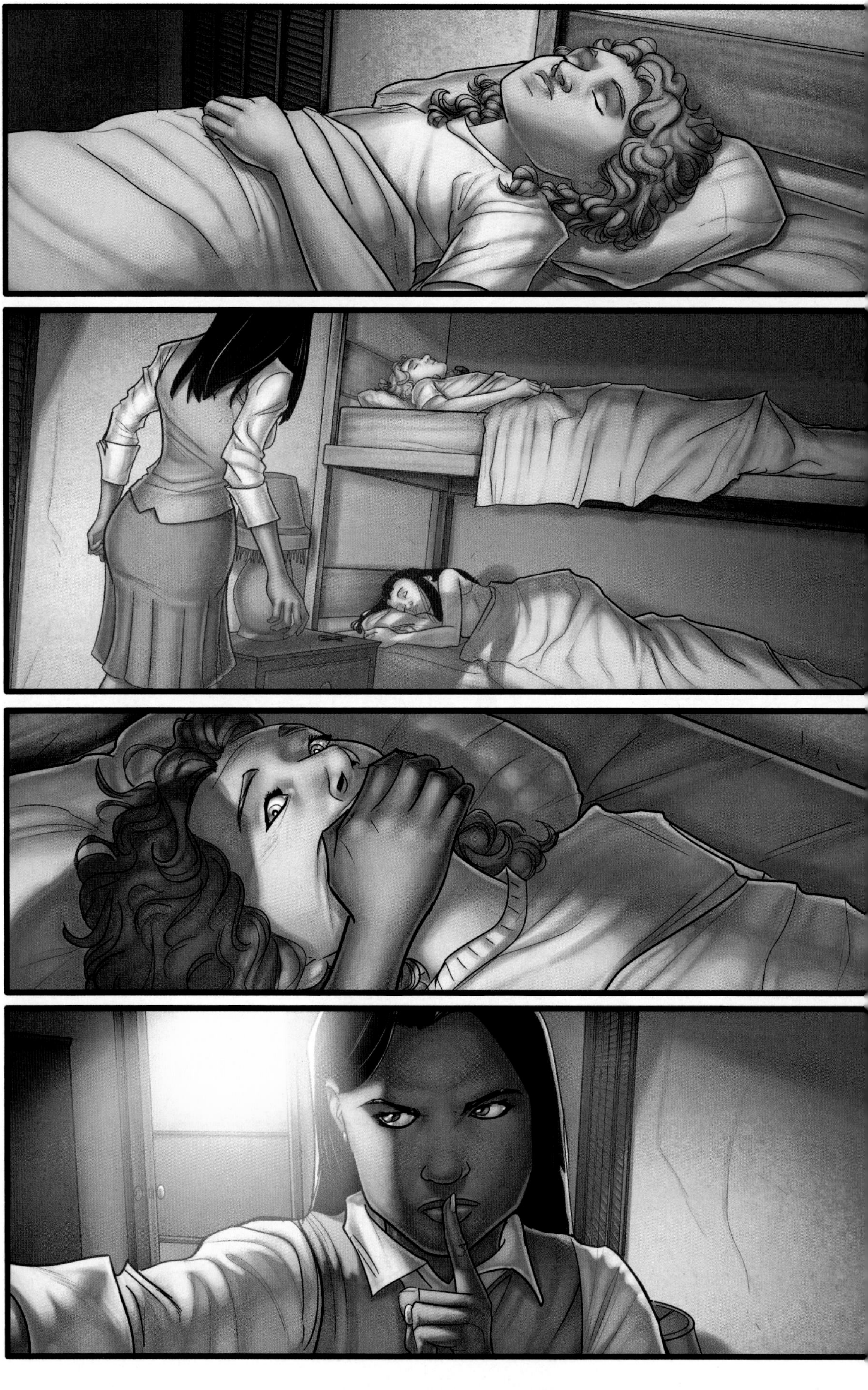

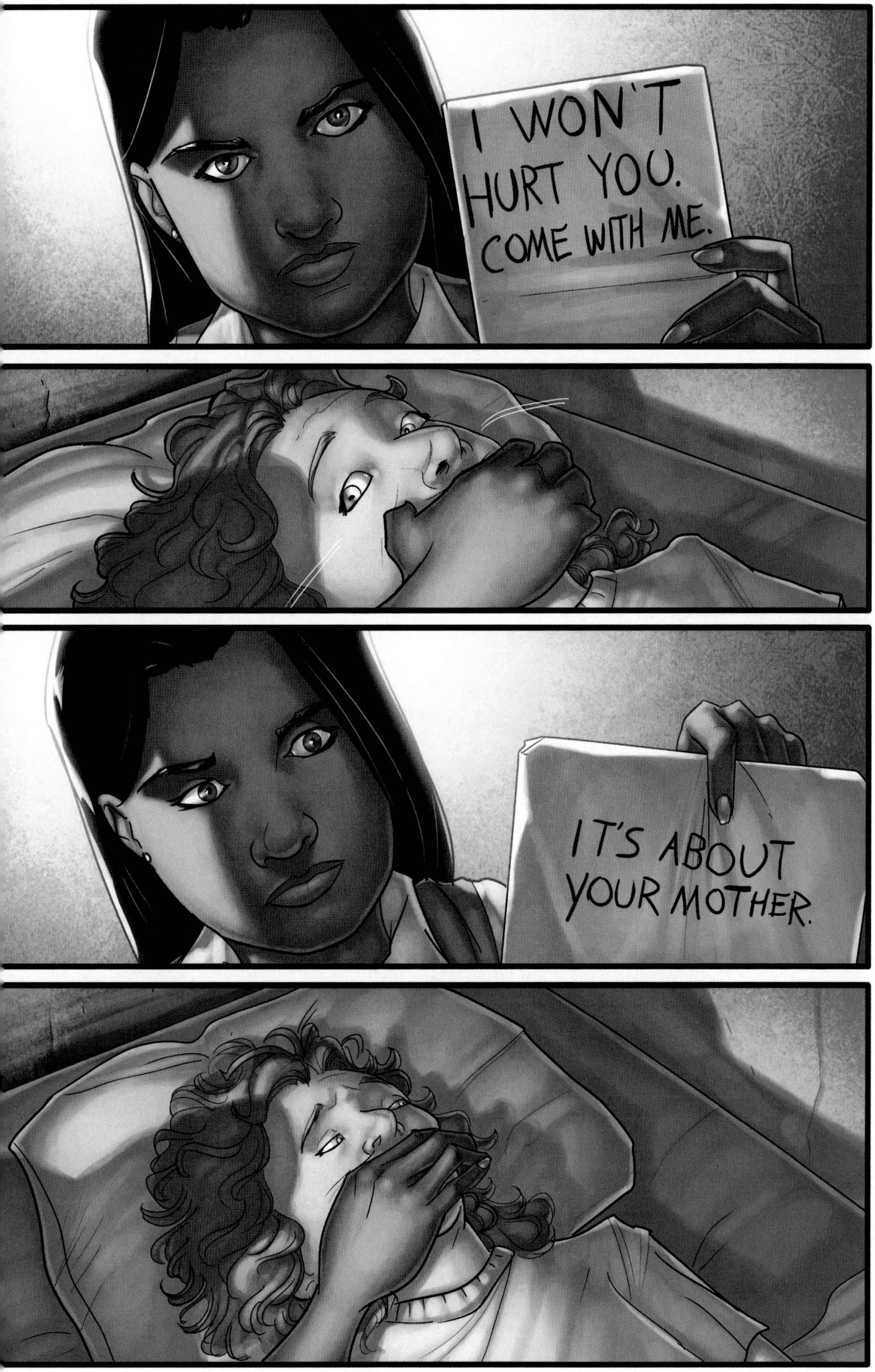
I WON'T HURT YOU. COME WITH ME.
IT'S ABOUT YOUR MOTHER.

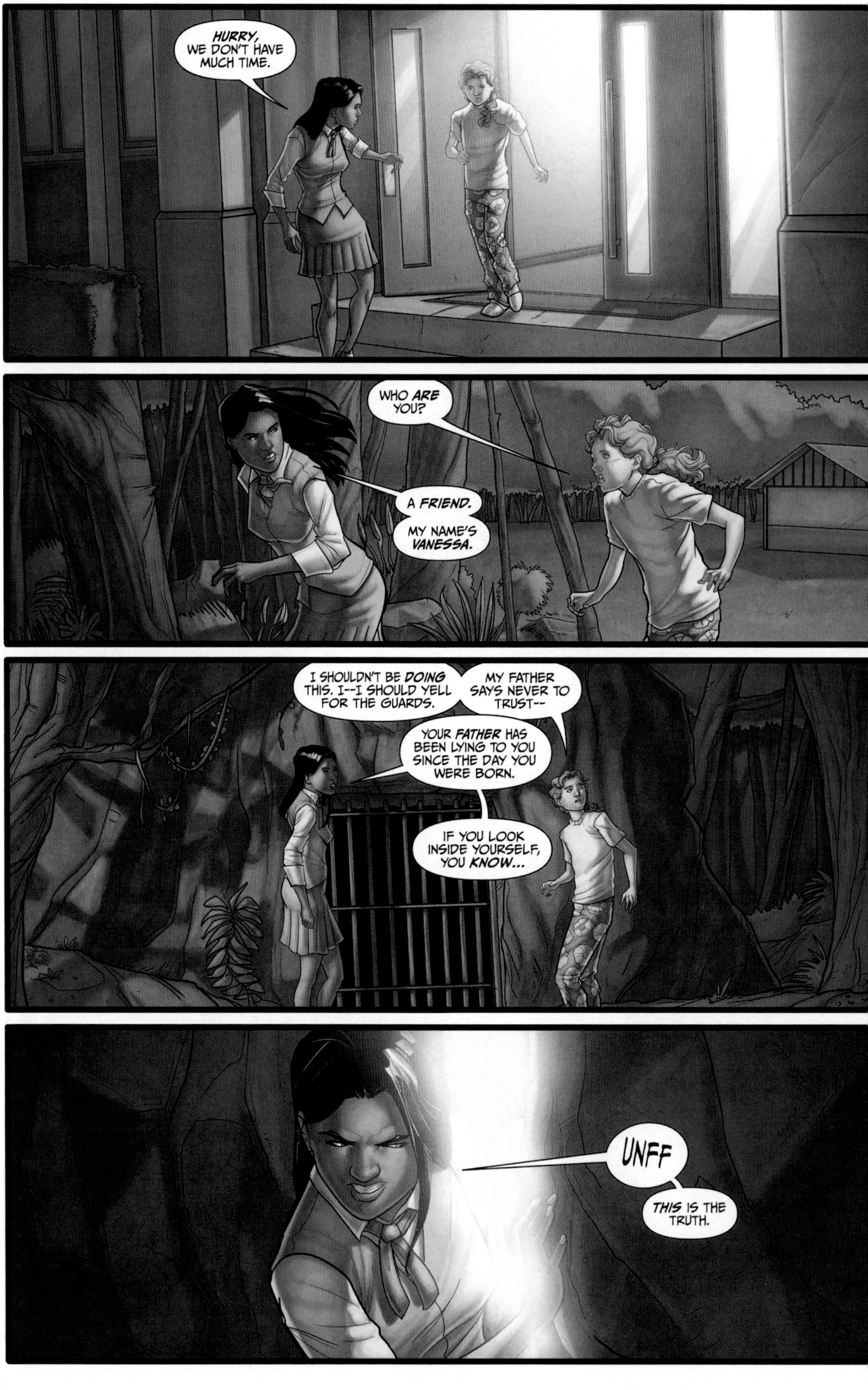
HURRY, WE DON'T HAVE MUCH TIME.
WHO ARE YOU?
A FRIEND.
MY NAME'S VANESSA.
I SHOULDN'T BE DOING THIS. I--I SHOULD YELL FOR THE GUARDS.
MY FATHER SAYS NEVER TO TRUST--
YOUR FATHER HAS BEEN LYING TO YOU SINCE THE DAY YOU WERE BORN.
IF YOU LOOK INSIDE YOURSELF, YOU KNOW...
UNFF
THIS IS THE TRUTH.

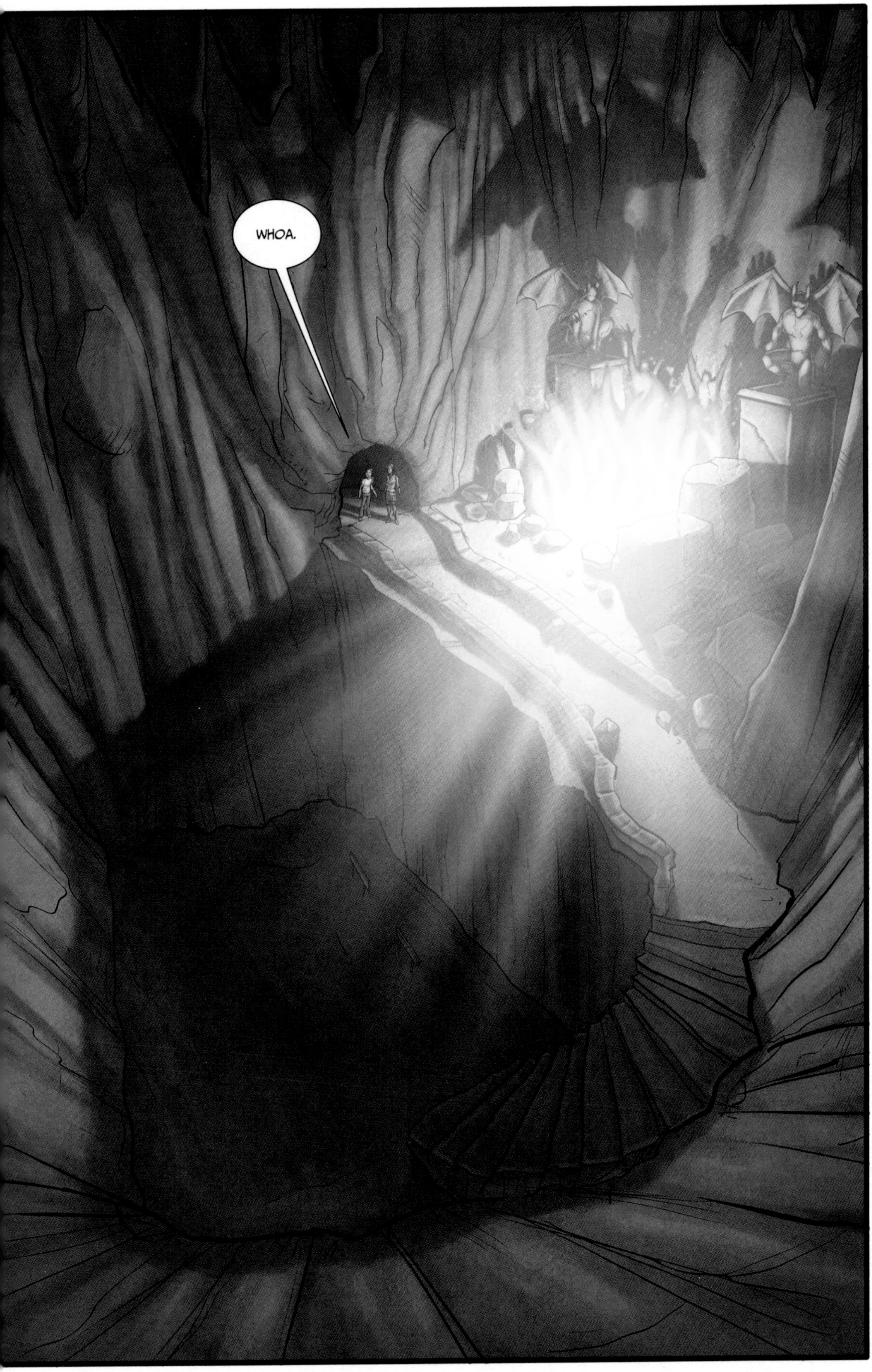
WHOA.

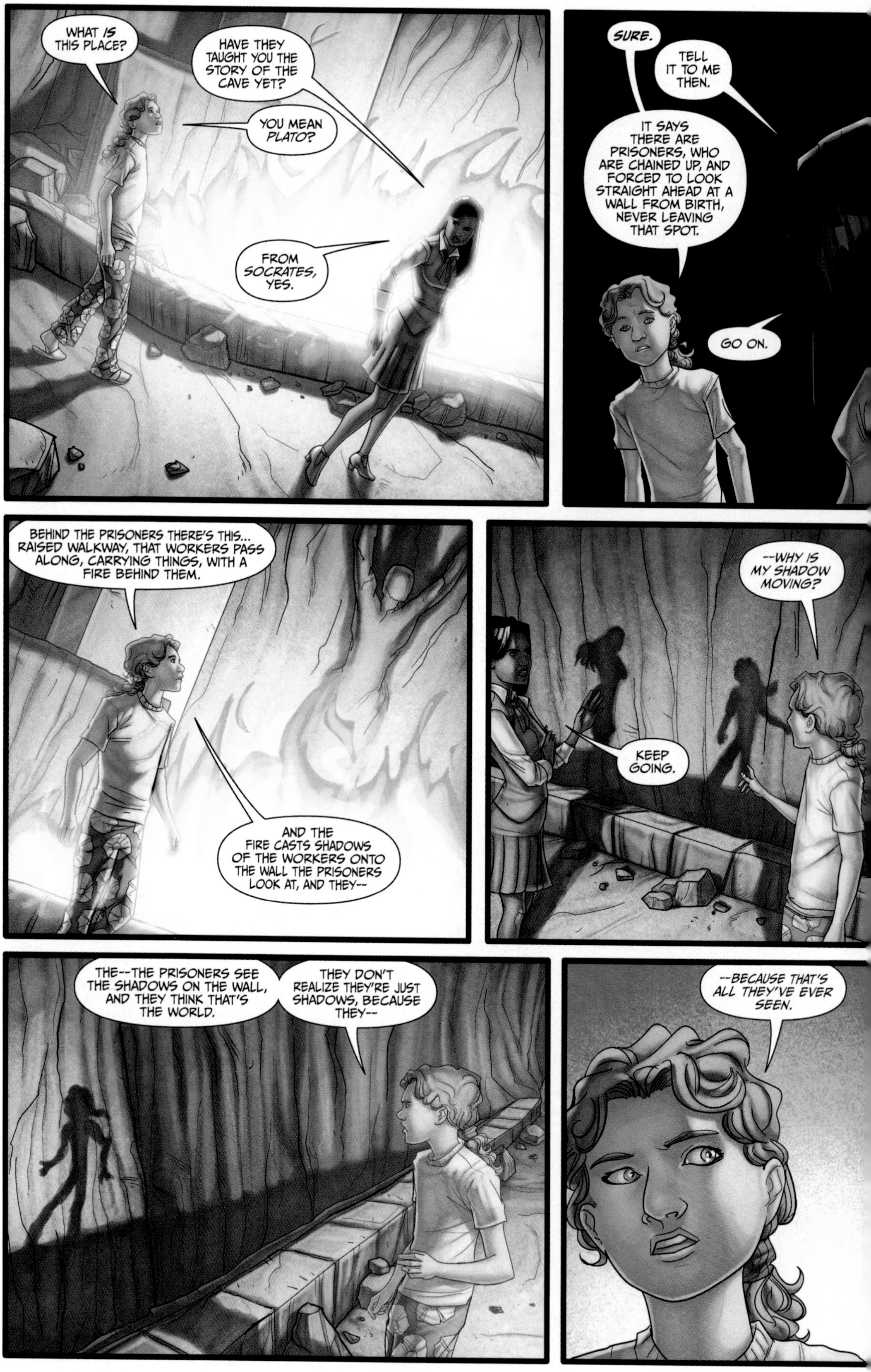
WHAT IS THIS PLACE?
HAVE THEY TAUGHT YOU THE STORY OF THE CAVE YET?
YOU MEAN PLATO?
FROM SOCRATES, YES.
SURE.
TELL IT TO ME THEN.
IT SAYS THERE ARE PRISONERS, WHO ARE CHAINED UP, AND FORCED TO LOOK STRAIGHT AHEAD AT A WALL FROM BIRTH, NEVER LEAVING THAT SPOT.
GO ON.
BEHIND THE PRISONERS THERE'S THIS... RAISED WALKWAY, THAT WORKERS PASS ALONG, CARRYING THINGS, WITH A FIRE BEHIND THEM.
AND THE FIRE CASTS SHADOWS OF THE WORKERS ONTO THE WALL THE PRISONERS LOOK AT, AND THEY--
--WHY IS MY SHADOW MOVING?
KEEP GOING.
THE--THE PRISONERS SEE THE SHADOWS ON THE WALL, AND THEY THINK THAT'S THE WORLD.
THEY DON'T REALIZE THEY'RE JUST SHADOWS, BECAUSE THEY--
--BECAUSE THAT'S ALL THEY'VE EVER SEEN.

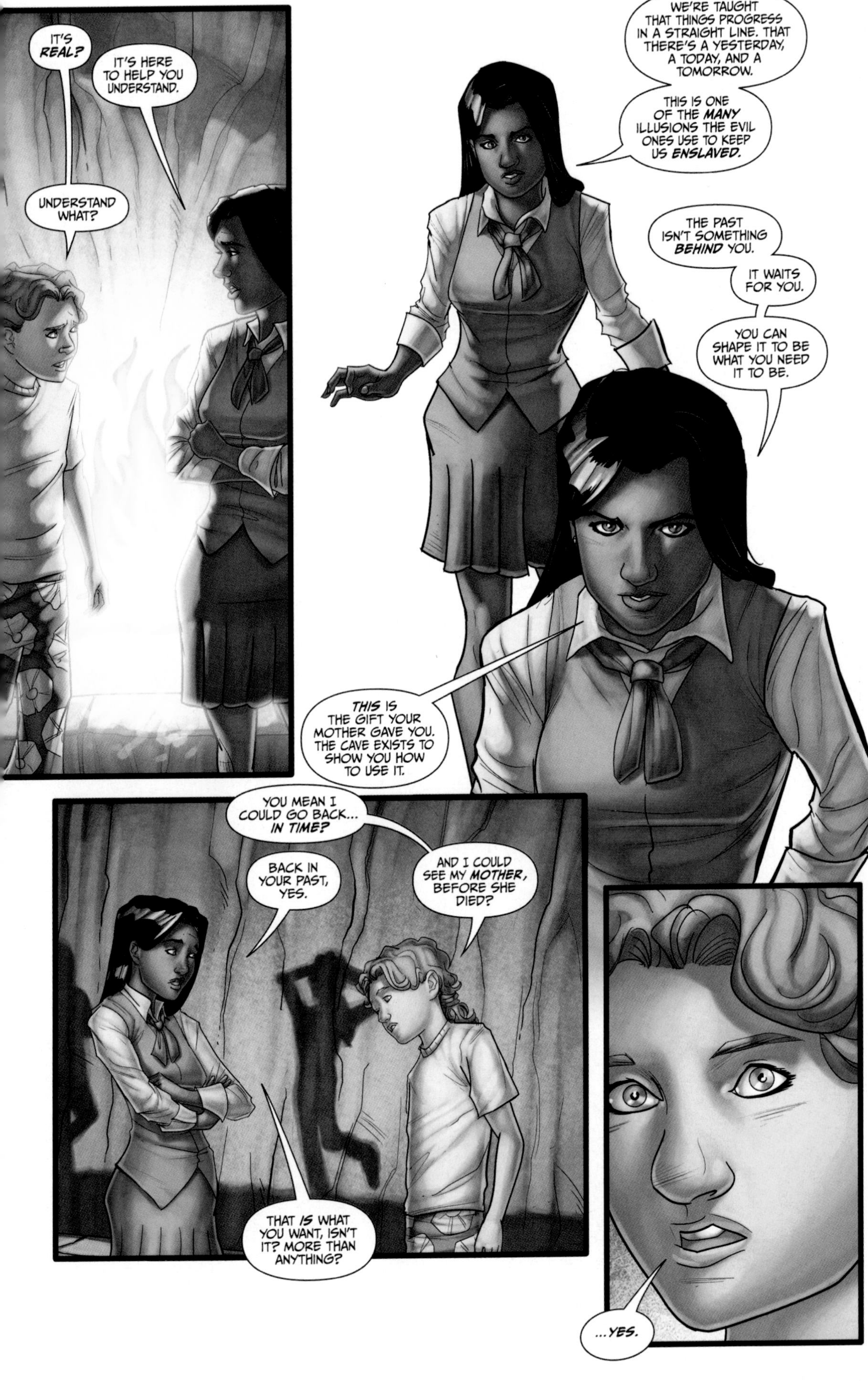
IT'S REAL?
IT'S HERE TO HELP YOU UNDERSTAND.
UNDERSTAND WHAT?
WE'RE TAUGHT THAT THINGS PROGRESS IN A STRAIGHT LINE. THAT THERE'S A YESTERDAY, A TODAY, AND A TOMORROW.
THIS IS ONE OF THE MANY ILLUSIONS THE EVIL ONES USE TO KEEP US ENSLAVED.
THE PAST ISN'T SOMETHING BEHIND YOU.
IT WAITS FOR YOU.
YOU CAN SHAPE IT TO BE WHAT YOU NEED IT TO BE.
THIS IS THE GIFT YOUR MOTHER GAVE YOU. THE CAVE EXISTS TO SHOW YOU HOW TO USE IT.
YOU MEAN I COULD GO BACK... IN TIME?
BACK IN YOUR PAST, YES.
AND I COULD SEE MY MOTHER, BEFORE SHE DIED?
THAT IS WHAT YOU WANT, ISN'T IT? MORE THAN ANYTHING?
...YES.

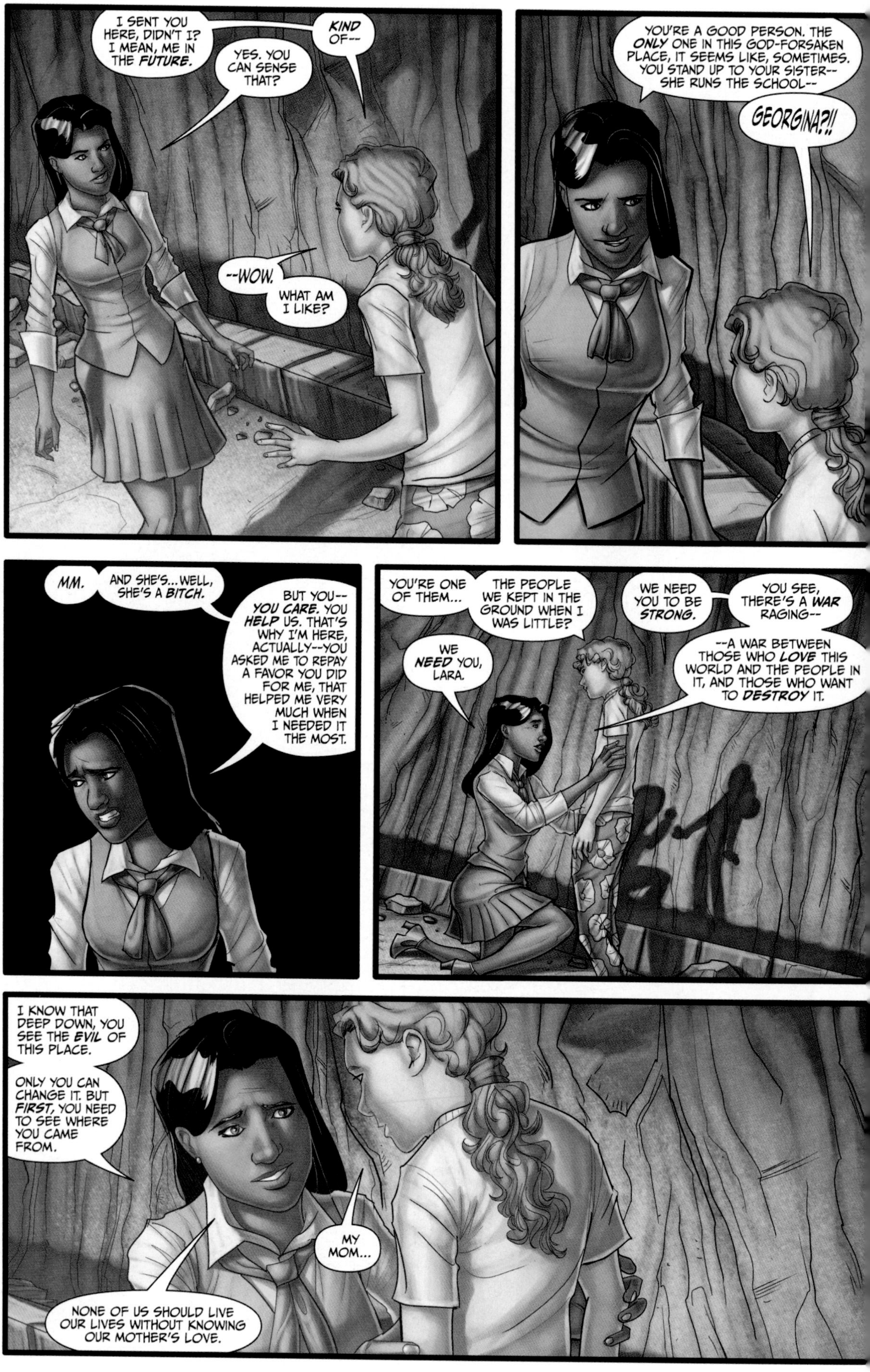

I SENT YOU HERE, DIDN'T I? I MEAN, ME IN THE *FUTURE.*
KIND OF--
YES. YOU CAN SENSE THAT?
--WOW.
WHAT AM I LIKE?
YOU'RE A GOOD PERSON. THE *ONLY* ONE IN THIS GOD-FORSAKEN PLACE, IT SEEMS LIKE, SOMETIMES. YOU STAND UP TO YOUR SISTER-- SHE RUNS THE SCHOOL--
GEORGINA?!!
MM.
AND SHE'S...WELL, SHE'S A *BITCH.*
BUT YOU-- *YOU CARE.* YOU *HELP* US. THAT'S WHY I'M HERE, ACTUALLY--YOU ASKED ME TO REPAY A FAVOR YOU DID FOR ME, THAT HELPED ME VERY MUCH WHEN I NEEDED IT THE MOST.
YOU'RE ONE OF THEM...
THE PEOPLE WE KEPT IN THE GROUND WHEN I WAS LITTLE?
WE NEED YOU TO BE *STRONG.*
YOU SEE, THERE'S A *WAR* RAGING--
--A WAR BETWEEN THOSE WHO *LOVE* THIS WORLD AND THE PEOPLE IN IT, AND THOSE WHO WANT TO *DESTROY* IT.
WE *NEED* YOU, LARA.
I KNOW THAT DEEP DOWN, YOU SEE THE *EVIL* OF THIS PLACE.
ONLY YOU CAN CHANGE IT. BUT *FIRST,* YOU NEED TO SEE WHERE YOU CAME FROM.
MY MOM...
NONE OF US SHOULD LIVE OUR LIVES WITHOUT KNOWING OUR MOTHER'S LOVE.

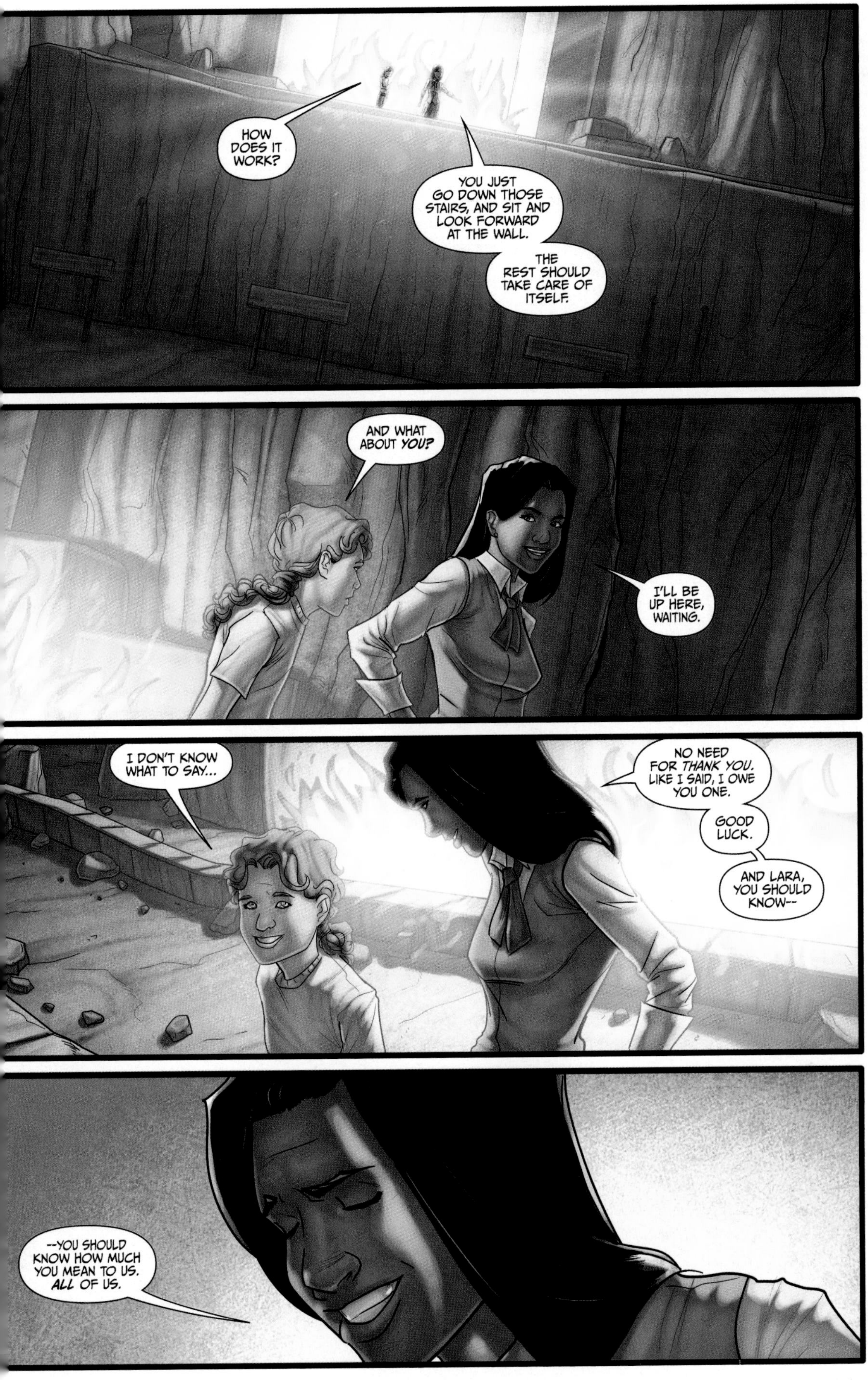
HOW DOES IT WORK?
YOU JUST GO DOWN THOSE STAIRS, AND SIT AND LOOK FORWARD AT THE WALL.
THE REST SHOULD TAKE CARE OF ITSELF.
AND WHAT ABOUT *YOU?*
I'LL BE UP HERE, WAITING.
I DON'T KNOW WHAT TO SAY...
NO NEED FOR *THANK YOU*. LIKE I SAID, I OWE YOU ONE.
GOOD LUCK.
AND LARA, YOU SHOULD KNOW--
--YOU SHOULD KNOW HOW MUCH YOU MEAN TO US. *ALL* OF US.

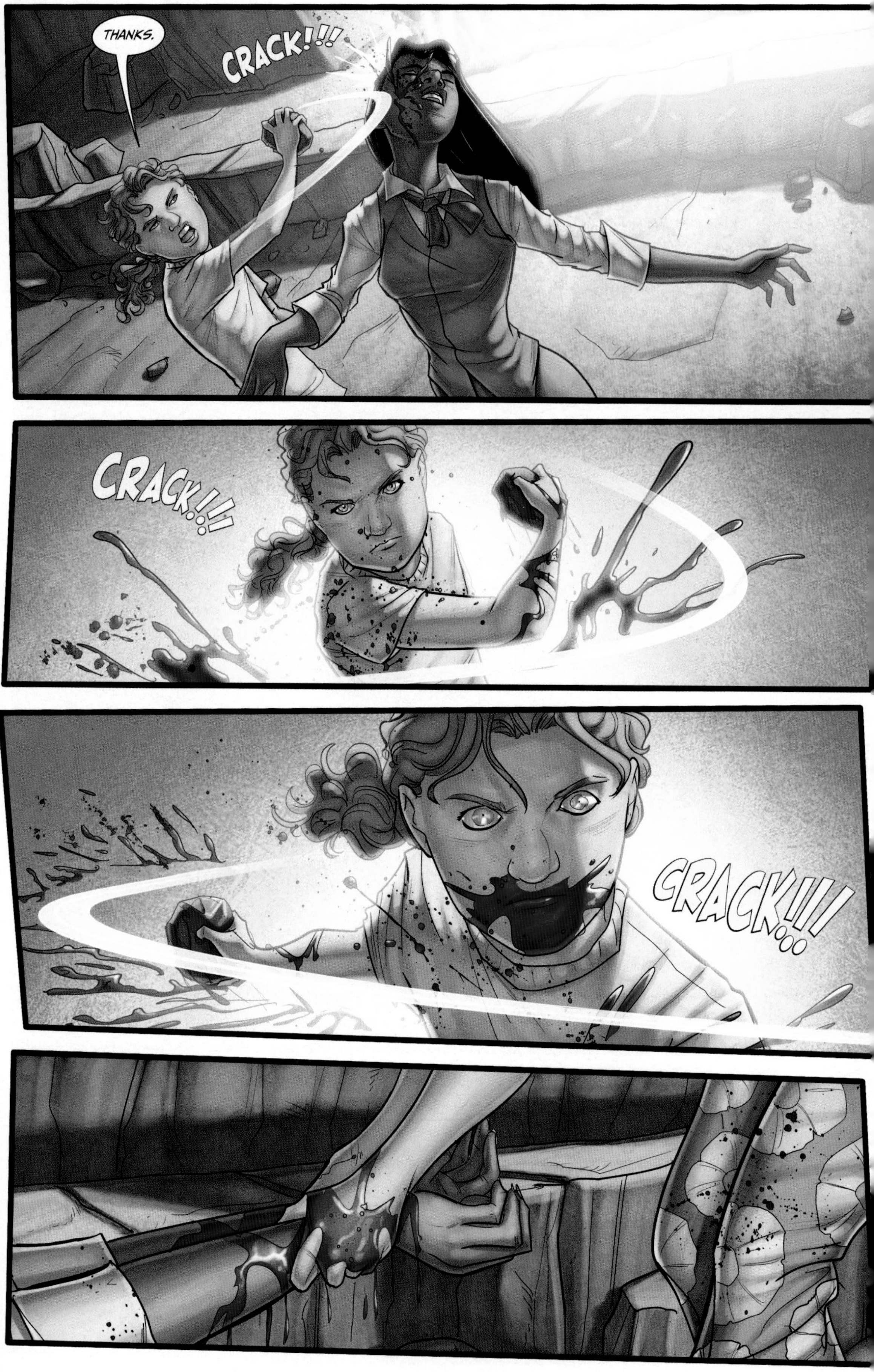
THANKS.
CRACK!!!
CRACK...!!!
CRACK...!!!

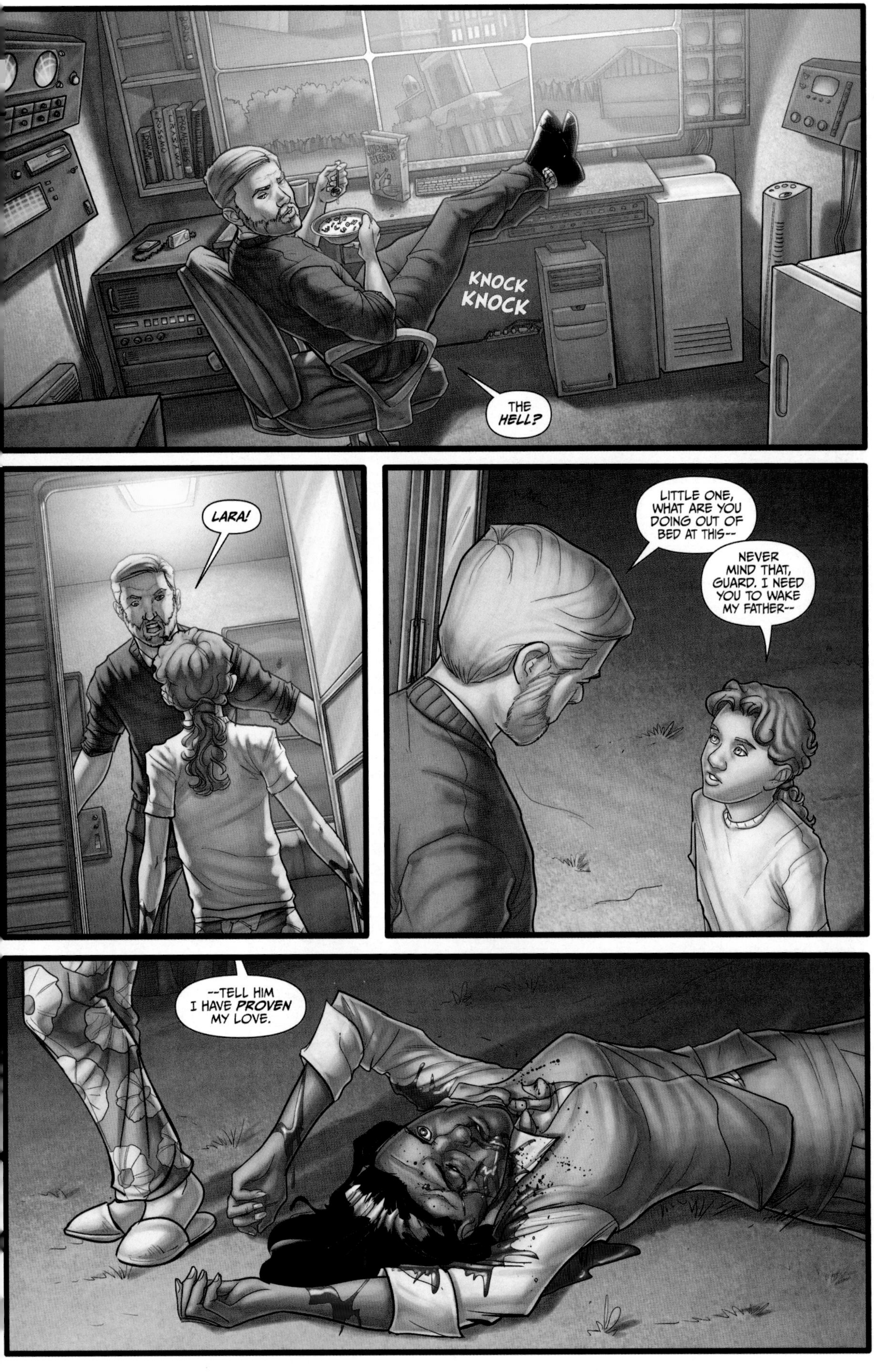
KNOCK KNOCK
THE HELL?
LARA!
LITTLE ONE, WHAT ARE YOU DOING OUT OF BED AT THIS--
NEVER MIND THAT, GUARD. I NEED YOU TO WAKE MY FATHER--
--TELL HIM I HAVE PROVEN MY LOVE.

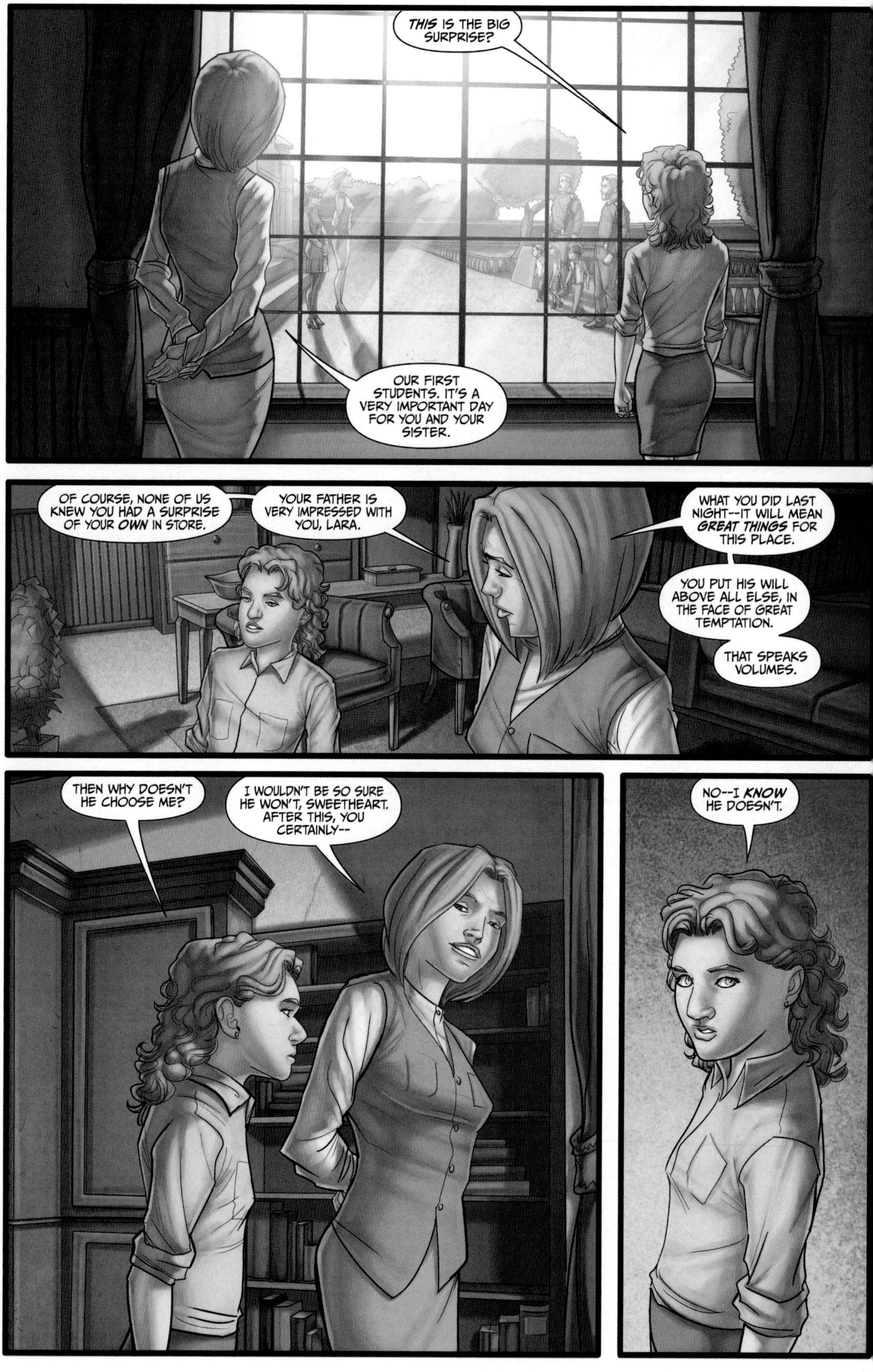
THIS IS THE BIG SURPRISE?
OUR FIRST STUDENTS. IT'S A VERY IMPORTANT DAY FOR YOU AND YOUR SISTER.
OF COURSE, NONE OF US KNEW YOU HAD A SURPRISE OF YOUR OWN IN STORE.
YOUR FATHER IS VERY IMPRESSED WITH YOU, LARA.
WHAT YOU DID LAST NIGHT--IT WILL MEAN GREAT THINGS FOR THIS PLACE.
YOU PUT HIS WILL ABOVE ALL ELSE, IN THE FACE OF GREAT TEMPTATION.
THAT SPEAKS VOLUMES.
THEN WHY DOESN'T HE CHOOSE ME?
I WOULDN'T BE SO SURE HE WON'T, SWEETHEART. AFTER THIS, YOU CERTAINLY--
NO--I KNOW HE DOESN'T.

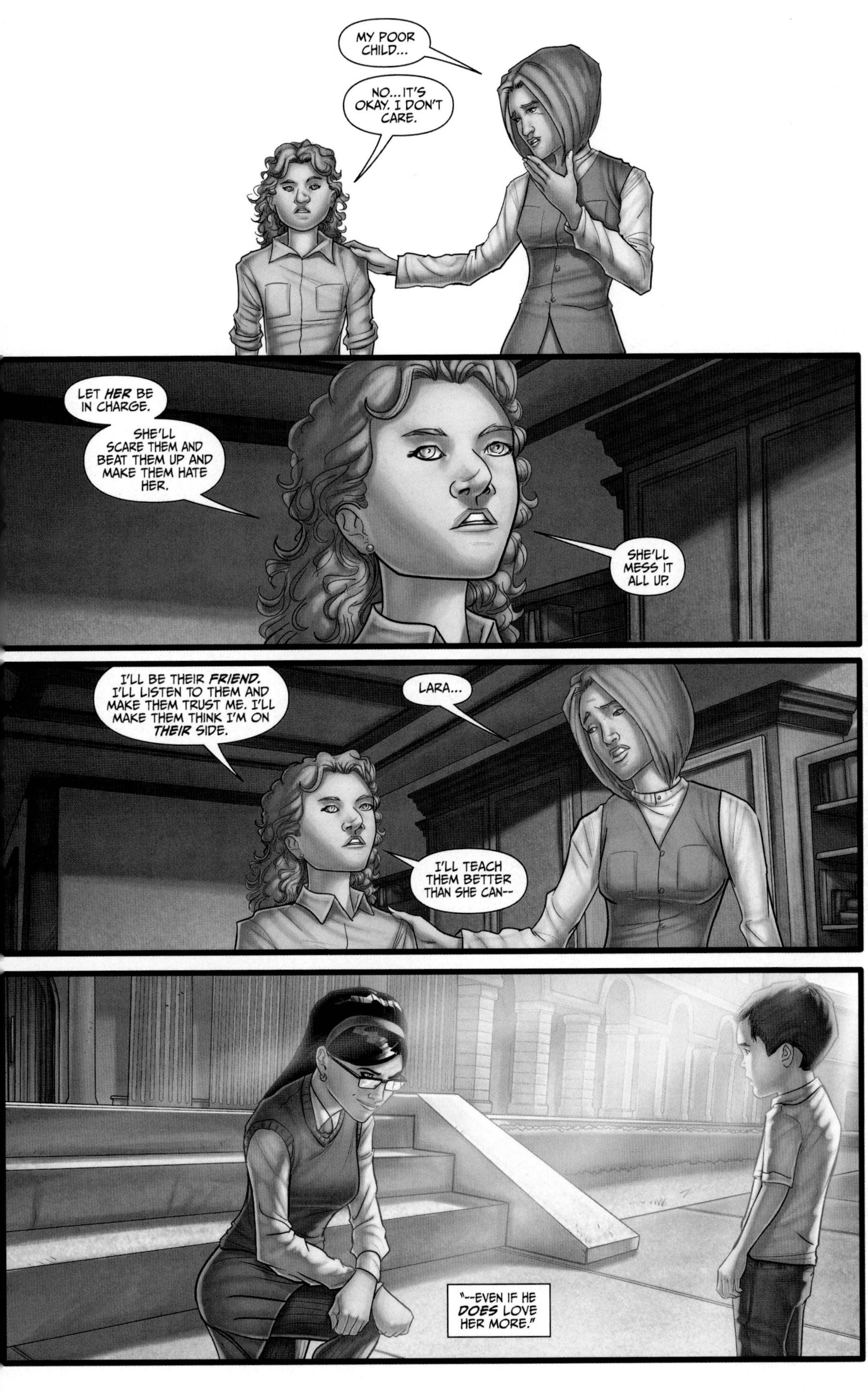
MY POOR CHILD...
NO...IT'S OKAY. I DON'T CARE.
LET *HER* BE IN CHARGE.
SHE'LL SCARE THEM AND BEAT THEM UP AND MAKE THEM HATE HER.
SHE'LL MESS IT ALL UP.
I'LL BE THEIR *FRIEND.* I'LL LISTEN TO THEM AND MAKE THEM TRUST ME. I'LL MAKE THEM THINK I'M ON *THEIR* SIDE.
LARA...
I'LL TEACH THEM BETTER THAN SHE CAN--
"--EVEN IF HE *DOES* LOVE HER MORE."

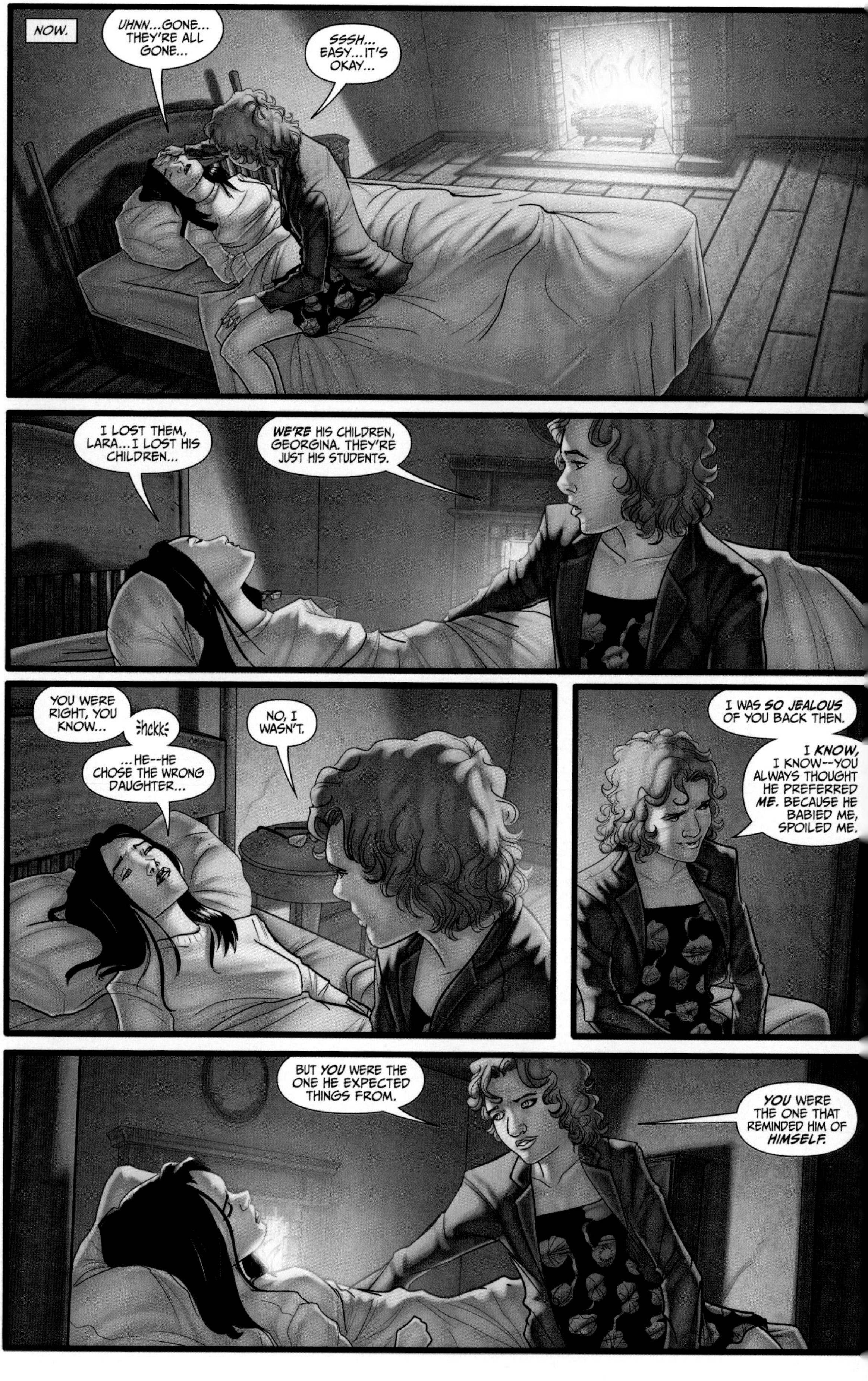
NOW.
UHNN...GONE... THEY'RE ALL GONE...
SSSH... EASY...IT'S OKAY...
I LOST THEM, LARA...I LOST HIS CHILDREN...
WE'RE HIS CHILDREN, GEORGINA. THEY'RE JUST HIS STUDENTS.
YOU WERE RIGHT, YOU KNOW...
hckk
...HE--HE CHOSE THE WRONG DAUGHTER...
NO, I WASN'T.
I WAS SO JEALOUS OF YOU BACK THEN.
I KNOW, I KNOW--YOU ALWAYS THOUGHT HE PREFERRED ME. BECAUSE HE BABIED ME, SPOILED ME.
BUT YOU WERE THE ONE HE EXPECTED THINGS FROM.
YOU WERE THE ONE THAT REMINDED HIM OF HIMSELF.

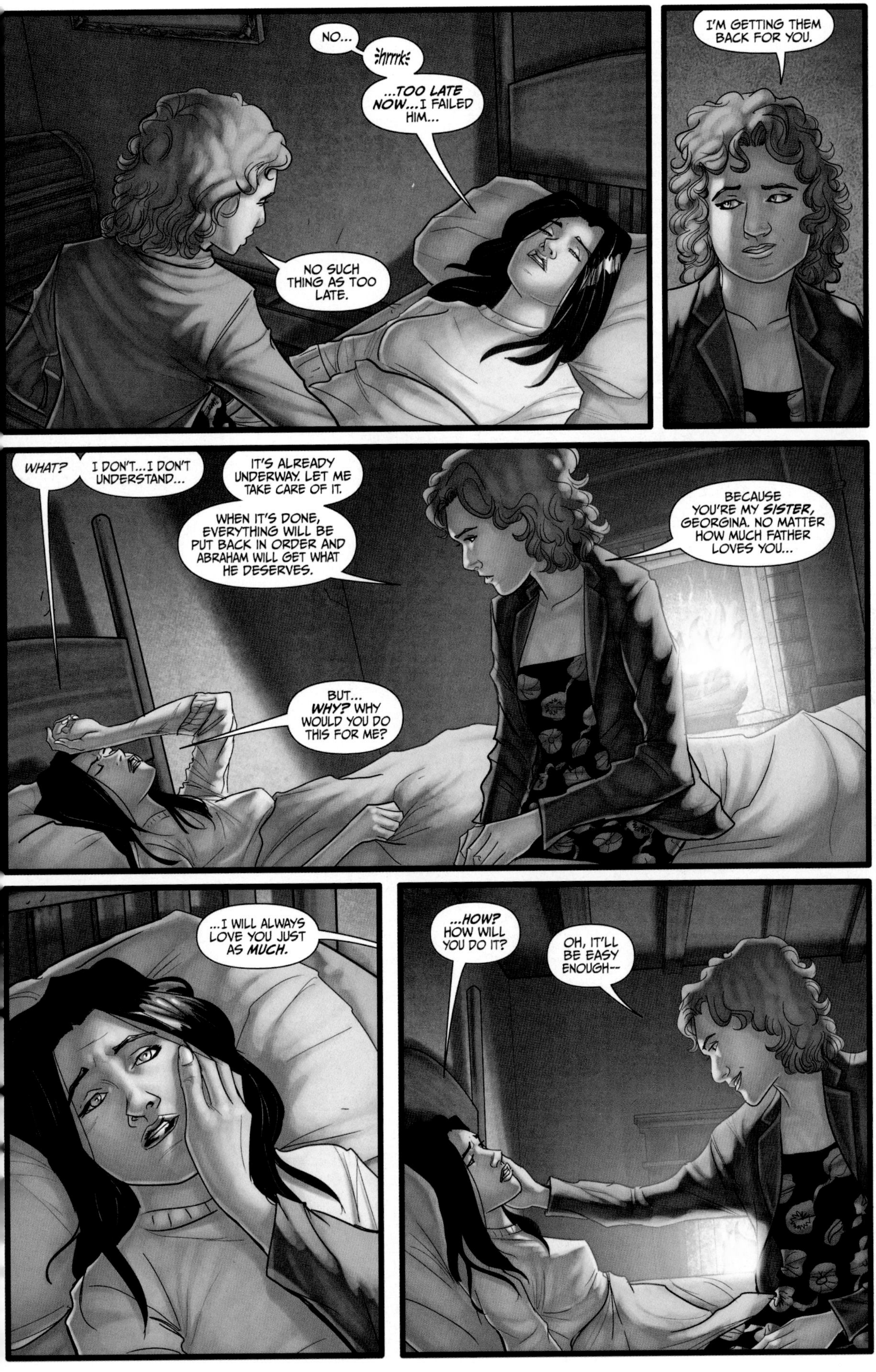
NO...
hrrrk
...TOO LATE NOW...I FAILED HIM...
NO SUCH THING AS TOO LATE.
I'M GETTING THEM BACK FOR YOU.
WHAT?
I DON'T...I DON'T UNDERSTAND...
IT'S ALREADY UNDERWAY. LET ME TAKE CARE OF IT.
WHEN IT'S DONE, EVERYTHING WILL BE PUT BACK IN ORDER AND ABRAHAM WILL GET WHAT HE DESERVES.
BUT... WHY? WHY WOULD YOU DO THIS FOR ME?
BECAUSE YOU'RE MY SISTER, GEORGINA. NO MATTER HOW MUCH FATHER LOVES YOU...
...I WILL ALWAYS LOVE YOU JUST AS MUCH.
...HOW? HOW WILL YOU DO IT?
OH, IT'LL BE EASY ENOUGH--

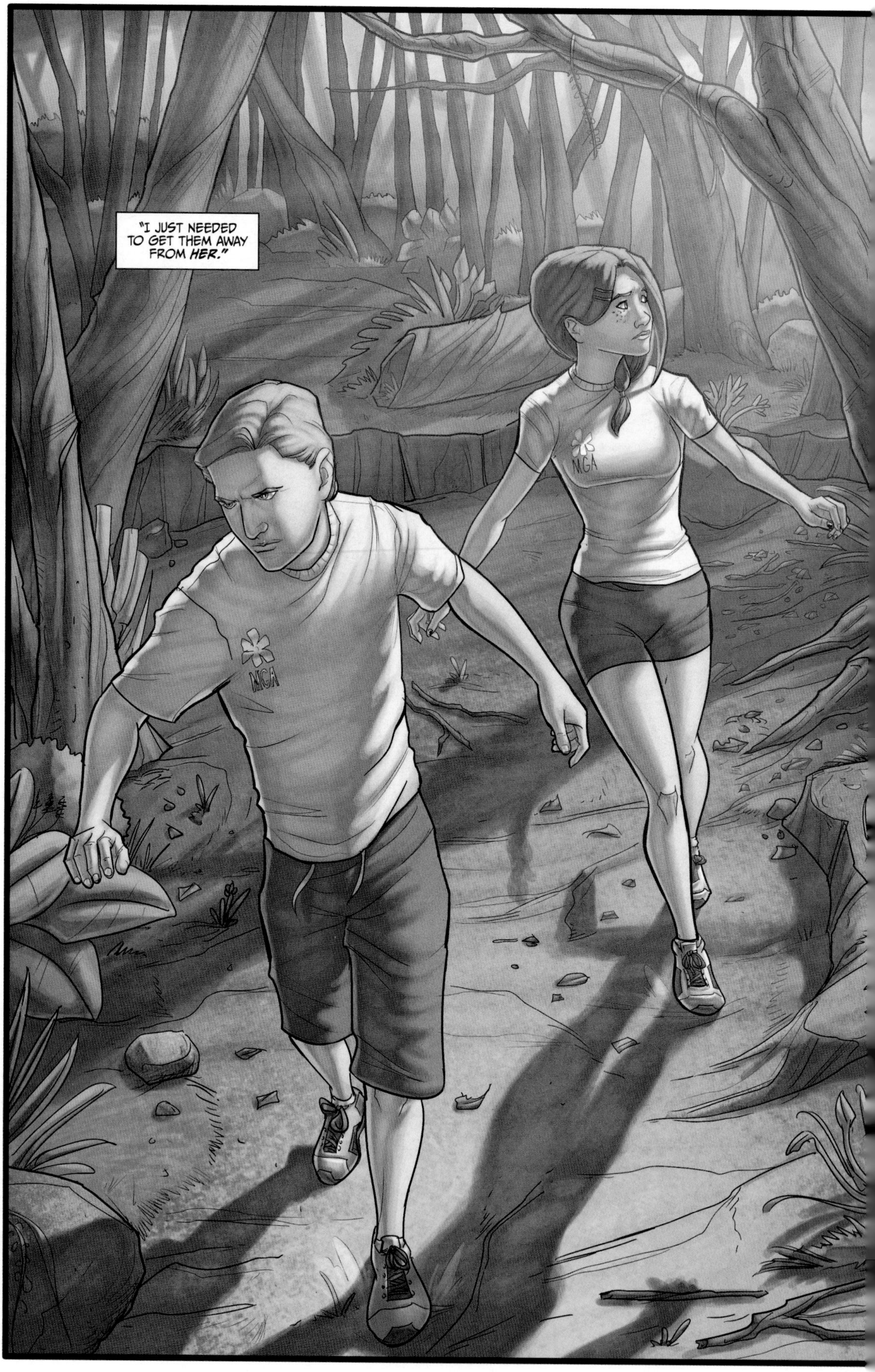
"I JUST NEEDED TO GET THEM AWAY FROM HER."

twentyone

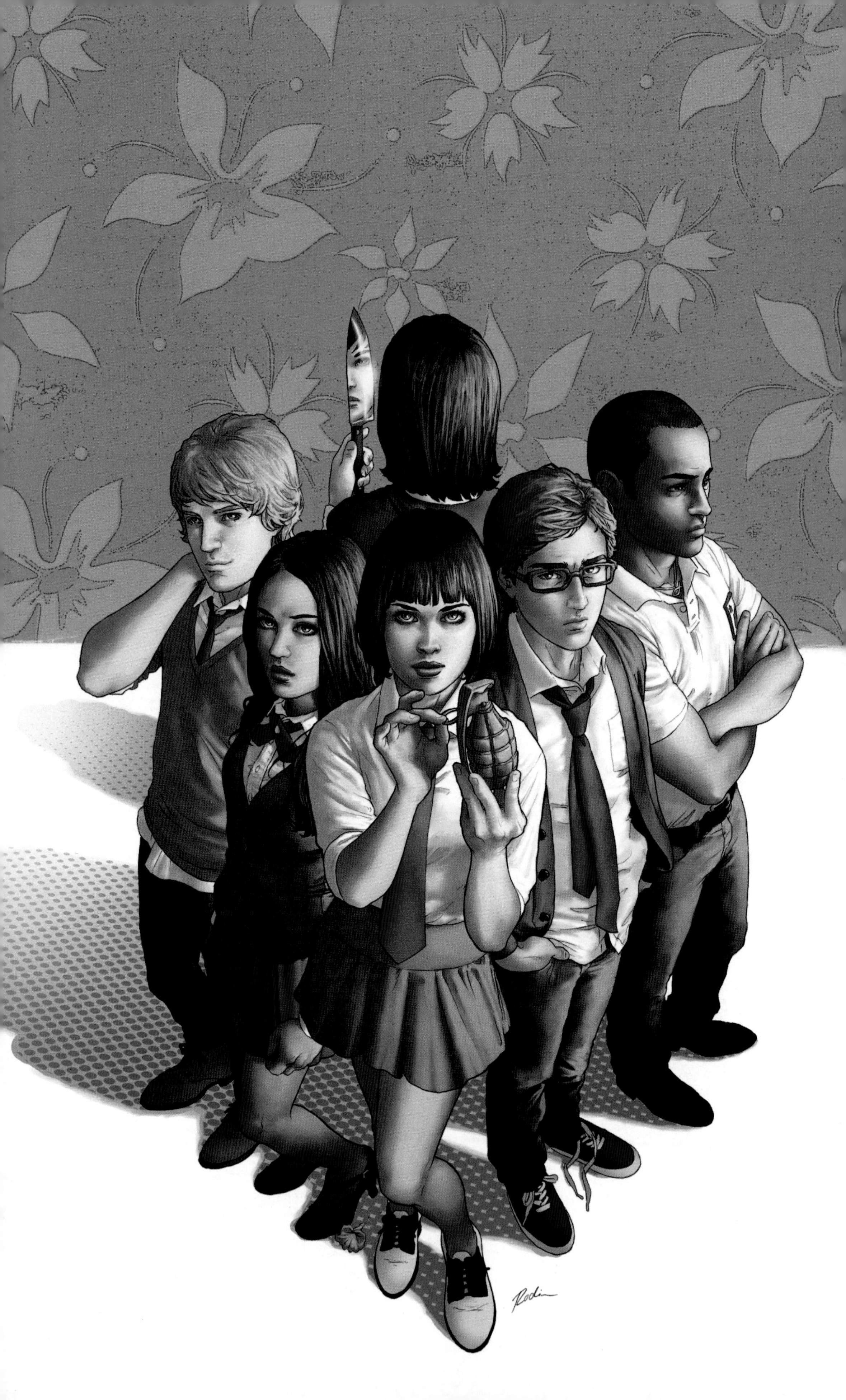

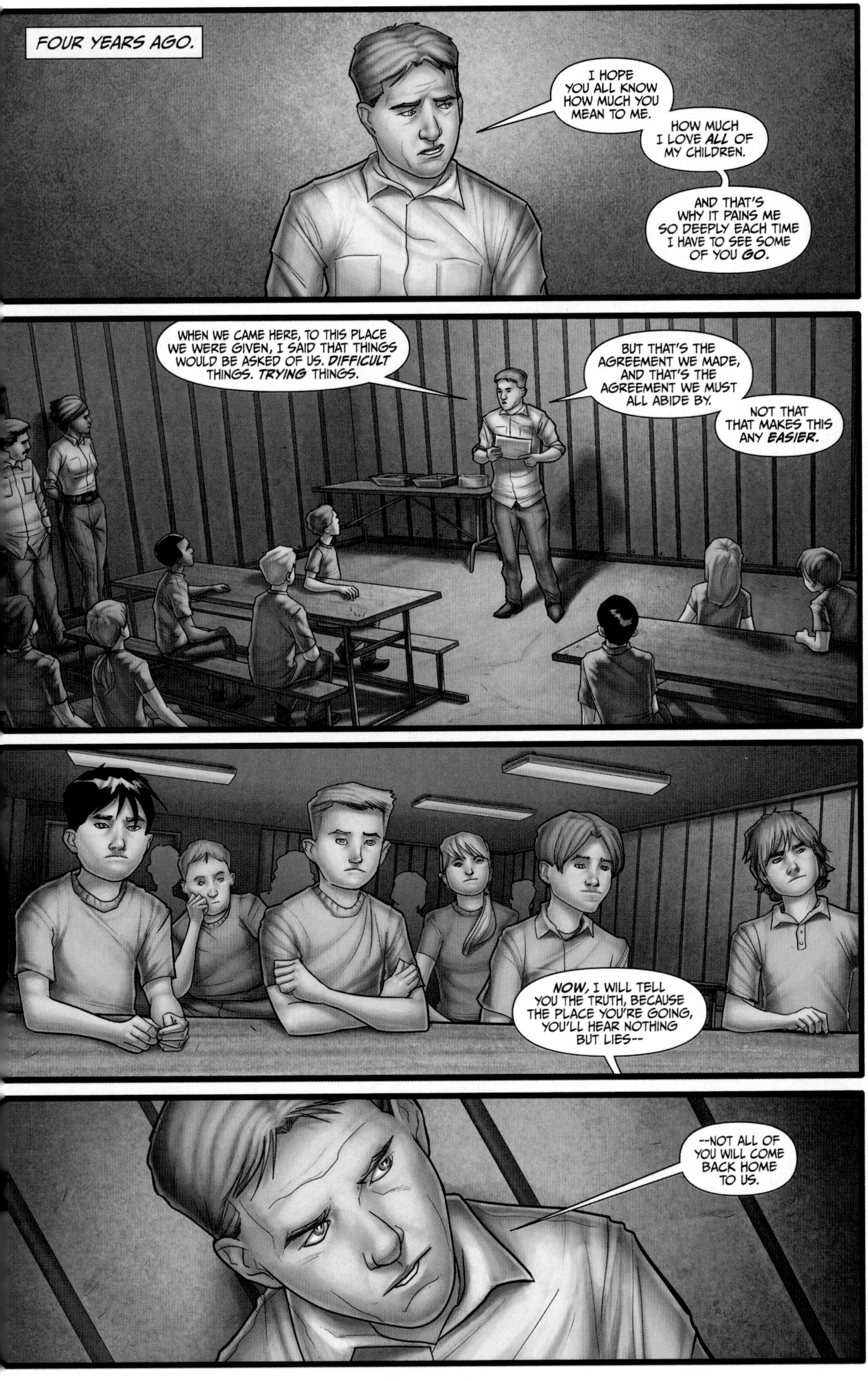
FOUR YEARS AGO.
I HOPE YOU ALL KNOW HOW MUCH YOU MEAN TO ME.
HOW MUCH I LOVE ALL OF MY CHILDREN.
AND THAT'S WHY IT PAINS ME SO DEEPLY EACH TIME I HAVE TO SEE SOME OF YOU GO.
WHEN WE CAME HERE, TO THIS PLACE WE WERE GIVEN, I SAID THAT THINGS WOULD BE ASKED OF US. DIFFICULT THINGS. TRYING THINGS.
BUT THAT'S THE AGREEMENT WE MADE, AND THAT'S THE AGREEMENT WE MUST ALL ABIDE BY.
NOT THAT THAT MAKES THIS ANY EASIER.
NOW, I WILL TELL YOU THE TRUTH, BECAUSE THE PLACE YOU'RE GOING, YOU'LL HEAR NOTHING BUT LIES--
--NOT ALL OF YOU WILL COME BACK HOME TO US.

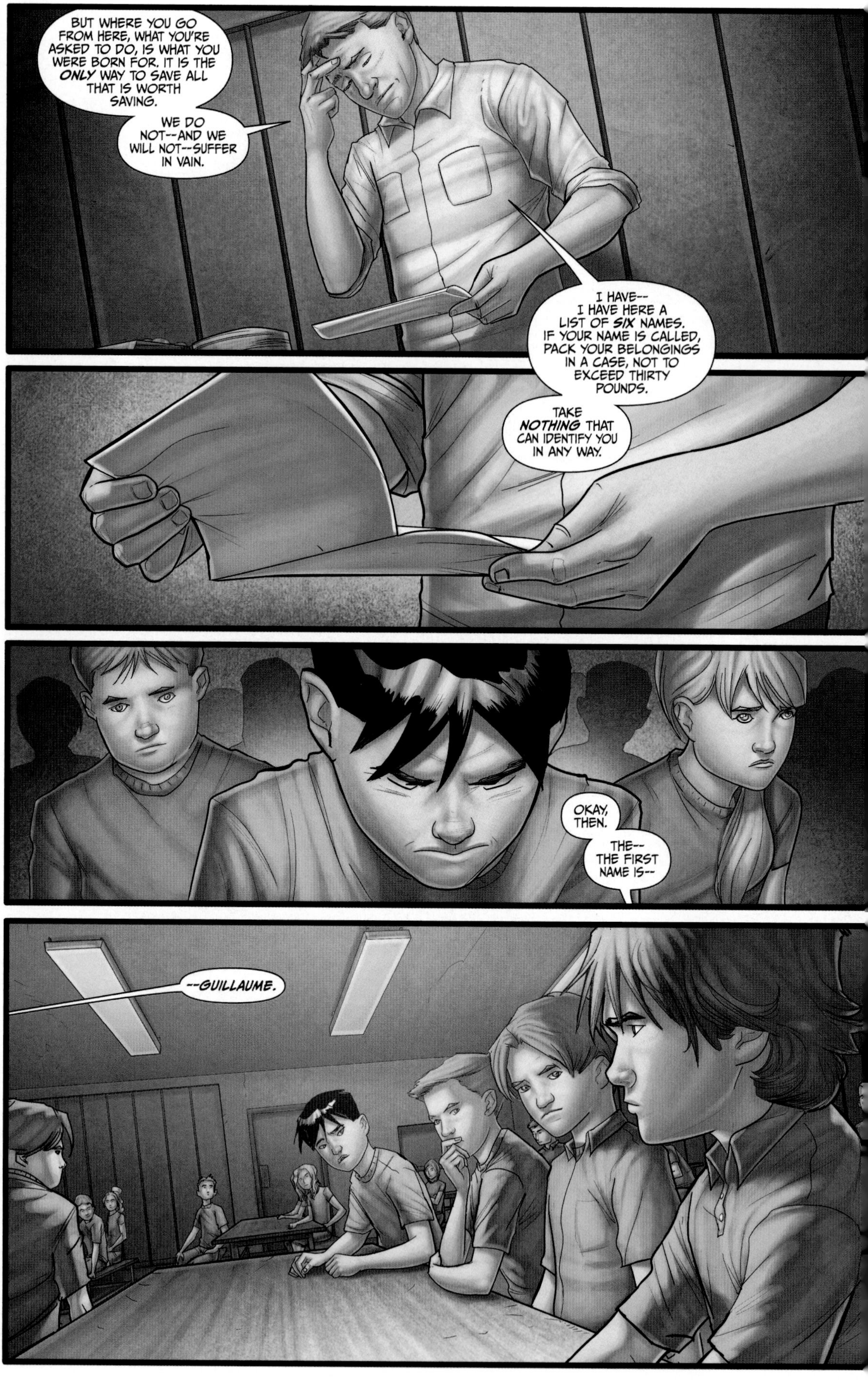
BUT WHERE YOU GO FROM HERE, WHAT YOU'RE ASKED TO DO, IS WHAT YOU WERE BORN FOR. IT IS THE ONLY WAY TO SAVE ALL THAT IS WORTH SAVING.
WE DO NOT--AND WE WILL NOT--SUFFER IN VAIN.
I HAVE-- I HAVE HERE A LIST OF SIX NAMES. IF YOUR NAME IS CALLED, PACK YOUR BELONGINGS IN A CASE, NOT TO EXCEED THIRTY POUNDS.
TAKE NOTHING THAT CAN IDENTIFY YOU IN ANY WAY.
OKAY, THEN.
THE-- THE FIRST NAME IS--
--GUILLAUME.

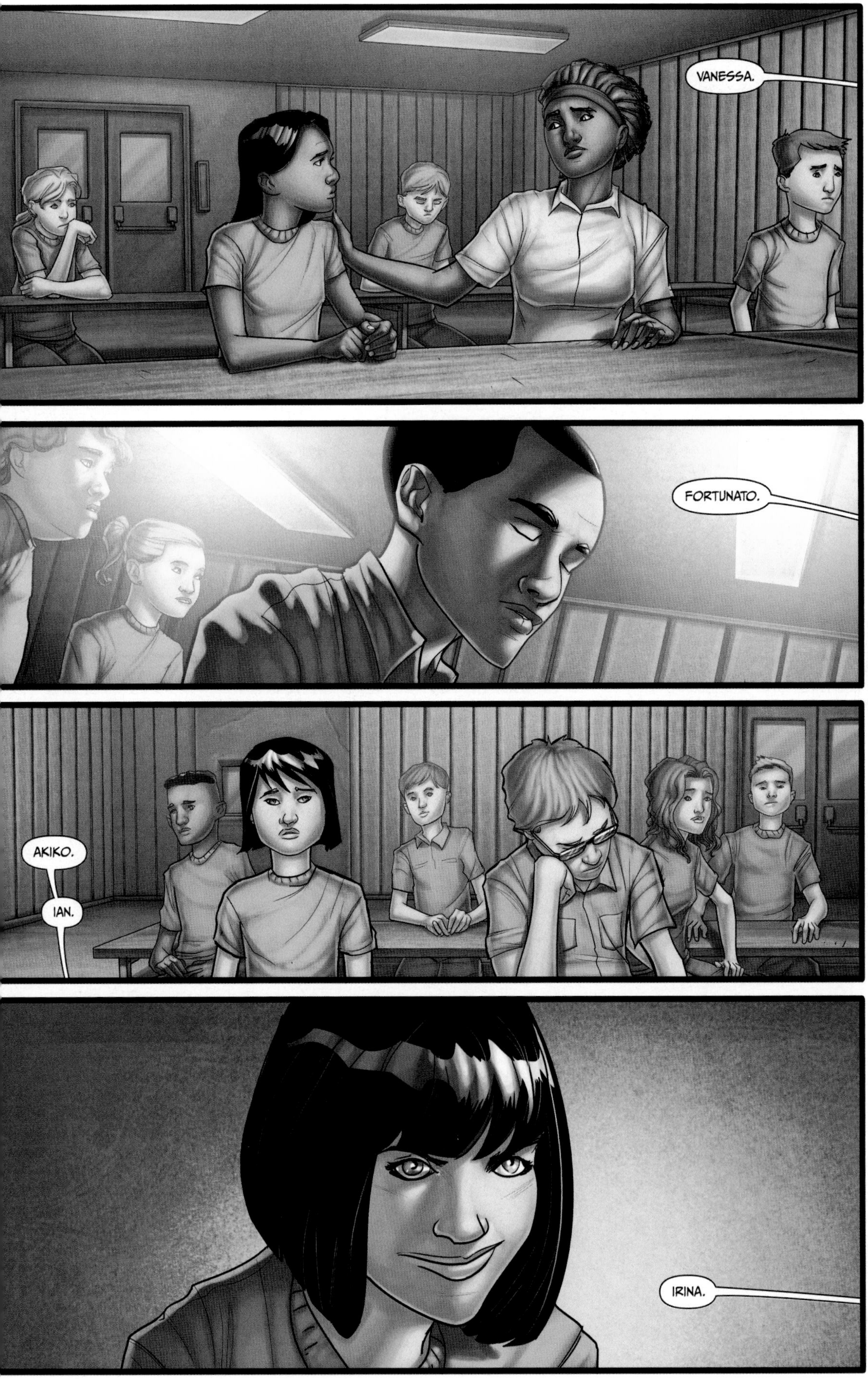
VANESSA.
FORTUNATO.
AKIKO.
IAN.
IRINA.

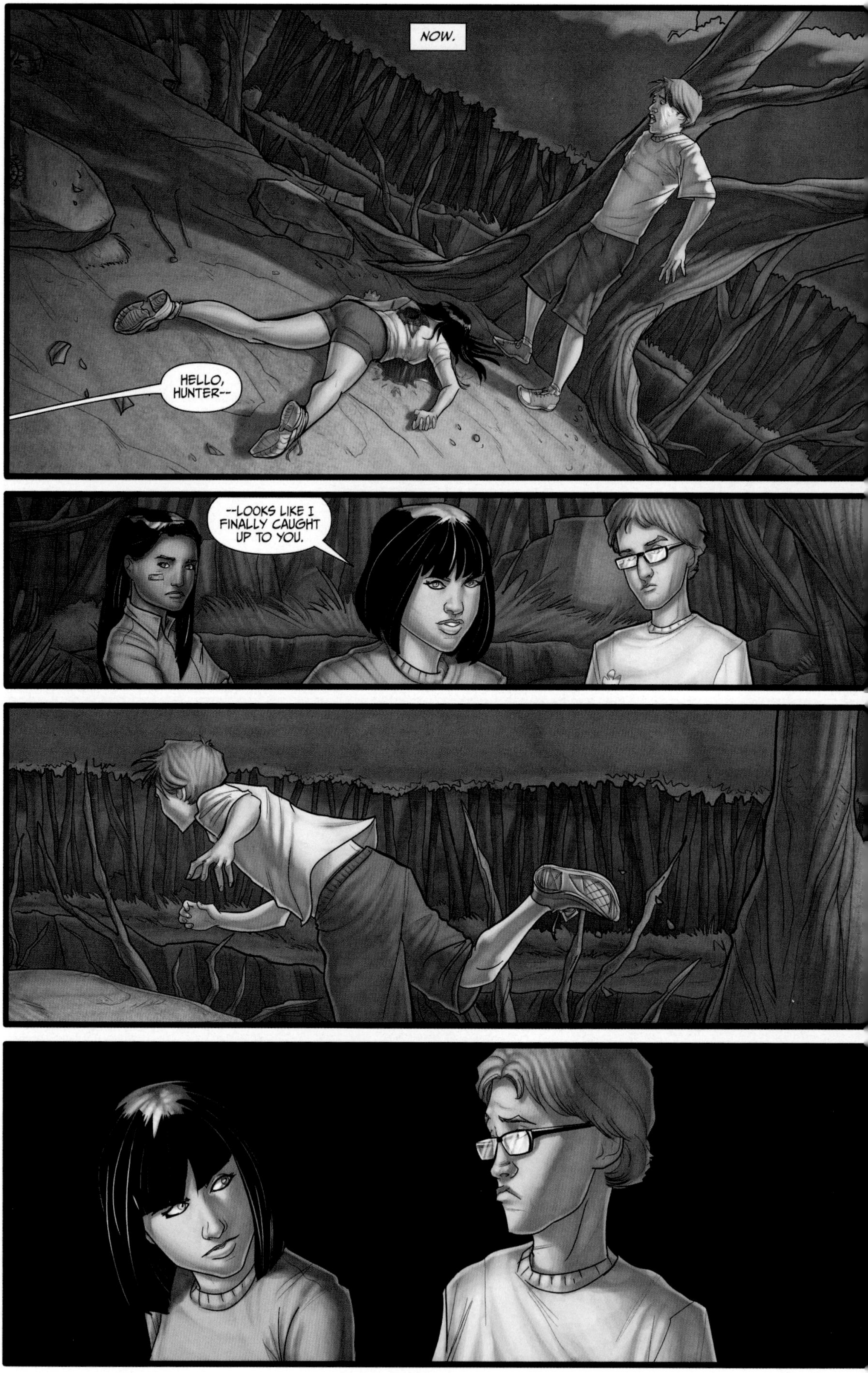
NOW.
HELLO, HUNTER--
--LOOKS LIKE I FINALLY CAUGHT UP TO YOU.

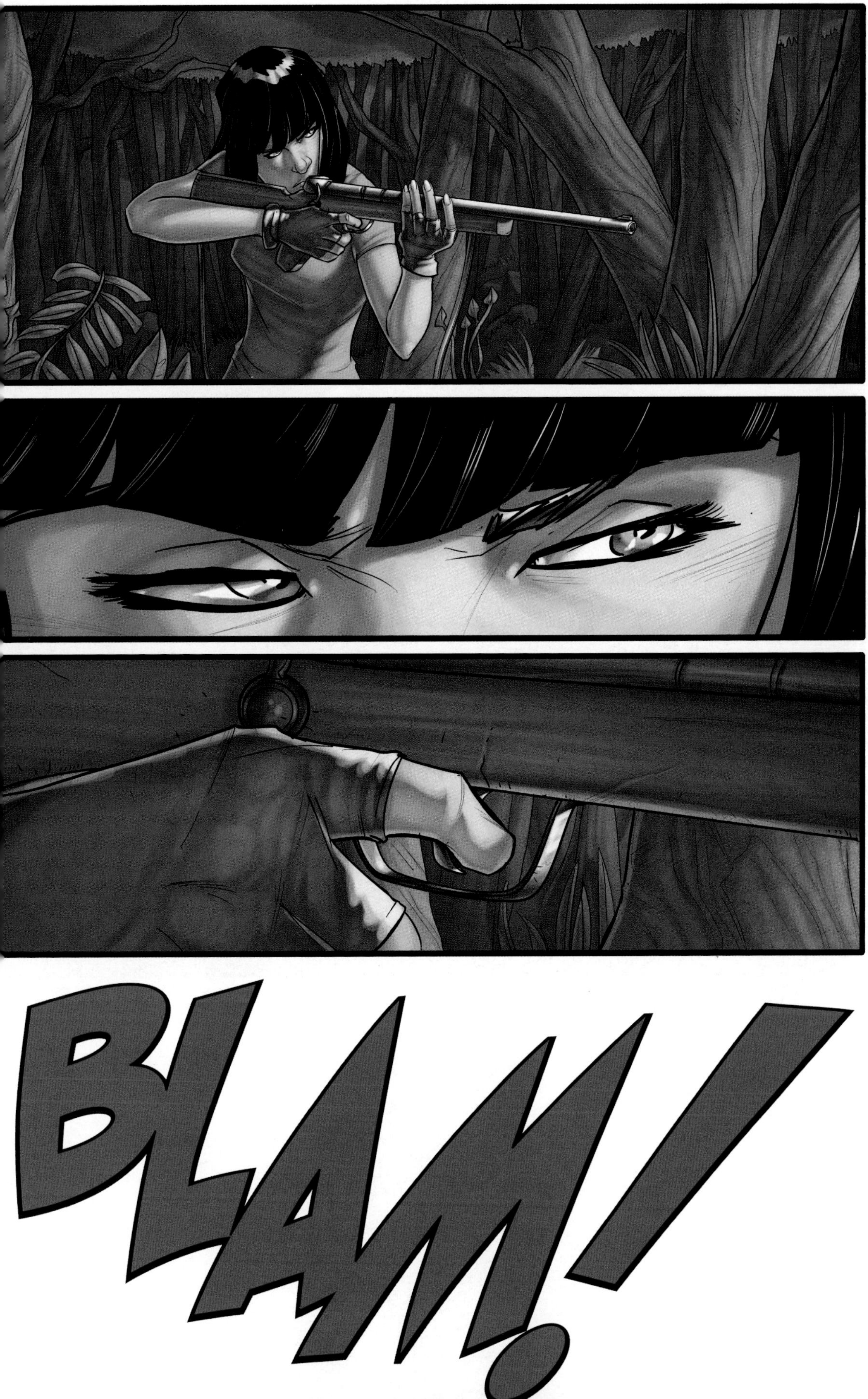
BLAM!

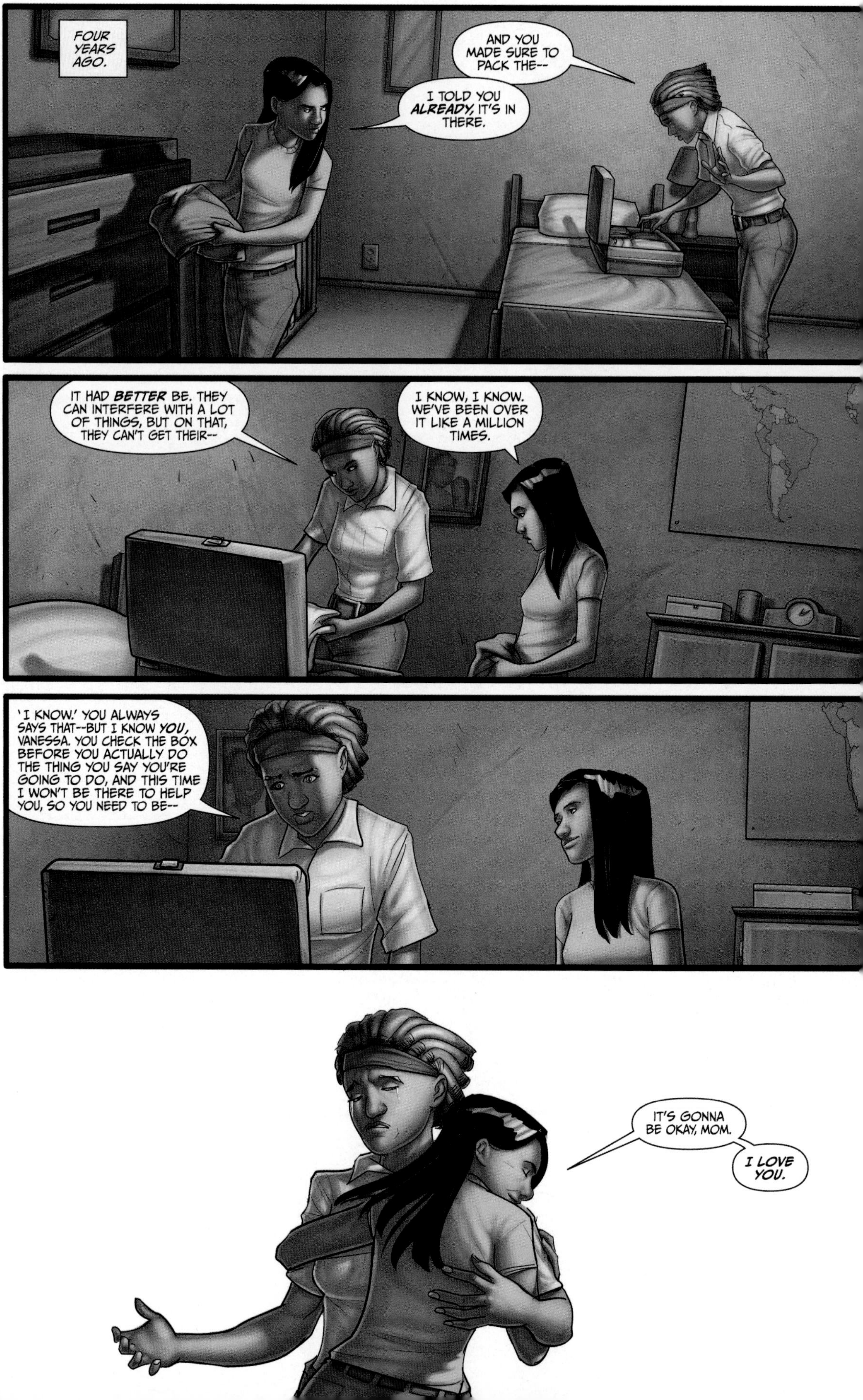
FOUR YEARS AGO.
AND YOU MADE SURE TO PACK THE--
I TOLD YOU ALREADY, IT'S IN THERE.
IT HAD BETTER BE. THEY CAN INTERFERE WITH A LOT OF THINGS, BUT ON THAT, THEY CAN'T GET THEIR--
I KNOW, I KNOW. WE'VE BEEN OVER IT LIKE A MILLION TIMES.
'I KNOW.' YOU ALWAYS SAYS THAT--BUT I KNOW YOU, VANESSA. YOU CHECK THE BOX BEFORE YOU ACTUALLY DO THE THING YOU SAY YOU'RE GOING TO DO, AND THIS TIME I WON'T BE THERE TO HELP YOU, SO YOU NEED TO BE--
IT'S GONNA BE OKAY, MOM.
I LOVE YOU.

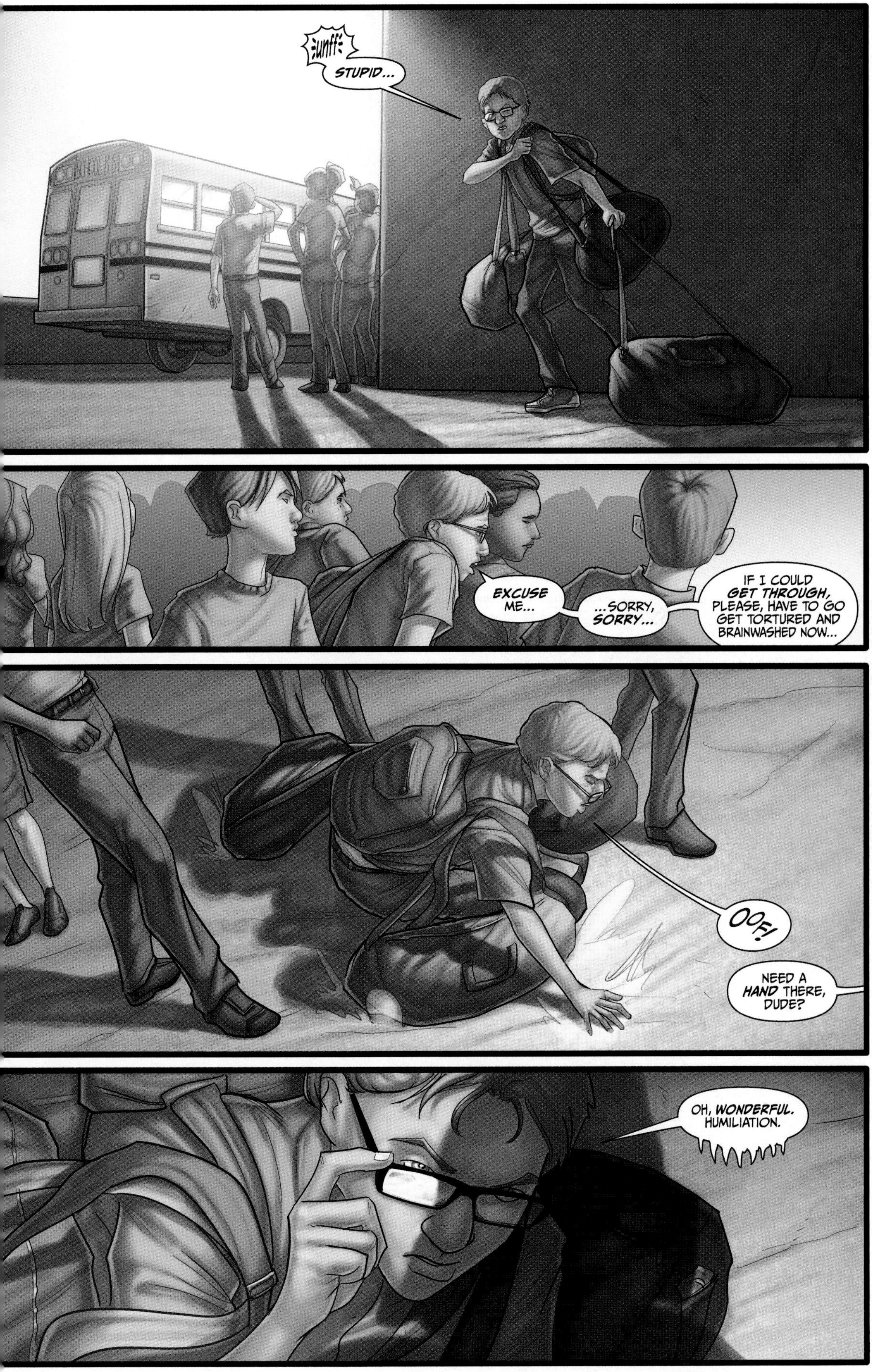
:unff:
STUPID...
SCHOOL BUS
EXCUSE ME...
...SORRY, SORRY...
IF I COULD GET THROUGH, PLEASE, HAVE TO GO GET TORTURED AND BRAINWASHED NOW...
OOF!
NEED A HAND THERE, DUDE?
OH, WONDERFUL. HUMILIATION.

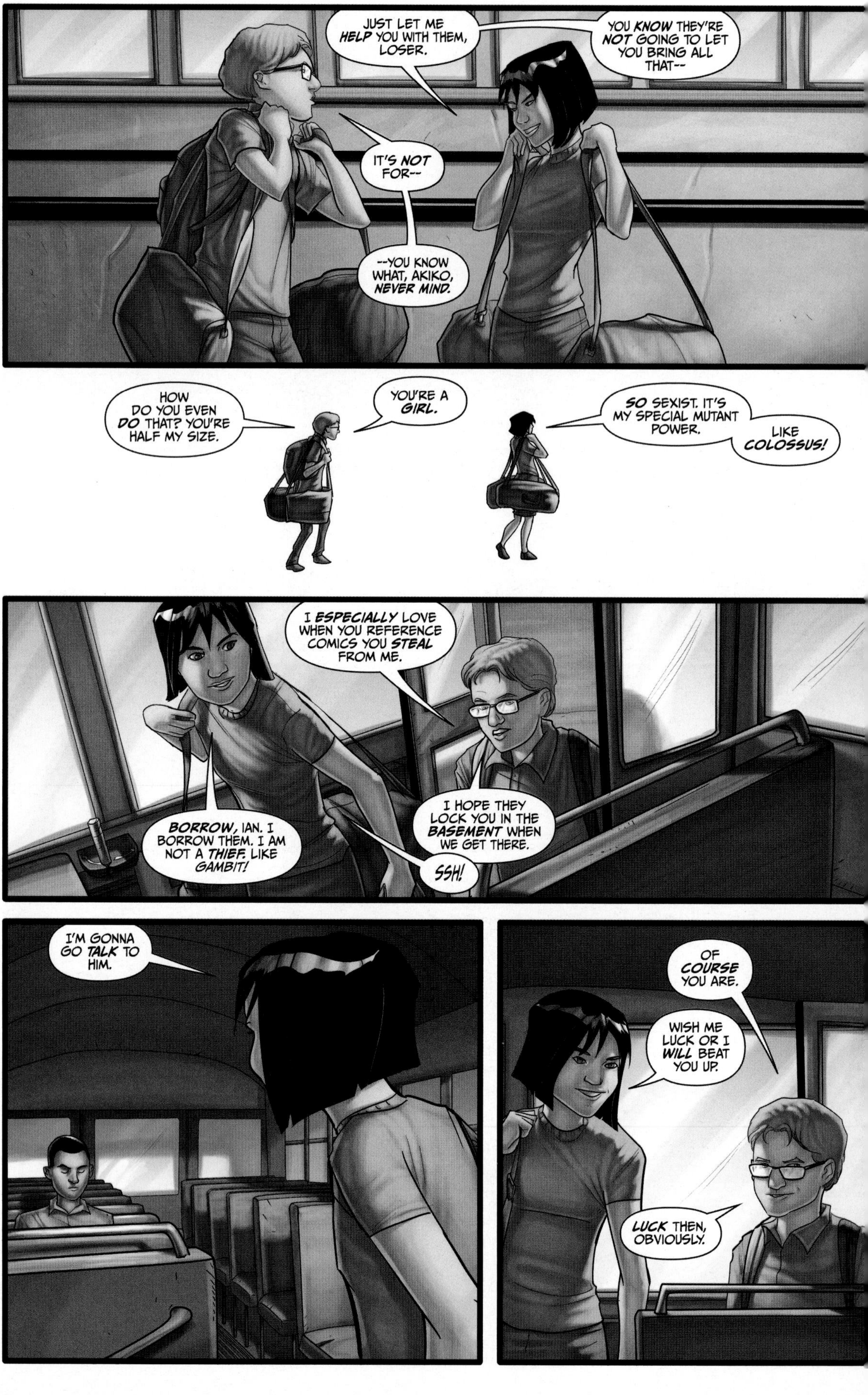
JUST LET ME HELP YOU WITH THEM, LOSER.
YOU KNOW THEY'RE NOT GOING TO LET YOU BRING ALL THAT--
IT'S NOT FOR--
--YOU KNOW WHAT, AKIKO, NEVER MIND.
HOW DO YOU EVEN DO THAT? YOU'RE HALF MY SIZE.
YOU'RE A GIRL.
SO SEXIST. IT'S MY SPECIAL MUTANT POWER.
LIKE COLOSSUS!
I ESPECIALLY LOVE WHEN YOU REFERENCE COMICS YOU STEAL FROM ME.
BORROW, IAN. I BORROW THEM. I AM NOT A THIEF. LIKE GAMBIT!
I HOPE THEY LOCK YOU IN THE BASEMENT WHEN WE GET THERE.
SSH!
I'M GONNA GO TALK TO HIM.
OF COURSE YOU ARE.
WISH ME LUCK OR I WILL BEAT YOU UP.
LUCK THEN, OBVIOUSLY.

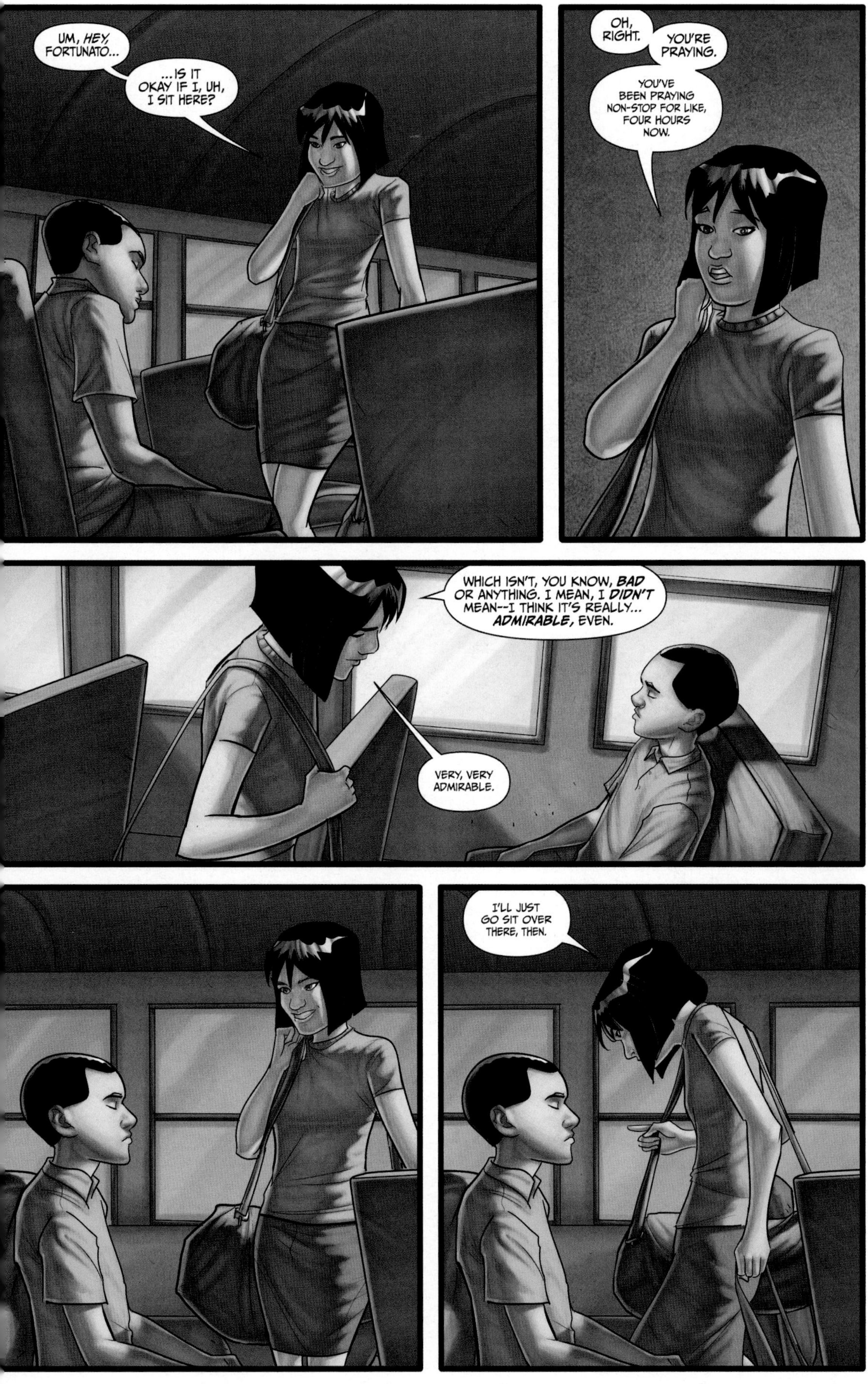
UM, HEY, FORTUNATO...
...IS IT OKAY IF I, UH, I SIT HERE?
OH, RIGHT.
YOU'RE PRAYING.
YOU'VE BEEN PRAYING NON-STOP FOR LIKE, FOUR HOURS NOW.
WHICH ISN'T, YOU KNOW, BAD OR ANYTHING. I MEAN, I DIDN'T MEAN--I THINK IT'S REALLY... ADMIRABLE, EVEN.
VERY, VERY ADMIRABLE.
I'LL JUST GO SIT OVER THERE, THEN.

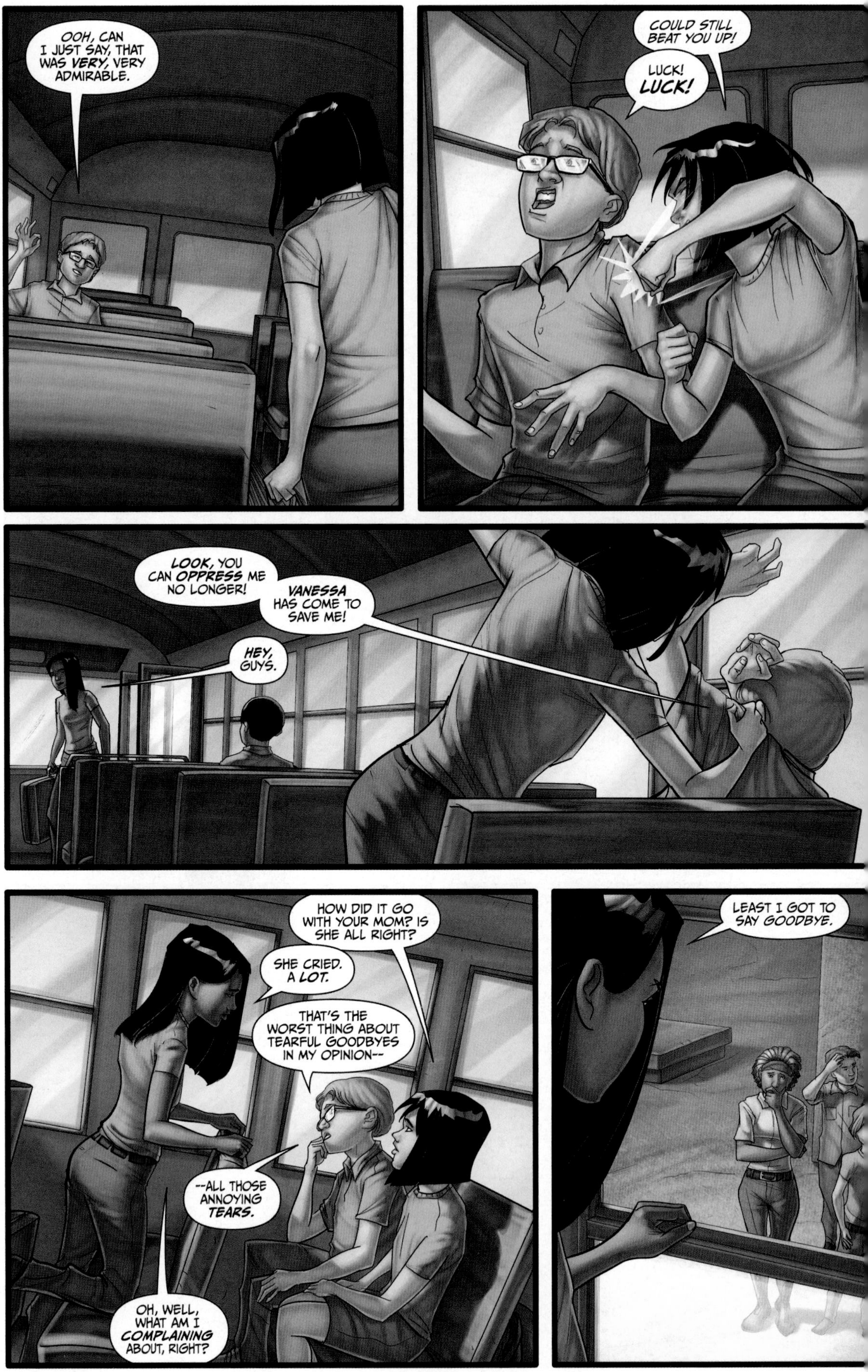

OOH, CAN I JUST SAY, THAT WAS VERY, VERY ADMIRABLE.
COULD STILL BEAT YOU UP!
LUCK! LUCK!
LOOK, YOU CAN OPPRESS ME NO LONGER!
VANESSA HAS COME TO SAVE ME!
HEY, GUYS.
HOW DID IT GO WITH YOUR MOM? IS SHE ALL RIGHT?
SHE CRIED. A LOT.
THAT'S THE WORST THING ABOUT TEARFUL GOODBYES IN MY OPINION--
--ALL THOSE ANNOYING TEARS.
OH, WELL, WHAT AM I COMPLAINING ABOUT, RIGHT?
LEAST I GOT TO SAY GOODBYE.

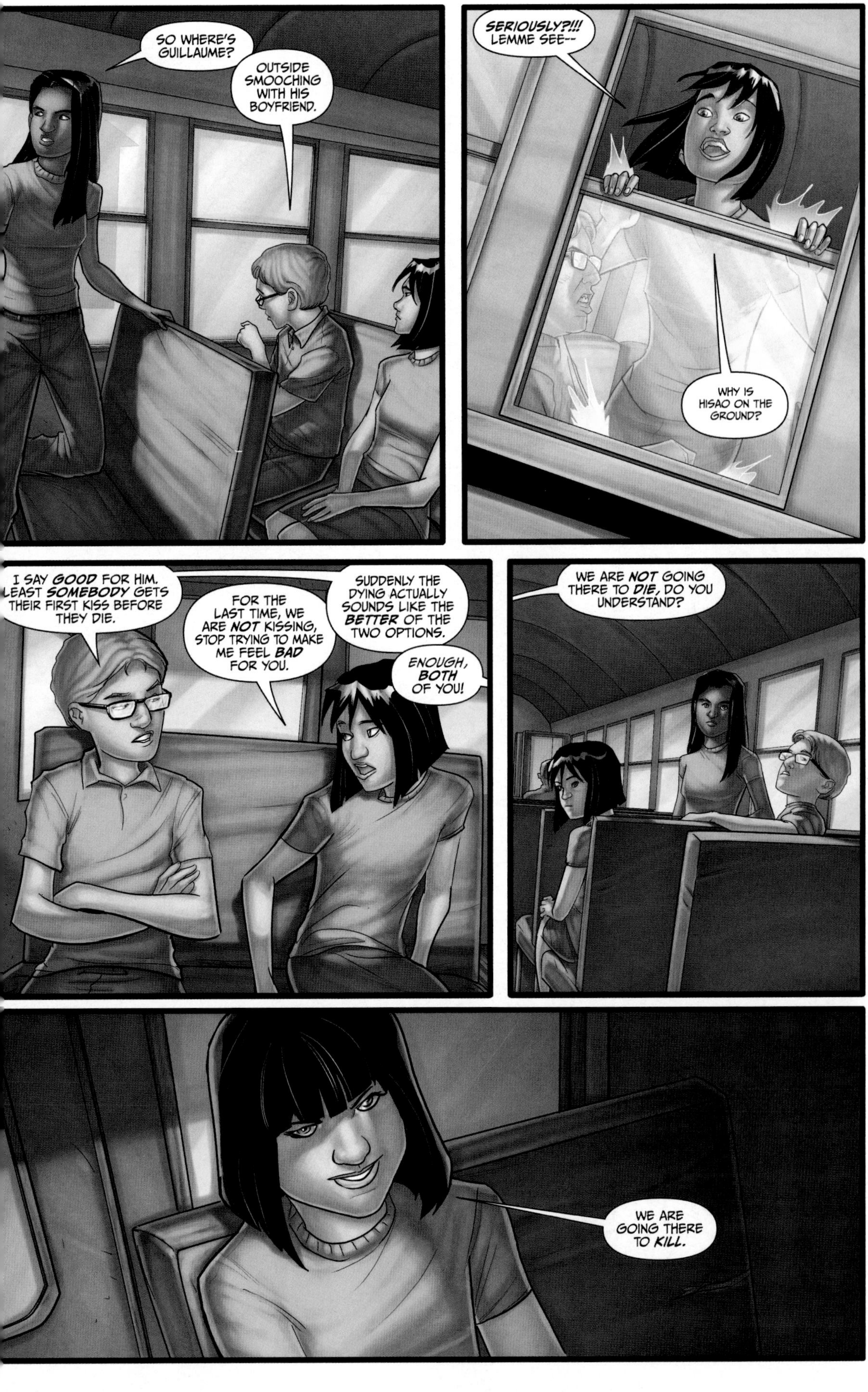
SO WHERE'S GUILLAUME?
OUTSIDE SMOOCHING WITH HIS BOYFRIEND.
SERIOUSLY?!!! LEMME SEE--
WHY IS HISAO ON THE GROUND?
I SAY GOOD FOR HIM. LEAST SOMEBODY GETS THEIR FIRST KISS BEFORE THEY DIE.
FOR THE LAST TIME, WE ARE NOT KISSING, STOP TRYING TO MAKE ME FEEL BAD FOR YOU.
SUDDENLY THE DYING ACTUALLY SOUNDS LIKE THE BETTER OF THE TWO OPTIONS.
ENOUGH, BOTH OF YOU!
WE ARE NOT GOING THERE TO DIE, DO YOU UNDERSTAND?
WE ARE GOING THERE TO KILL.

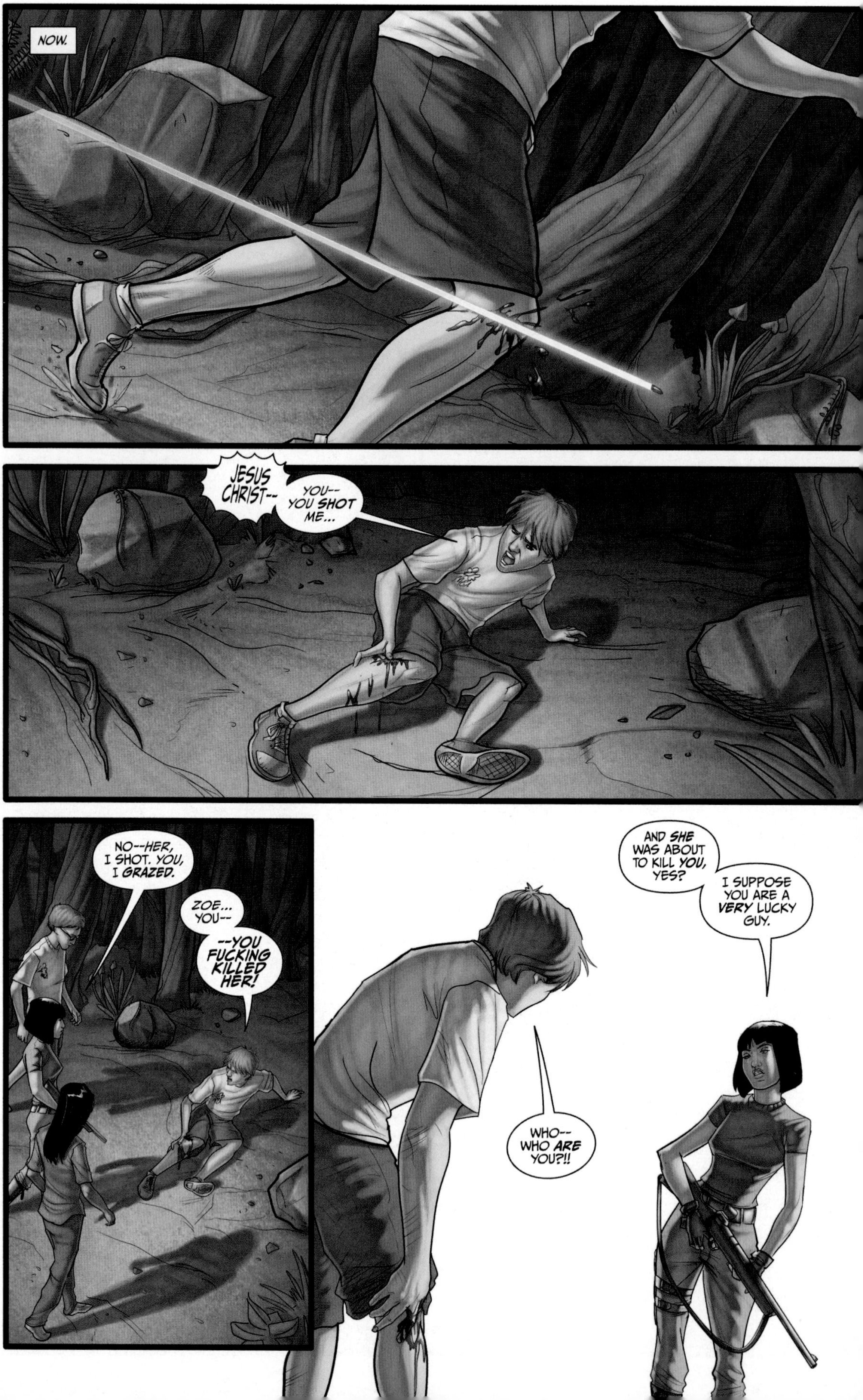
NOW.
JESUS CHRIST--
YOU-- YOU SHOT ME...
NO--HER, I SHOT. YOU, I GRAZED.
ZOE... YOU--
--YOU FUCKING KILLED HER!
AND SHE WAS ABOUT TO KILL YOU, YES?
I SUPPOSE YOU ARE A VERY LUCKY GUY.
WHO-- WHO ARE YOU?!!

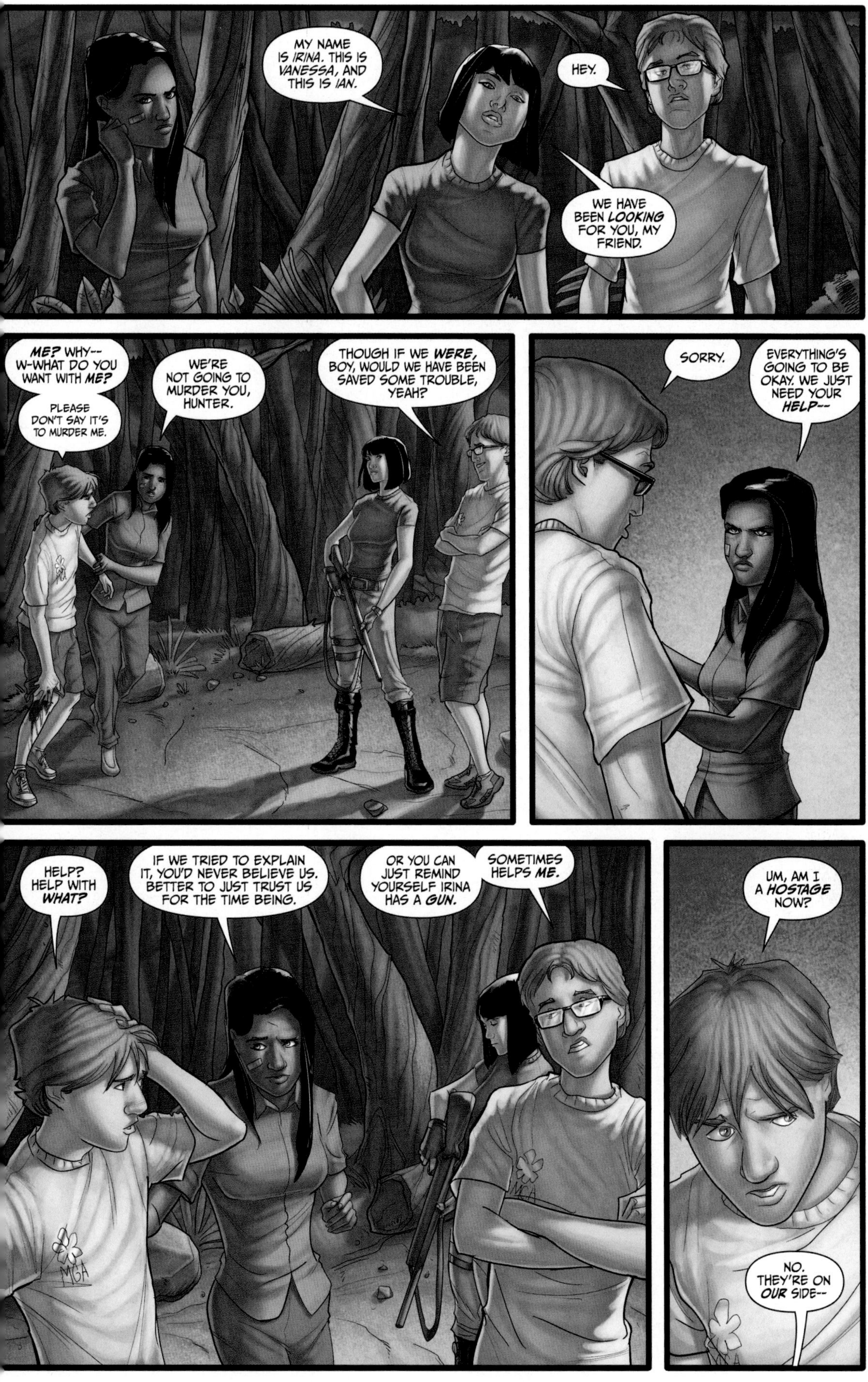

MY NAME IS IRINA. THIS IS VANESSA, AND THIS IS IAN.
HEY.
WE HAVE BEEN LOOKING FOR YOU, MY FRIEND.
ME? WHY-- W-WHAT DO YOU WANT WITH ME?
PLEASE DON'T SAY IT'S TO MURDER ME.
WE'RE NOT GOING TO MURDER YOU, HUNTER.
THOUGH IF WE WERE, BOY, WOULD WE HAVE BEEN SAVED SOME TROUBLE, YEAH?
SORRY.
EVERYTHING'S GOING TO BE OKAY. WE JUST NEED YOUR HELP--
HELP? HELP WITH WHAT?
IF WE TRIED TO EXPLAIN IT, YOU'D NEVER BELIEVE US. BETTER TO JUST TRUST US FOR THE TIME BEING.
OR YOU CAN JUST REMIND YOURSELF IRINA HAS A GUN.
SOMETIMES HELPS ME.
UM, AM I A HOSTAGE NOW?
NO. THEY'RE ON OUR SIDE--

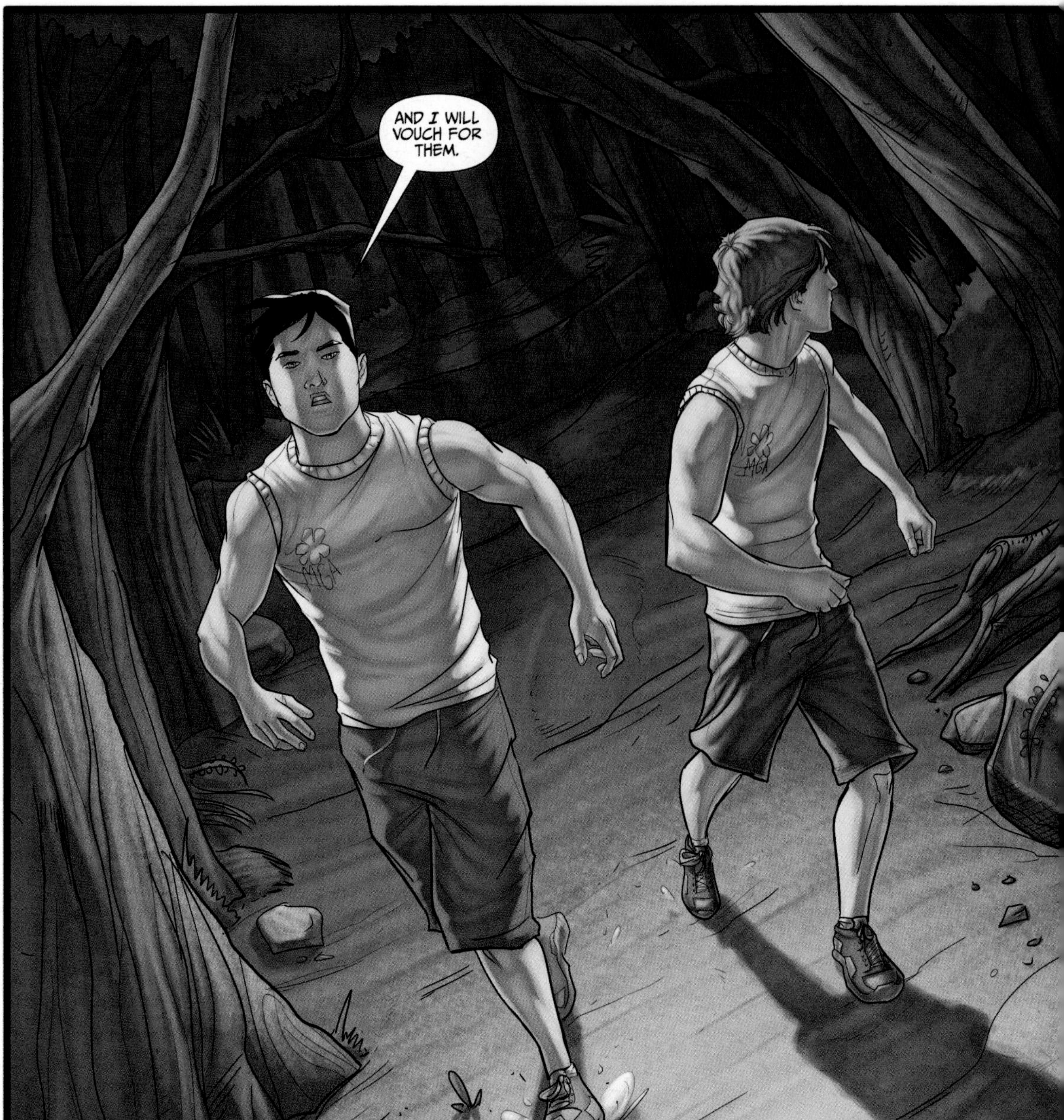
AND I WILL VOUCH FOR THEM.

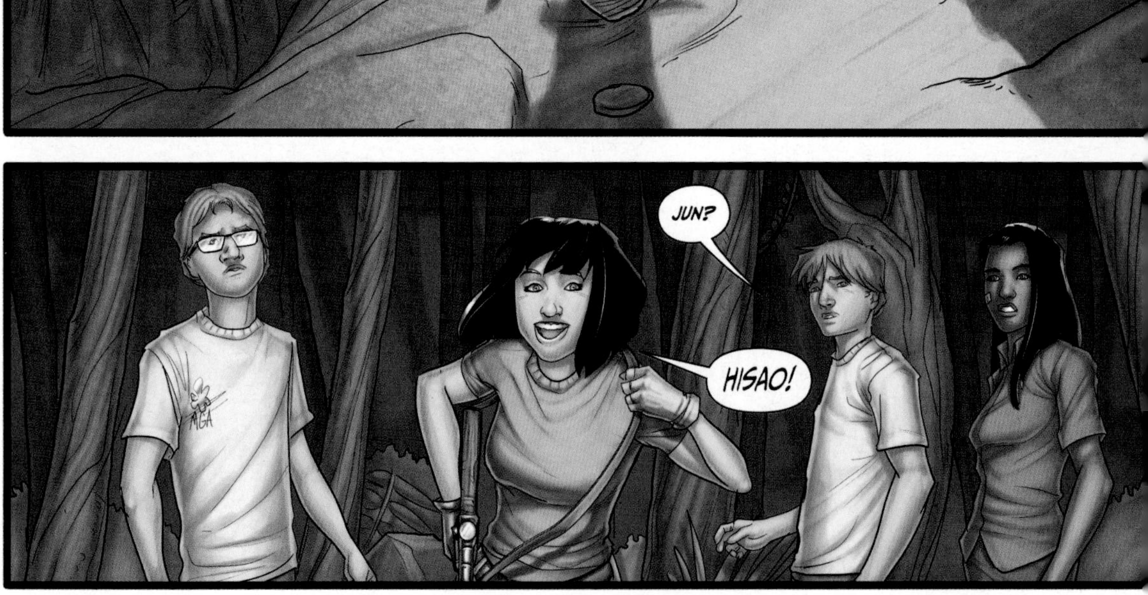
JUN?
HISAO!

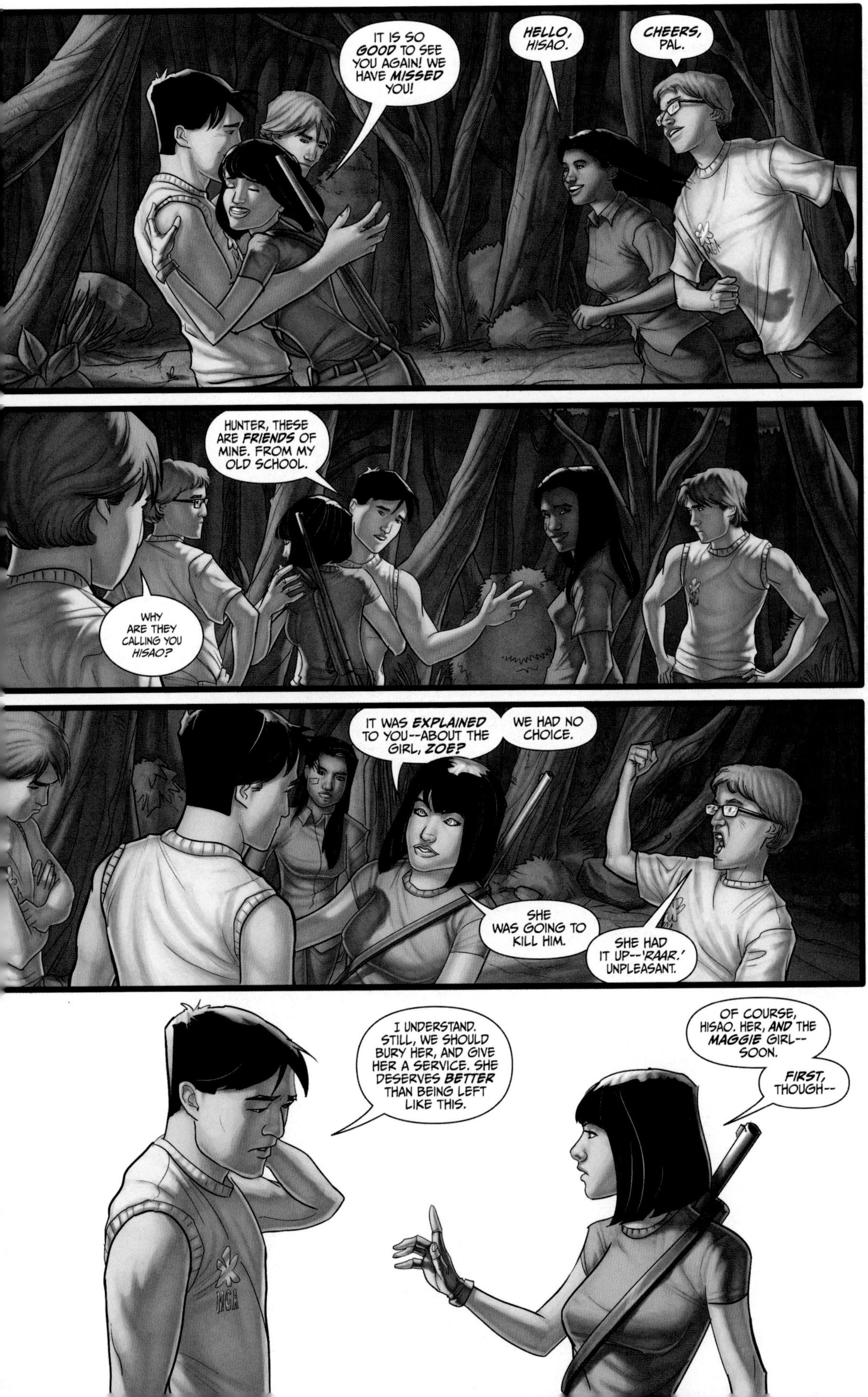

IT IS SO GOOD TO SEE YOU AGAIN! WE HAVE MISSED YOU!
HELLO, HISAO.
CHEERS, PAL.
HUNTER, THESE ARE FRIENDS OF MINE. FROM MY OLD SCHOOL.
WHY ARE THEY CALLING YOU HISAO?
IT WAS EXPLAINED TO YOU--ABOUT THE GIRL, ZOE?
WE HAD NO CHOICE.
SHE WAS GOING TO KILL HIM.
SHE HAD IT UP--'RAAR.' UNPLEASANT.
I UNDERSTAND. STILL, WE SHOULD BURY HER, AND GIVE HER A SERVICE. SHE DESERVES BETTER THAN BEING LEFT LIKE THIS.
OF COURSE, HISAO. HER, AND THE MAGGIE GIRL-- SOON.
FIRST, THOUGH--

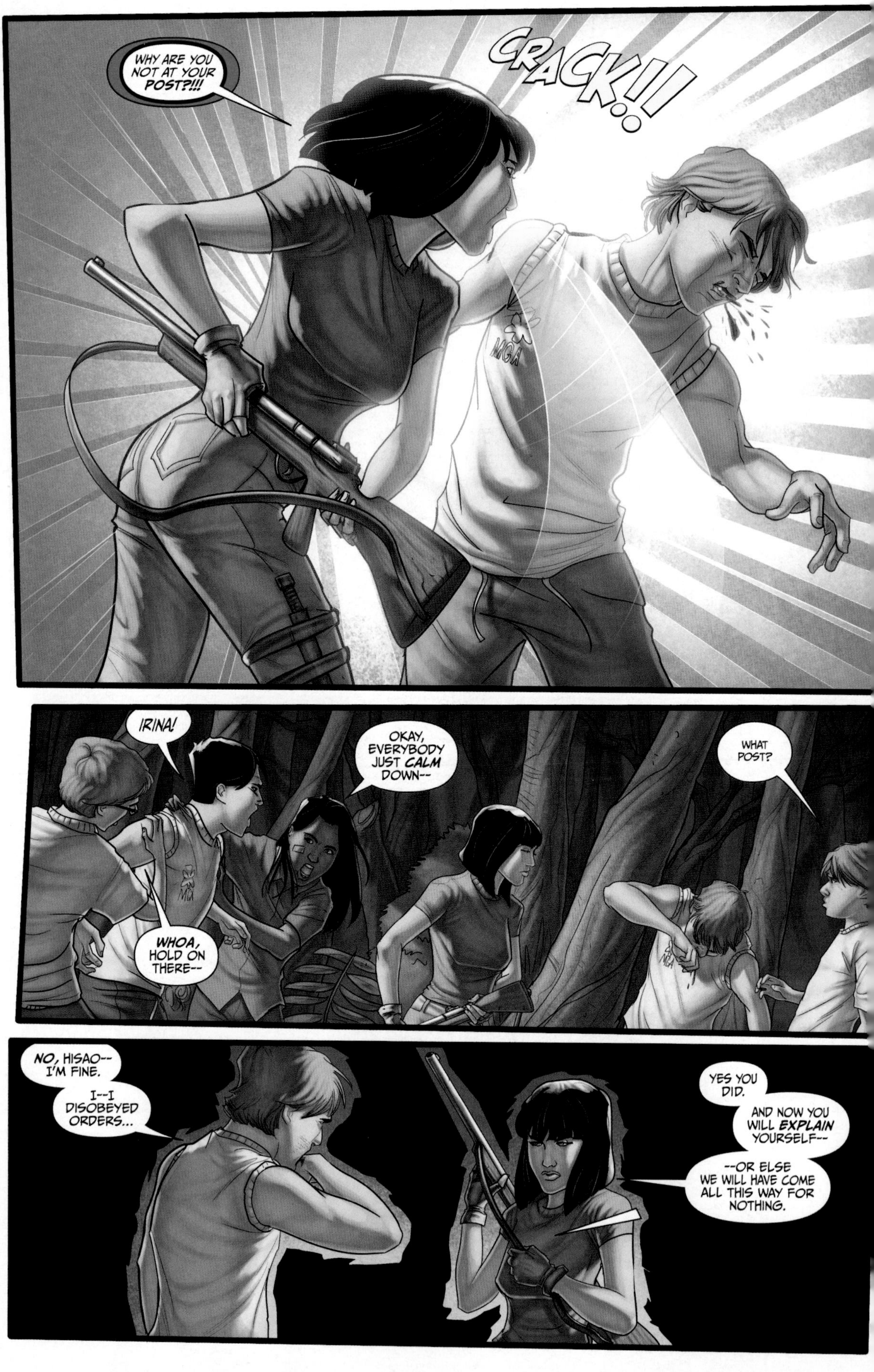

WHY ARE YOU NOT AT YOUR POST?!!!
CRACK!!!
IRINA!
OKAY, EVERYBODY JUST CALM DOWN--
WHOA, HOLD ON THERE--
WHAT POST?
NO, HISAO-- I'M FINE.
I--I DISOBEYED ORDERS...
YES YOU DID.
AND NOW YOU WILL EXPLAIN YOURSELF--
--OR ELSE WE WILL HAVE COME ALL THIS WAY FOR NOTHING.

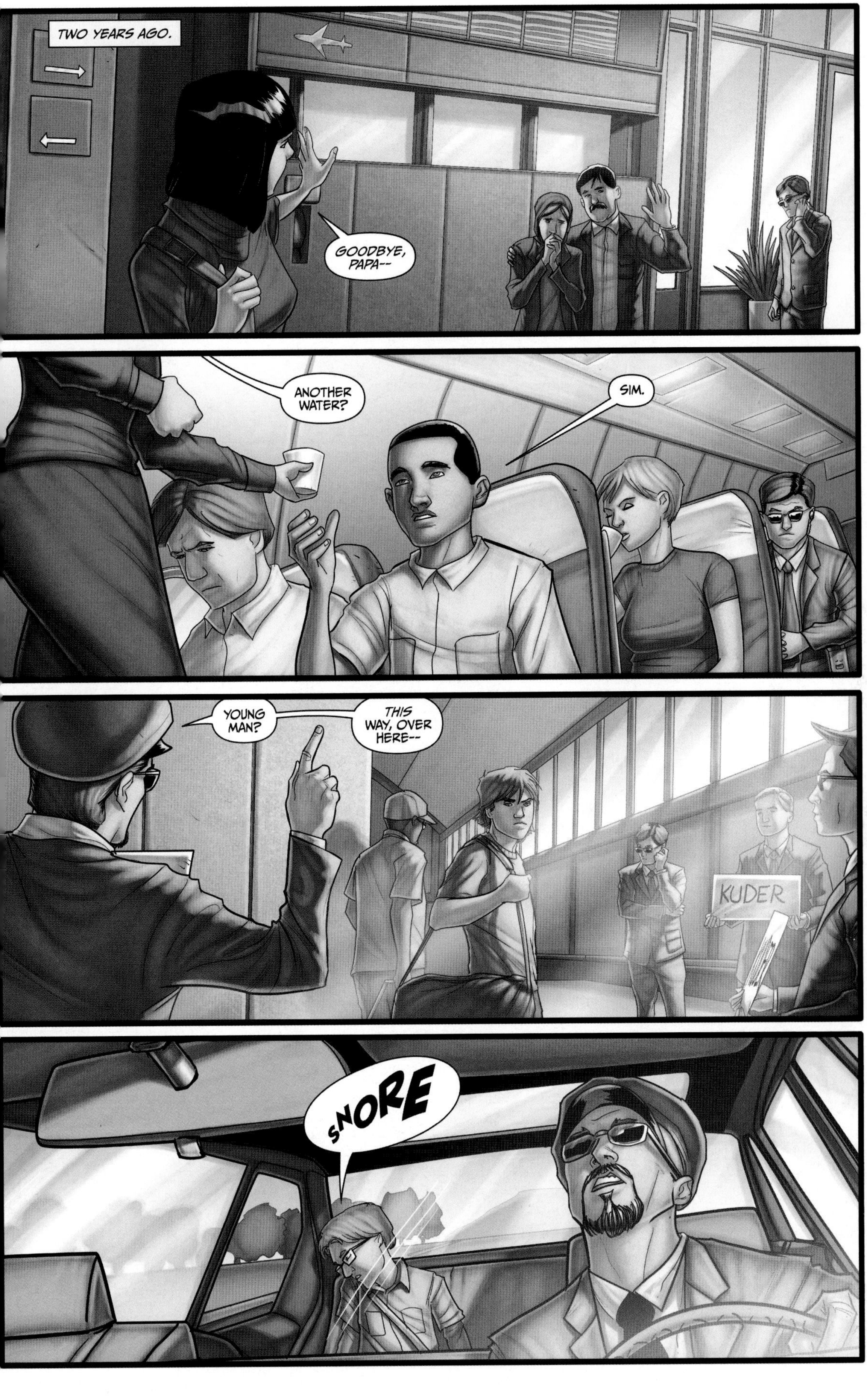

TWO YEARS AGO.
GOODBYE, PAPA--
ANOTHER WATER?
SIM.
YOUNG MAN?
THIS WAY, OVER HERE--
KUDER
SNORE

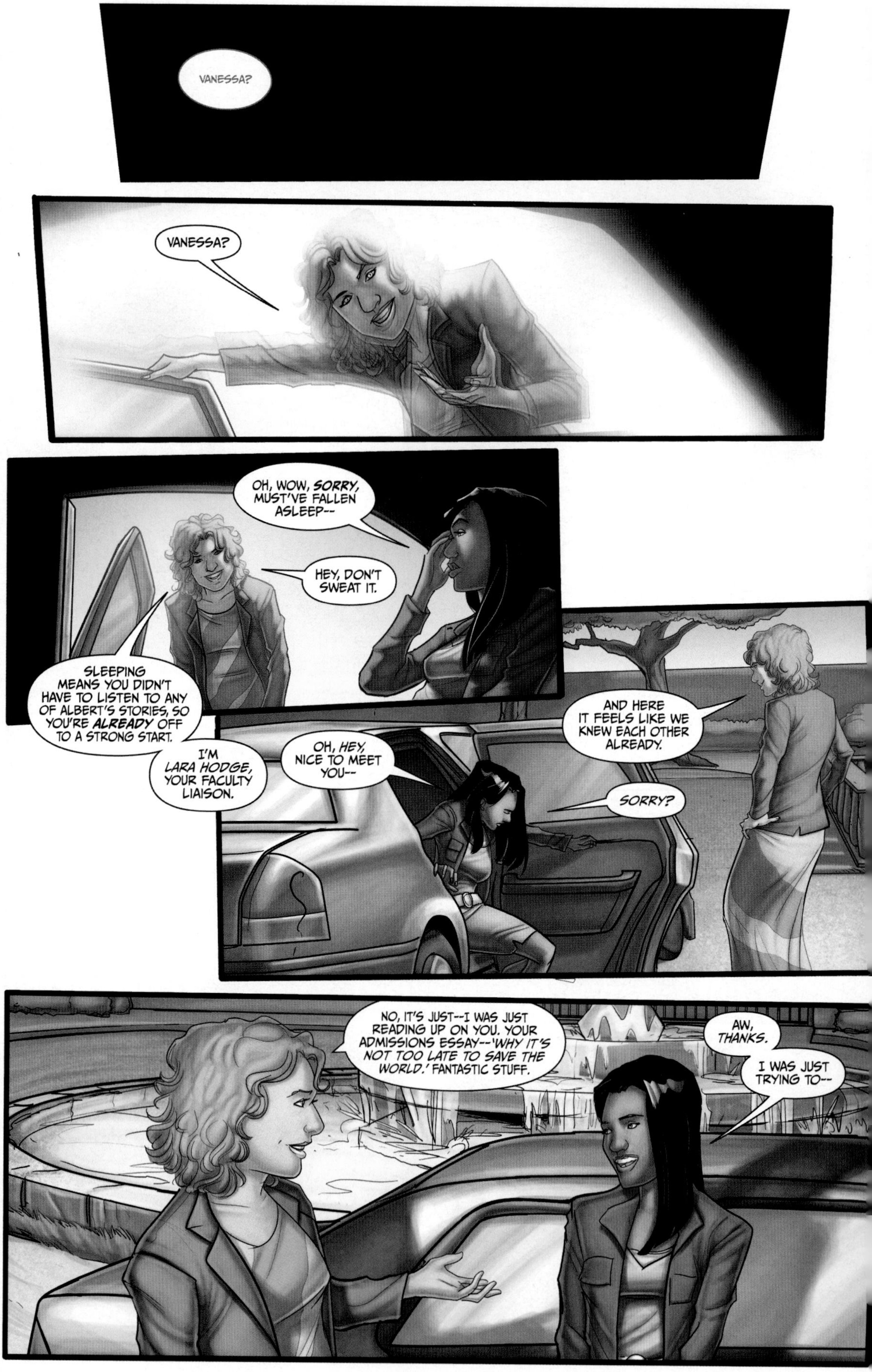
VANESSA?
VANESSA?
OH, WOW, SORRY, MUST'VE FALLEN ASLEEP--
HEY, DON'T SWEAT IT.
SLEEPING MEANS YOU DIDN'T HAVE TO LISTEN TO ANY OF ALBERT'S STORIES, SO YOU'RE ALREADY OFF TO A STRONG START.
I'M LARA HODGE, YOUR FACULTY LIAISON.
OH, HEY, NICE TO MEET YOU--
AND HERE IT FEELS LIKE WE KNEW EACH OTHER ALREADY.
SORRY?
NO, IT'S JUST--I WAS JUST READING UP ON YOU. YOUR ADMISSIONS ESSAY--'WHY IT'S NOT TOO LATE TO SAVE THE WORLD.' FANTASTIC STUFF.
AW, THANKS.
I WAS JUST TRYING TO--

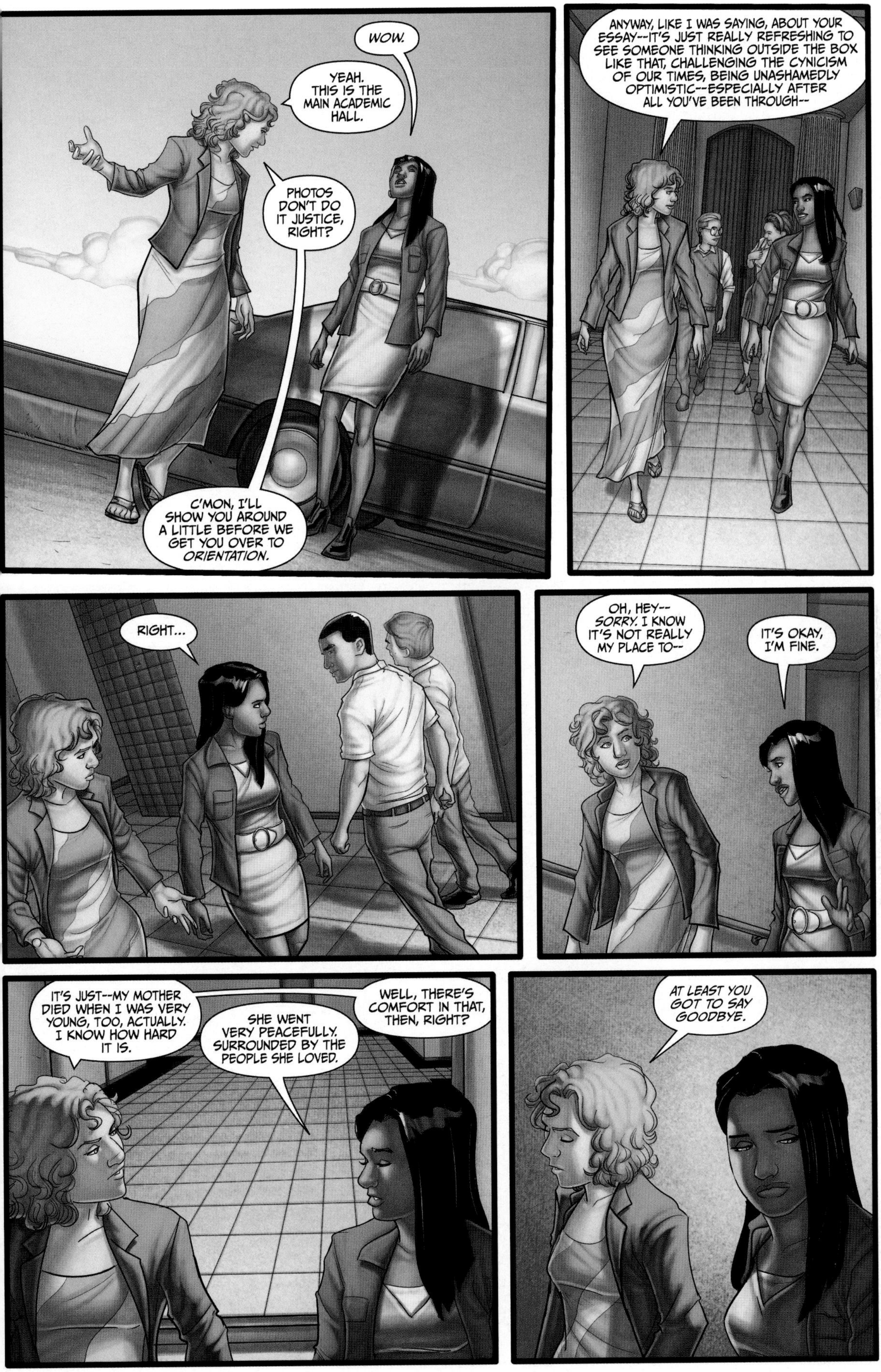
WOW.
YEAH. THIS IS THE MAIN ACADEMIC HALL.
PHOTOS DON'T DO IT JUSTICE, RIGHT?
C'MON, I'LL SHOW YOU AROUND A LITTLE BEFORE WE GET YOU OVER TO ORIENTATION.
ANYWAY, LIKE I WAS SAYING, ABOUT YOUR ESSAY--IT'S JUST REALLY REFRESHING TO SEE SOMEONE THINKING OUTSIDE THE BOX LIKE THAT, CHALLENGING THE CYNICISM OF OUR TIMES, BEING UNASHAMEDLY OPTIMISTIC--ESPECIALLY AFTER ALL YOU'VE BEEN THROUGH--
RIGHT...
OH, HEY-- SORRY. I KNOW IT'S NOT REALLY MY PLACE TO--
IT'S OKAY, I'M FINE.
IT'S JUST--MY MOTHER DIED WHEN I WAS VERY YOUNG, TOO, ACTUALLY. I KNOW HOW HARD IT IS.
SHE WENT VERY PEACEFULLY. SURROUNDED BY THE PEOPLE SHE LOVED.
WELL, THERE'S COMFORT IN THAT, THEN, RIGHT?
AT LEAST YOU GOT TO SAY GOODBYE.

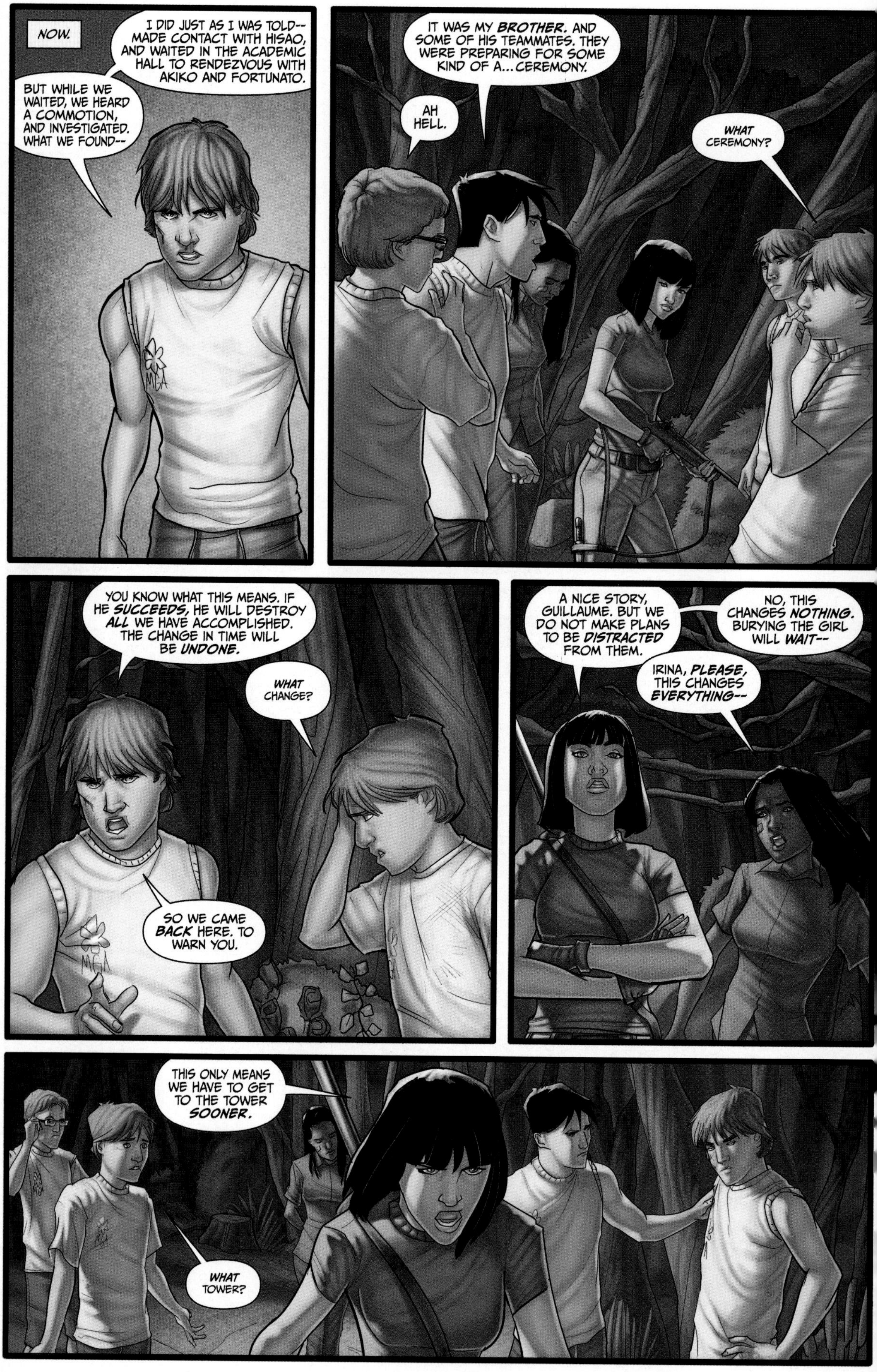
NOW.
I DID JUST AS I WAS TOLD-- MADE CONTACT WITH HISAO, AND WAITED IN THE ACADEMIC HALL TO RENDEZVOUS WITH AKIKO AND FORTUNATO.
BUT WHILE WE WAITED, WE HEARD A COMMOTION, AND INVESTIGATED. WHAT WE FOUND--
IT WAS MY BROTHER. AND SOME OF HIS TEAMMATES. THEY WERE PREPARING FOR SOME KIND OF A...CEREMONY.
AH HELL.
WHAT CEREMONY?
YOU KNOW WHAT THIS MEANS. IF HE SUCCEEDS, HE WILL DESTROY ALL WE HAVE ACCOMPLISHED. THE CHANGE IN TIME WILL BE UNDONE.
WHAT CHANGE?
SO WE CAME BACK HERE. TO WARN YOU.
A NICE STORY, GUILLAUME. BUT WE DO NOT MAKE PLANS TO BE DISTRACTED FROM THEM.
NO, THIS CHANGES NOTHING. BURYING THE GIRL WILL WAIT--
IRINA, PLEASE, THIS CHANGES EVERYTHING--
THIS ONLY MEANS WE HAVE TO GET TO THE TOWER SOONER.
WHAT TOWER?

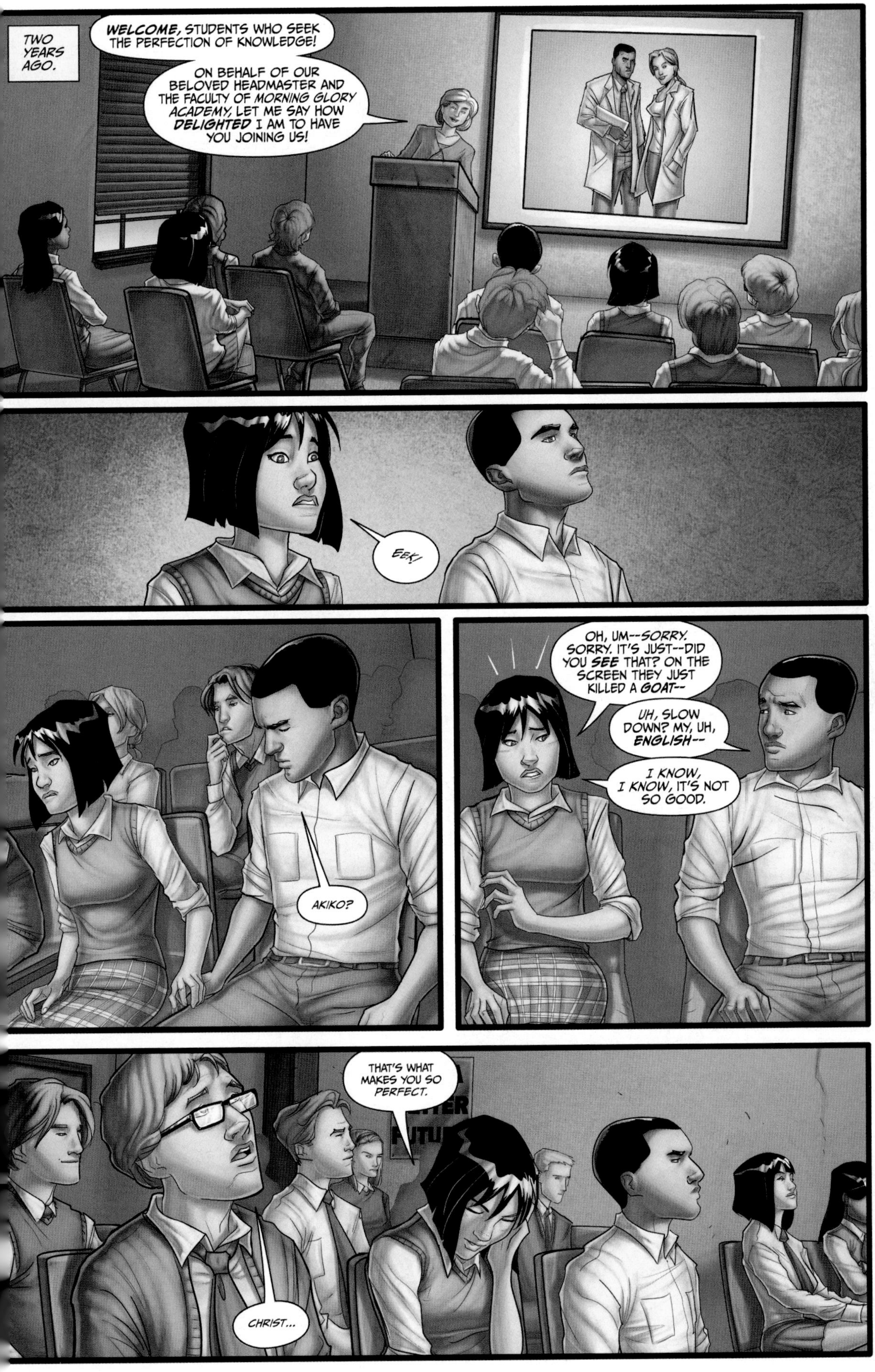
TWO YEARS AGO.
WELCOME, STUDENTS WHO SEEK THE PERFECTION OF KNOWLEDGE!
ON BEHALF OF OUR BELOVED HEADMASTER AND THE FACULTY OF MORNING GLORY ACADEMY, LET ME SAY HOW DELIGHTED I AM TO HAVE YOU JOINING US!
EEK!
AKIKO?
OH, UM--SORRY. SORRY. IT'S JUST--DID YOU SEE THAT? ON THE SCREEN THEY JUST KILLED A GOAT--
UH, SLOW DOWN? MY, UH, ENGLISH--
I KNOW, I KNOW, IT'S NOT SO GOOD.
THAT'S WHAT MAKES YOU SO PERFECT.
CHRIST...

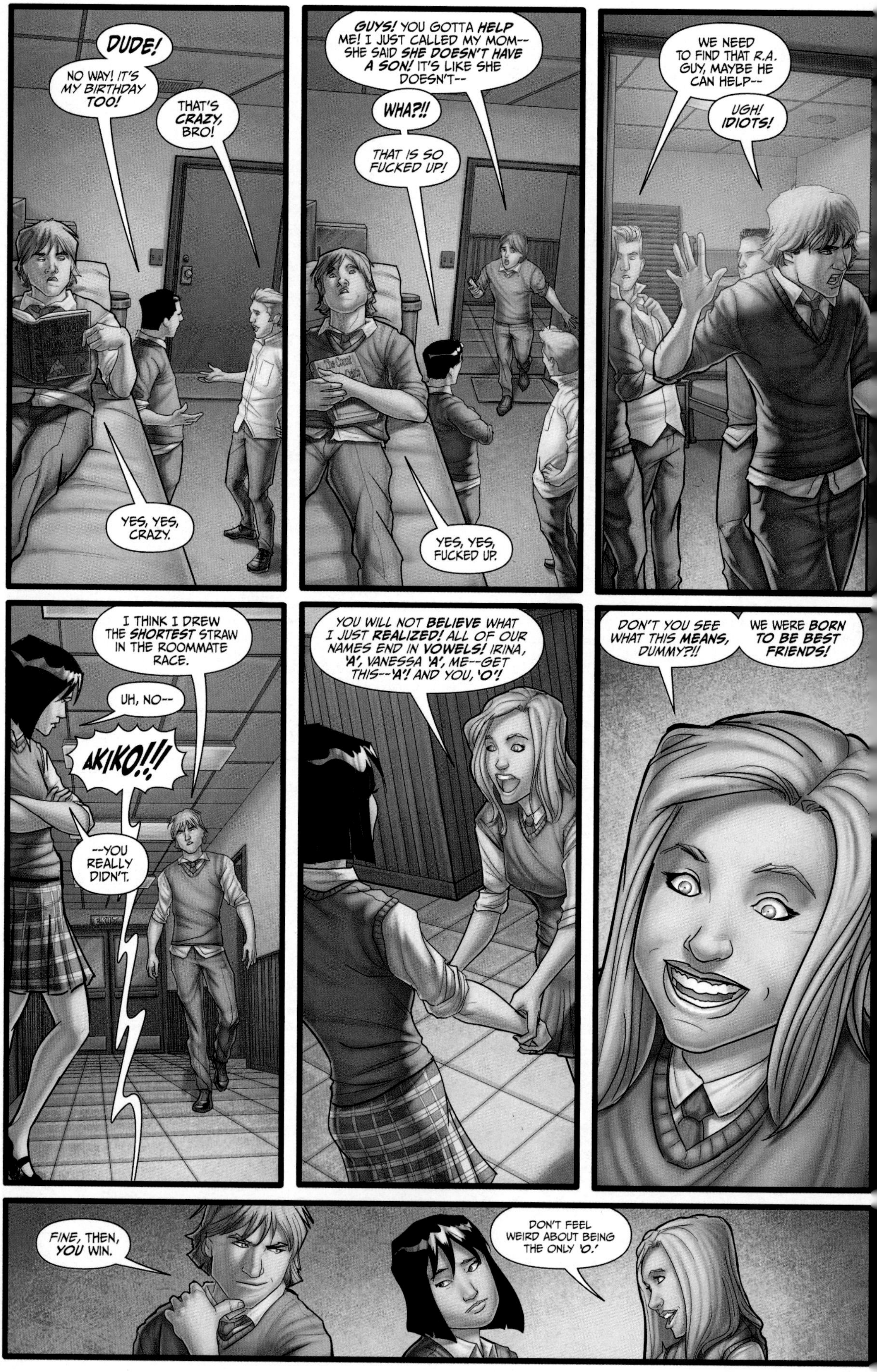
DUDE!
NO WAY! IT'S MY BIRTHDAY TOO!
THAT'S CRAZY, BRO!
YES, YES, CRAZY.
GUYS! YOU GOTTA HELP ME! I JUST CALLED MY MOM-- SHE SAID SHE DOESN'T HAVE A SON! IT'S LIKE SHE DOESN'T--
WHA?!!
THAT IS SO FUCKED UP!
YES, YES, FUCKED UP.
WE NEED TO FIND THAT R.A. GUY, MAYBE HE CAN HELP--
UGH! IDIOTS!
I THINK I DREW THE SHORTEST STRAW IN THE ROOMMATE RACE.
UH, NO--
AKIKO!!!
--YOU REALLY DIDN'T.
YOU WILL NOT BELIEVE WHAT I JUST REALIZED! ALL OF OUR NAMES END IN VOWELS! IRINA, 'A', VANESSA 'A', ME--GET THIS--'A'! AND YOU, 'O'!
DON'T YOU SEE WHAT THIS MEANS, DUMMY?!!
WE WERE BORN TO BE BEST FRIENDS!
FINE, THEN, YOU WIN.
DON'T FEEL WEIRD ABOUT BEING THE ONLY 'O.'

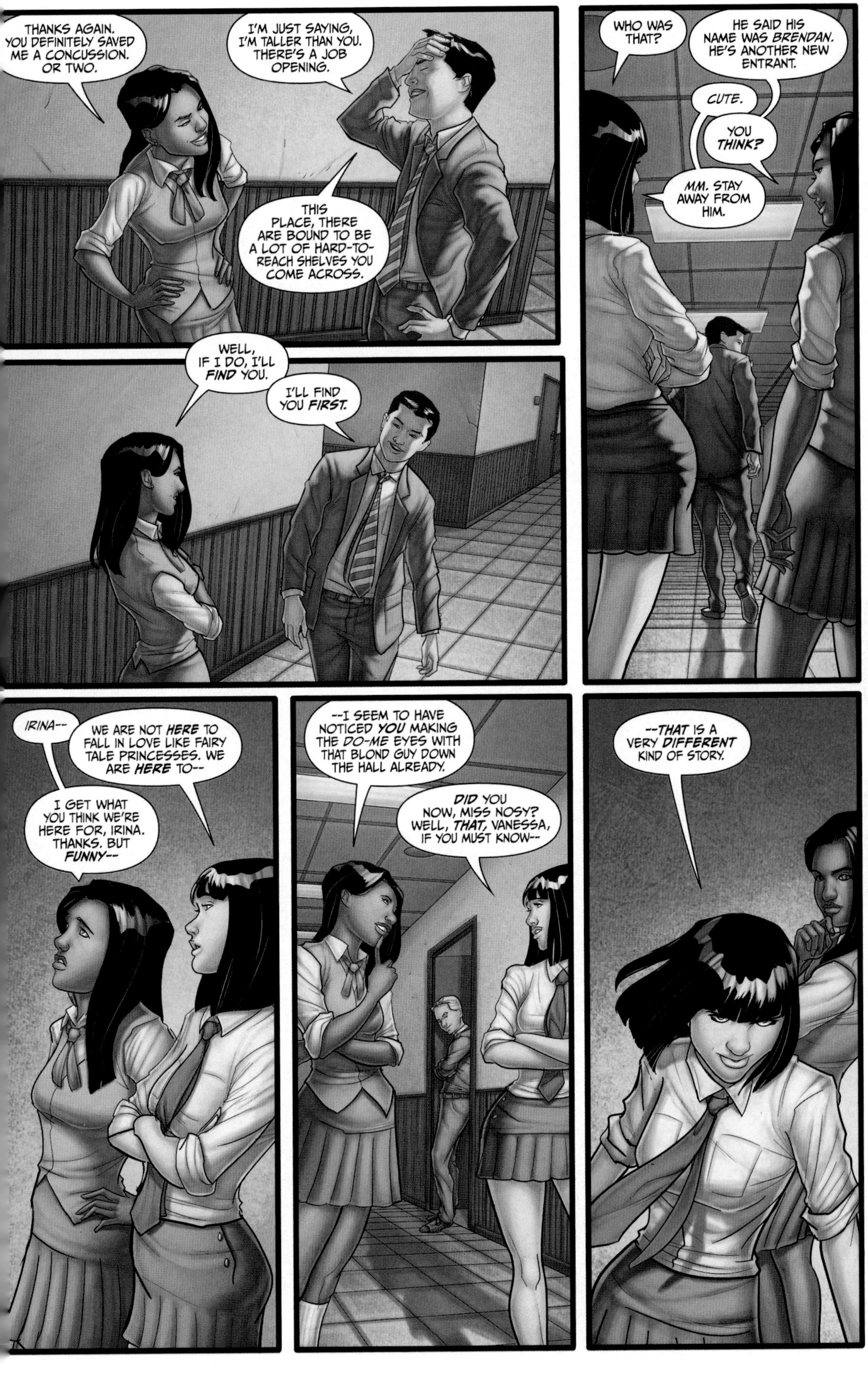
THANKS AGAIN. YOU DEFINITELY SAVED ME A CONCUSSION. OR TWO.
I'M JUST SAYING, I'M TALLER THAN YOU. THERE'S A JOB OPENING.
THIS PLACE, THERE ARE BOUND TO BE A LOT OF HARD-TO-REACH SHELVES YOU COME ACROSS.
WELL, IF I DO, I'LL FIND YOU.
I'LL FIND YOU FIRST.
WHO WAS THAT?
HE SAID HIS NAME WAS BRENDAN. HE'S ANOTHER NEW ENTRANT.
CUTE.
YOU THINK?
MM. STAY AWAY FROM HIM.
IRINA--
WE ARE NOT HERE TO FALL IN LOVE LIKE FAIRY TALE PRINCESSES. WE ARE HERE TO--
I GET WHAT YOU THINK WE'RE HERE FOR, IRINA. THANKS. BUT FUNNY--
--I SEEM TO HAVE NOTICED YOU MAKING THE DO-ME EYES WITH THAT BLOND GUY DOWN THE HALL ALREADY.
DID YOU NOW, MISS NOSY? WELL, THAT, VANESSA, IF YOU MUST KNOW--
--THAT IS A VERY DIFFERENT KIND OF STORY.

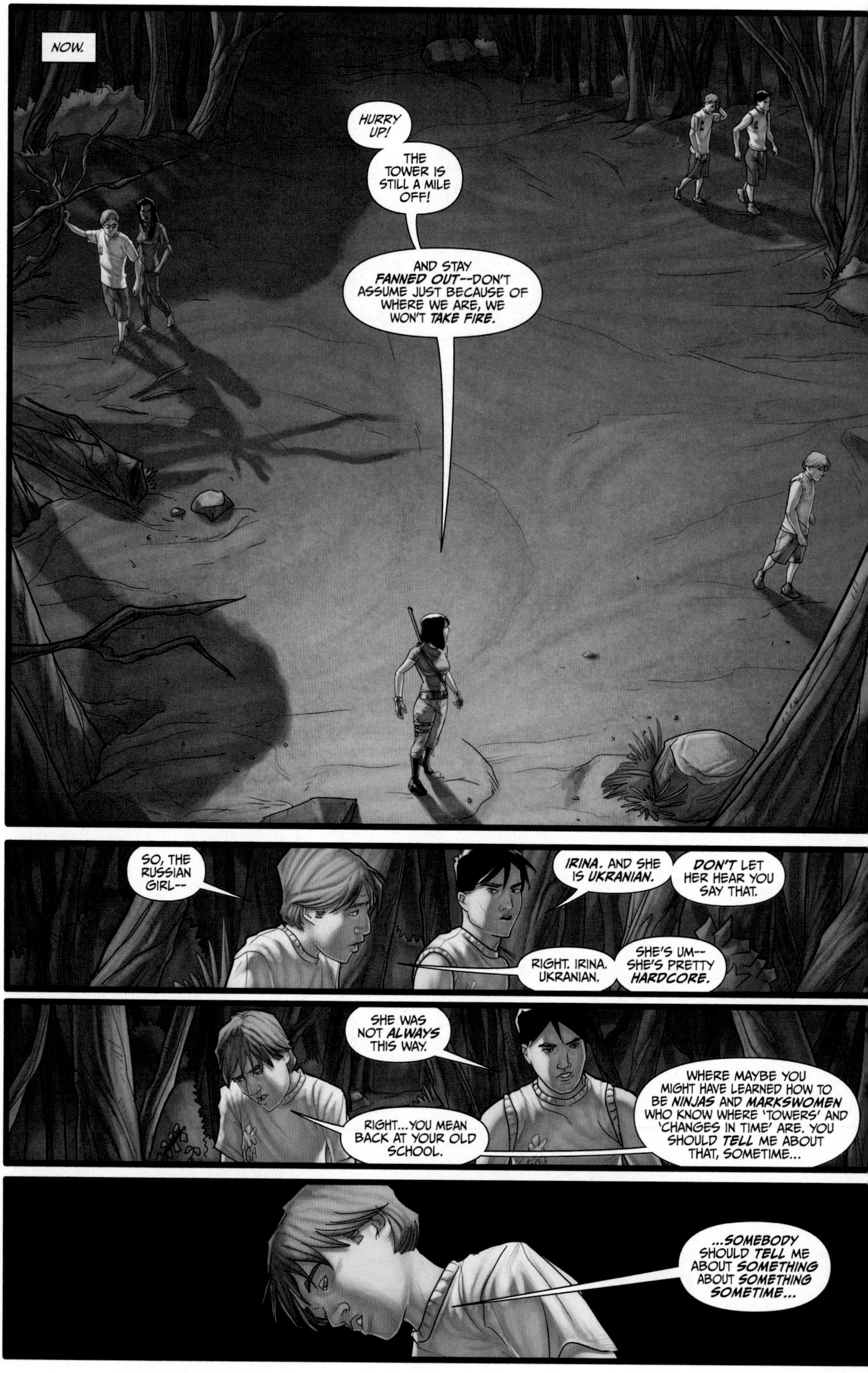
NOW.
HURRY UP!
THE TOWER IS STILL A MILE OFF!
AND STAY FANNED OUT--DON'T ASSUME JUST BECAUSE OF WHERE WE ARE, WE WON'T TAKE FIRE.
SO, THE RUSSIAN GIRL--
IRINA. AND SHE IS UKRANIAN.
DON'T LET HER HEAR YOU SAY THAT.
RIGHT. IRINA. UKRANIAN.
SHE'S UM-- SHE'S PRETTY HARDCORE.
SHE WAS NOT ALWAYS THIS WAY.
RIGHT...YOU MEAN BACK AT YOUR OLD SCHOOL.
WHERE MAYBE YOU MIGHT HAVE LEARNED HOW TO BE NINJAS AND MARKSWOMEN WHO KNOW WHERE 'TOWERS' AND 'CHANGES IN TIME' ARE. YOU SHOULD TELL ME ABOUT THAT, SOMETIME...
...SOMEBODY SHOULD TELL ME ABOUT SOMETHING ABOUT SOMETHING SOMETIME...

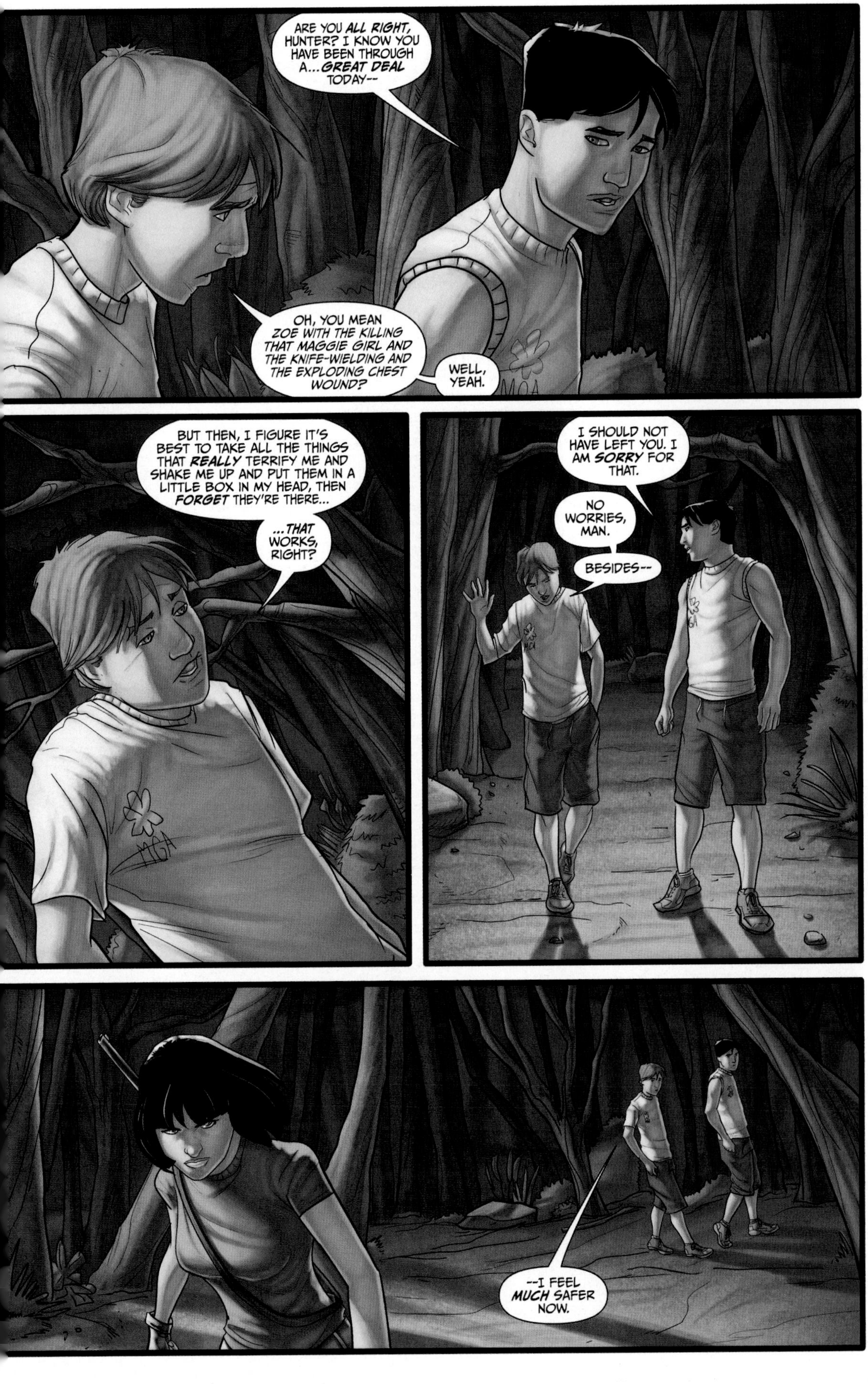
ARE YOU ALL RIGHT, HUNTER? I KNOW YOU HAVE BEEN THROUGH A...GREAT DEAL TODAY--
OH, YOU MEAN ZOE WITH THE KILLING THAT MAGGIE GIRL AND THE KNIFE-WIELDING AND THE EXPLODING CHEST WOUND?
WELL, YEAH.
BUT THEN, I FIGURE IT'S BEST TO TAKE ALL THE THINGS THAT REALLY TERRIFY ME AND SHAKE ME UP AND PUT THEM IN A LITTLE BOX IN MY HEAD, THEN FORGET THEY'RE THERE...
...THAT WORKS, RIGHT?
I SHOULD NOT HAVE LEFT YOU. I AM SORRY FOR THAT.
NO WORRIES, MAN.
BESIDES--
--I FEEL MUCH SAFER NOW.

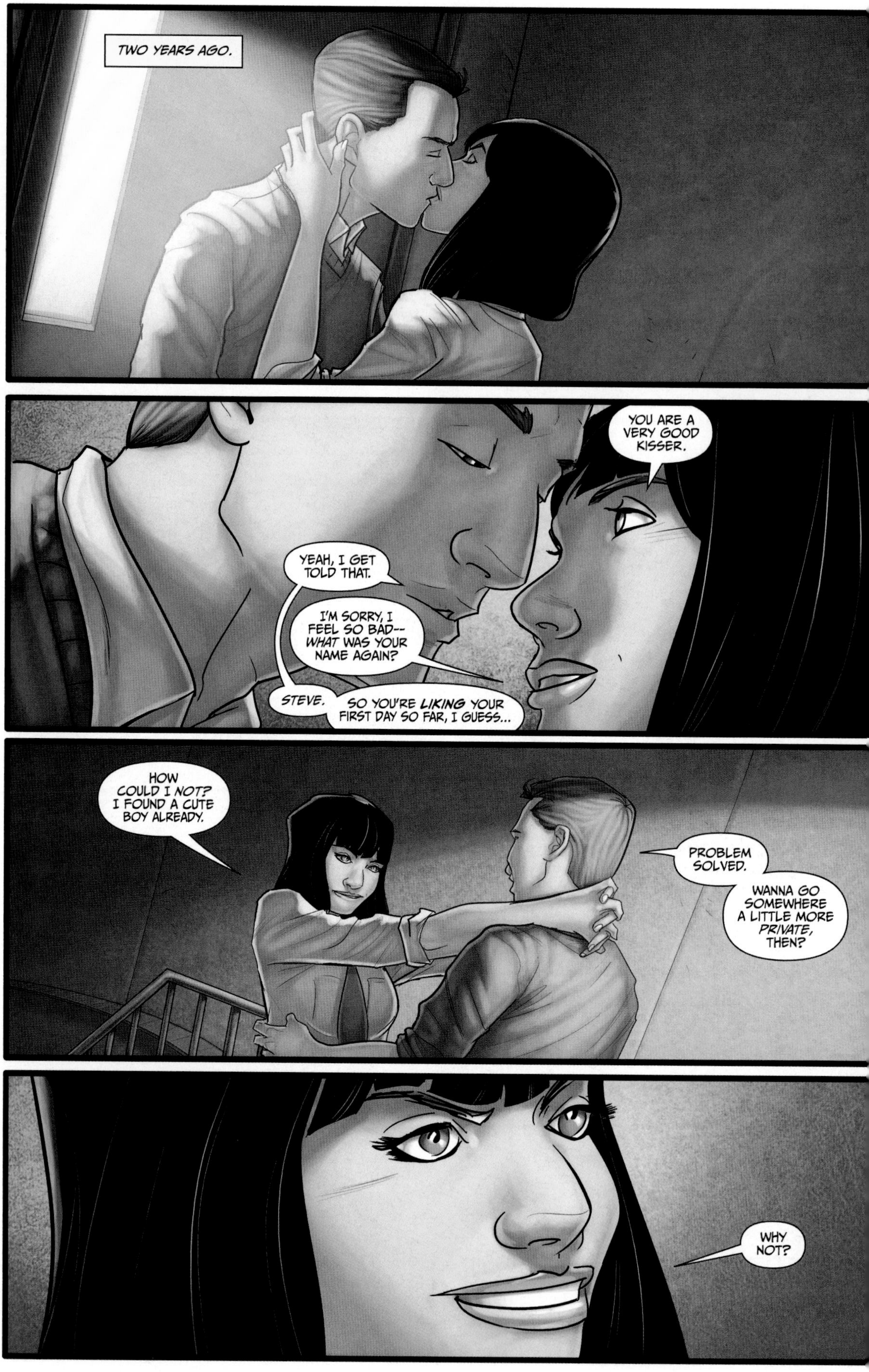
TWO YEARS AGO.
YOU ARE A VERY GOOD KISSER.
YEAH, I GET TOLD THAT.
I'M SORRY, I FEEL SO BAD-- *WHAT* WAS YOUR NAME AGAIN?
STEVE.
SO YOU'RE *LIKING* YOUR FIRST DAY SO FAR, I GUESS...
HOW COULD I *NOT?* I FOUND A CUTE BOY ALREADY.
PROBLEM SOLVED.
WANNA GO SOMEWHERE A LITTLE MORE *PRIVATE,* THEN?
WHY NOT?

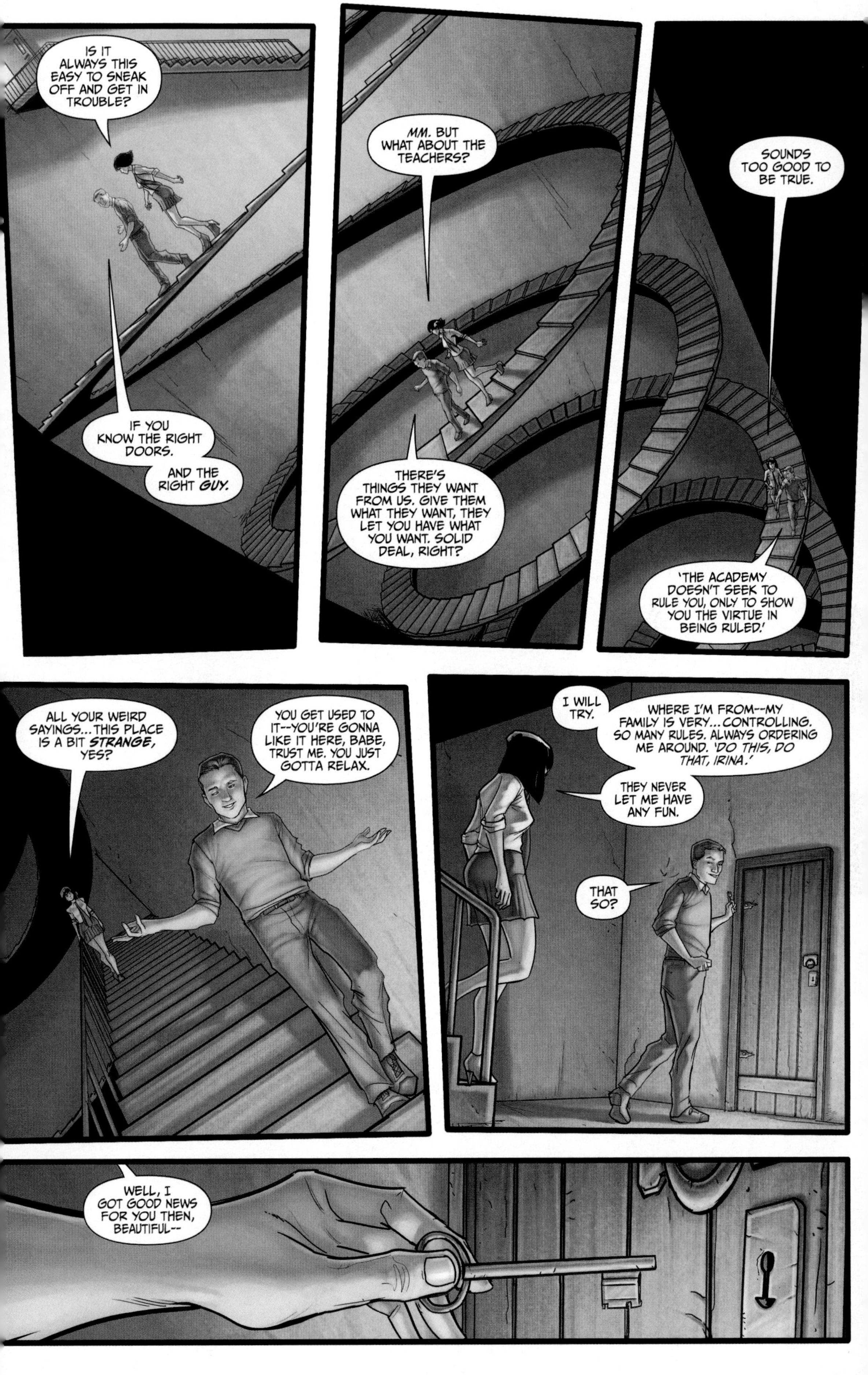
IS IT ALWAYS THIS EASY TO SNEAK OFF AND GET IN TROUBLE?
IF YOU KNOW THE RIGHT DOORS.
AND THE RIGHT GUY.
MM. BUT WHAT ABOUT THE TEACHERS?
THERE'S THINGS THEY WANT FROM US. GIVE THEM WHAT THEY WANT, THEY LET YOU HAVE WHAT YOU WANT. SOLID DEAL, RIGHT?
SOUNDS TOO GOOD TO BE TRUE.
'THE ACADEMY DOESN'T SEEK TO RULE YOU, ONLY TO SHOW YOU THE VIRTUE IN BEING RULED.'
ALL YOUR WEIRD SAYINGS... THIS PLACE IS A BIT STRANGE, YES?
YOU GET USED TO IT--YOU'RE GONNA LIKE IT HERE, BABE, TRUST ME. YOU JUST GOTTA RELAX.
I WILL TRY.
WHERE I'M FROM--MY FAMILY IS VERY... CONTROLLING. SO MANY RULES. ALWAYS ORDERING ME AROUND. 'DO THIS, DO THAT, IRINA.'
THEY NEVER LET ME HAVE ANY FUN.
THAT SO?
WELL, I GOT GOOD NEWS FOR YOU THEN, BEAUTIFUL--

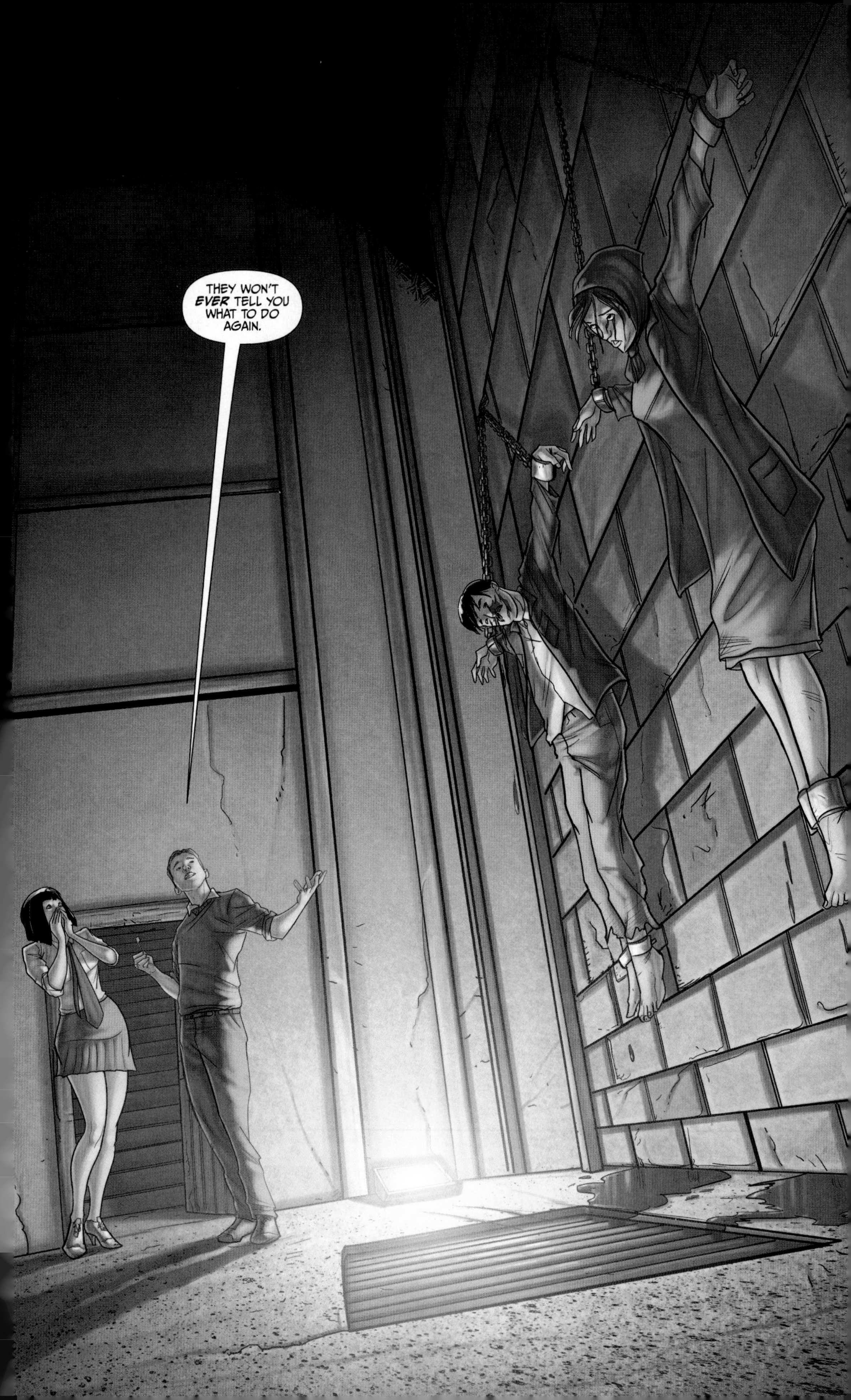
THEY WON'T EVER TELL YOU WHAT TO DO AGAIN.

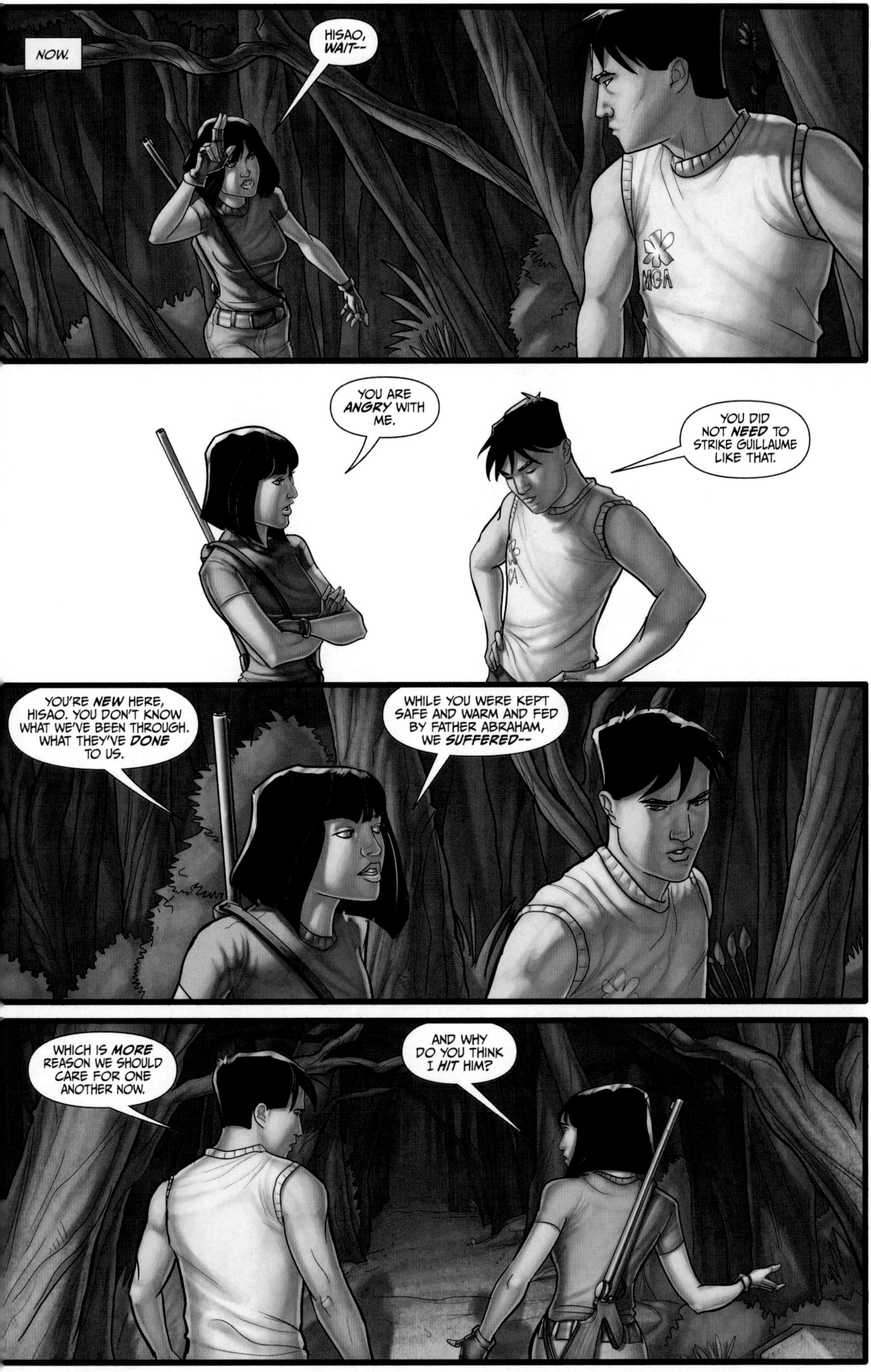
NOW.
HISAO, WAIT--
YOU ARE ANGRY WITH ME.
YOU DID NOT NEED TO STRIKE GUILLAUME LIKE THAT.
YOU'RE NEW HERE, HISAO. YOU DON'T KNOW WHAT WE'VE BEEN THROUGH. WHAT THEY'VE DONE TO US.
WHILE YOU WERE KEPT SAFE AND WARM AND FED BY FATHER ABRAHAM, WE SUFFERED--
WHICH IS MORE REASON WE SHOULD CARE FOR ONE ANOTHER NOW.
AND WHY DO YOU THINK I HIT HIM?

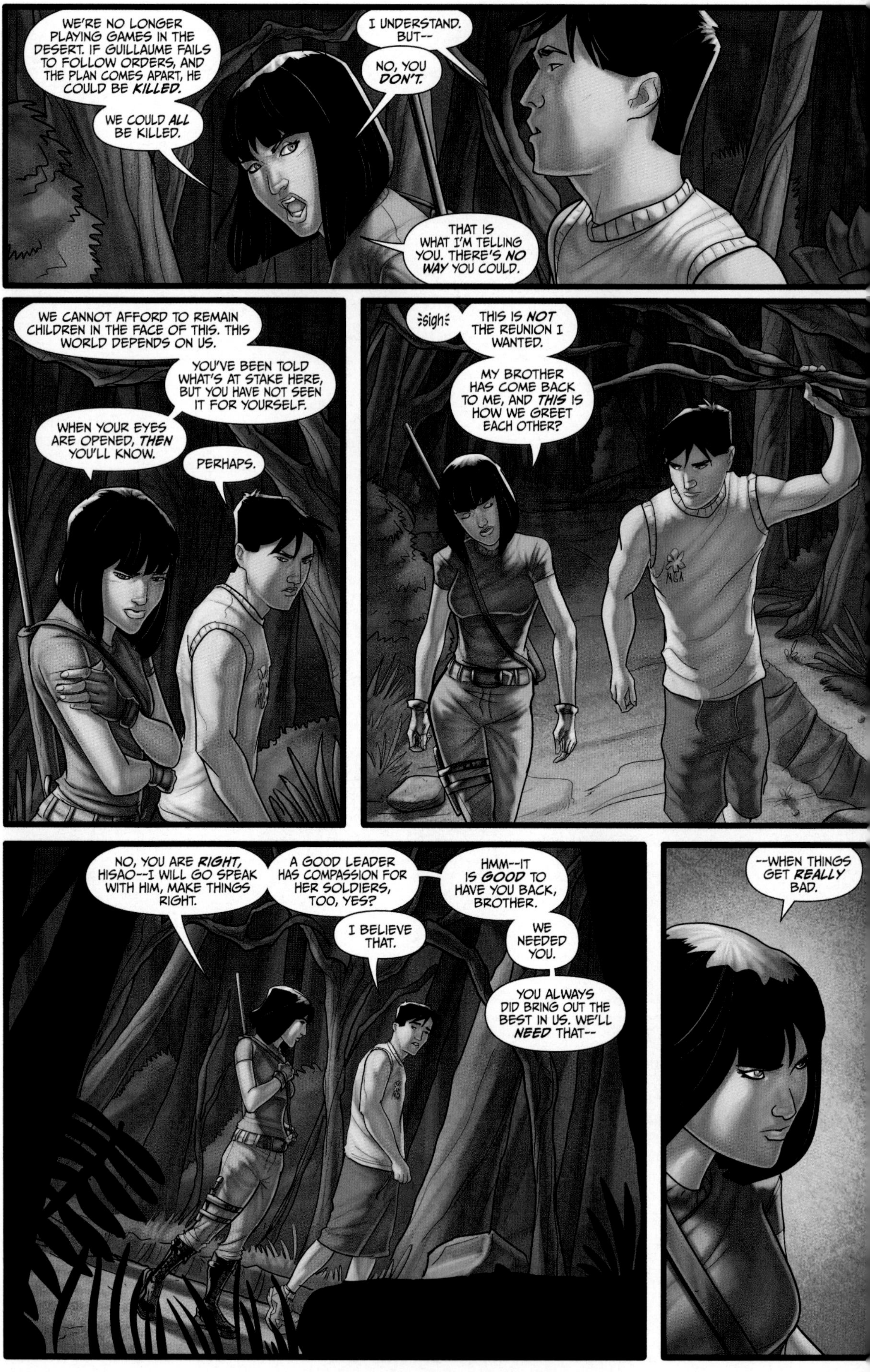
WE'RE NO LONGER PLAYING GAMES IN THE DESERT. IF GUILLAUME FAILS TO FOLLOW ORDERS, AND THE PLAN COMES APART, HE COULD BE KILLED.
WE COULD ALL BE KILLED.
I UNDERSTAND. BUT--
NO, YOU DON'T.
THAT IS WHAT I'M TELLING YOU. THERE'S NO WAY YOU COULD.
WE CANNOT AFFORD TO REMAIN CHILDREN IN THE FACE OF THIS. THIS WORLD DEPENDS ON US.
YOU'VE BEEN TOLD WHAT'S AT STAKE HERE, BUT YOU HAVE NOT SEEN IT FOR YOURSELF.
WHEN YOUR EYES ARE OPENED, THEN YOU'LL KNOW.
PERHAPS.
sigh
THIS IS NOT THE REUNION I WANTED.
MY BROTHER HAS COME BACK TO ME, AND THIS IS HOW WE GREET EACH OTHER?
NO, YOU ARE RIGHT, HISAO--I WILL GO SPEAK WITH HIM, MAKE THINGS RIGHT.
A GOOD LEADER HAS COMPASSION FOR HER SOLDIERS, TOO, YES?
I BELIEVE THAT.
HMM--IT IS GOOD TO HAVE YOU BACK, BROTHER.
WE NEEDED YOU.
YOU ALWAYS DID BRING OUT THE BEST IN US. WE'LL NEED THAT--
--WHEN THINGS GET REALLY BAD.

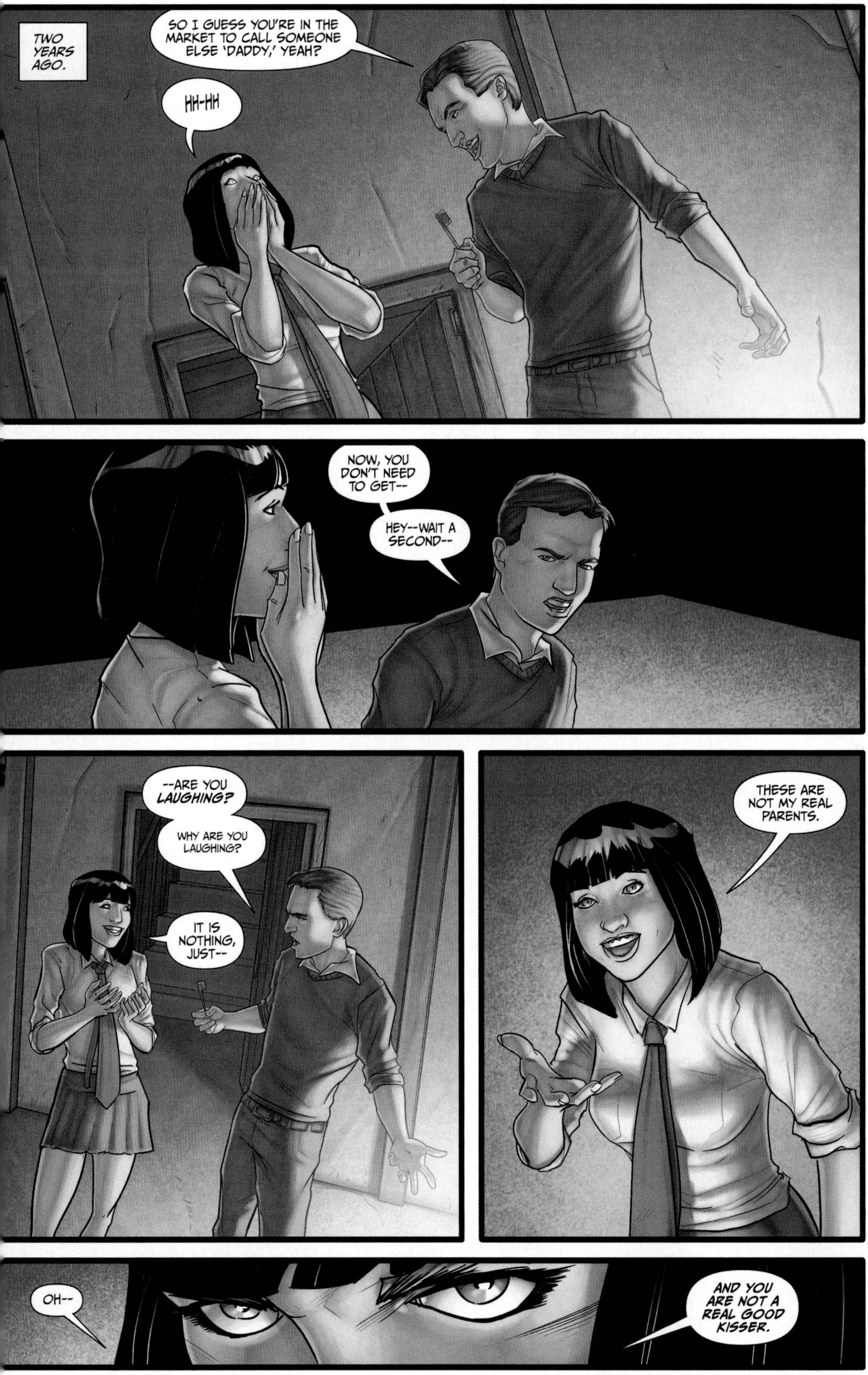
TWO YEARS AGO.
SO I GUESS YOU'RE IN THE MARKET TO CALL SOMEONE ELSE 'DADDY,' YEAH?
HH-HH
NOW, YOU DON'T NEED TO GET--
HEY--WAIT A SECOND--
--ARE YOU LAUGHING?
WHY ARE YOU LAUGHING?
IT IS NOTHING, JUST--
THESE ARE NOT MY REAL PARENTS.
OH--
AND YOU ARE NOT A REAL GOOD KISSER.

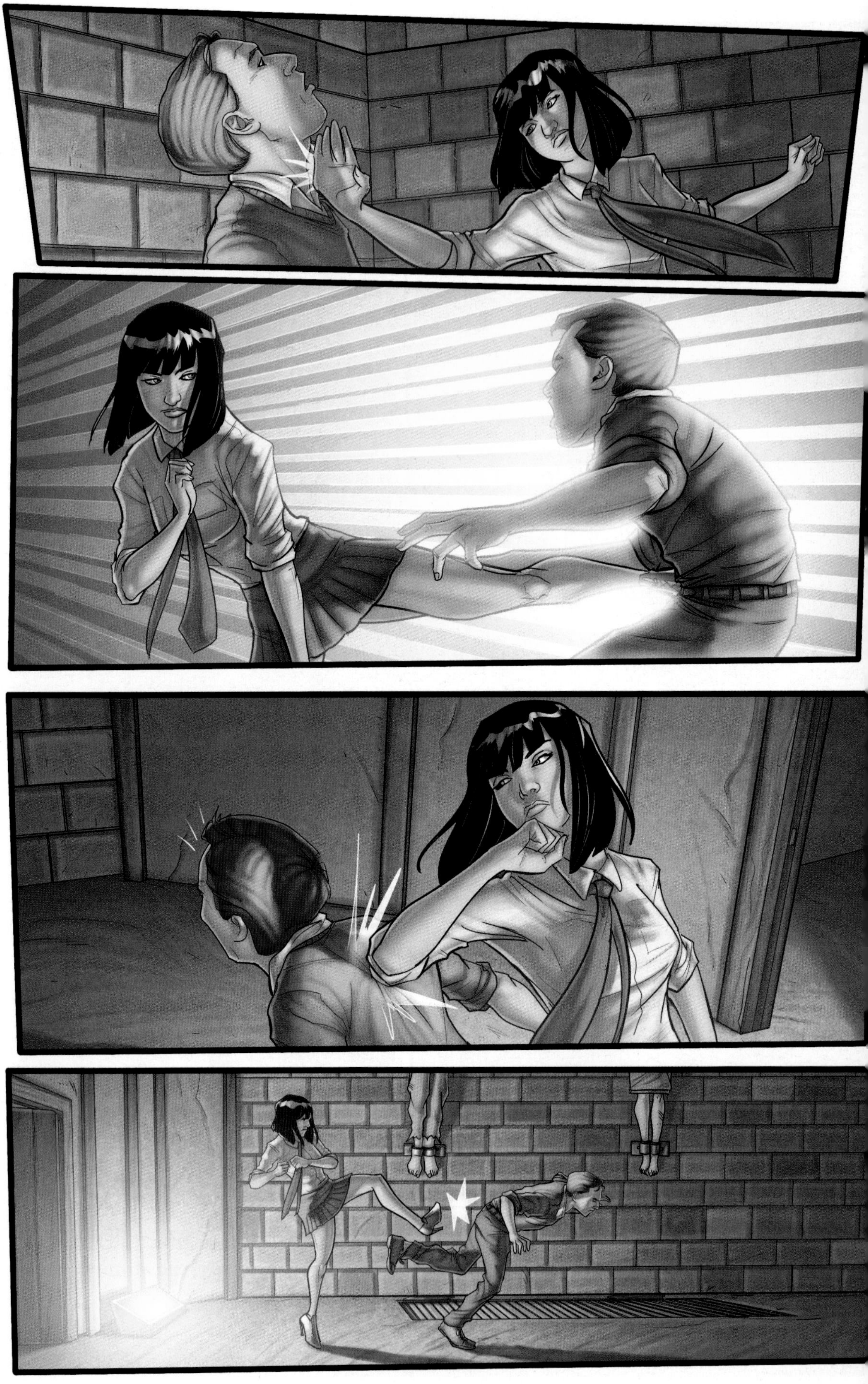

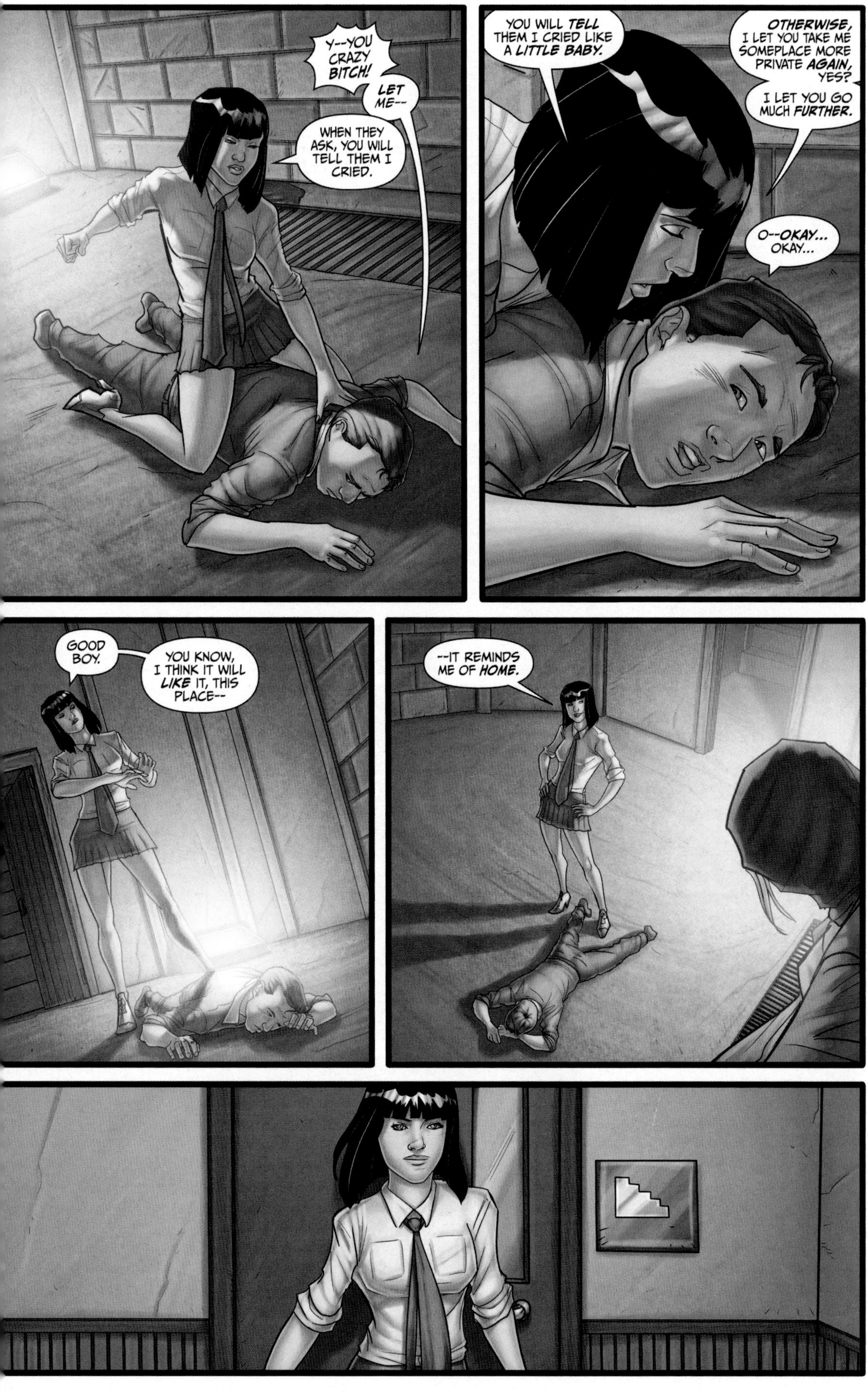
Y--YOU CRAZY *BITCH!*
LET ME--
WHEN THEY ASK, YOU WILL TELL THEM I CRIED.
YOU WILL *TELL* THEM I CRIED LIKE A *LITTLE BABY.*
OTHERWISE, I LET YOU TAKE ME SOMEPLACE MORE PRIVATE *AGAIN,* YES?
I LET YOU GO MUCH *FURTHER.*
O--*OKAY...* OKAY...
GOOD BOY.
YOU KNOW, I THINK IT WILL *LIKE* IT, THIS PLACE--
--IT REMINDS ME OF *HOME.*

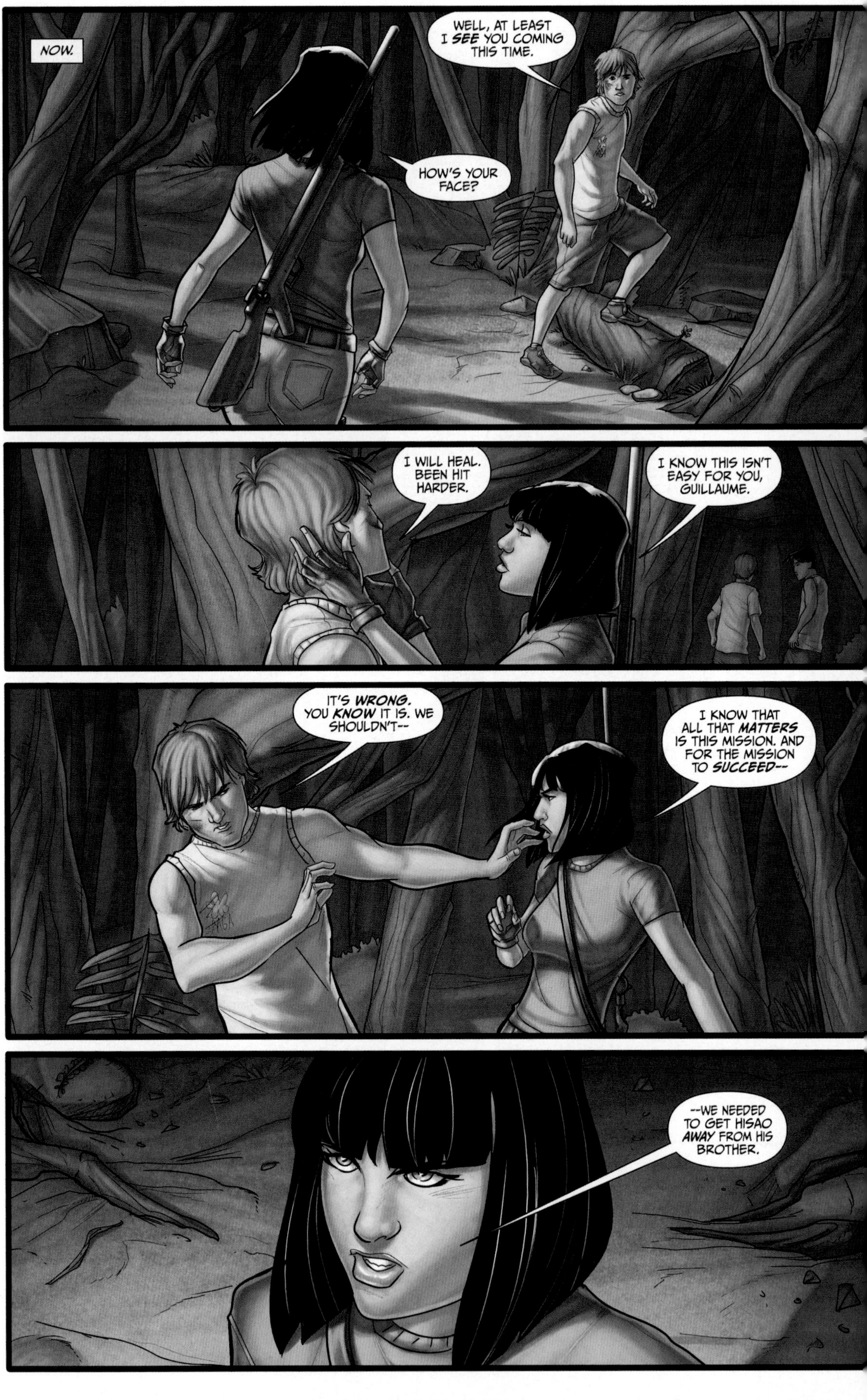
NOW.
WELL, AT LEAST I SEE YOU COMING THIS TIME.
HOW'S YOUR FACE?
I WILL HEAL. BEEN HIT HARDER.
I KNOW THIS ISN'T EASY FOR YOU, GUILLAUME.
IT'S WRONG. YOU KNOW IT IS. WE SHOULDN'T--
I KNOW THAT ALL THAT MATTERS IS THIS MISSION. AND FOR THE MISSION TO SUCCEED--
--WE NEEDED TO GET HISAO AWAY FROM HIS BROTHER.

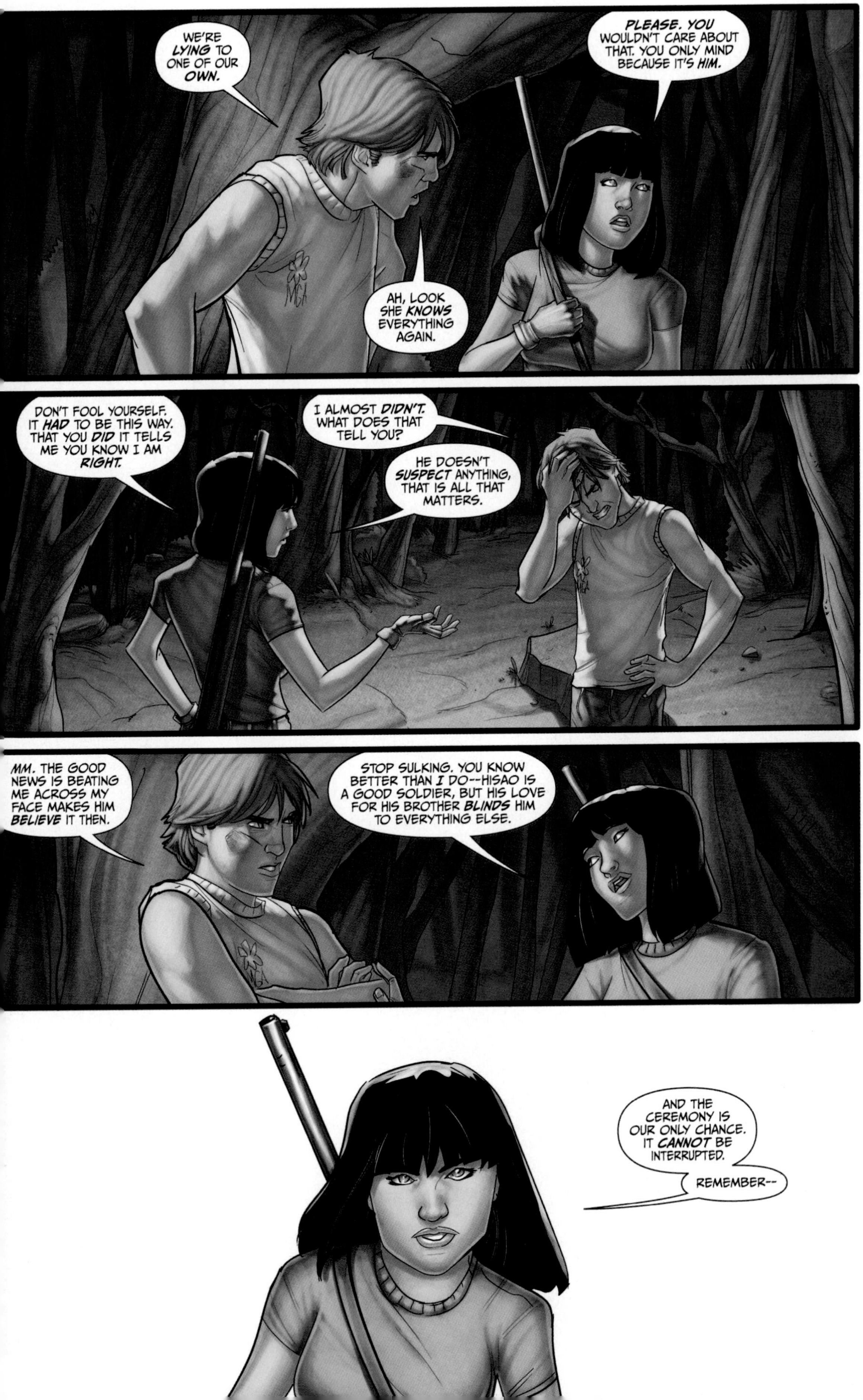
WE'RE LYING TO ONE OF OUR OWN.
PLEASE. YOU WOULDN'T CARE ABOUT THAT. YOU ONLY MIND BECAUSE IT'S HIM.
AH, LOOK SHE KNOWS EVERYTHING AGAIN.
DON'T FOOL YOURSELF. IT HAD TO BE THIS WAY. THAT YOU DID IT TELLS ME YOU KNOW I AM RIGHT.
I ALMOST DIDN'T. WHAT DOES THAT TELL YOU?
HE DOESN'T SUSPECT ANYTHING, THAT IS ALL THAT MATTERS.
MM. THE GOOD NEWS IS BEATING ME ACROSS MY FACE MAKES HIM BELIEVE IT THEN.
STOP SULKING. YOU KNOW BETTER THAN I DO--HISAO IS A GOOD SOLDIER, BUT HIS LOVE FOR HIS BROTHER BLINDS HIM TO EVERYTHING ELSE.
AND THE CEREMONY IS OUR ONLY CHANCE. IT CANNOT BE INTERRUPTED.
REMEMBER--

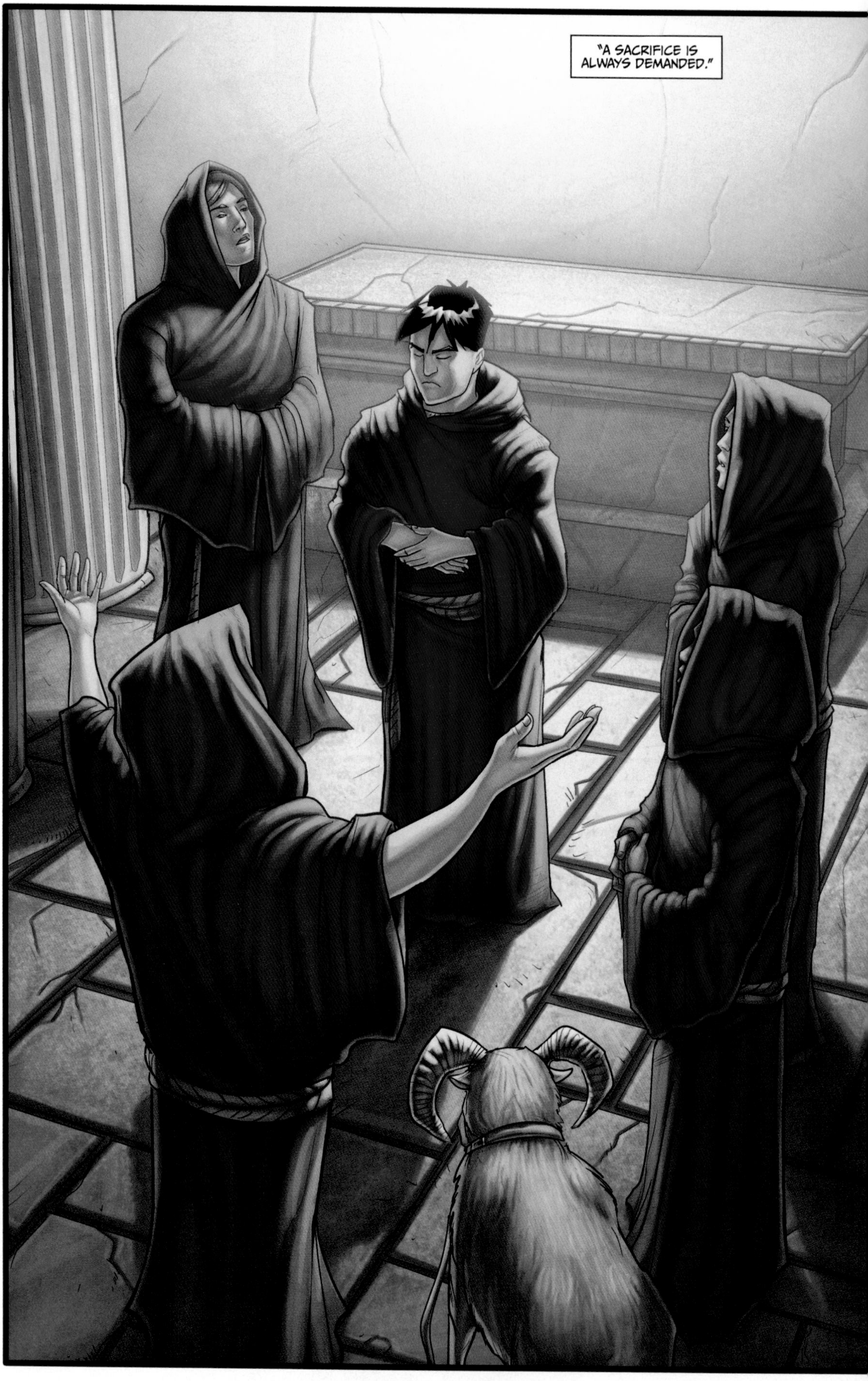
"A SACRIFICE IS ALWAYS DEMANDED."

twentytwo

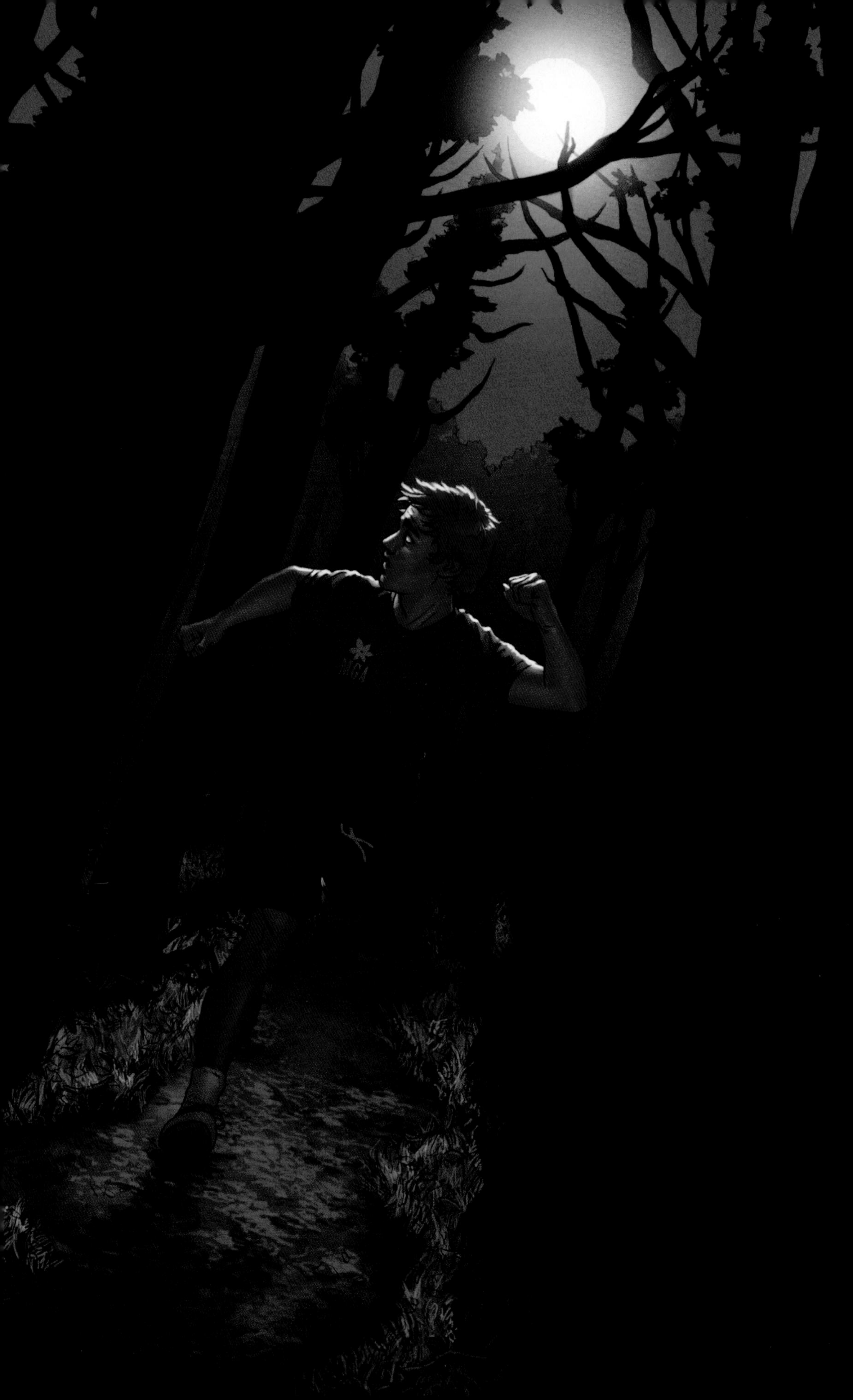

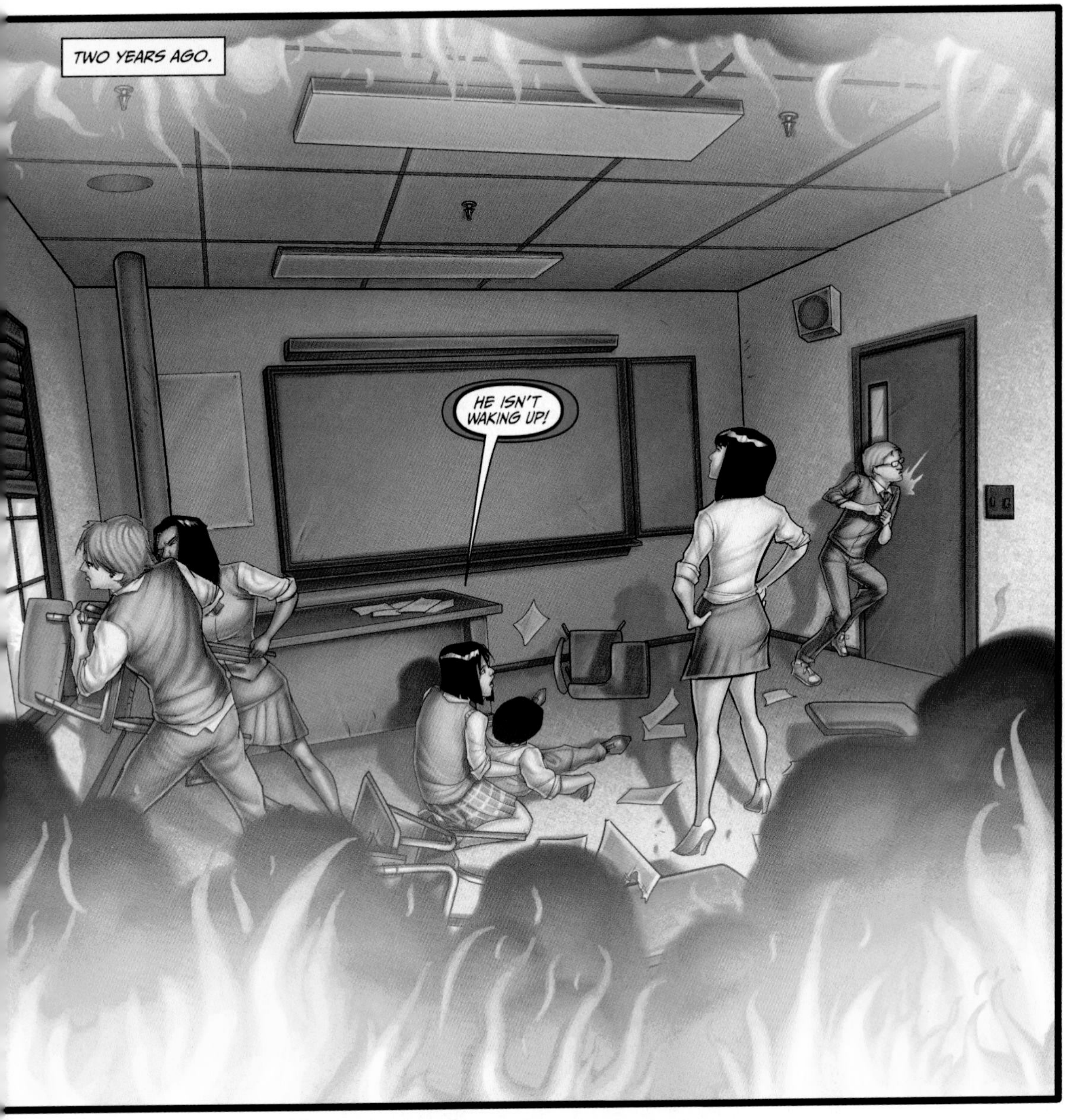
TWO YEARS AGO.
HE ISN'T WAKING UP!

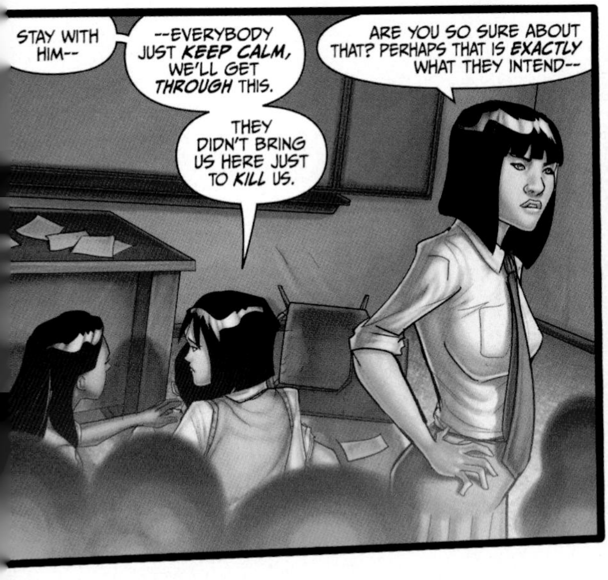
STAY WITH HIM--
--EVERYBODY JUST KEEP CALM, WE'LL GET THROUGH THIS.
THEY DIDN'T BRING US HERE JUST TO KILL US.
ARE YOU SO SURE ABOUT THAT? PERHAPS THAT IS EXACTLY WHAT THEY INTEND--

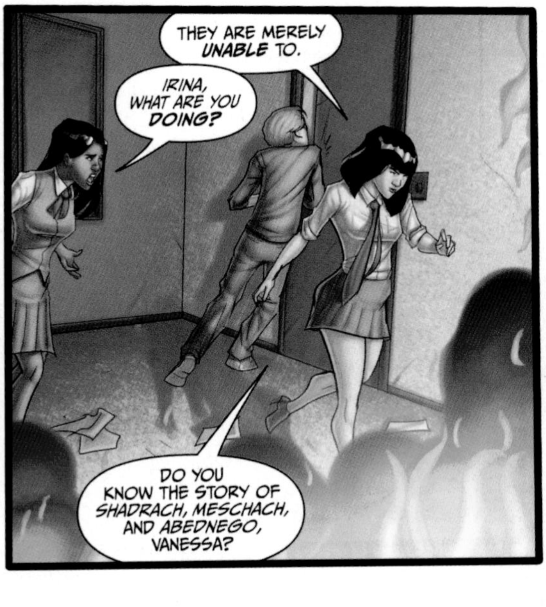
THEY ARE MERELY UNABLE TO.
IRINA, WHAT ARE YOU DOING?
DO YOU KNOW THE STORY OF SHADRACH, MESCHACH, AND ABEDNEGO, VANESSA?

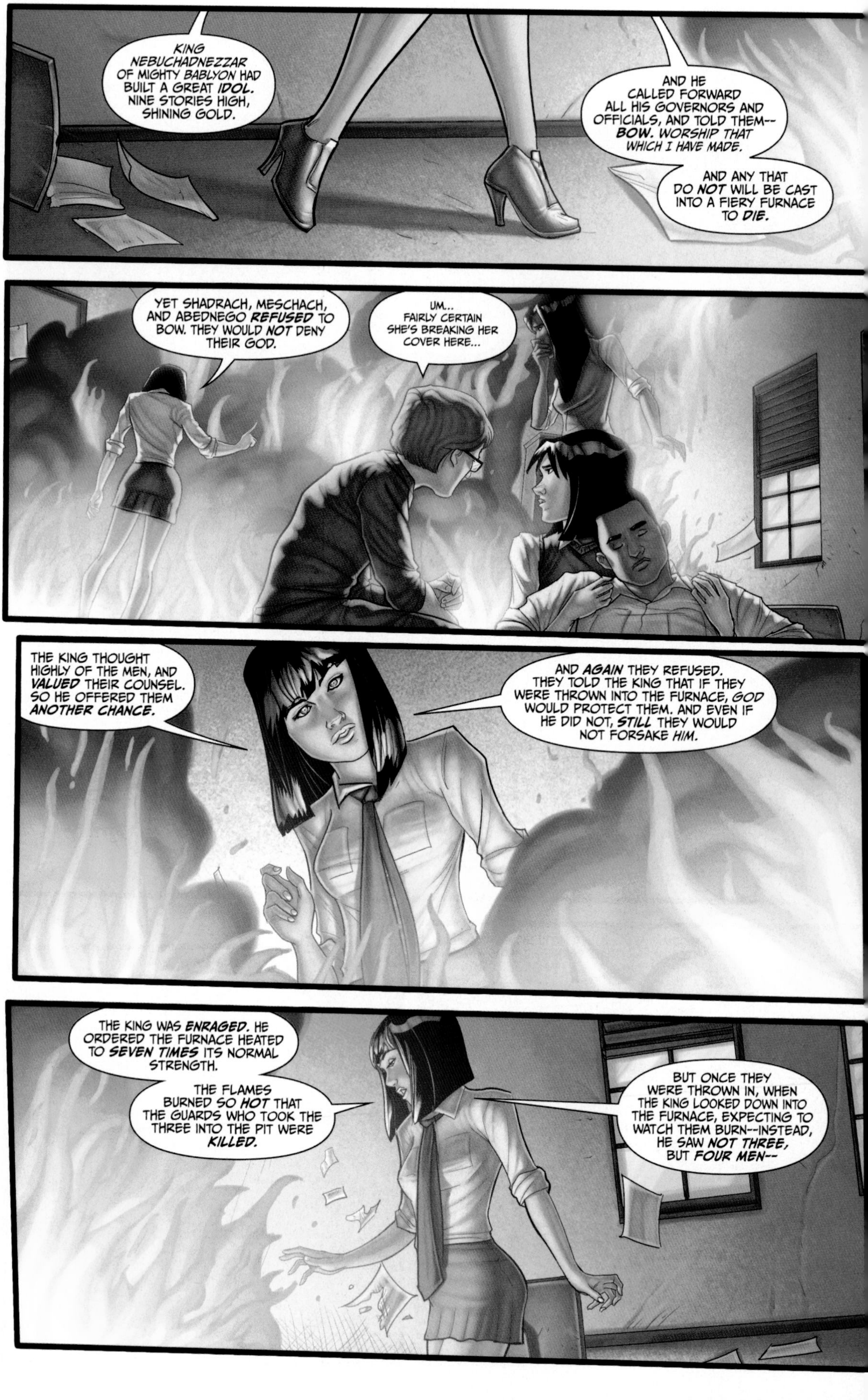
KING NEBUCHADNEZZAR OF MIGHTY BABLYON HAD BUILT A GREAT IDOL. NINE STORIES HIGH, SHINING GOLD.
AND HE CALLED FORWARD ALL HIS GOVERNORS AND OFFICIALS, AND TOLD THEM--BOW. WORSHIP THAT WHICH I HAVE MADE.
AND ANY THAT DO NOT WILL BE CAST INTO A FIERY FURNACE TO DIE.
YET SHADRACH, MESCHACH, AND ABEDNEGO REFUSED TO BOW. THEY WOULD NOT DENY THEIR GOD.
UM... FAIRLY CERTAIN SHE'S BREAKING HER COVER HERE...
THE KING THOUGHT HIGHLY OF THE MEN, AND VALUED THEIR COUNSEL. SO HE OFFERED THEM ANOTHER CHANCE.
AND AGAIN THEY REFUSED. THEY TOLD THE KING THAT IF THEY WERE THROWN INTO THE FURNACE, GOD WOULD PROTECT THEM. AND EVEN IF HE DID NOT, STILL THEY WOULD NOT FORSAKE HIM.
THE KING WAS ENRAGED. HE ORDERED THE FURNACE HEATED TO SEVEN TIMES ITS NORMAL STRENGTH.
THE FLAMES BURNED SO HOT THAT THE GUARDS WHO TOOK THE THREE INTO THE PIT WERE KILLED.
BUT ONCE THEY WERE THROWN IN, WHEN THE KING LOOKED DOWN INTO THE FURNACE, EXPECTING TO WATCH THEM BURN--INSTEAD, HE SAW NOT THREE, BUT FOUR MEN--

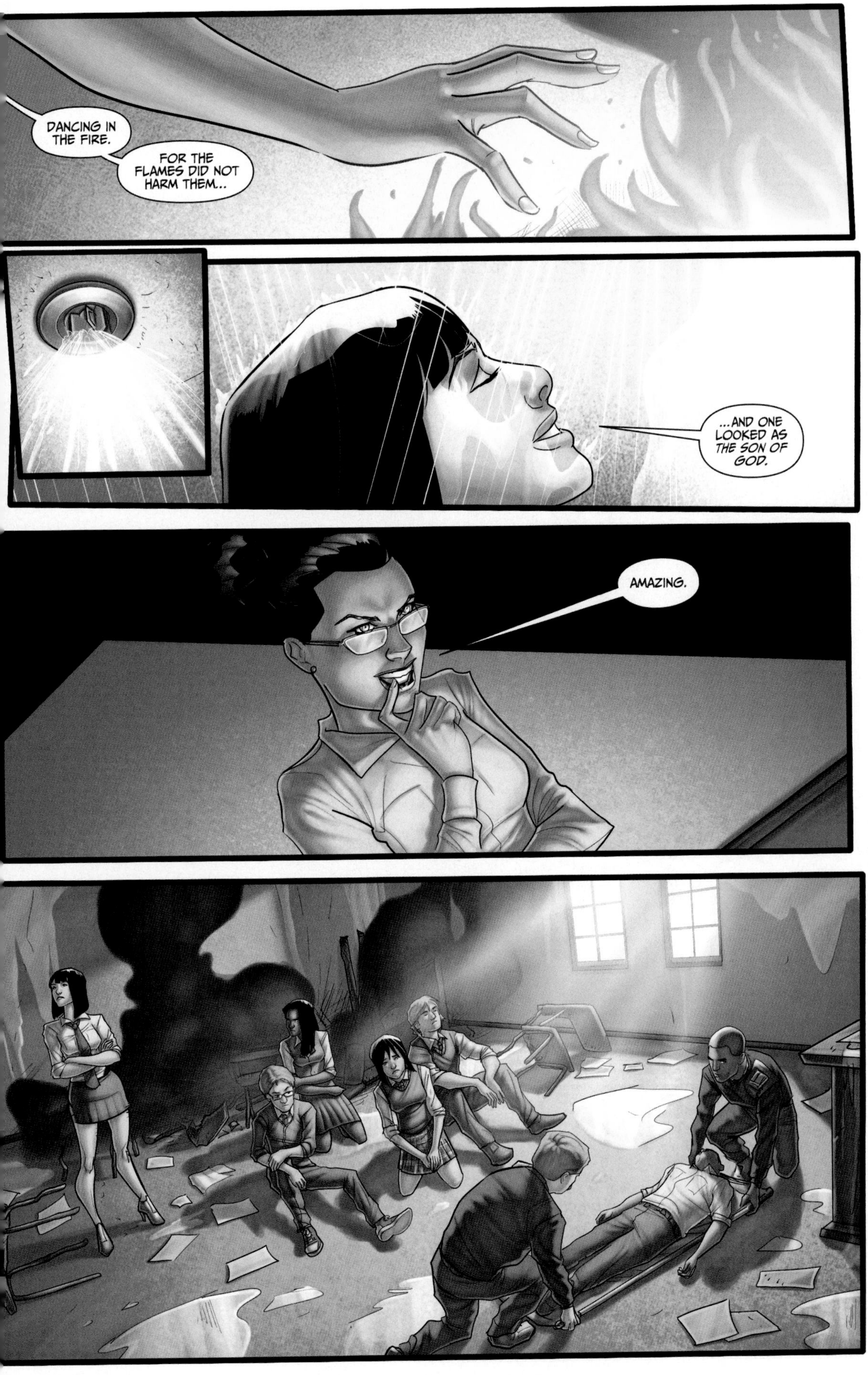
DANCING IN THE FIRE.
FOR THE FLAMES DID NOT HARM THEM...
...AND ONE LOOKED AS THE SON OF GOD.
AMAZING.

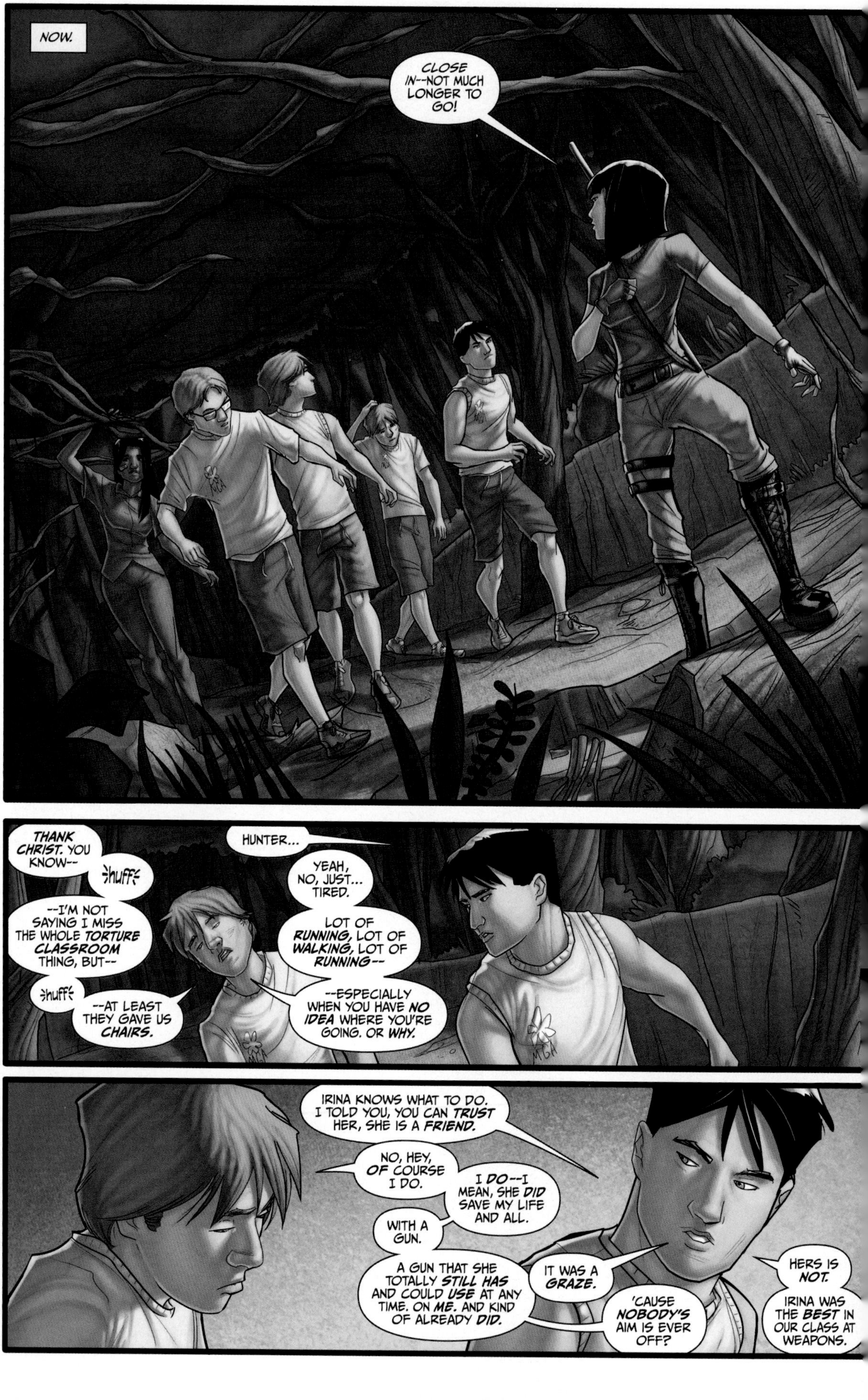
NOW.
CLOSE IN--NOT MUCH LONGER TO GO!
THANK CHRIST. YOU KNOW--
HUNTER...
huff
YEAH, NO, JUST... TIRED.
--I'M NOT SAYING I MISS THE WHOLE TORTURE CLASSROOM THING, BUT--
LOT OF RUNNING, LOT OF WALKING, LOT OF RUNNING--
huff
--AT LEAST THEY GAVE US CHAIRS.
--ESPECIALLY WHEN YOU HAVE NO IDEA WHERE YOU'RE GOING. OR WHY.
IRINA KNOWS WHAT TO DO. I TOLD YOU, YOU CAN TRUST HER, SHE IS A FRIEND.
NO, HEY, OF COURSE I DO.
I DO--I MEAN, SHE DID SAVE MY LIFE AND ALL.
WITH A GUN.
A GUN THAT SHE TOTALLY STILL HAS AND COULD USE AT ANY TIME. ON ME. AND KIND OF ALREADY DID.
IT WAS A GRAZE.
'CAUSE NOBODY'S AIM IS EVER OFF?
HERS IS NOT.
IRINA WAS THE BEST IN OUR CLASS AT WEAPONS.

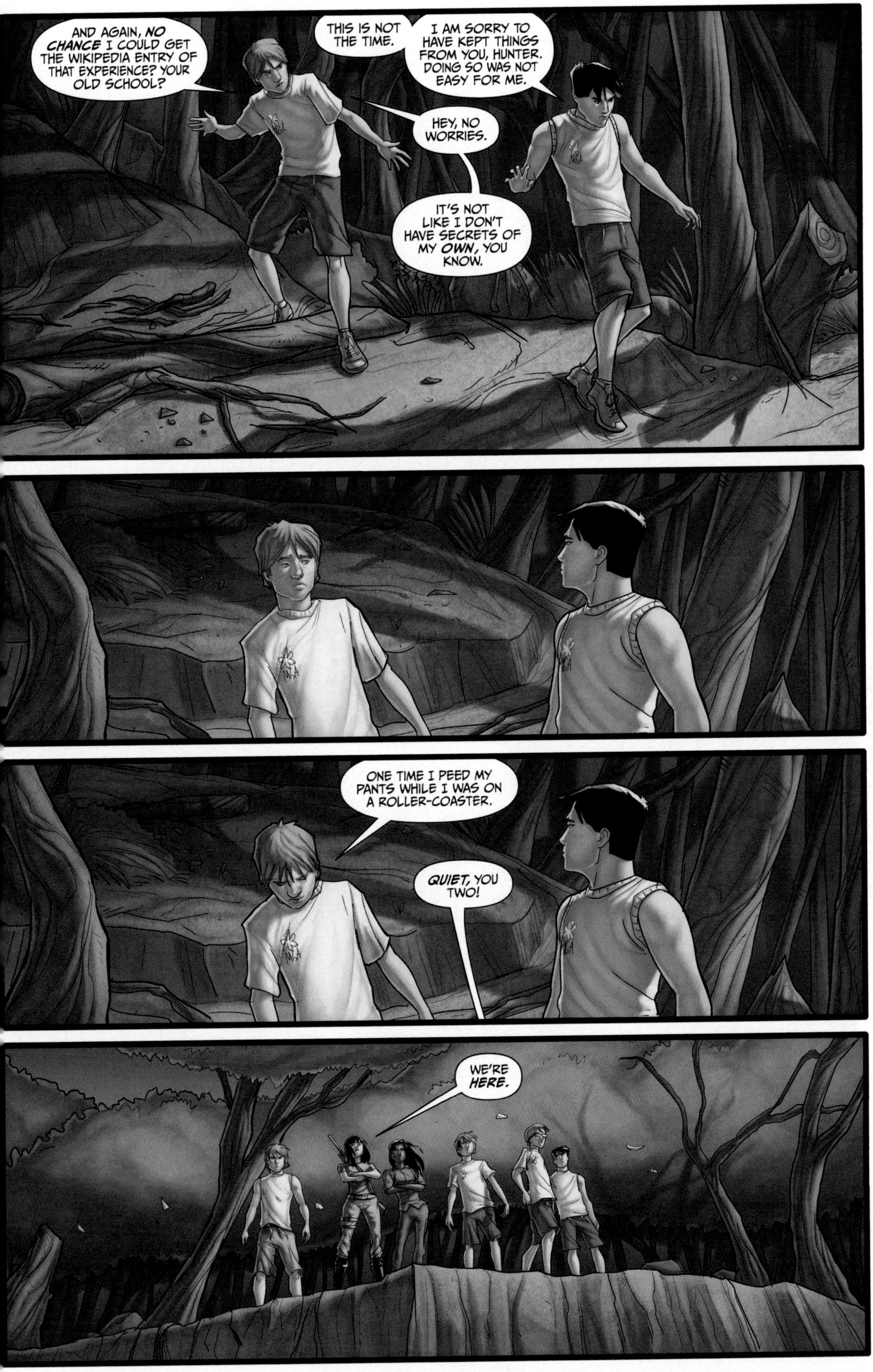
AND AGAIN, NO CHANCE I COULD GET THE WIKIPEDIA ENTRY OF THAT EXPERIENCE? YOUR OLD SCHOOL?
THIS IS NOT THE TIME.
I AM SORRY TO HAVE KEPT THINGS FROM YOU, HUNTER. DOING SO WAS NOT EASY FOR ME.
HEY, NO WORRIES.
IT'S NOT LIKE I DON'T HAVE SECRETS OF MY OWN, YOU KNOW.
ONE TIME I PEED MY PANTS WHILE I WAS ON A ROLLER-COASTER.
QUIET, YOU TWO!
WE'RE HERE.

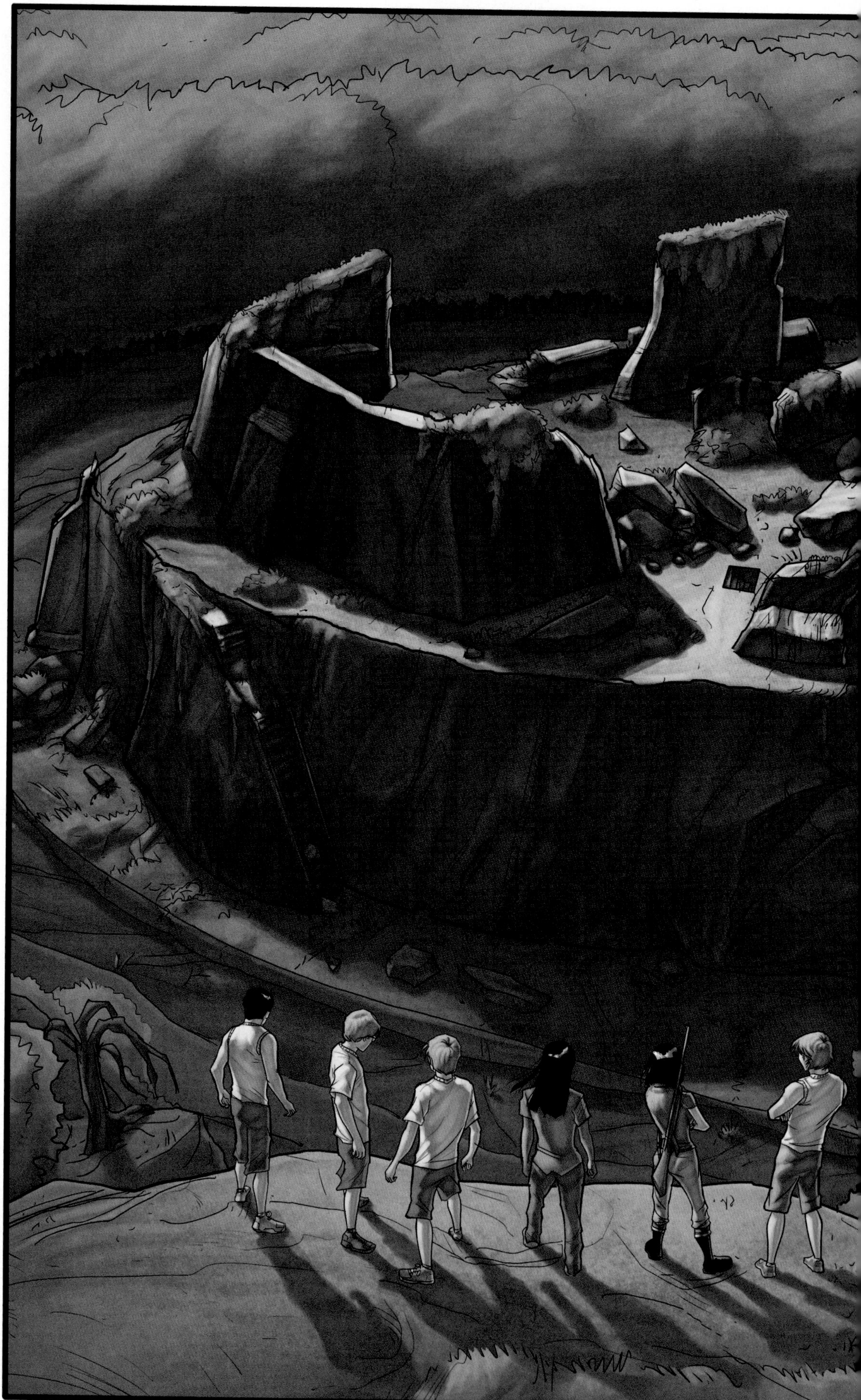

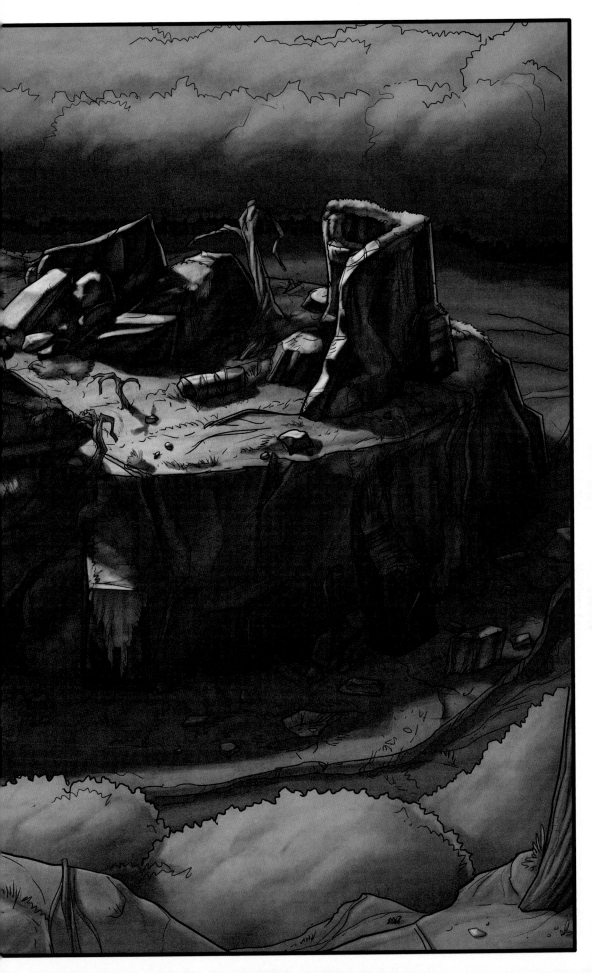

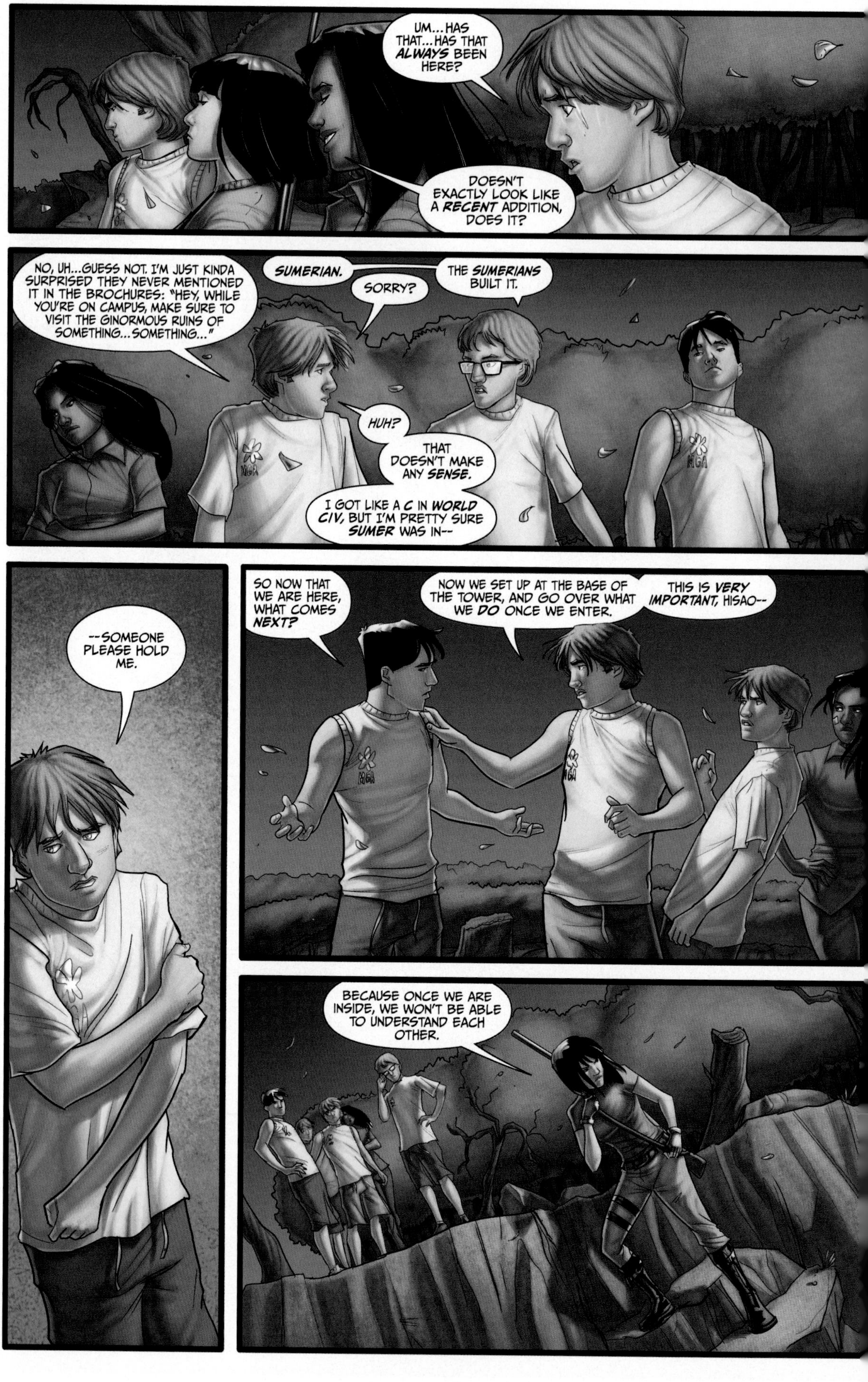
UM... HAS THAT... HAS THAT ALWAYS BEEN HERE?
DOESN'T EXACTLY LOOK LIKE A RECENT ADDITION, DOES IT?
NO, UH...GUESS NOT. I'M JUST KINDA SURPRISED THEY NEVER MENTIONED IT IN THE BROCHURES: "HEY, WHILE YOU'RE ON CAMPUS, MAKE SURE TO VISIT THE GINORMOUS RUINS OF SOMETHING...SOMETHING..."
SUMERIAN.
SORRY?
THE SUMERIANS BUILT IT.
HUH?
THAT DOESN'T MAKE ANY SENSE.
I GOT LIKE A C IN WORLD CIV, BUT I'M PRETTY SURE SUMER WAS IN--
--SOMEONE PLEASE HOLD ME.
SO NOW THAT WE ARE HERE, WHAT COMES NEXT?
NOW WE SET UP AT THE BASE OF THE TOWER, AND GO OVER WHAT WE DO ONCE WE ENTER.
THIS IS VERY IMPORTANT, HISAO--
BECAUSE ONCE WE ARE INSIDE, WE WON'T BE ABLE TO UNDERSTAND EACH OTHER.

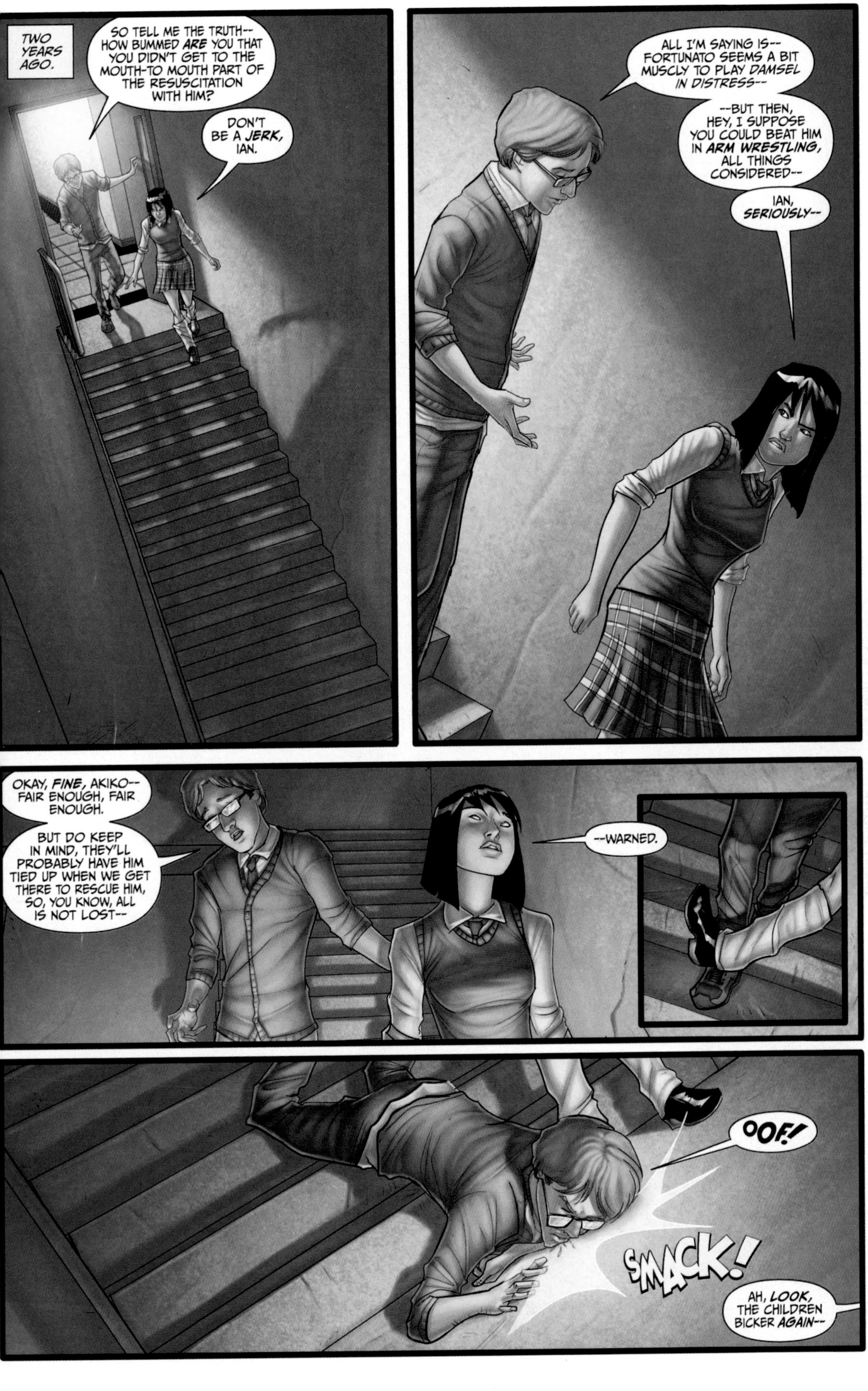
TWO YEARS AGO.
SO TELL ME THE TRUTH-- HOW BUMMED ARE YOU THAT YOU DIDN'T GET TO THE MOUTH-TO MOUTH PART OF THE RESUSCITATION WITH HIM?
DON'T BE A JERK, IAN.
ALL I'M SAYING IS-- FORTUNATO SEEMS A BIT MUSCLY TO PLAY DAMSEL IN DISTRESS--
--BUT THEN, HEY, I SUPPOSE YOU COULD BEAT HIM IN ARM WRESTLING, ALL THINGS CONSIDERED--
IAN, SERIOUSLY--
OKAY, FINE, AKIKO-- FAIR ENOUGH, FAIR ENOUGH.
BUT DO KEEP IN MIND, THEY'LL PROBABLY HAVE HIM TIED UP WHEN WE GET THERE TO RESCUE HIM, SO, YOU KNOW, ALL IS NOT LOST--
--WARNED.
OOF!
SMACK!
AH, LOOK, THE CHILDREN BICKER AGAIN--

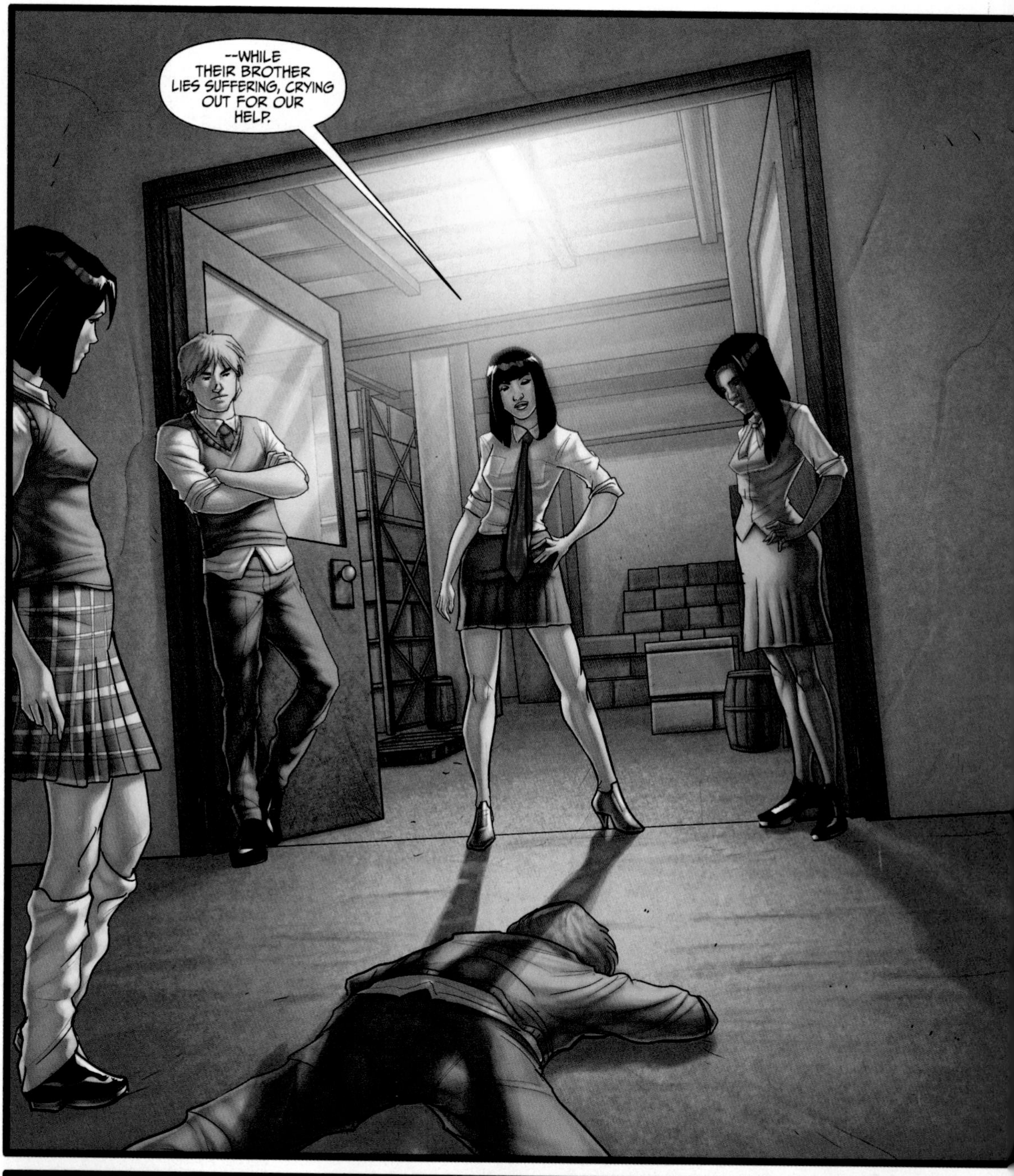
--WHILE THEIR BROTHER LIES SUFFERING, CRYING OUT FOR OUR HELP.

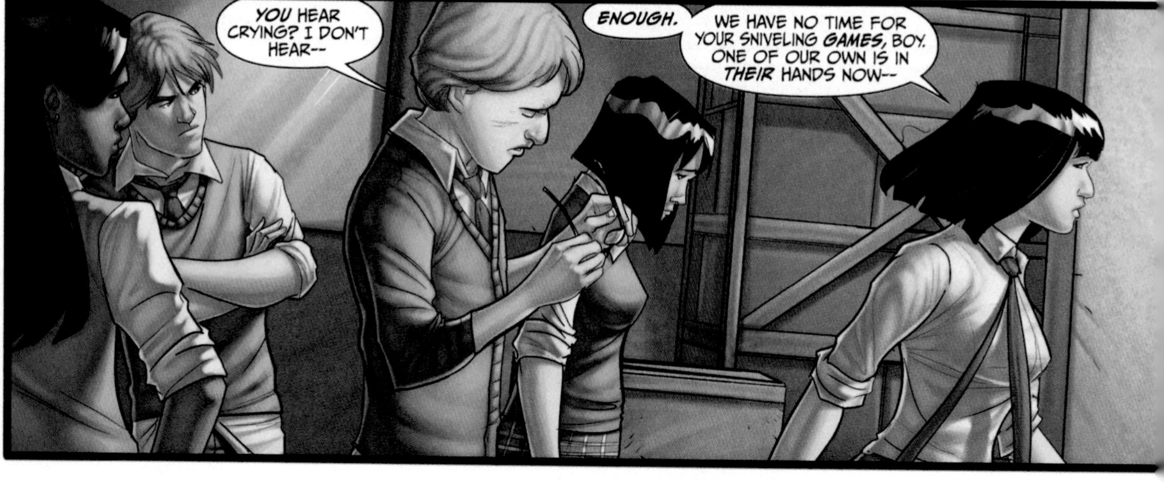
YOU HEAR CRYING? I DON'T HEAR--
ENOUGH.
WE HAVE NO TIME FOR YOUR SNIVELING GAMES, BOY. ONE OF OUR OWN IS IN THEIR HANDS NOW--

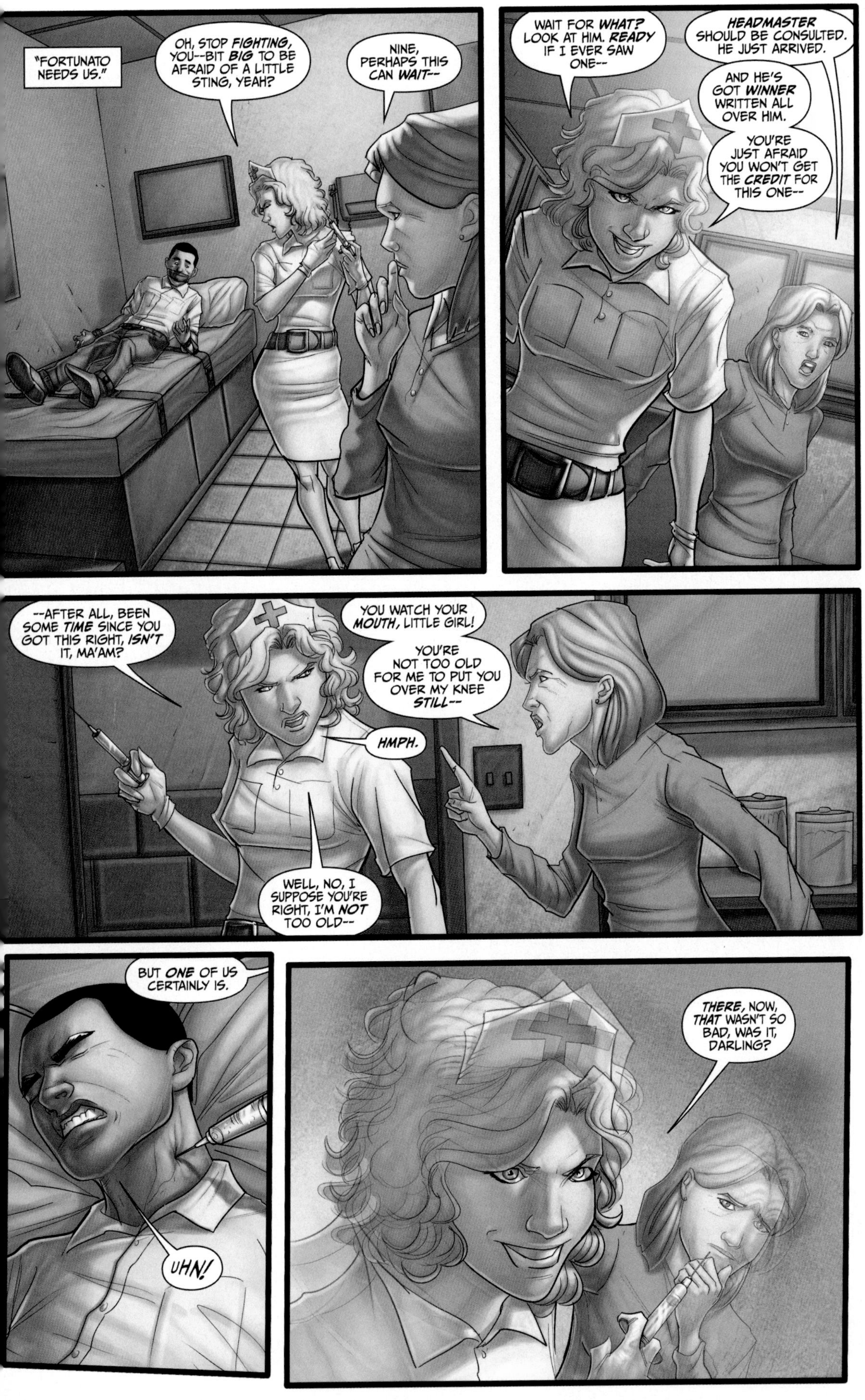

"FORTUNATO NEEDS US."
OH, STOP FIGHTING, YOU--BIT BIG TO BE AFRAID OF A LITTLE STING, YEAH?
NINE, PERHAPS THIS CAN WAIT--
WAIT FOR WHAT? LOOK AT HIM. READY IF I EVER SAW ONE--
HEADMASTER SHOULD BE CONSULTED. HE JUST ARRIVED.
AND HE'S GOT WINNER WRITTEN ALL OVER HIM.
YOU'RE JUST AFRAID YOU WON'T GET THE CREDIT FOR THIS ONE--
--AFTER ALL, BEEN SOME TIME SINCE YOU GOT THIS RIGHT, ISN'T IT, MA'AM?
YOU WATCH YOUR MOUTH, LITTLE GIRL!
YOU'RE NOT TOO OLD FOR ME TO PUT YOU OVER MY KNEE STILL--
HMPH.
WELL, NO, I SUPPOSE YOU'RE RIGHT, I'M NOT TOO OLD--
BUT ONE OF US CERTAINLY IS.
UHN!
THERE, NOW, THAT WASN'T SO BAD, WAS IT, DARLING?

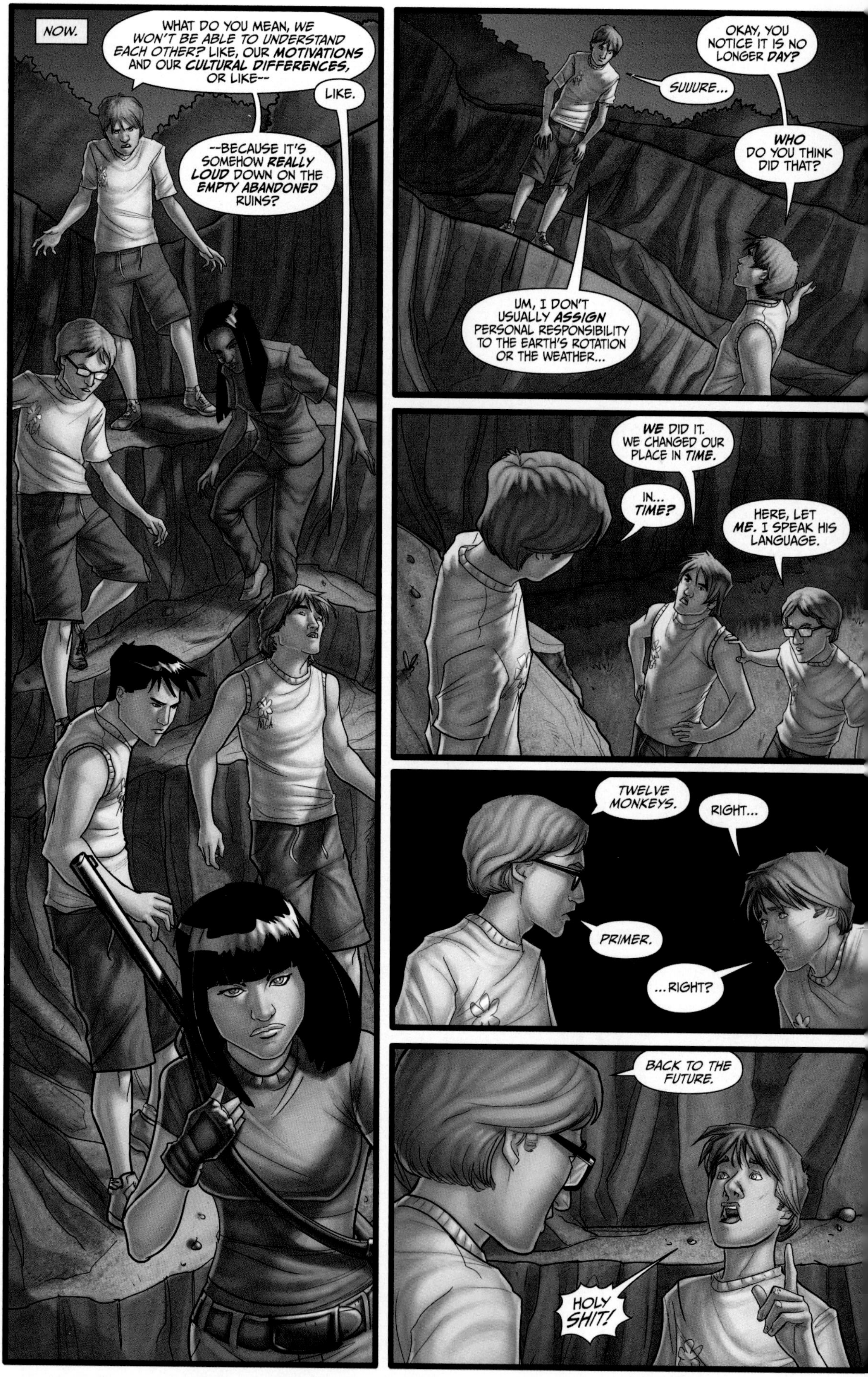
NOW.
WHAT DO YOU MEAN, WE WON'T BE ABLE TO UNDERSTAND EACH OTHER? LIKE, OUR MOTIVATIONS AND OUR CULTURAL DIFFERENCES, OR LIKE--
--BECAUSE IT'S SOMEHOW REALLY LOUD DOWN ON THE EMPTY ABANDONED RUINS?
LIKE.
OKAY, YOU NOTICE IT IS NO LONGER DAY?
SUUURE...
WHO DO YOU THINK DID THAT?
UM, I DON'T USUALLY ASSIGN PERSONAL RESPONSIBILITY TO THE EARTH'S ROTATION OR THE WEATHER...
WE DID IT. WE CHANGED OUR PLACE IN TIME.
IN... TIME?
HERE, LET ME. I SPEAK HIS LANGUAGE.
TWELVE MONKEYS.
RIGHT...
PRIMER.
...RIGHT?
BACK TO THE FUTURE.
HOLY SHIT!

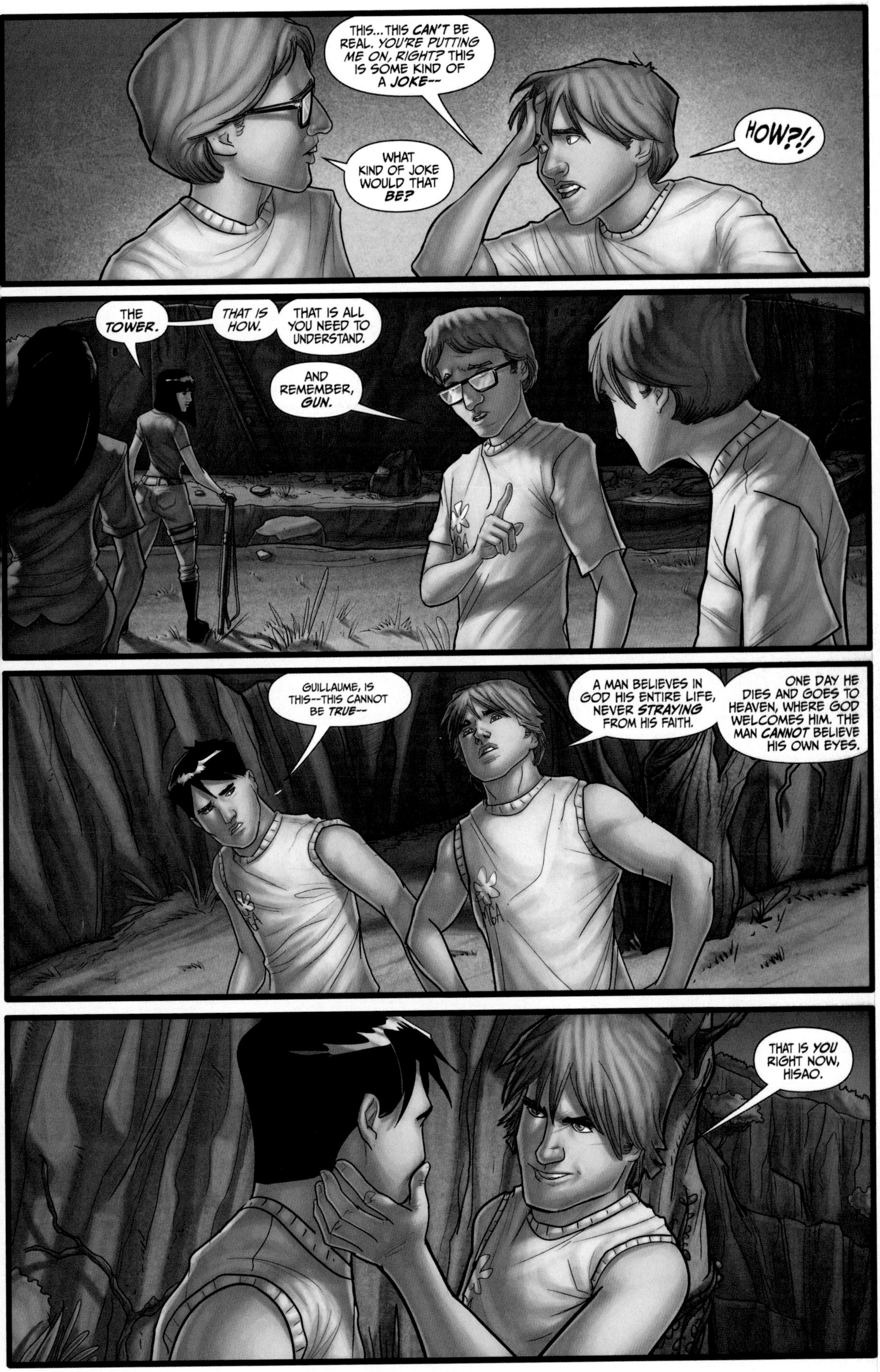
THIS...THIS CAN'T BE REAL. YOU'RE PUTTING ME ON, RIGHT? THIS IS SOME KIND OF A JOKE--
WHAT KIND OF JOKE WOULD THAT BE?
HOW?!!
THE TOWER.
THAT IS HOW.
THAT IS ALL YOU NEED TO UNDERSTAND.
AND REMEMBER, GUN.
GUILLAUME, IS THIS--THIS CANNOT BE TRUE--
A MAN BELIEVES IN GOD HIS ENTIRE LIFE, NEVER STRAYING FROM HIS FAITH.
ONE DAY HE DIES AND GOES TO HEAVEN, WHERE GOD WELCOMES HIM. THE MAN CANNOT BELIEVE HIS OWN EYES.
THAT IS YOU RIGHT NOW, HISAO.

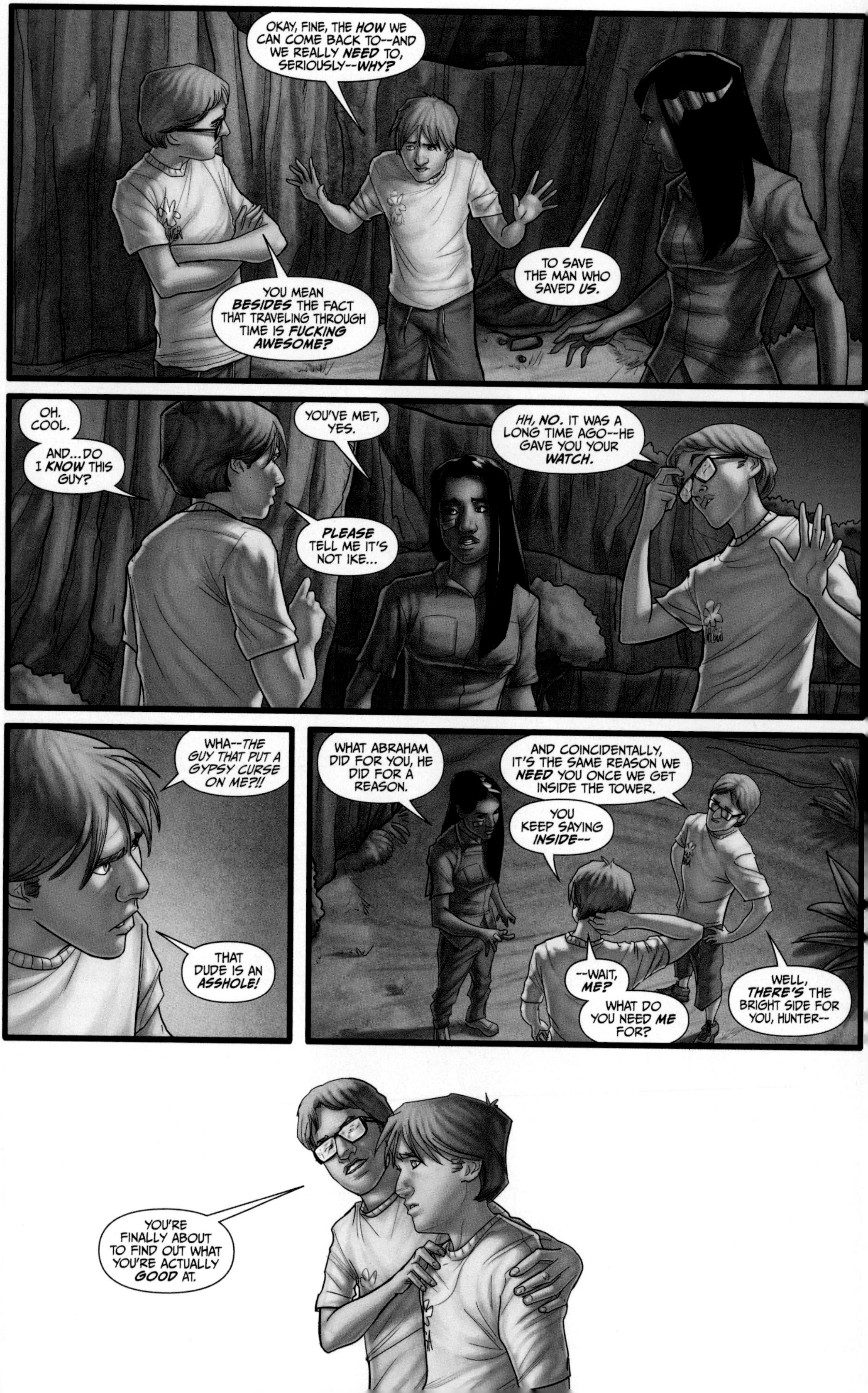

OKAY, FINE, THE HOW WE CAN COME BACK TO--AND WE REALLY NEED TO, SERIOUSLY--WHY?
YOU MEAN BESIDES THE FACT THAT TRAVELING THROUGH TIME IS FUCKING AWESOME?
TO SAVE THE MAN WHO SAVED US.
OH. COOL.
AND...DO I KNOW THIS GUY?
YOU'VE MET, YES.
HH, NO. IT WAS A LONG TIME AGO--HE GAVE YOU YOUR WATCH.
PLEASE TELL ME IT'S NOT IKE...
WHA--THE GUY THAT PUT A GYPSY CURSE ON ME?!!
THAT DUDE IS AN ASSHOLE!
WHAT ABRAHAM DID FOR YOU, HE DID FOR A REASON.
AND COINCIDENTALLY, IT'S THE SAME REASON WE NEED YOU ONCE WE GET INSIDE THE TOWER.
YOU KEEP SAYING INSIDE--
--WAIT, ME?
WHAT DO YOU NEED ME FOR?
WELL, THERE'S THE BRIGHT SIDE FOR YOU, HUNTER--
YOU'RE FINALLY ABOUT TO FIND OUT WHAT YOU'RE ACTUALLY GOOD AT.

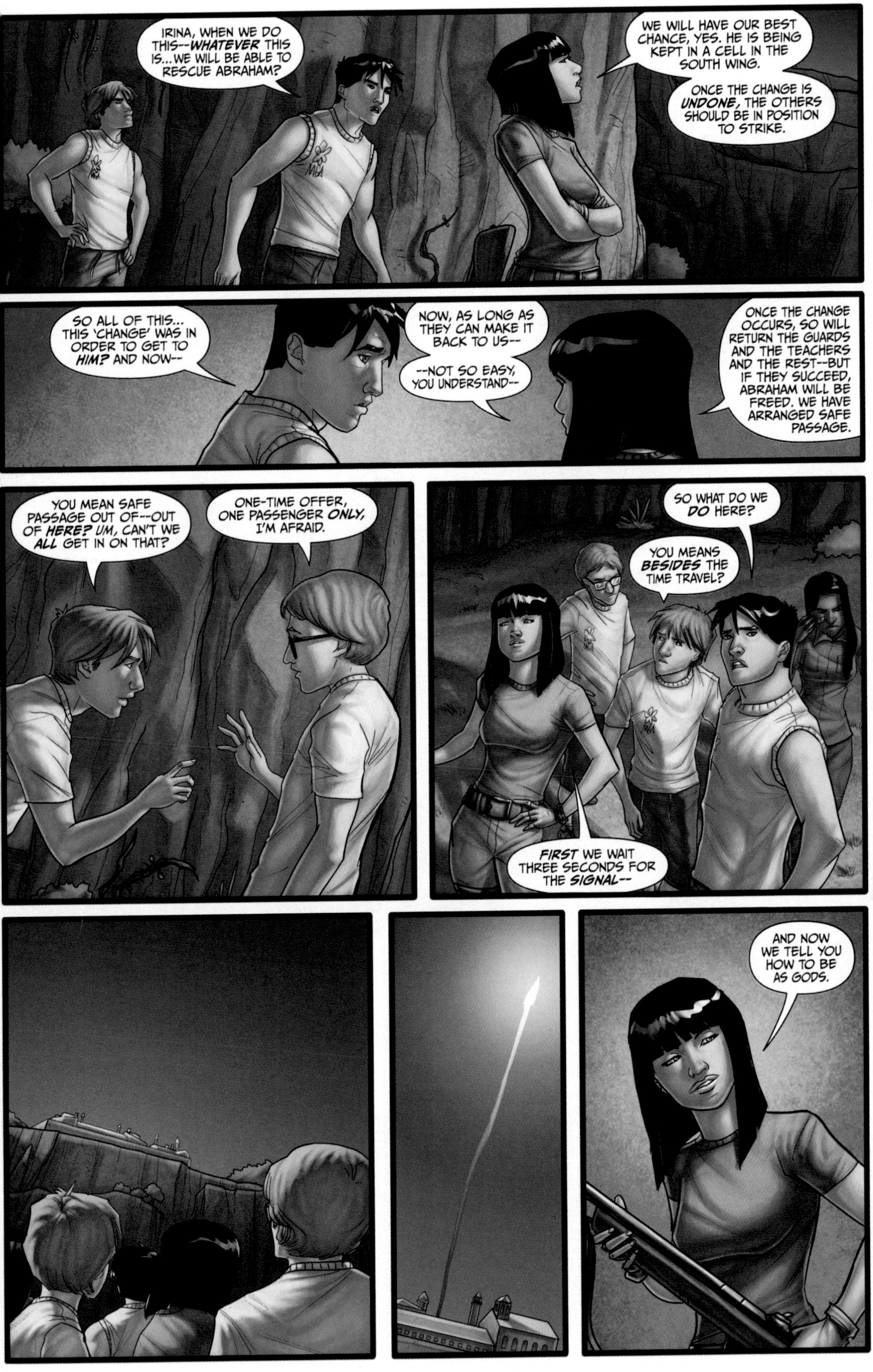
IRINA, WHEN WE DO THIS--WHATEVER THIS IS...WE WILL BE ABLE TO RESCUE ABRAHAM?
WE WILL HAVE OUR BEST CHANCE, YES. HE IS BEING KEPT IN A CELL IN THE SOUTH WING.
ONCE THE CHANGE IS UNDONE, THE OTHERS SHOULD BE IN POSITION TO STRIKE.
SO ALL OF THIS... THIS 'CHANGE' WAS IN ORDER TO GET TO HIM? AND NOW--
NOW, AS LONG AS THEY CAN MAKE IT BACK TO US--
--NOT SO EASY, YOU UNDERSTAND--
ONCE THE CHANGE OCCURS, SO WILL RETURN THE GUARDS AND THE TEACHERS AND THE REST--BUT IF THEY SUCCEED, ABRAHAM WILL BE FREED. WE HAVE ARRANGED SAFE PASSAGE.
YOU MEAN SAFE PASSAGE OUT OF--OUT OF HERE? UM, CAN'T WE ALL GET IN ON THAT?
ONE-TIME OFFER, ONE PASSENGER ONLY, I'M AFRAID.
SO WHAT DO WE DO HERE?
YOU MEANS BESIDES THE TIME TRAVEL?
FIRST WE WAIT THREE SECONDS FOR THE SIGNAL--
AND NOW WE TELL YOU HOW TO BE AS GODS.

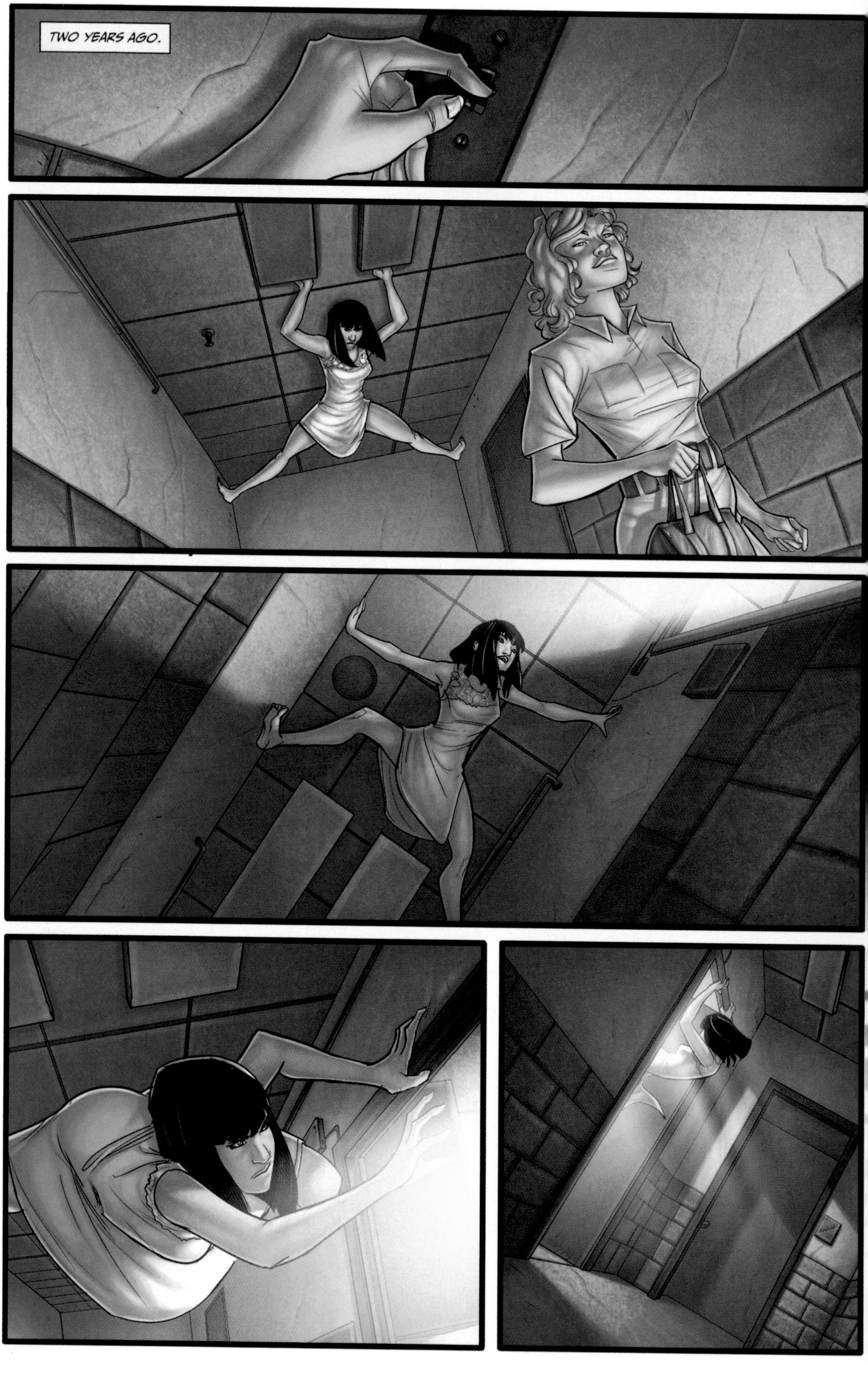
TWO YEARS AGO.

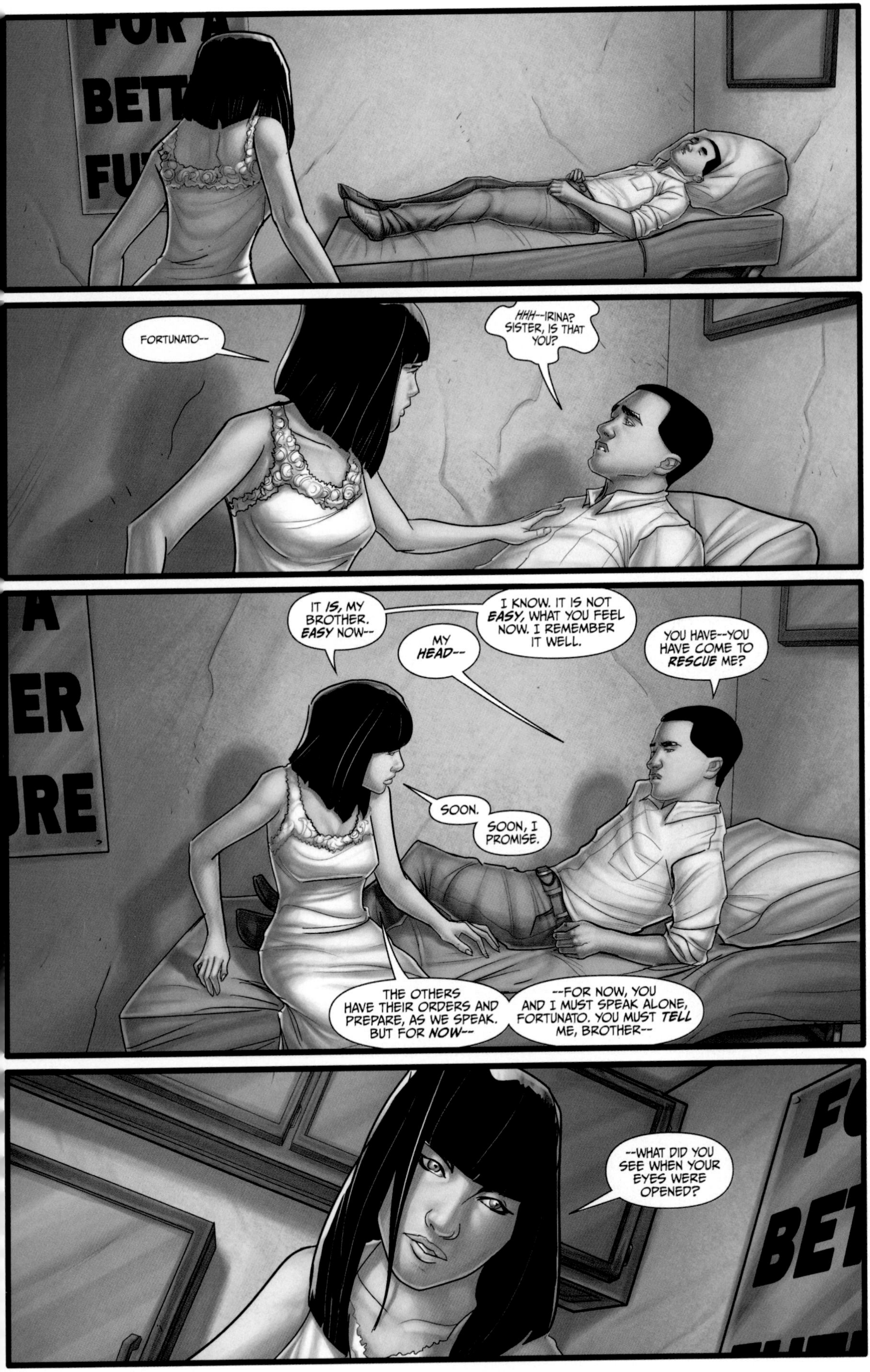
FOR A
BETT
FUT
FORTUNATO--
HHH--IRINA? SISTER, IS THAT YOU?
IT IS, MY BROTHER. EASY NOW--
I KNOW. IT IS NOT EASY, WHAT YOU FEEL NOW. I REMEMBER IT WELL.
MY HEAD--
YOU HAVE--YOU HAVE COME TO RESCUE ME?
A
ER
URE
SOON.
SOON, I PROMISE.
THE OTHERS HAVE THEIR ORDERS AND PREPARE, AS WE SPEAK. BUT FOR NOW--
--FOR NOW, YOU AND I MUST SPEAK ALONE, FORTUNATO. YOU MUST TELL ME, BROTHER--
--WHAT DID YOU SEE WHEN YOUR EYES WERE OPENED?
BE

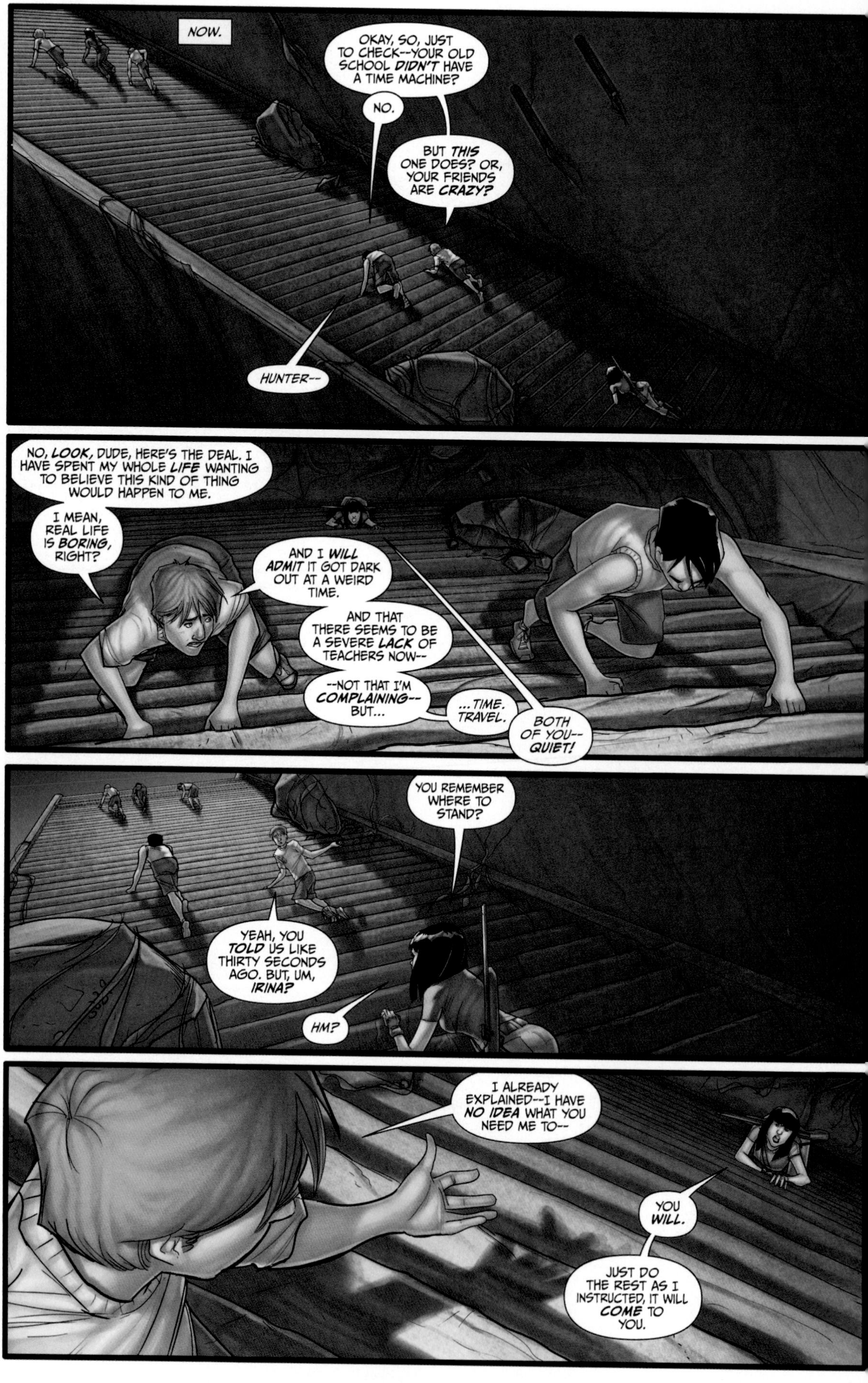
NOW.
OKAY, SO, JUST TO CHECK--YOUR OLD SCHOOL DIDN'T HAVE A TIME MACHINE?
NO.
BUT THIS ONE DOES? OR, YOUR FRIENDS ARE CRAZY?
HUNTER--
NO, LOOK, DUDE, HERE'S THE DEAL. I HAVE SPENT MY WHOLE LIFE WANTING TO BELIEVE THIS KIND OF THING WOULD HAPPEN TO ME.
I MEAN, REAL LIFE IS BORING, RIGHT?
AND I WILL ADMIT IT GOT DARK OUT AT A WEIRD TIME.
AND THAT THERE SEEMS TO BE A SEVERE LACK OF TEACHERS NOW--
--NOT THAT I'M COMPLAINING-- BUT...
...TIME. TRAVEL.
BOTH OF YOU-- QUIET!
YOU REMEMBER WHERE TO STAND?
YEAH, YOU TOLD US LIKE THIRTY SECONDS AGO. BUT, UM, IRINA?
HM?
I ALREADY EXPLAINED--I HAVE NO IDEA WHAT YOU NEED ME TO--
YOU WILL.
JUST DO THE REST AS I INSTRUCTED, IT WILL COME TO YOU.

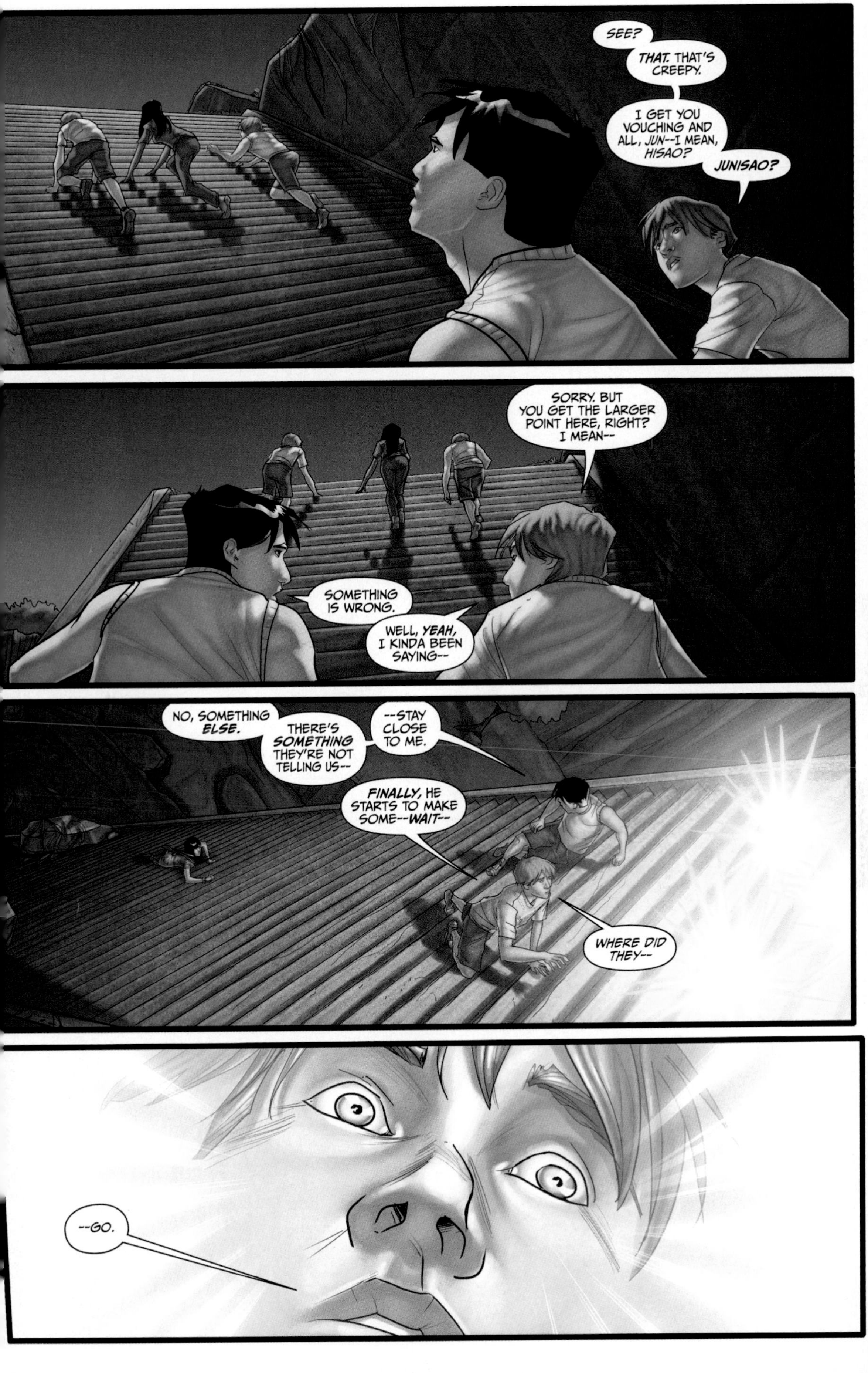
SEE?
THAT. THAT'S CREEPY.
I GET YOU VOUCHING AND ALL, JUN--I MEAN, HISAO?
JUNISAO?
SORRY. BUT YOU GET THE LARGER POINT HERE, RIGHT? I MEAN--
SOMETHING IS WRONG.
WELL, YEAH, I KINDA BEEN SAYING--
NO, SOMETHING ELSE.
THERE'S SOMETHING THEY'RE NOT TELLING US--
--STAY CLOSE TO ME.
FINALLY, HE STARTS TO MAKE SOME--WAIT--
WHERE DID THEY--
--GO.

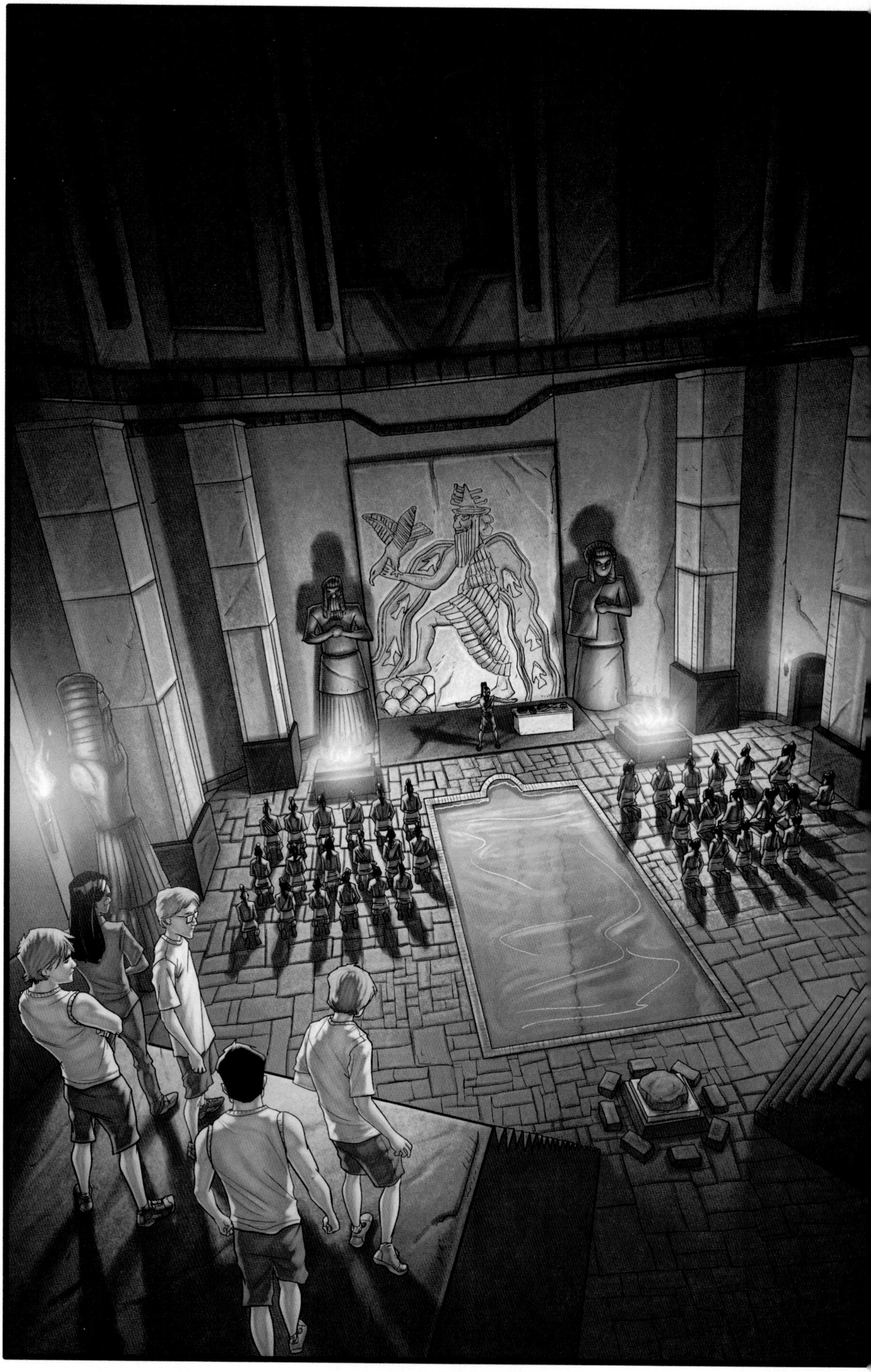

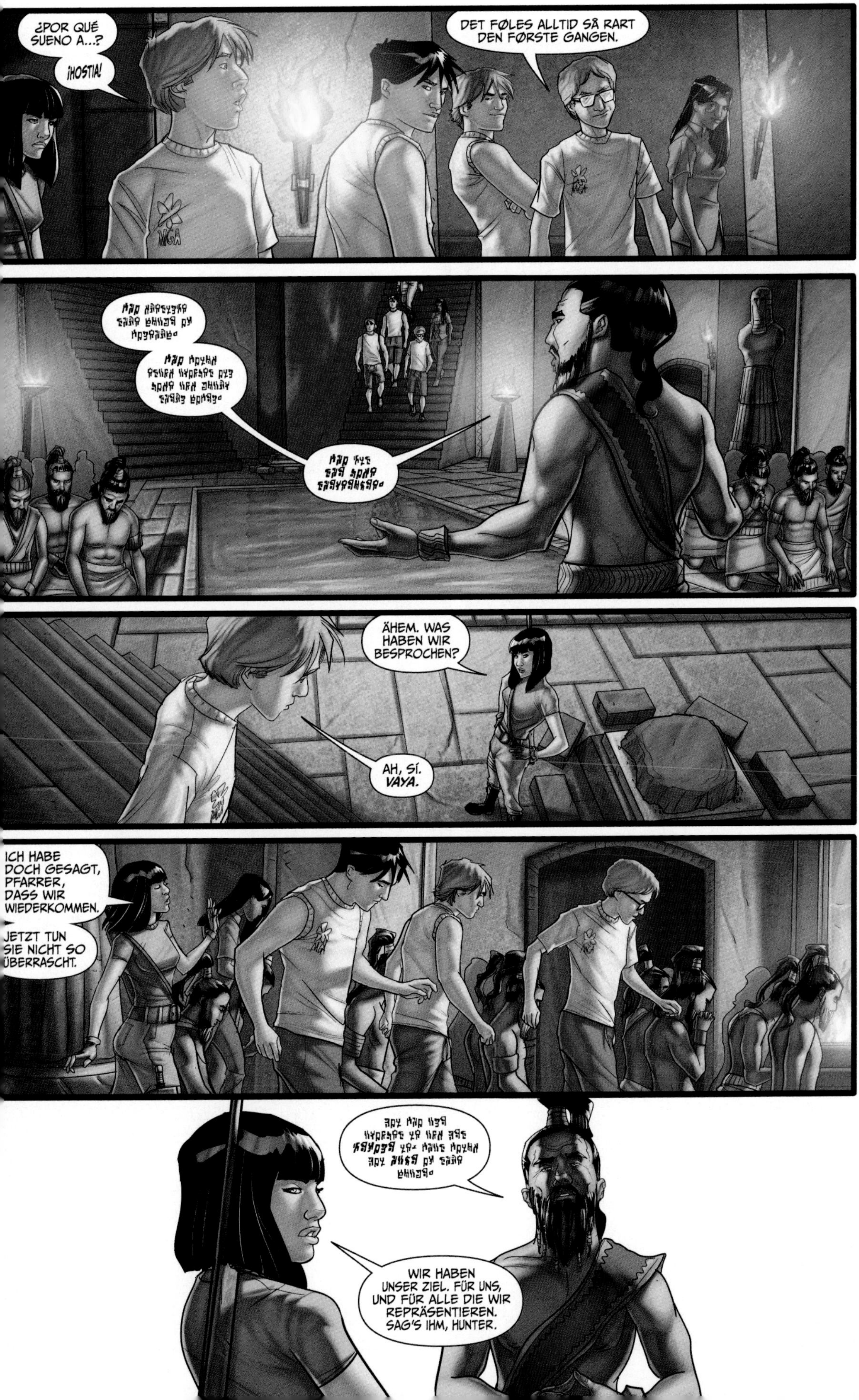
¿POR QUÉ SUENO A...?
¡HOSTIA!
DET FØLES ALLTID SÅ RART DEN FØRSTE GANGEN.
ÄHEM. WAS HABEN WIR BESPROCHEN?
AH, SÍ. VAYA.
ICH HABE DOCH GESAGT, PFARRER, DASS WIR WIEDERKOMMEN.
JETZT TUN SIE NICHT SO ÜBERRASCHT.
WIR HABEN UNSER ZIEL. FÜR UNS, UND FÜR ALLE DIE WIR REPRÄSENTIEREN. SAG'S IHM, HUNTER.

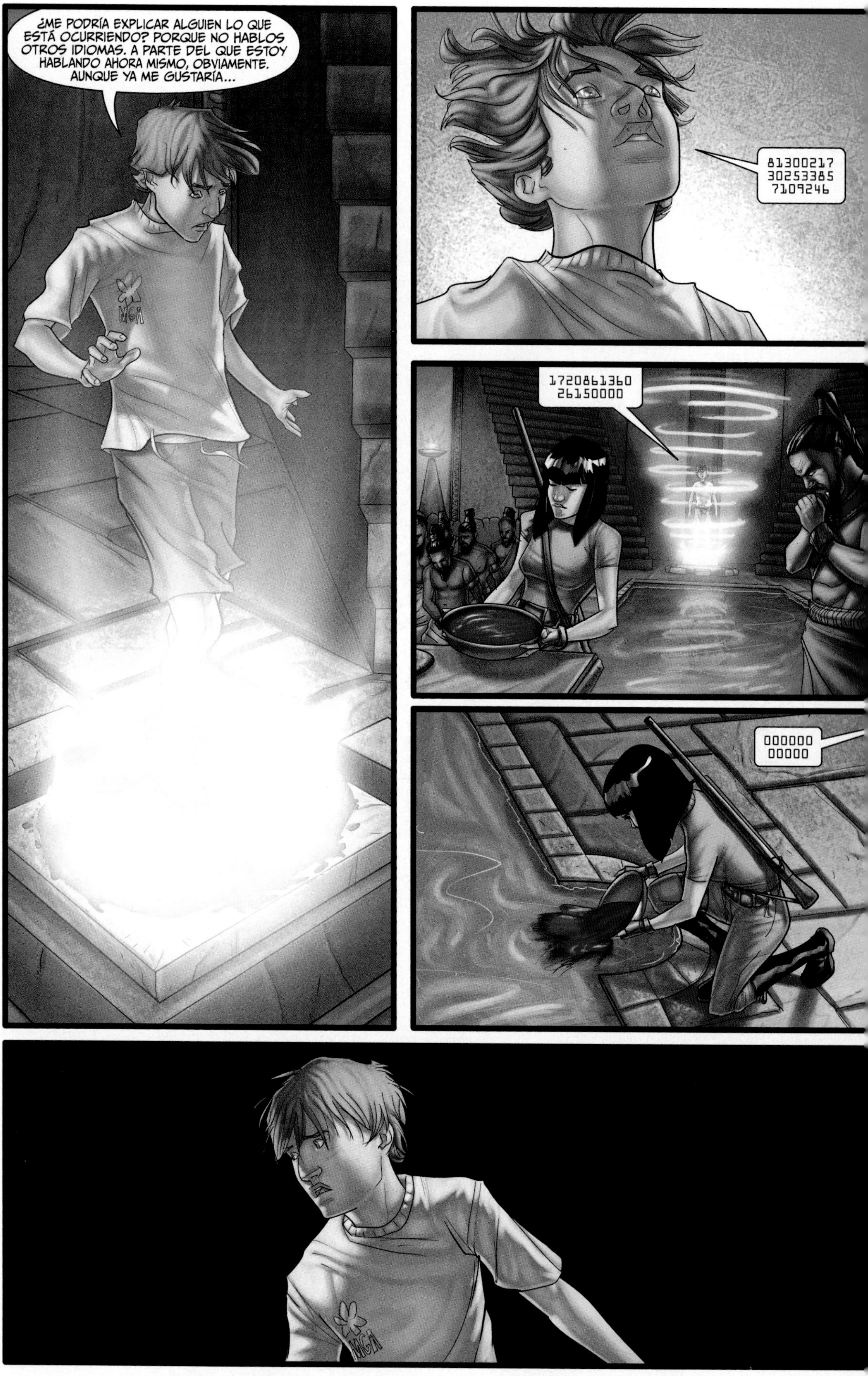
¿ME PODRÍA EXPLICAR ALGUIEN LO QUE ESTÁ OCURRIENDO? PORQUE NO HABLOS OTROS IDIOMAS. A PARTE DEL QUE ESTOY HABLANDO AHORA MISMO, OBVIAMENTE. AUNQUE YA ME GUSTARÍA...
81300217 30253385 7109246
1720861360 26150000
000000 00000

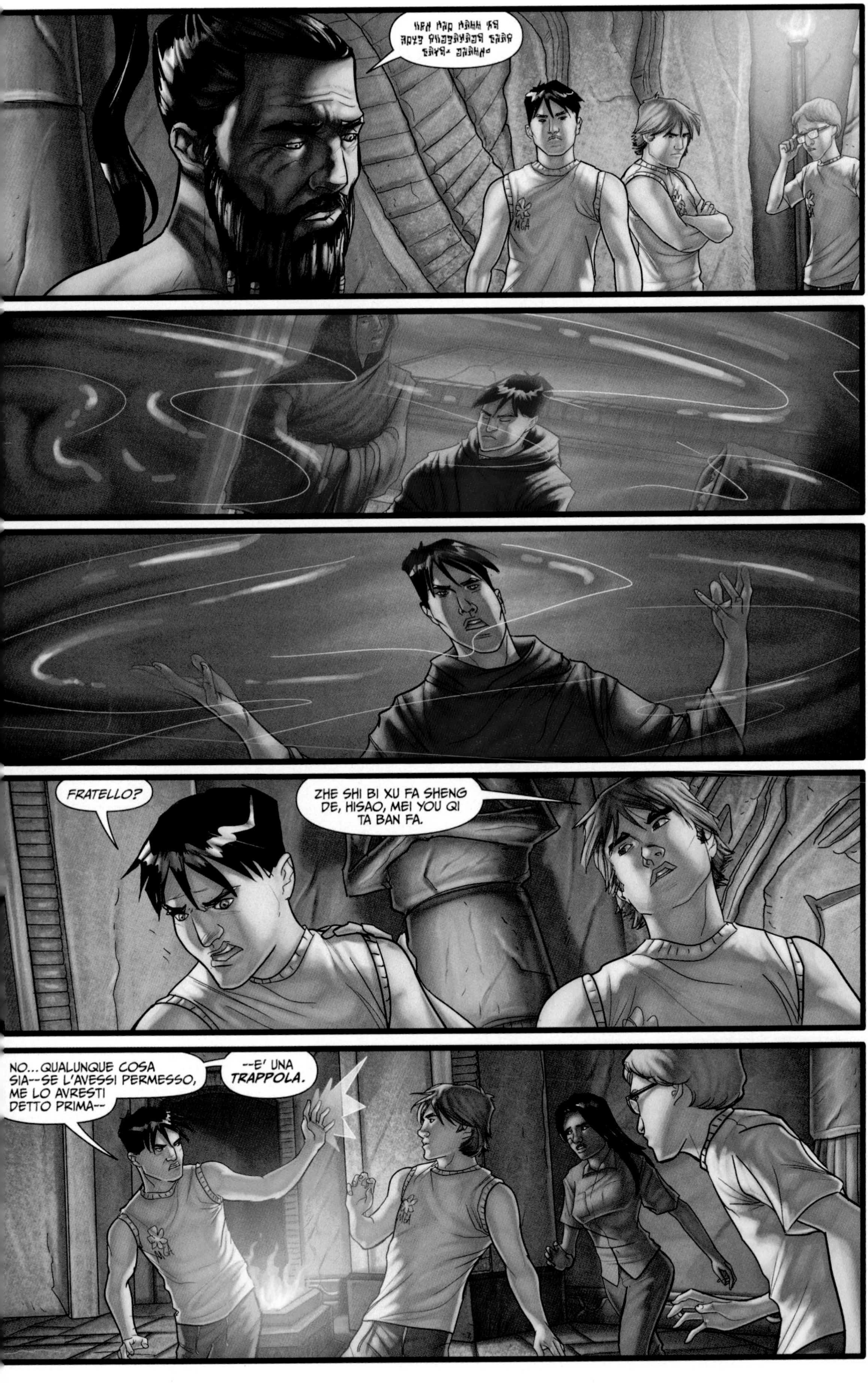
FRATELLO?
ZHE SHI BI XU FA SHENG DE, HISAO, MEI YOU QI TA BAN FA.
NO... QUALUNQUE COSA SIA--SE L'AVESSI PERMESSO, ME LO AVRESTI DETTO PRIMA--
--E' UNA TRAPPOLA.

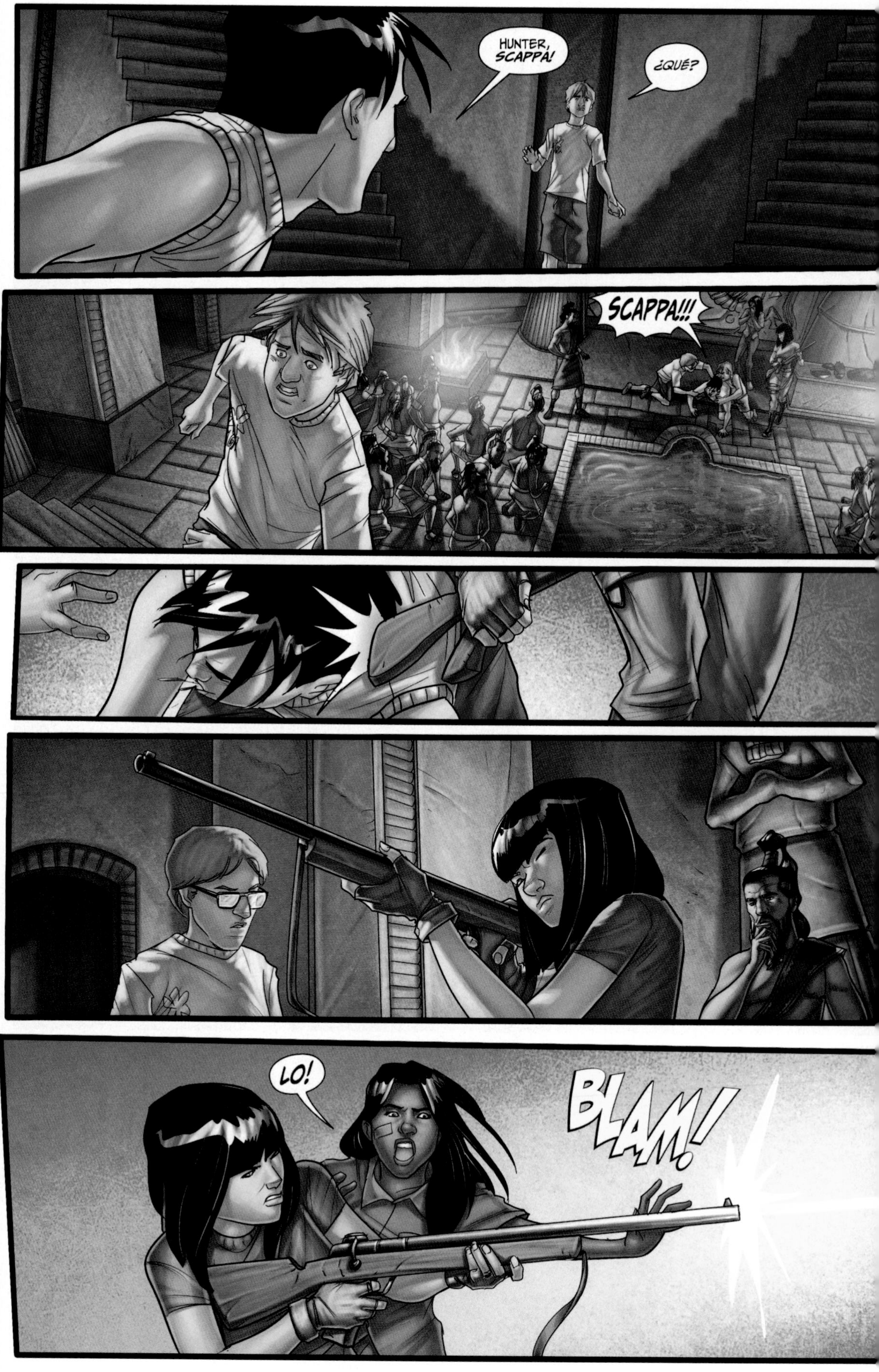
HUNTER, SCAPPA!
¿QUÉ?
SCAPPA!!!
LO!
BLAM!

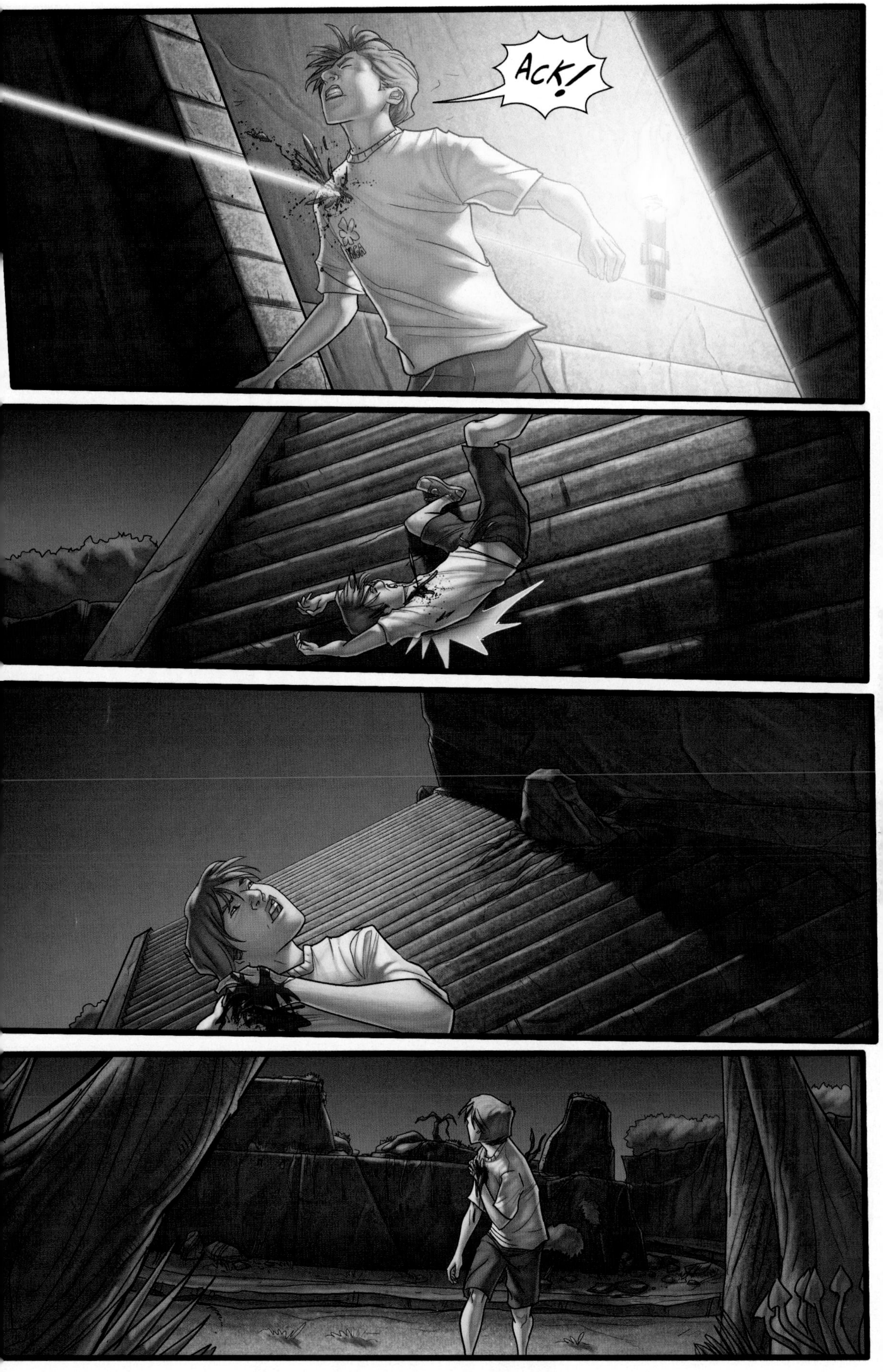
ACK!

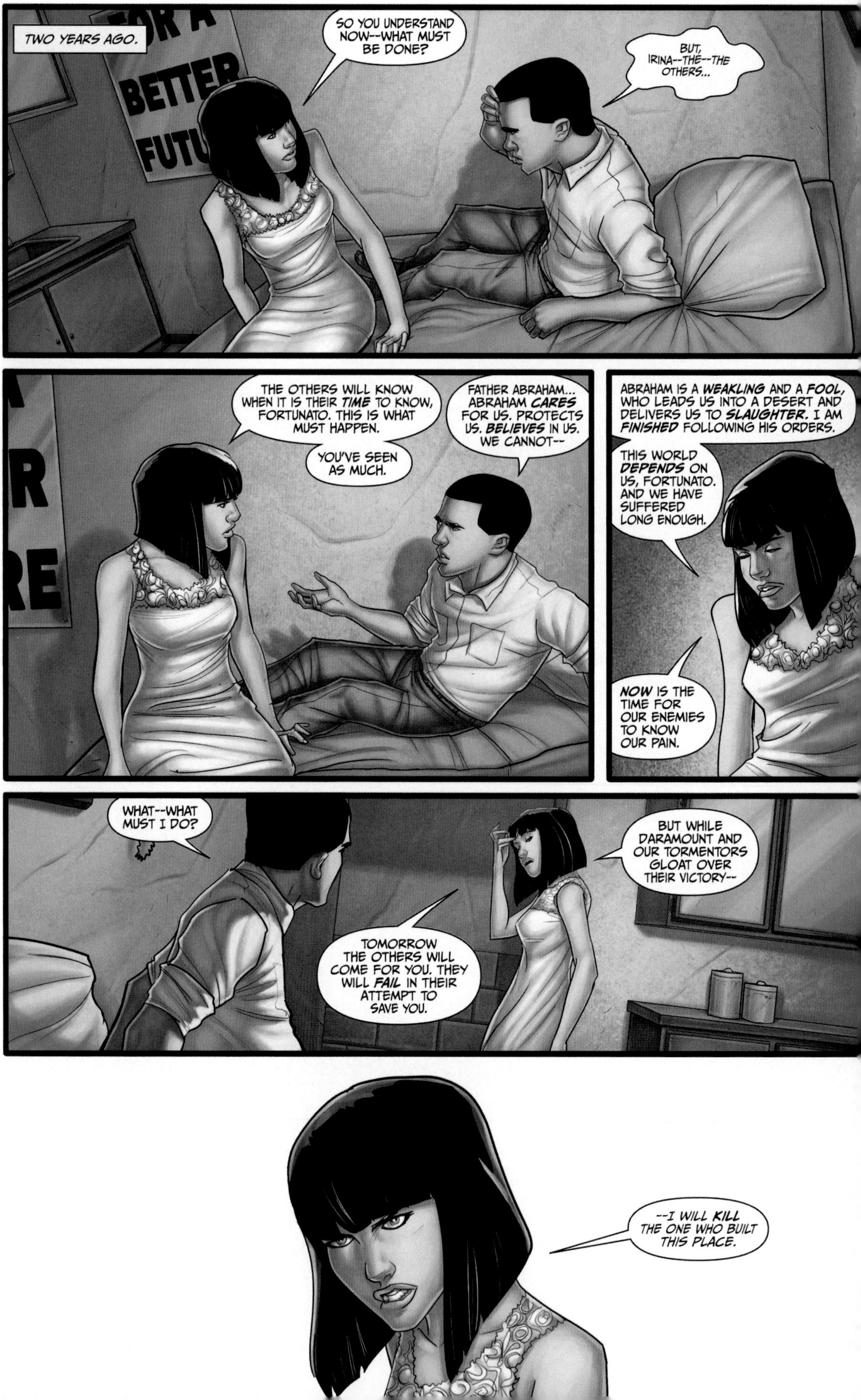
TWO YEARS AGO.
FOR A BETTER FUTU
SO YOU UNDERSTAND NOW--WHAT MUST BE DONE?
BUT, IRINA--THE--THE OTHERS...
THE OTHERS WILL KNOW WHEN IT IS THEIR TIME TO KNOW, FORTUNATO. THIS IS WHAT MUST HAPPEN.
YOU'VE SEEN AS MUCH.
FATHER ABRAHAM... ABRAHAM CARES FOR US. PROTECTS US. BELIEVES IN US. WE CANNOT--
ABRAHAM IS A WEAKLING AND A FOOL, WHO LEADS US INTO A DESERT AND DELIVERS US TO SLAUGHTER. I AM FINISHED FOLLOWING HIS ORDERS.
THIS WORLD DEPENDS ON US, FORTUNATO. AND WE HAVE SUFFERED LONG ENOUGH.
NOW IS THE TIME FOR OUR ENEMIES TO KNOW OUR PAIN.
WHAT--WHAT MUST I DO?
TOMORROW THE OTHERS WILL COME FOR YOU. THEY WILL FAIL IN THEIR ATTEMPT TO SAVE YOU.
BUT WHILE DARAMOUNT AND OUR TORMENTORS GLOAT OVER THEIR VICTORY--
--I WILL KILL THE ONE WHO BUILT THIS PLACE.

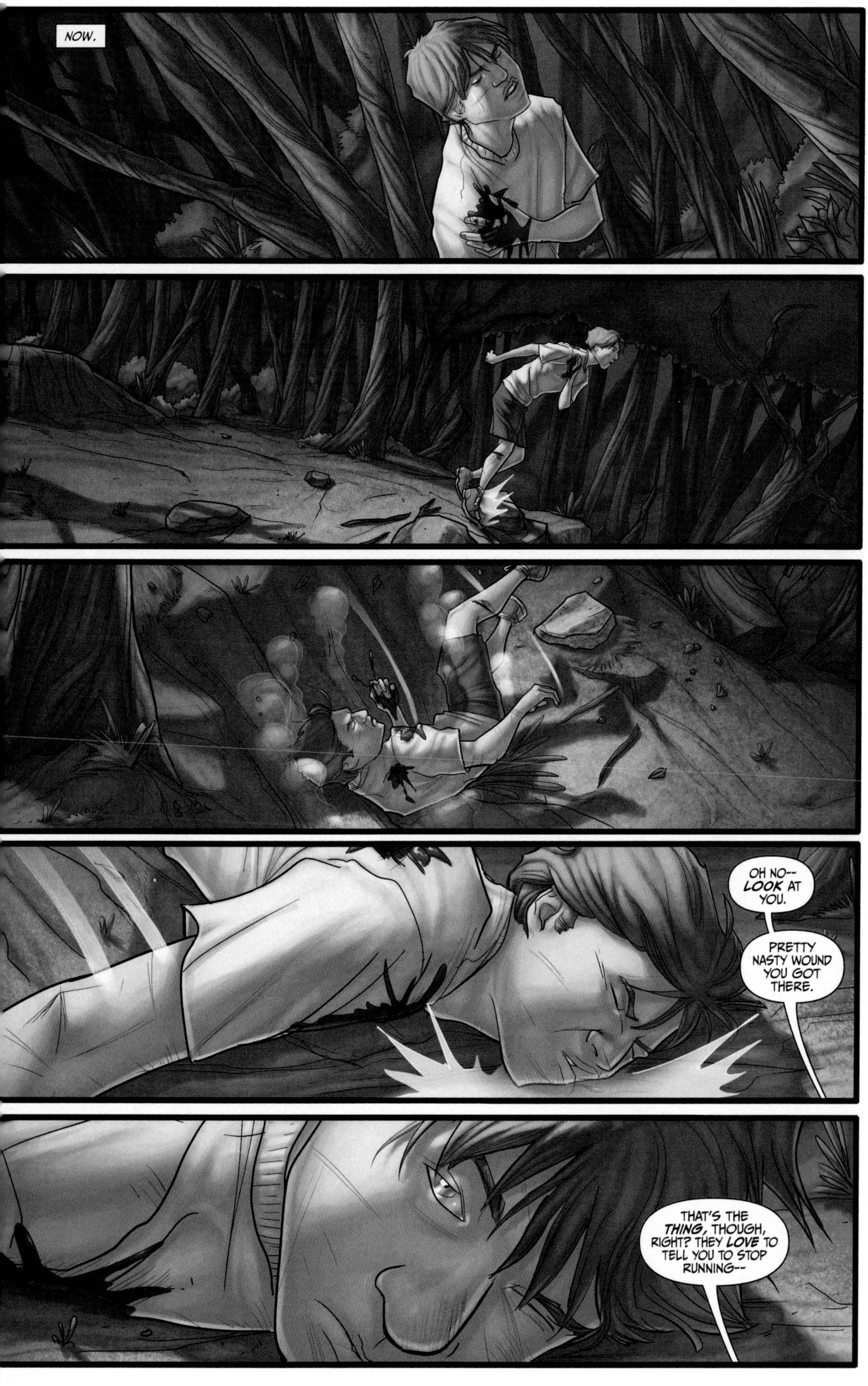
NOW.
OH NO-- LOOK AT YOU.
PRETTY NASTY WOUND YOU GOT THERE.
THAT'S THE THING, THOUGH, RIGHT? THEY LOVE TO TELL YOU TO STOP RUNNING--

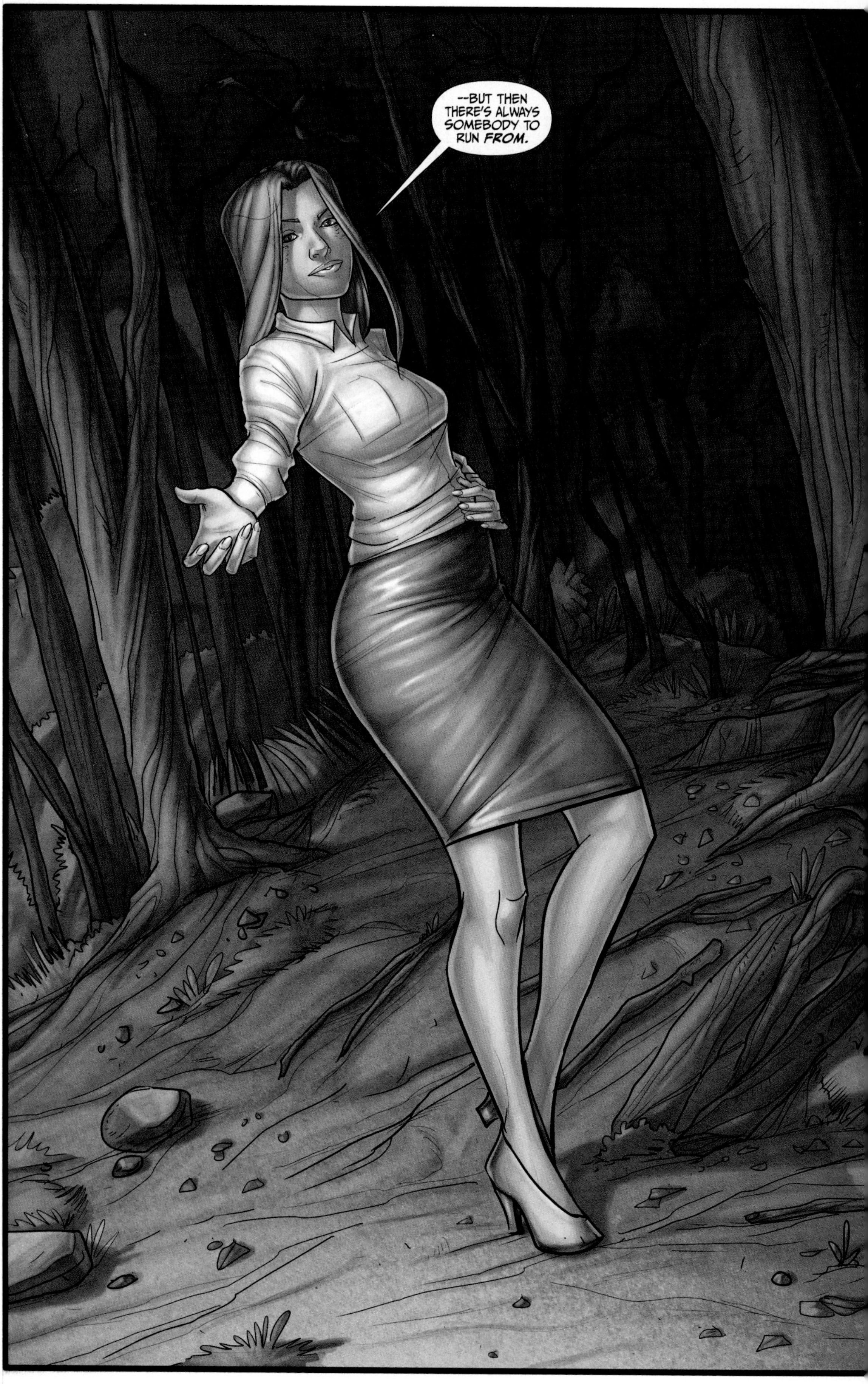
--BUT THEN THERE'S ALWAYS SOMEBODY TO RUN *FROM*.

twenty**three**

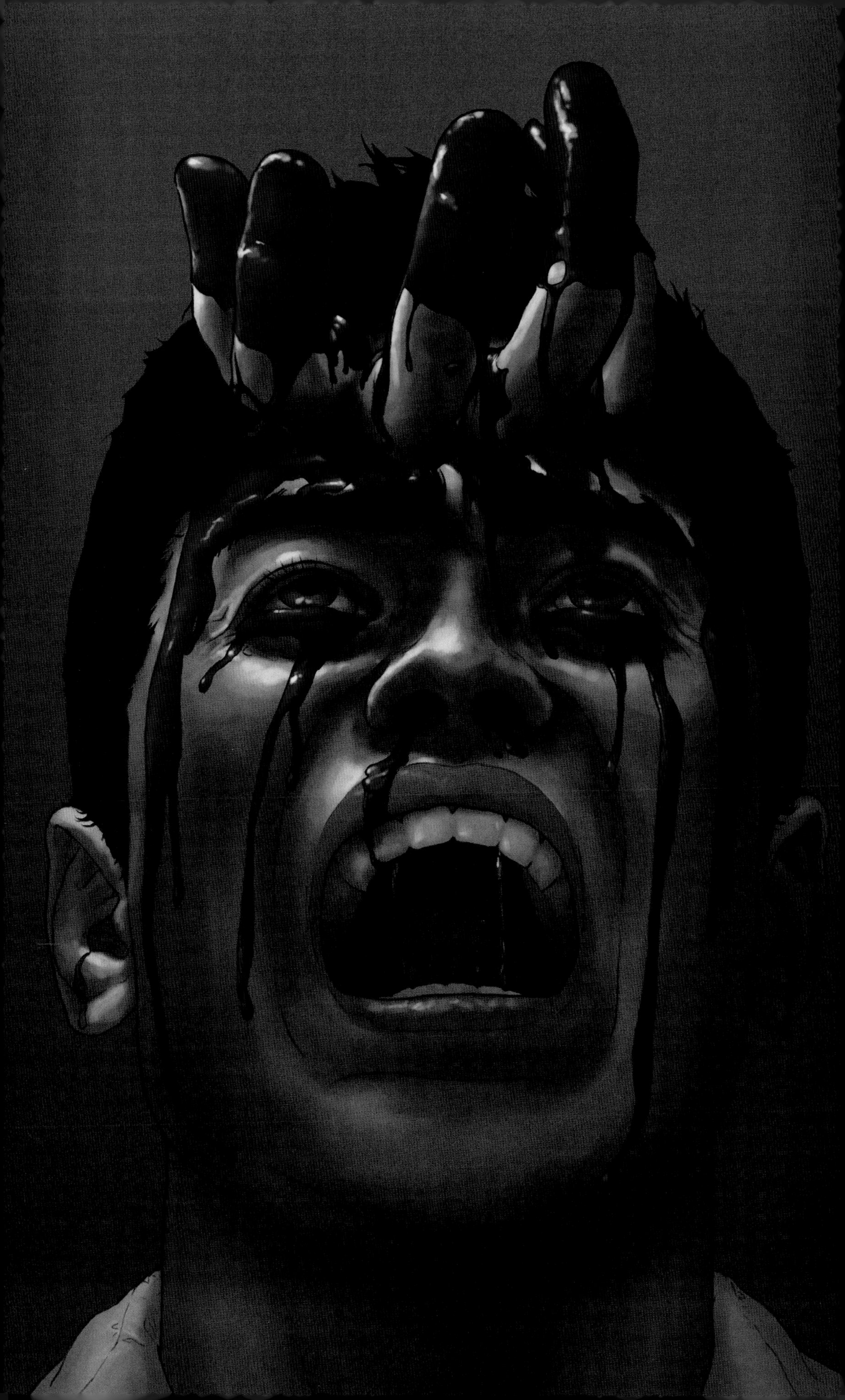

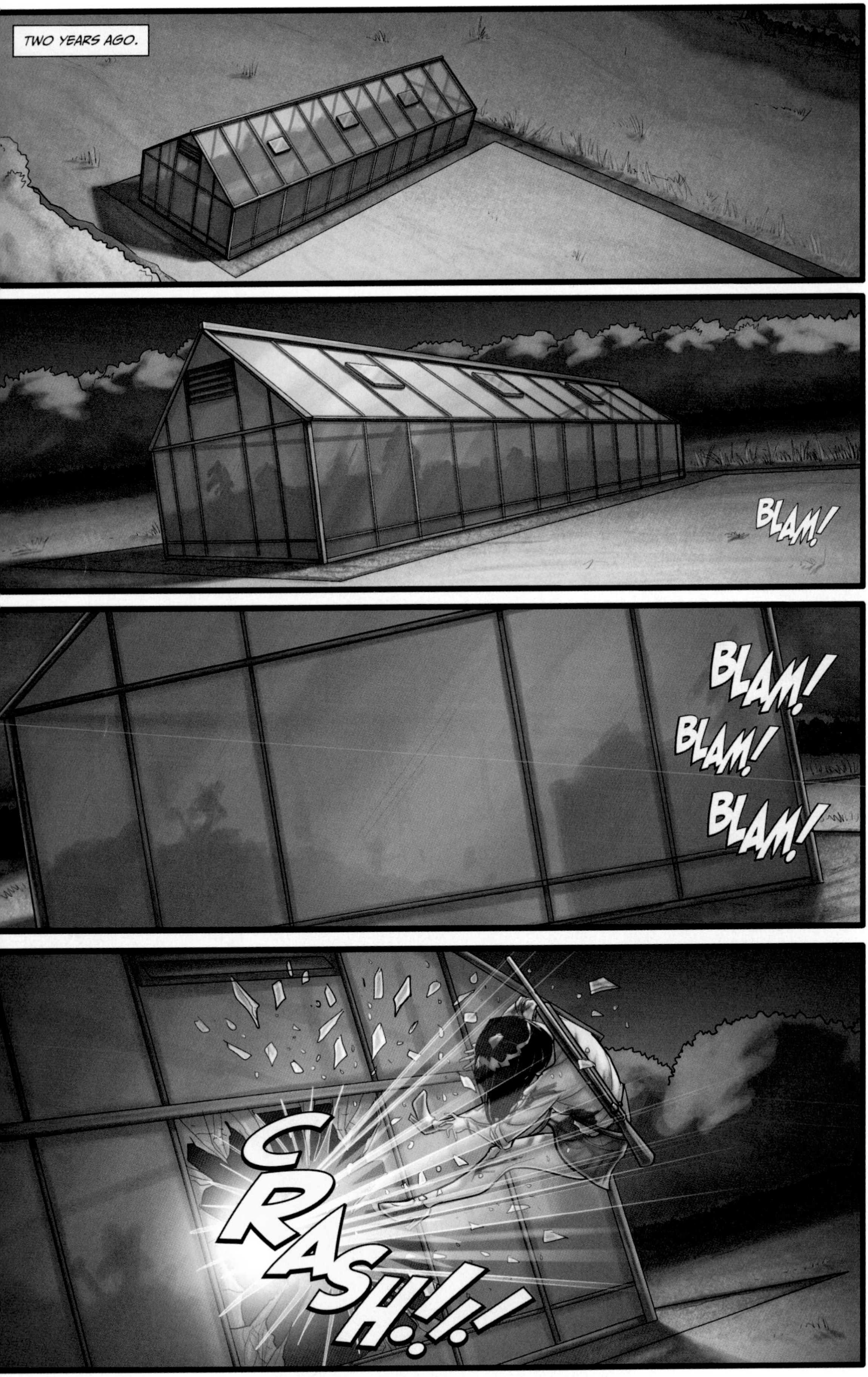
TWO YEARS AGO.
BLAM!
BLAM!
BLAM!
BLAM!
CRASH!!!

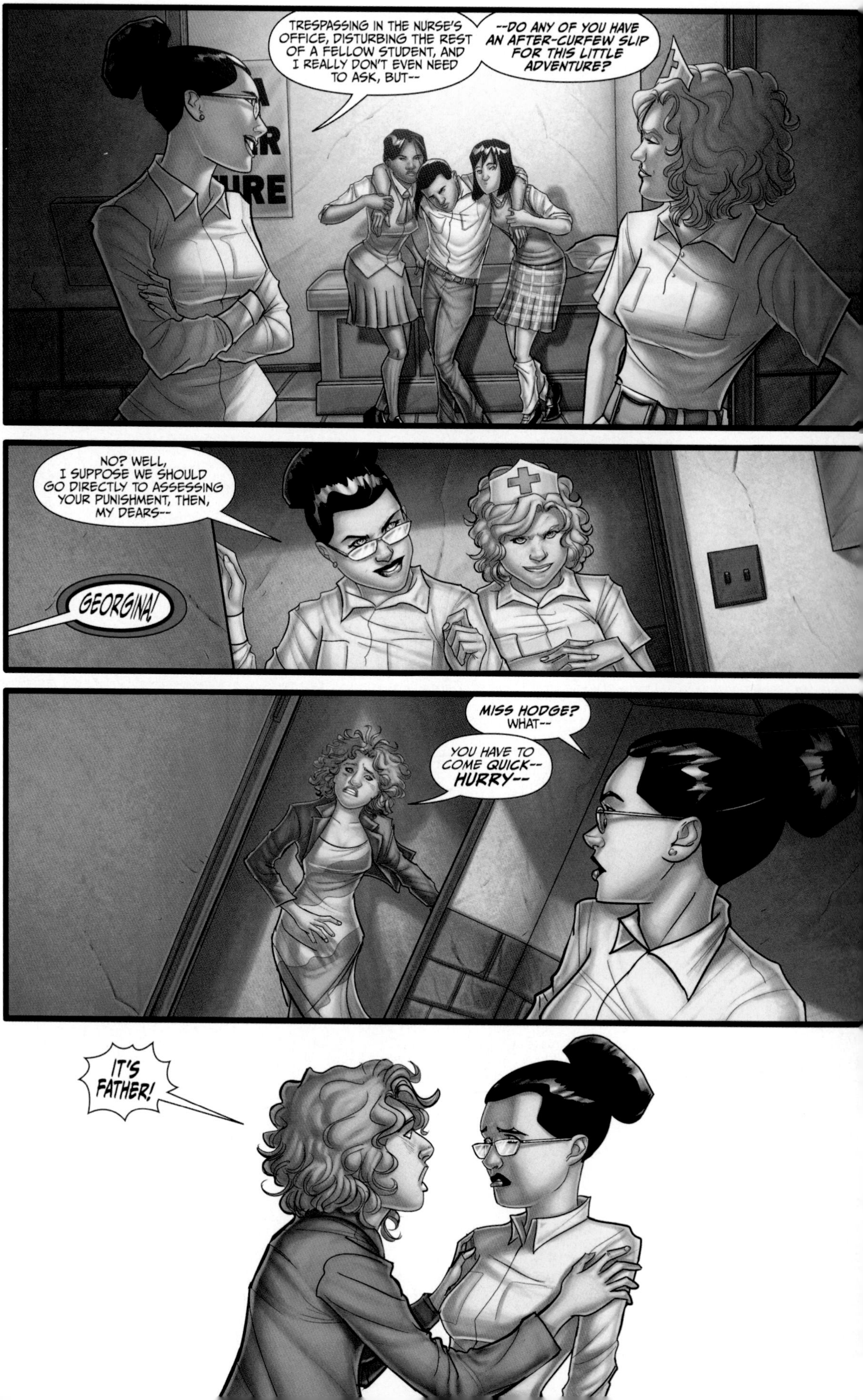
TRESPASSING IN THE NURSE'S OFFICE, DISTURBING THE REST OF A FELLOW STUDENT, AND I REALLY DON'T EVEN NEED TO ASK, BUT--
--DO ANY OF YOU HAVE AN AFTER-CURFEW SLIP FOR THIS LITTLE ADVENTURE?
NO? WELL, I SUPPOSE WE SHOULD GO DIRECTLY TO ASSESSING YOUR PUNISHMENT, THEN, MY DEARS--
GEORGINA!
MISS HODGE? WHAT--
YOU HAVE TO COME QUICK-- HURRY--
IT'S FATHER!

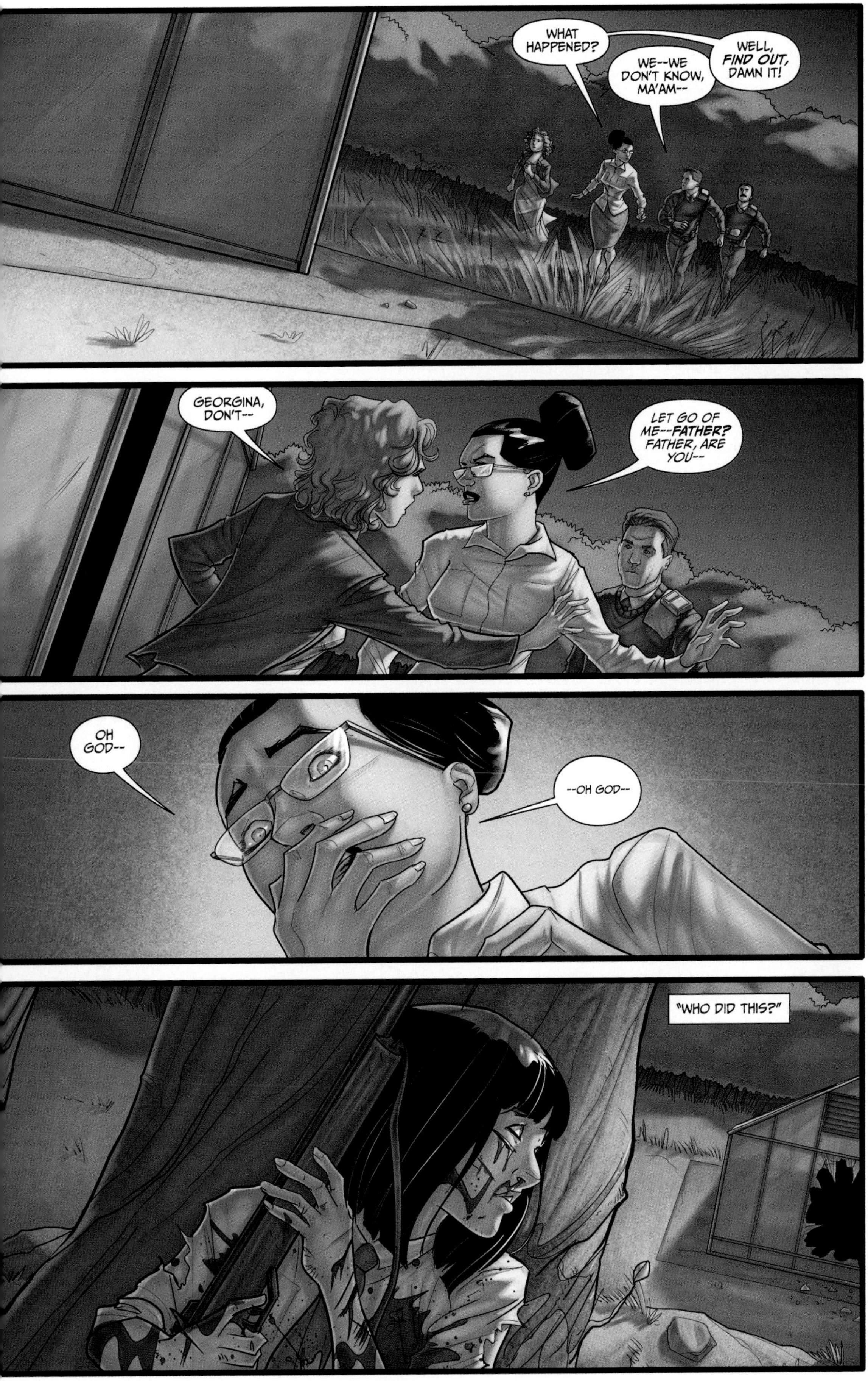
WHAT HAPPENED?
WE--WE DON'T KNOW, MA'AM--
WELL, FIND OUT, DAMN IT!
GEORGINA, DON'T--
LET GO OF ME--FATHER? FATHER, ARE YOU--
OH GOD--
--OH GOD--
"WHO DID THIS?"

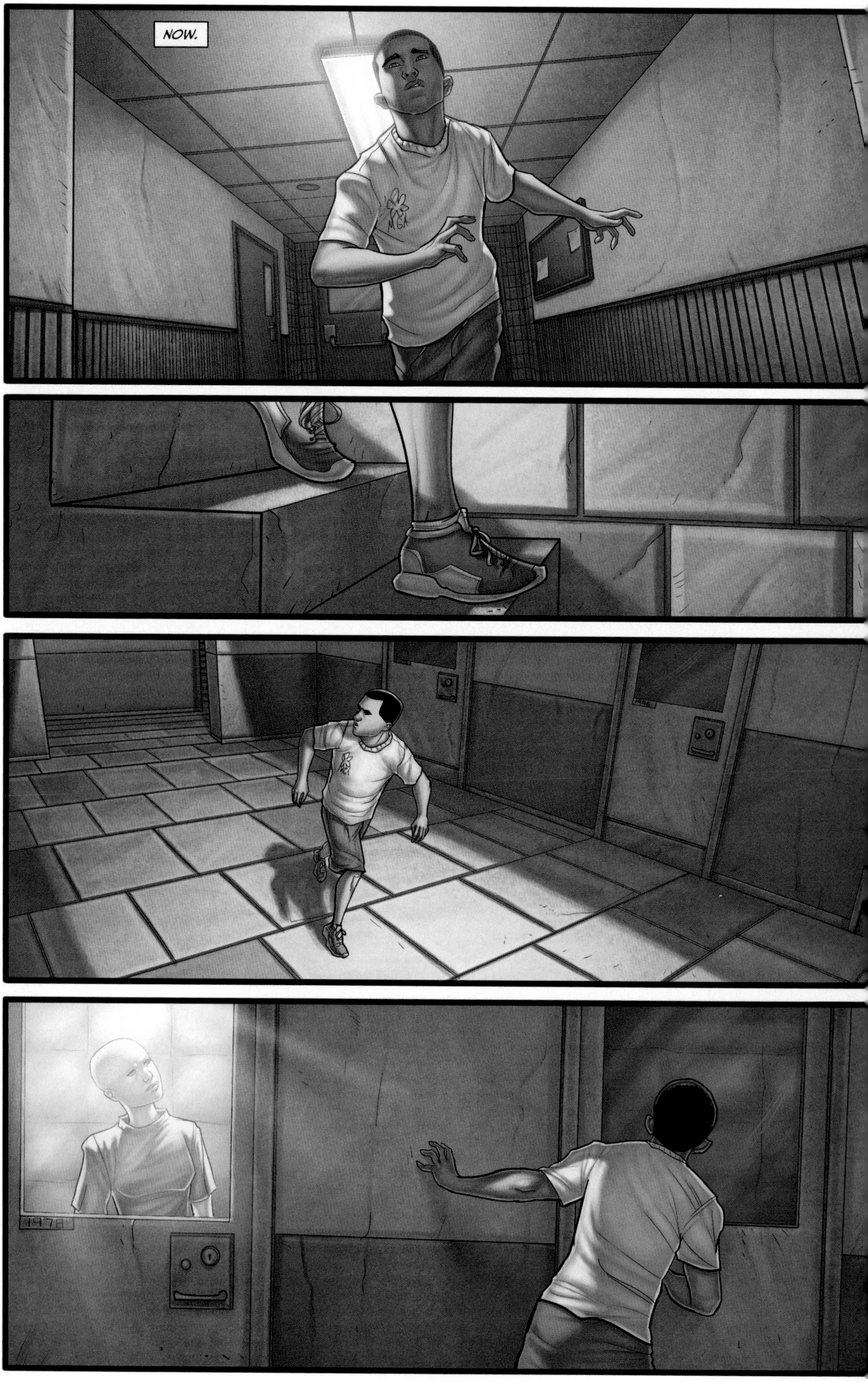

NOW.

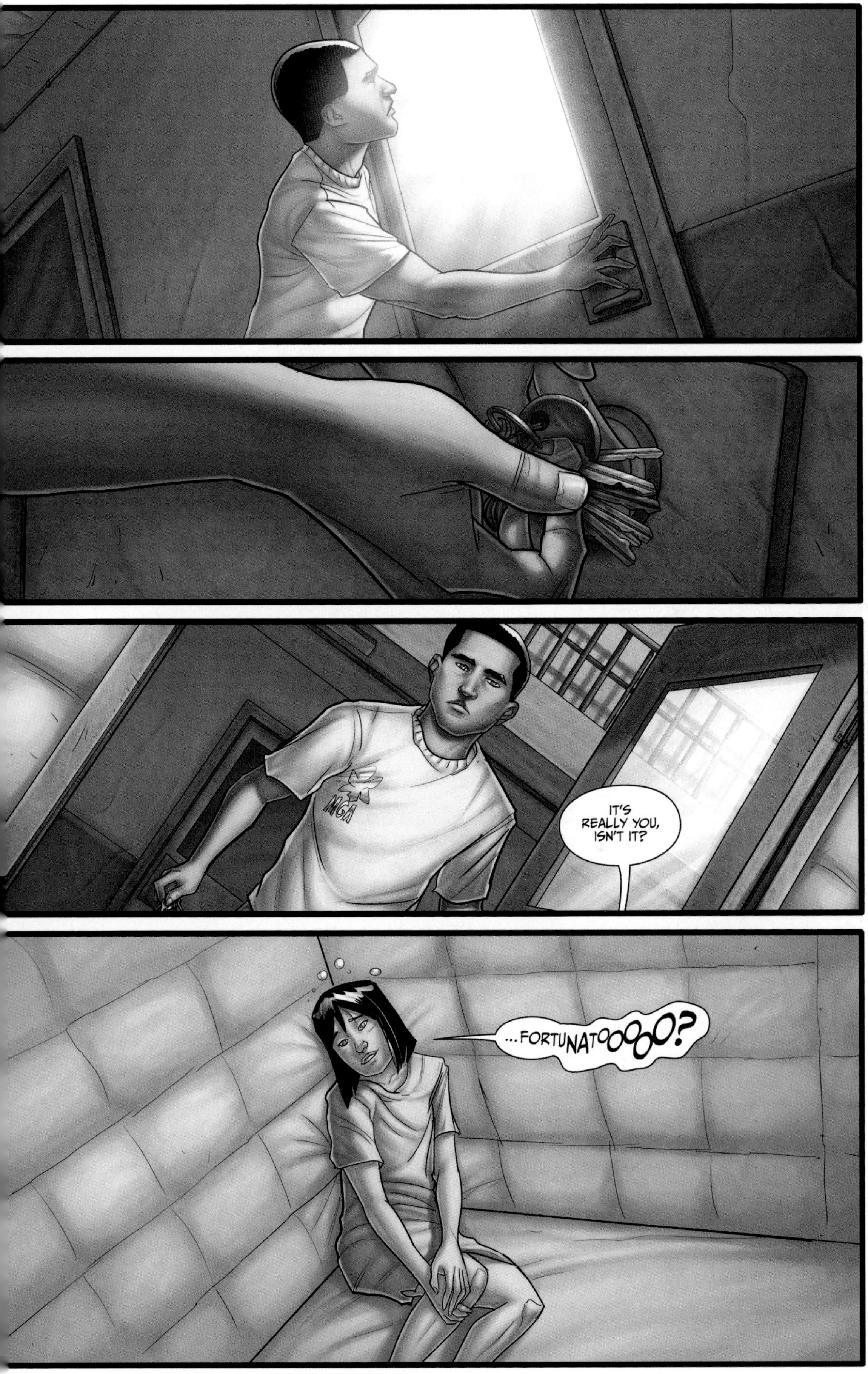
IT'S REALLY YOU, ISN'T IT?
...FORTUNATOOOOO?

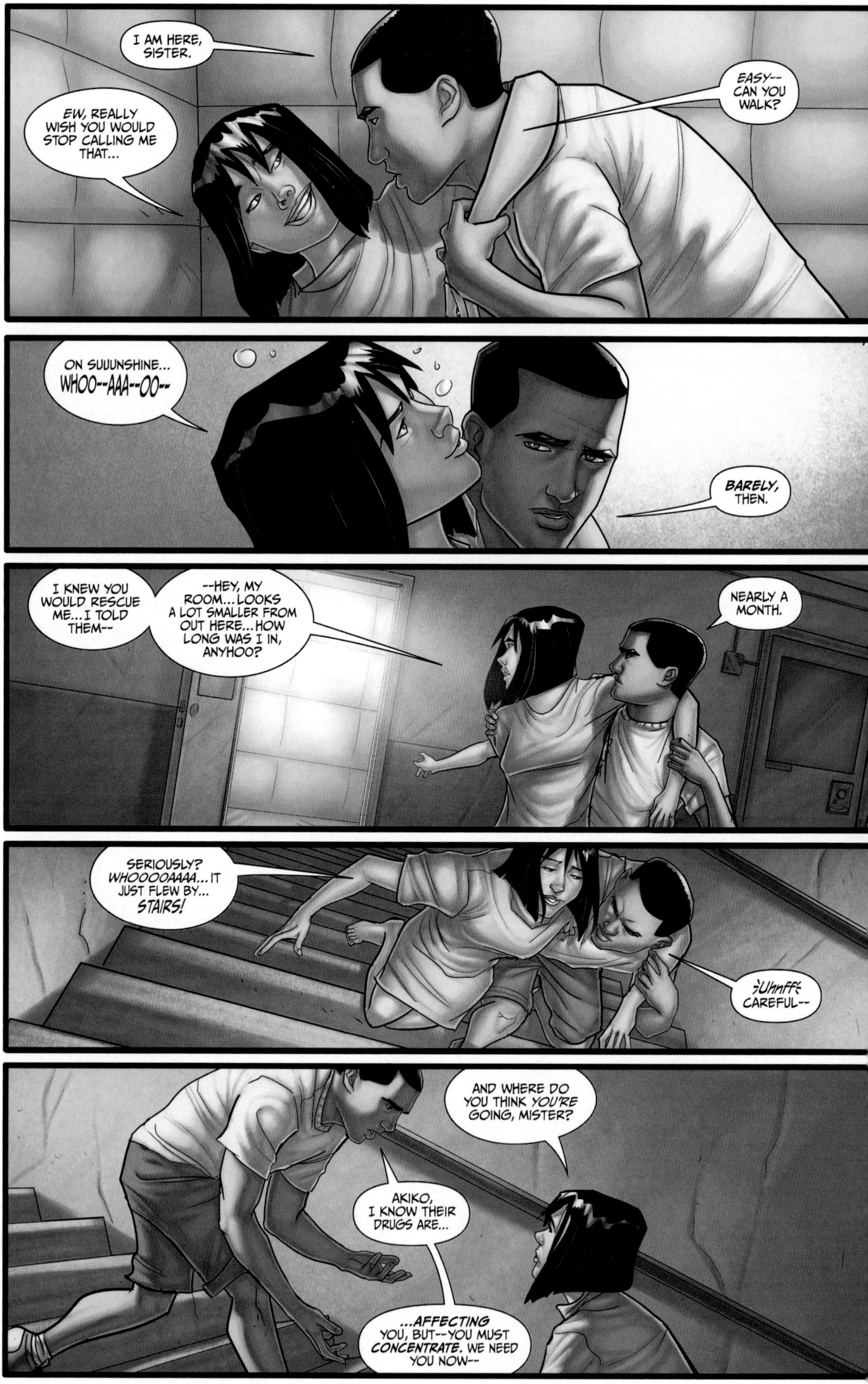
I AM HERE, SISTER.
EW, REALLY WISH YOU WOULD STOP CALLING ME THAT...
EASY-- CAN YOU WALK?
ON SUUUNSHINE... WHOO--AAA--OO--
BARELY, THEN.
I KNEW YOU WOULD RESCUE ME...I TOLD THEM--
--HEY, MY ROOM...LOOKS A LOT SMALLER FROM OUT HERE...HOW LONG WAS I IN, ANYHOO?
NEARLY A MONTH.
SERIOUSLY? WHOOOOAAAA...IT JUST FLEW BY... STAIRS!
UHNFF CAREFUL--
AND WHERE DO YOU THINK YOU'RE GOING, MISTER?
AKIKO, I KNOW THEIR DRUGS ARE...
...AFFECTING YOU, BUT--YOU MUST CONCENTRATE. WE NEED YOU NOW--

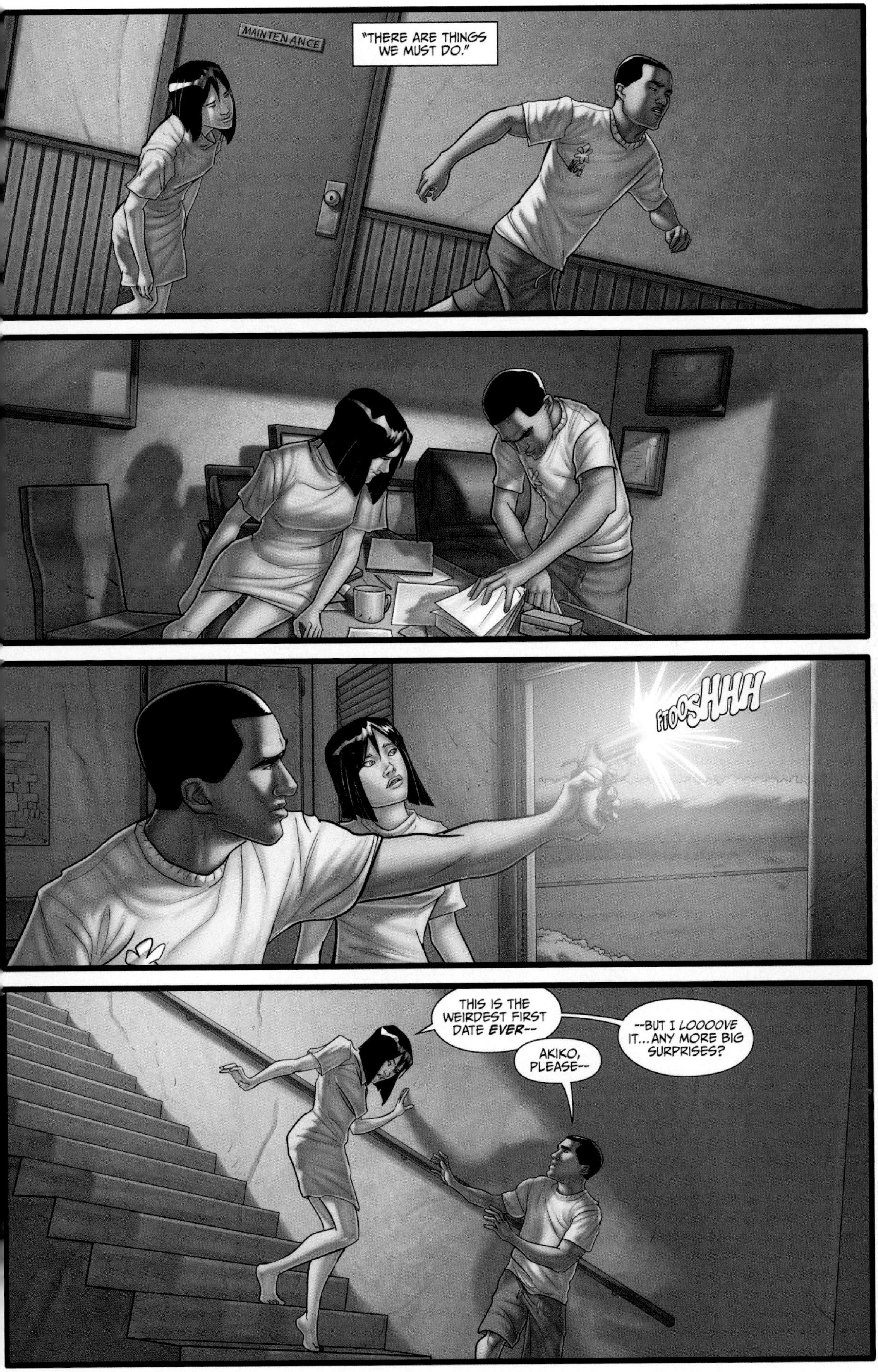
MAINTENANCE
"THERE ARE THINGS WE MUST DO."
FTOOSHHH
THIS IS THE WEIRDEST FIRST DATE *EVER*--
AKIKO, PLEASE--
--BUT I *LOOOOVE* IT...ANY MORE BIG SURPRISES?

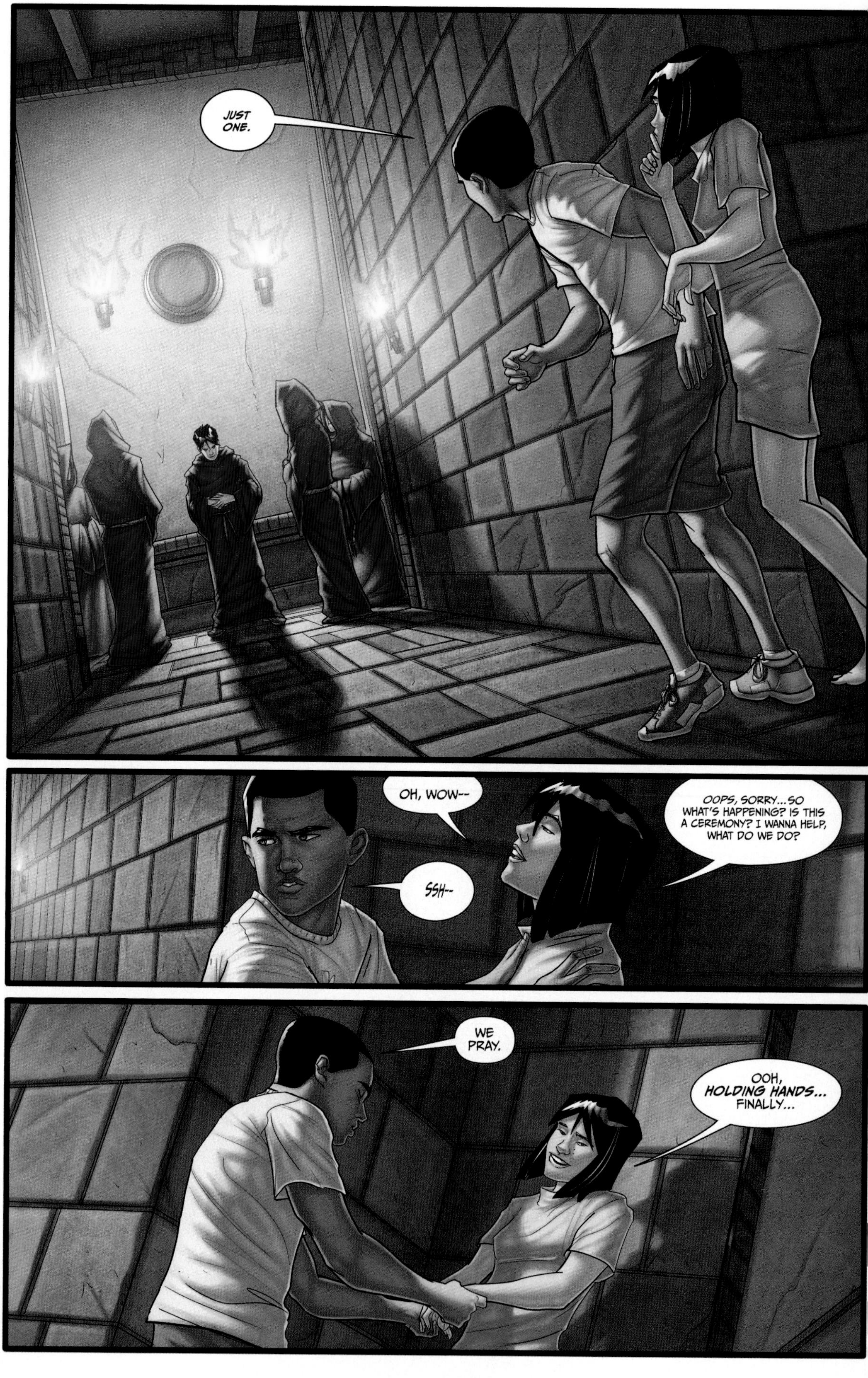
JUST ONE.
OH, WOW--
SSH--
OOPS, SORRY... SO WHAT'S HAPPENING? IS THIS A CEREMONY? I WANNA HELP, WHAT DO WE DO?
WE PRAY.
OOH, HOLDING HANDS... FINALLY...

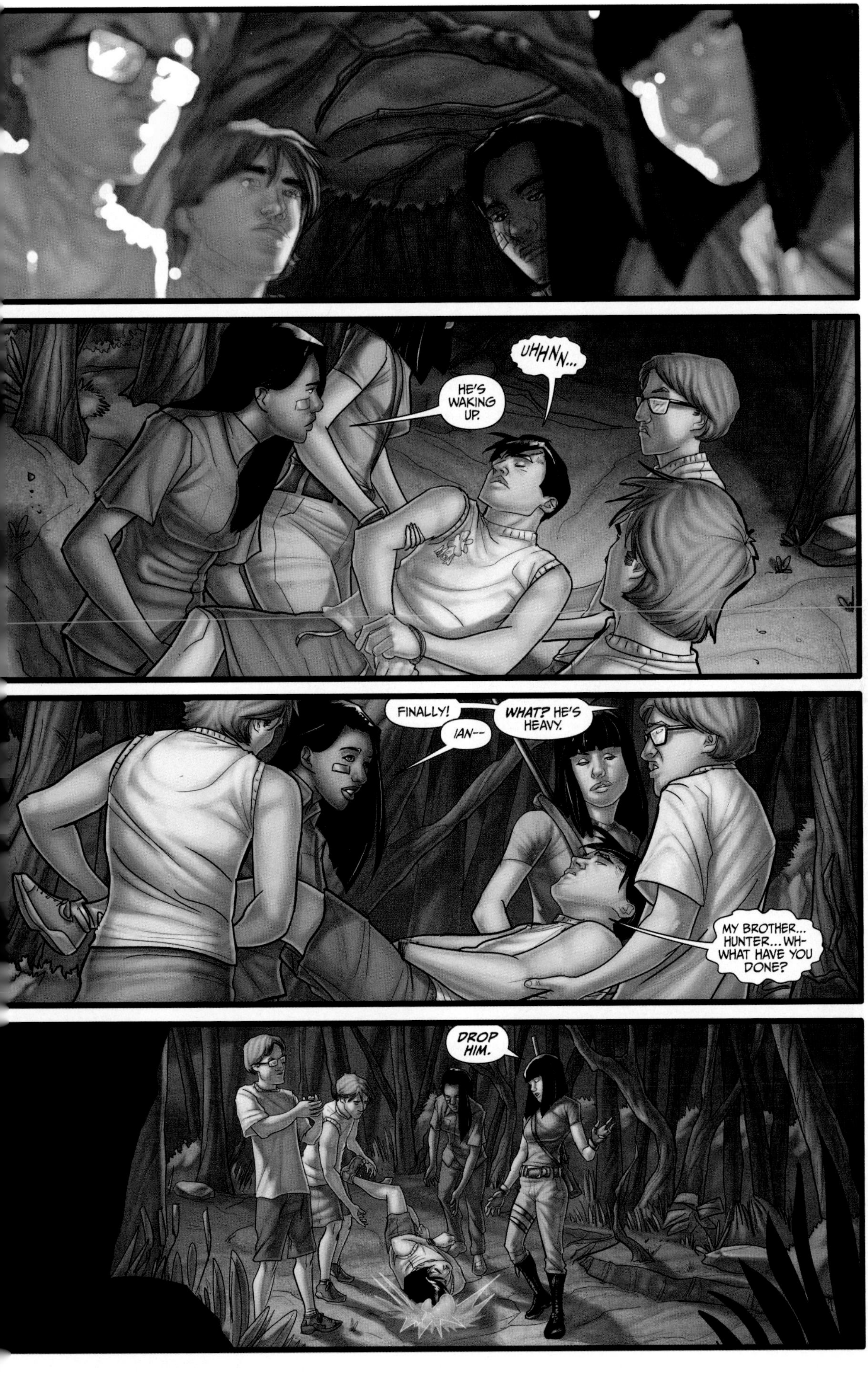
HE'S WAKING UP.
UHHNN...
FINALLY!
IAN--
WHAT? HE'S HEAVY.
MY BROTHER... HUNTER... WH-WHAT HAVE YOU DONE?
DROP HIM.

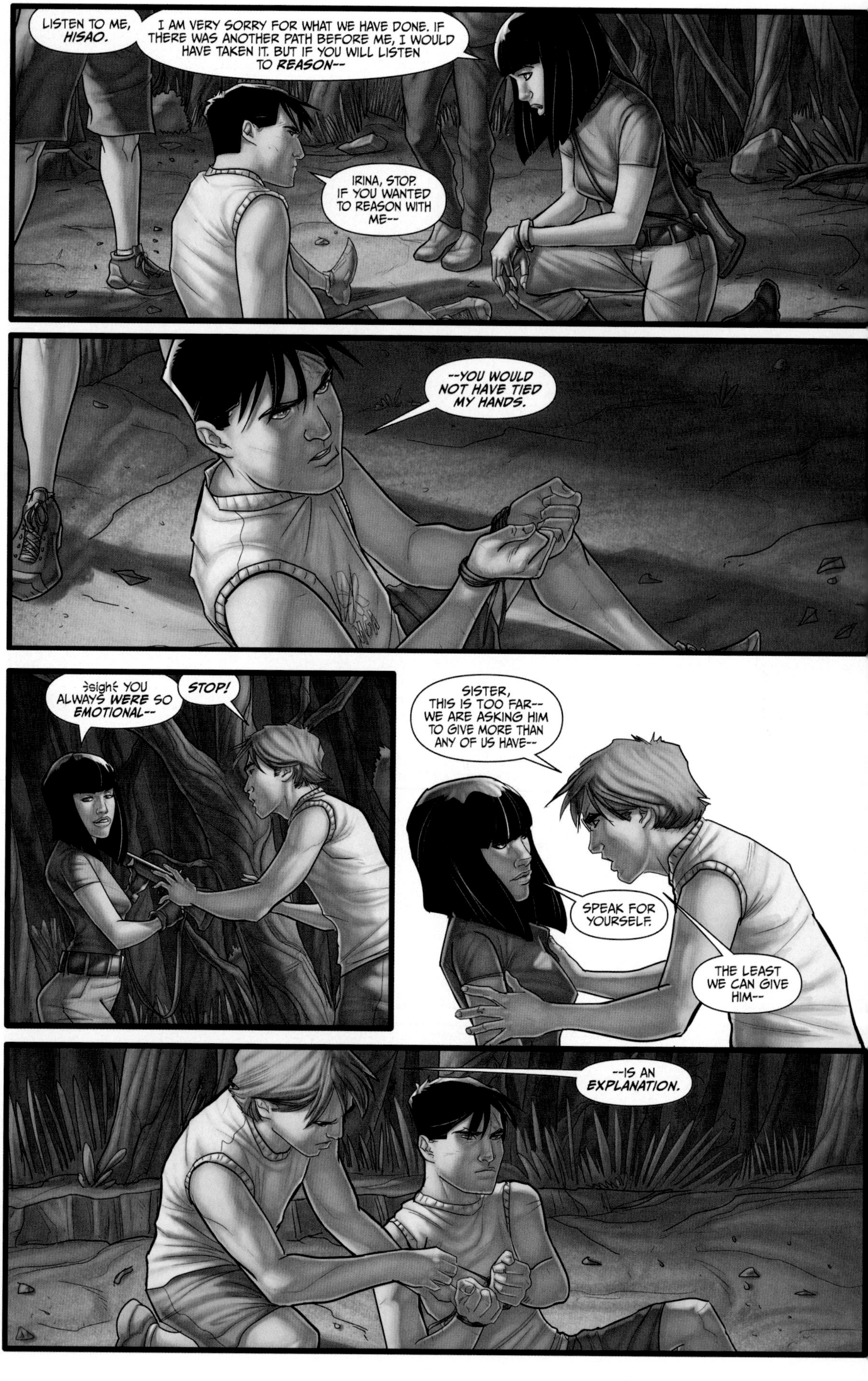
LISTEN TO ME, HISAO.
I AM VERY SORRY FOR WHAT WE HAVE DONE. IF THERE WAS ANOTHER PATH BEFORE ME, I WOULD HAVE TAKEN IT. BUT IF YOU WILL LISTEN TO REASON--
IRINA, STOP. IF YOU WANTED TO REASON WITH ME--
--YOU WOULD NOT HAVE TIED MY HANDS.
sigh YOU ALWAYS WERE SO EMOTIONAL--
STOP!
SISTER, THIS IS TOO FAR-- WE ARE ASKING HIM TO GIVE MORE THAN ANY OF US HAVE--
SPEAK FOR YOURSELF.
THE LEAST WE CAN GIVE HIM--
--IS AN EXPLANATION.

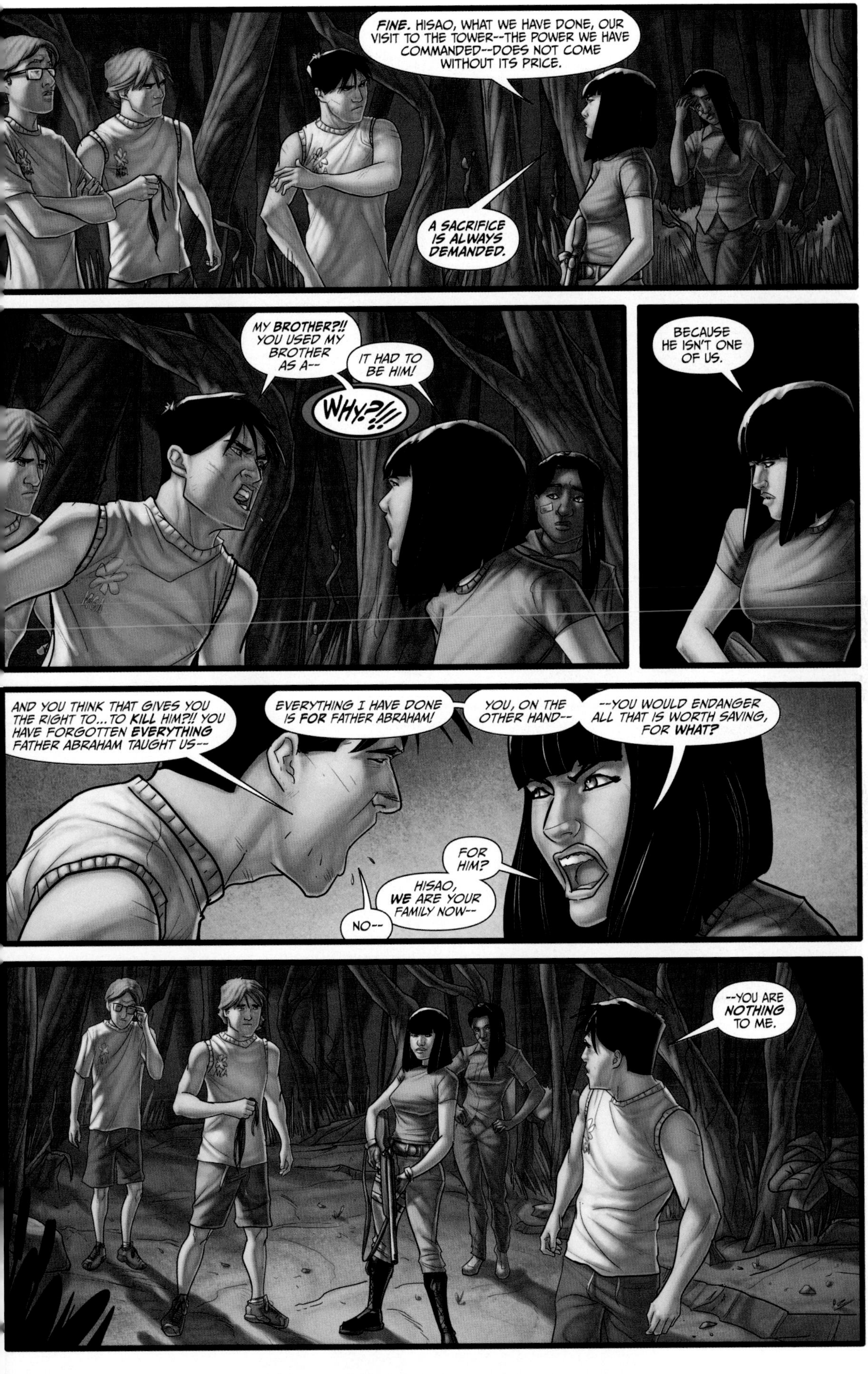
FINE. HISAO, WHAT WE HAVE DONE, OUR VISIT TO THE TOWER--THE POWER WE HAVE COMMANDED--DOES NOT COME WITHOUT ITS PRICE.
A SACRIFICE IS ALWAYS DEMANDED.
MY BROTHER?!! YOU USED MY BROTHER AS A--
IT HAD TO BE HIM!
WHY?!!!
BECAUSE HE ISN'T ONE OF US.
AND YOU THINK THAT GIVES YOU THE RIGHT TO...TO KILL HIM?!! YOU HAVE FORGOTTEN EVERYTHING FATHER ABRAHAM TAUGHT US--
EVERYTHING I HAVE DONE IS FOR FATHER ABRAHAM!
YOU, ON THE OTHER HAND--
--YOU WOULD ENDANGER ALL THAT IS WORTH SAVING, FOR WHAT?
FOR HIM?
HISAO, WE ARE YOUR FAMILY NOW--
NO--
--YOU ARE NOTHING TO ME.

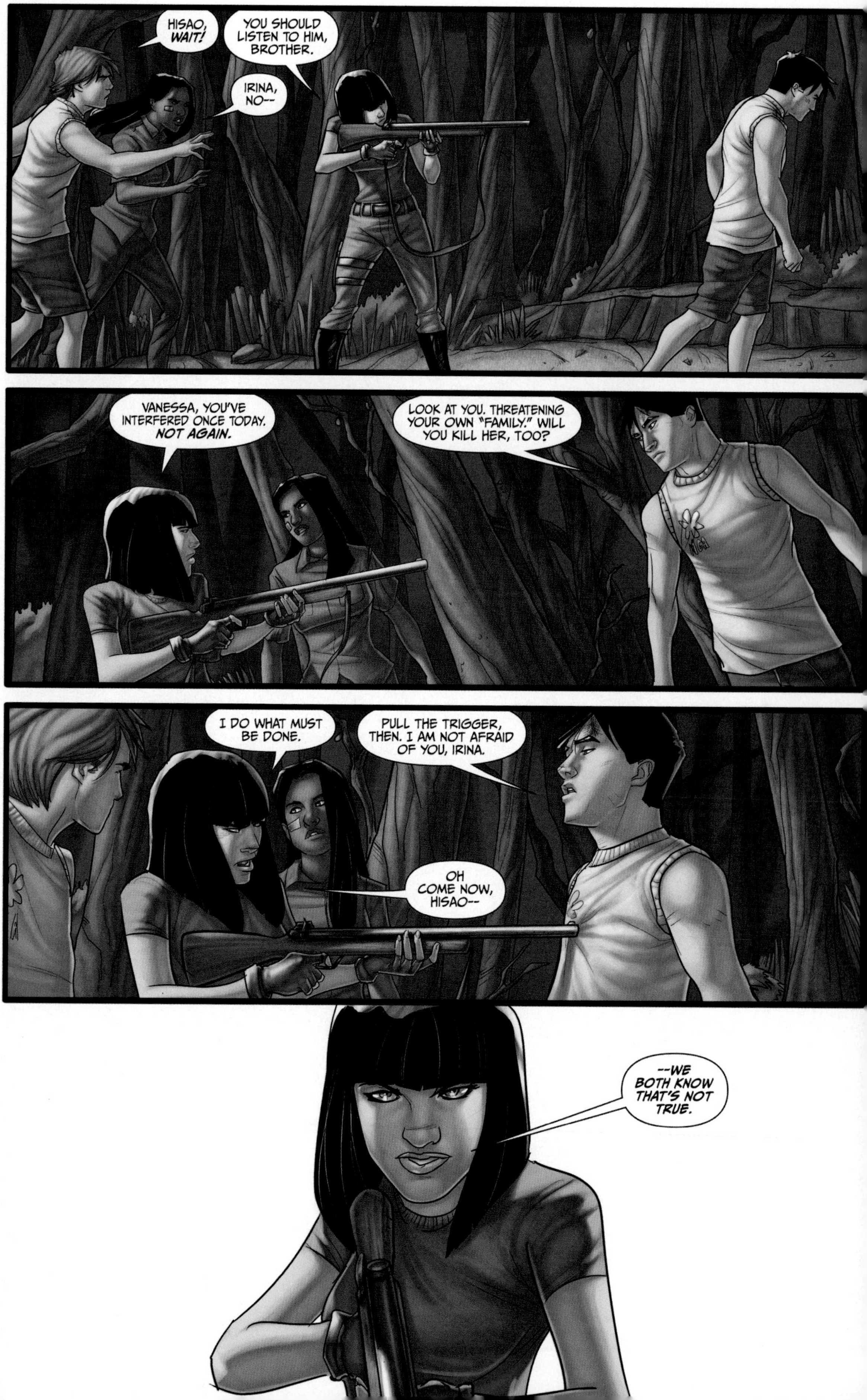
HISAO, WAIT!
YOU SHOULD LISTEN TO HIM, BROTHER.
IRINA, NO--
VANESSA, YOU'VE INTERFERED ONCE TODAY. NOT AGAIN.
LOOK AT YOU. THREATENING YOUR OWN "FAMILY." WILL YOU KILL HER, TOO?
I DO WHAT MUST BE DONE.
PULL THE TRIGGER, THEN. I AM NOT AFRAID OF YOU, IRINA.
OH COME NOW, HISAO--
--WE BOTH KNOW THAT'S NOT TRUE.

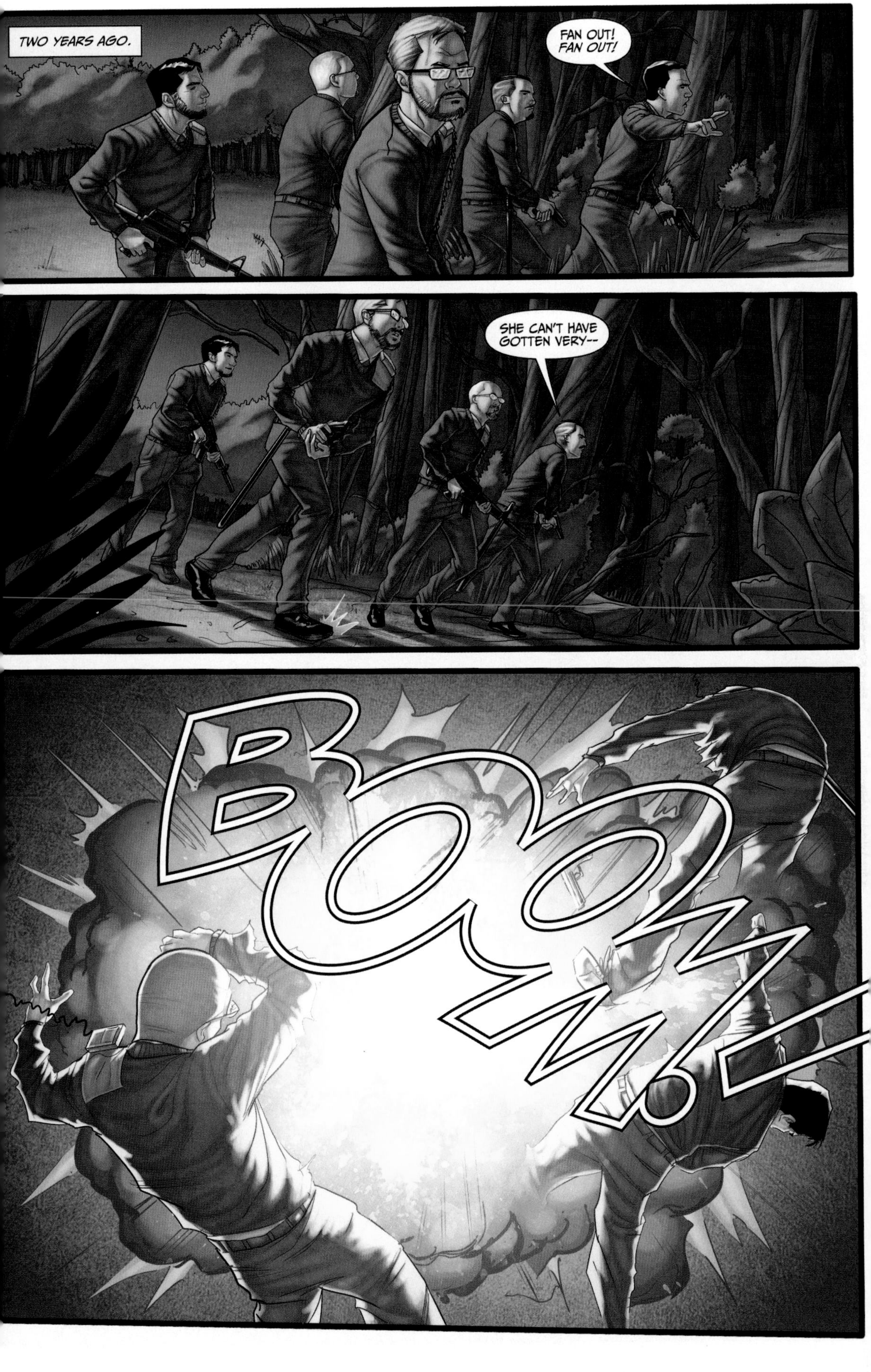
TWO YEARS AGO.
FAN OUT! FAN OUT!
SHE CAN'T HAVE GOTTEN VERY--
BOOM!!

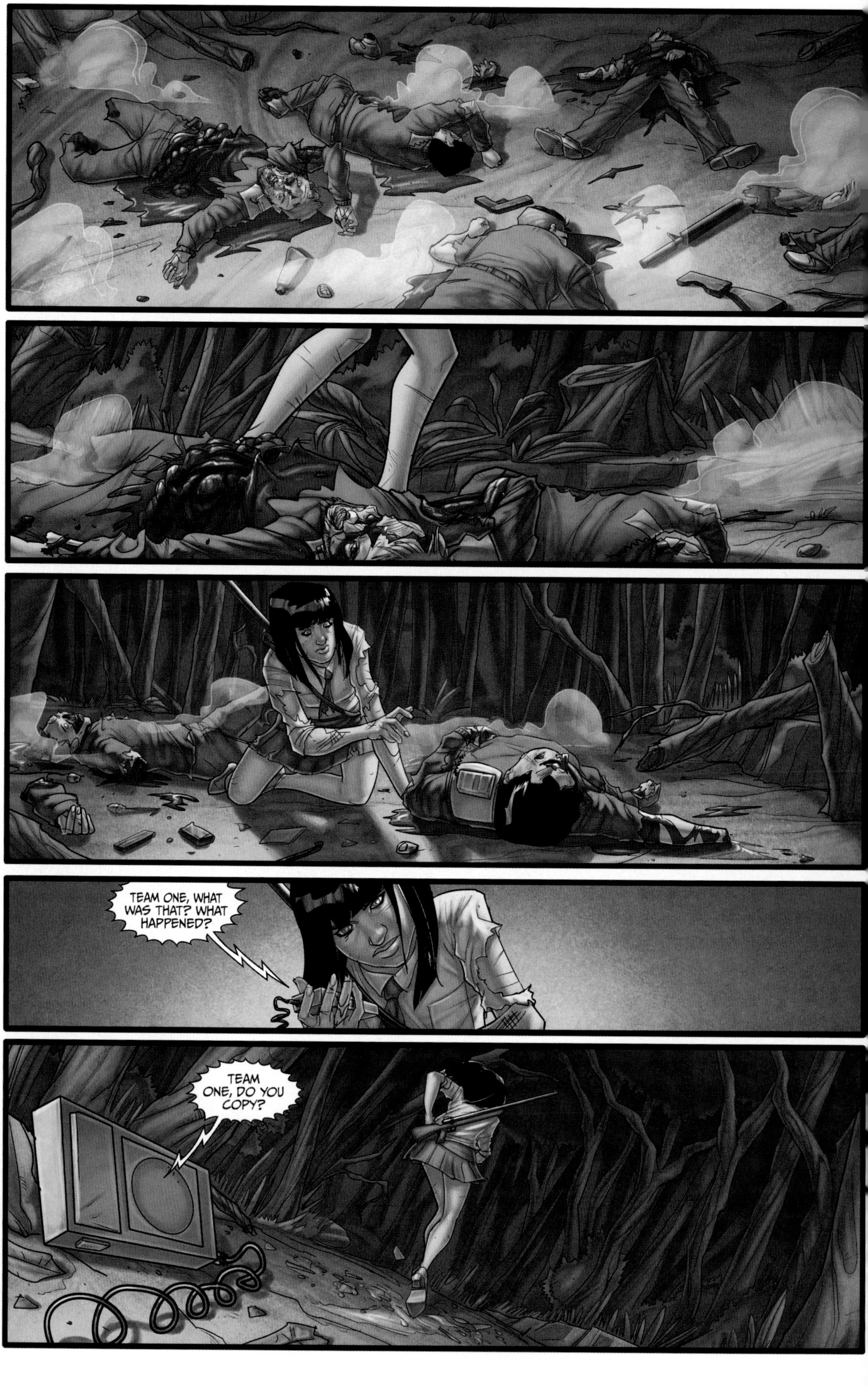
TEAM ONE, WHAT WAS THAT? WHAT HAPPENED?
TEAM ONE, DO YOU COPY?

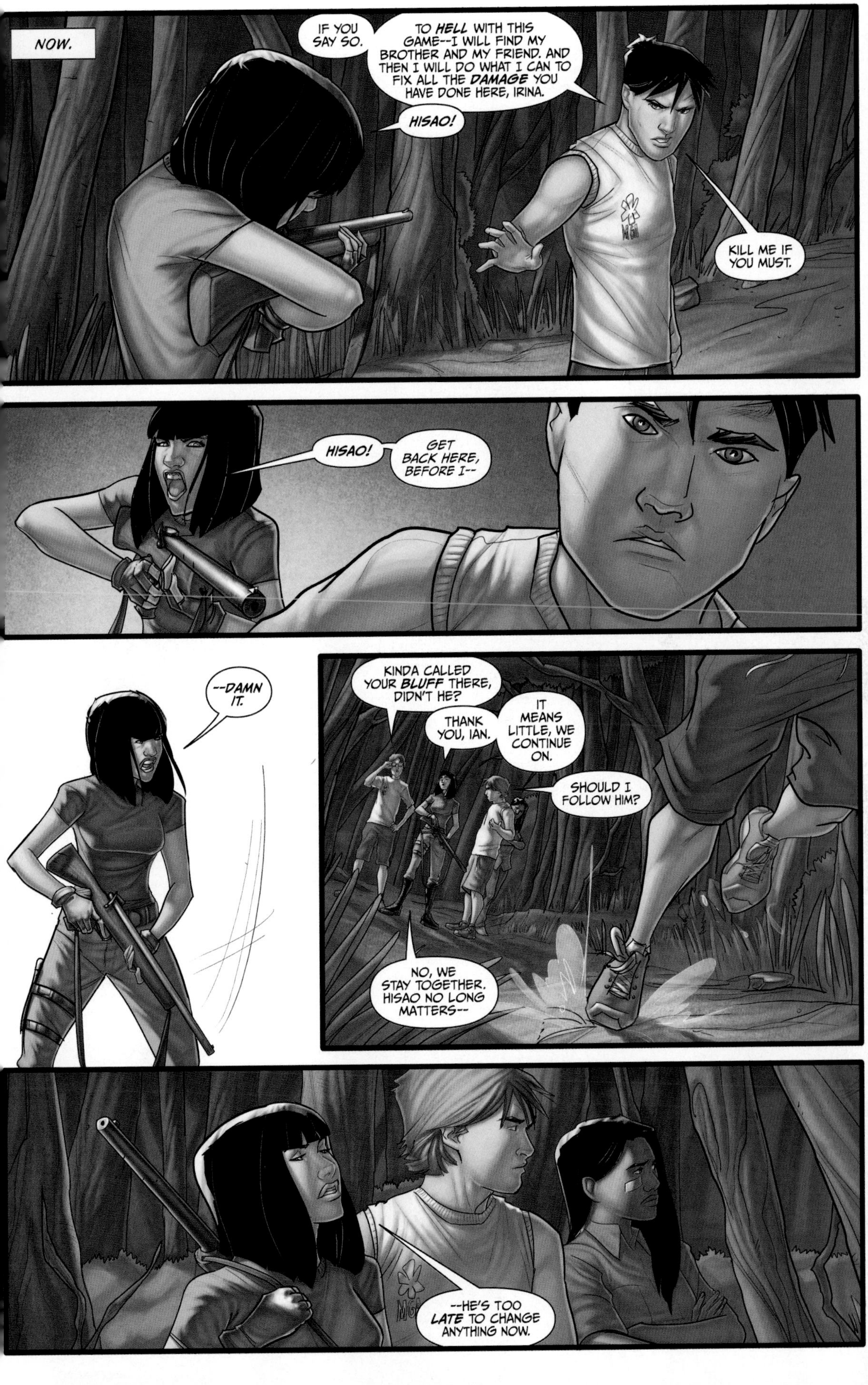
NOW.
IF YOU SAY SO.
TO HELL WITH THIS GAME--I WILL FIND MY BROTHER AND MY FRIEND. AND THEN I WILL DO WHAT I CAN TO FIX ALL THE DAMAGE YOU HAVE DONE HERE, IRINA.
HISAO!
KILL ME IF YOU MUST.
HISAO!
GET BACK HERE, BEFORE I--
--DAMN IT.
KINDA CALLED YOUR BLUFF THERE, DIDN'T HE?
THANK YOU, IAN.
IT MEANS LITTLE, WE CONTINUE ON.
SHOULD I FOLLOW HIM?
NO, WE STAY TOGETHER. HISAO NO LONG MATTERS--
--HE'S TOO LATE TO CHANGE ANYTHING NOW.

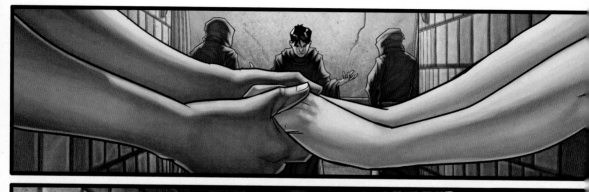

OH.

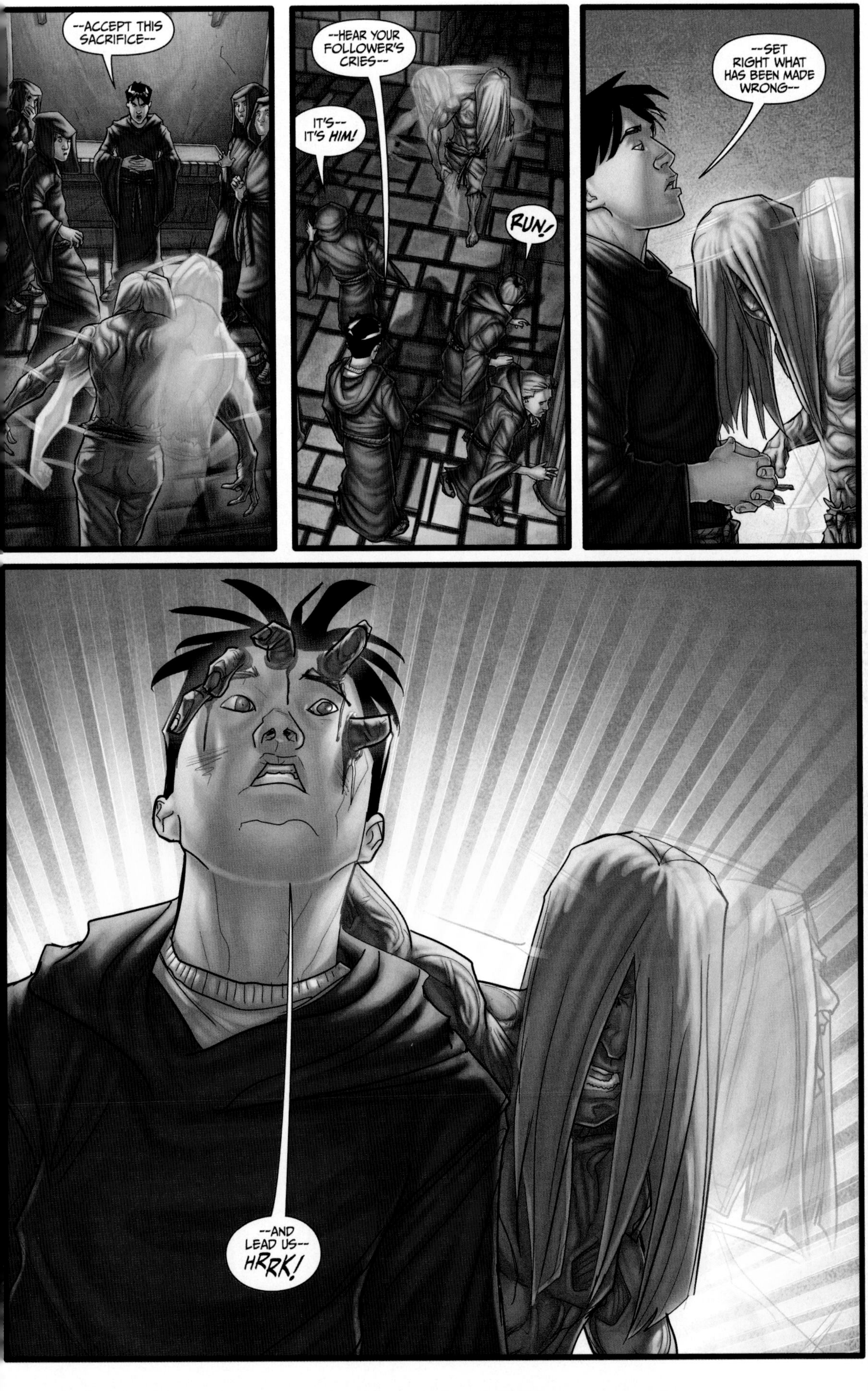
--ACCEPT THIS SACRIFICE--
--HEAR YOUR FOLLOWER'S CRIES--
IT'S-- IT'S HIM!
RUN!
--SET RIGHT WHAT HAS BEEN MADE WRONG--
--AND LEAD US-- HRRK!

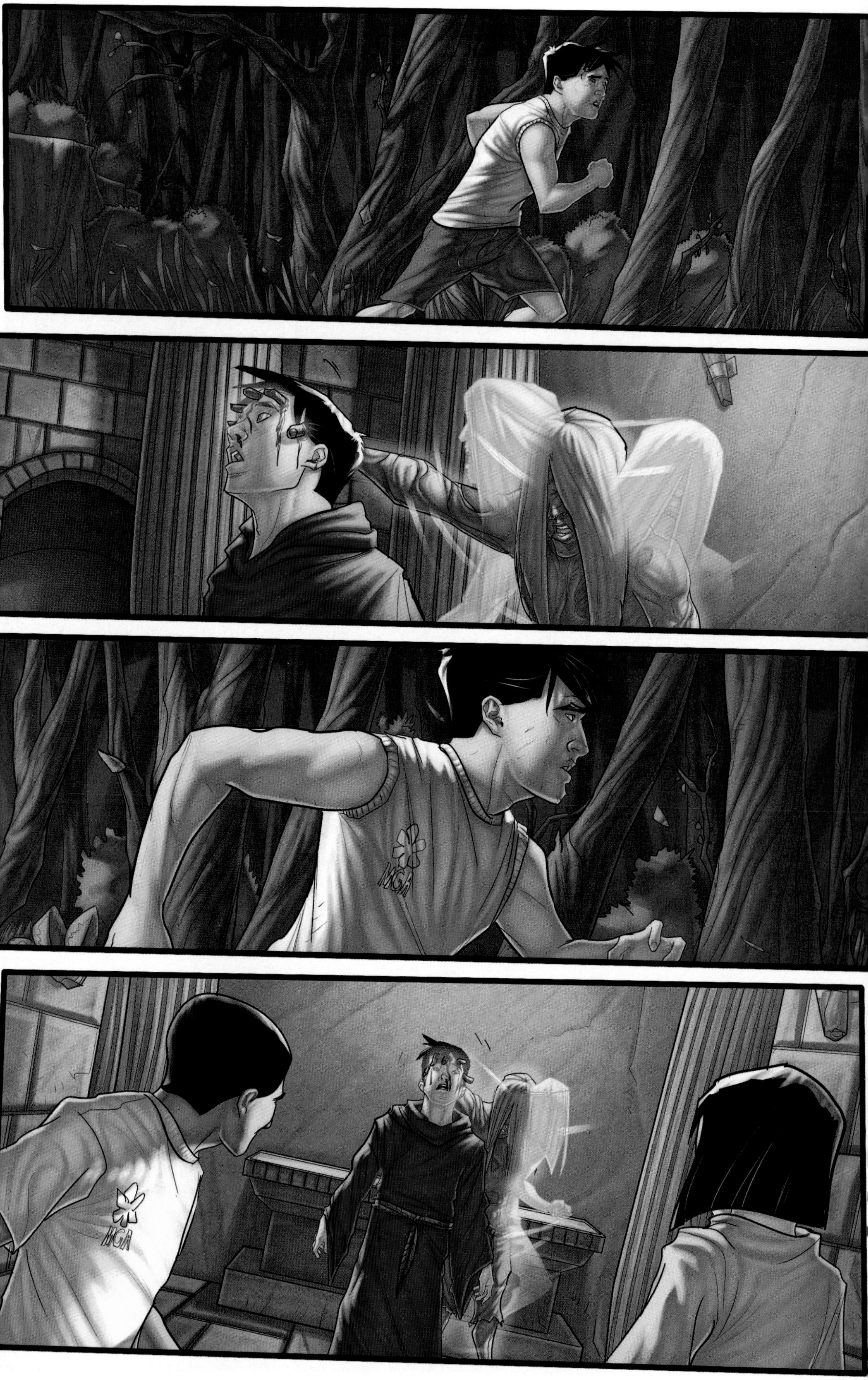
MGA

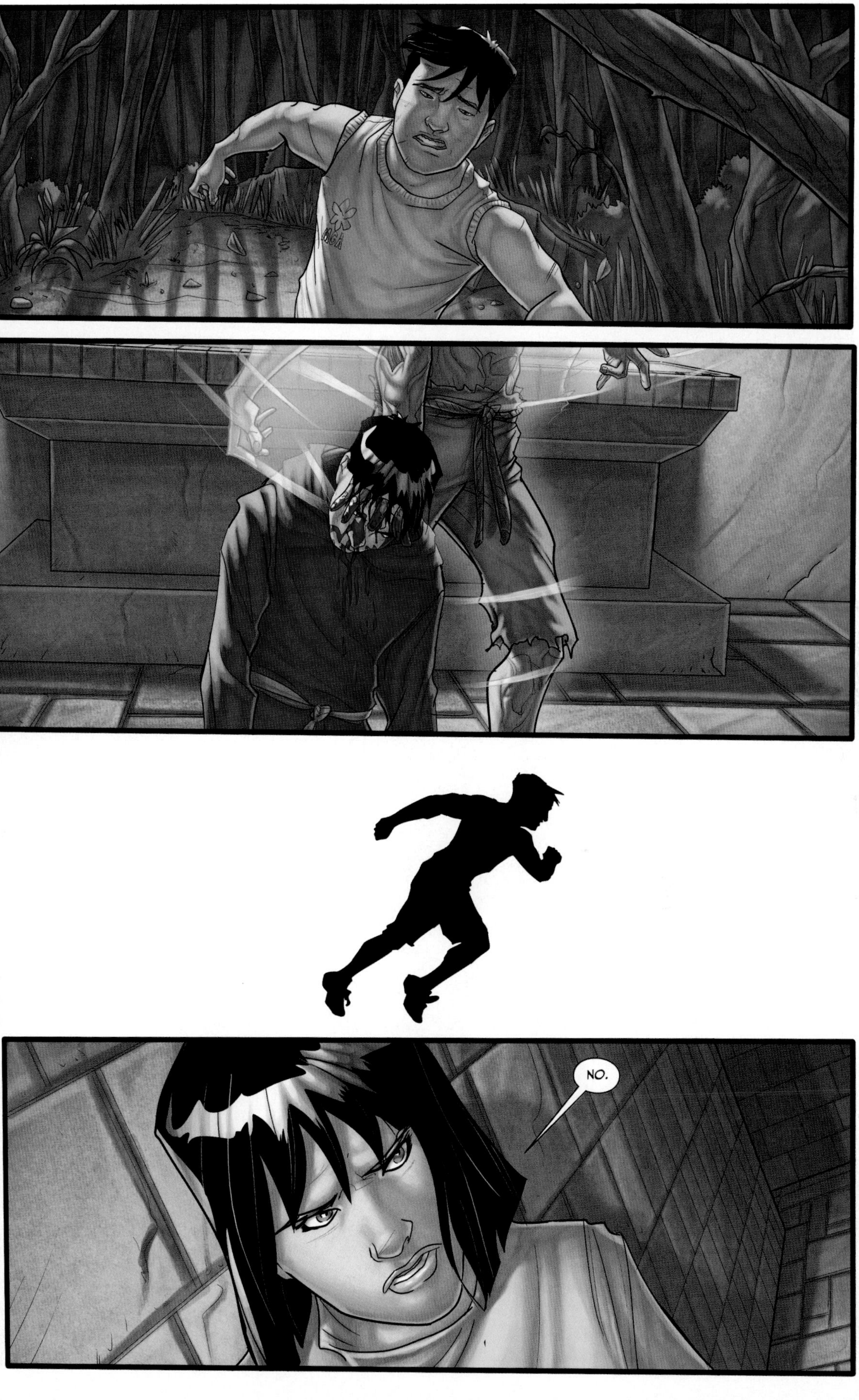
NO.

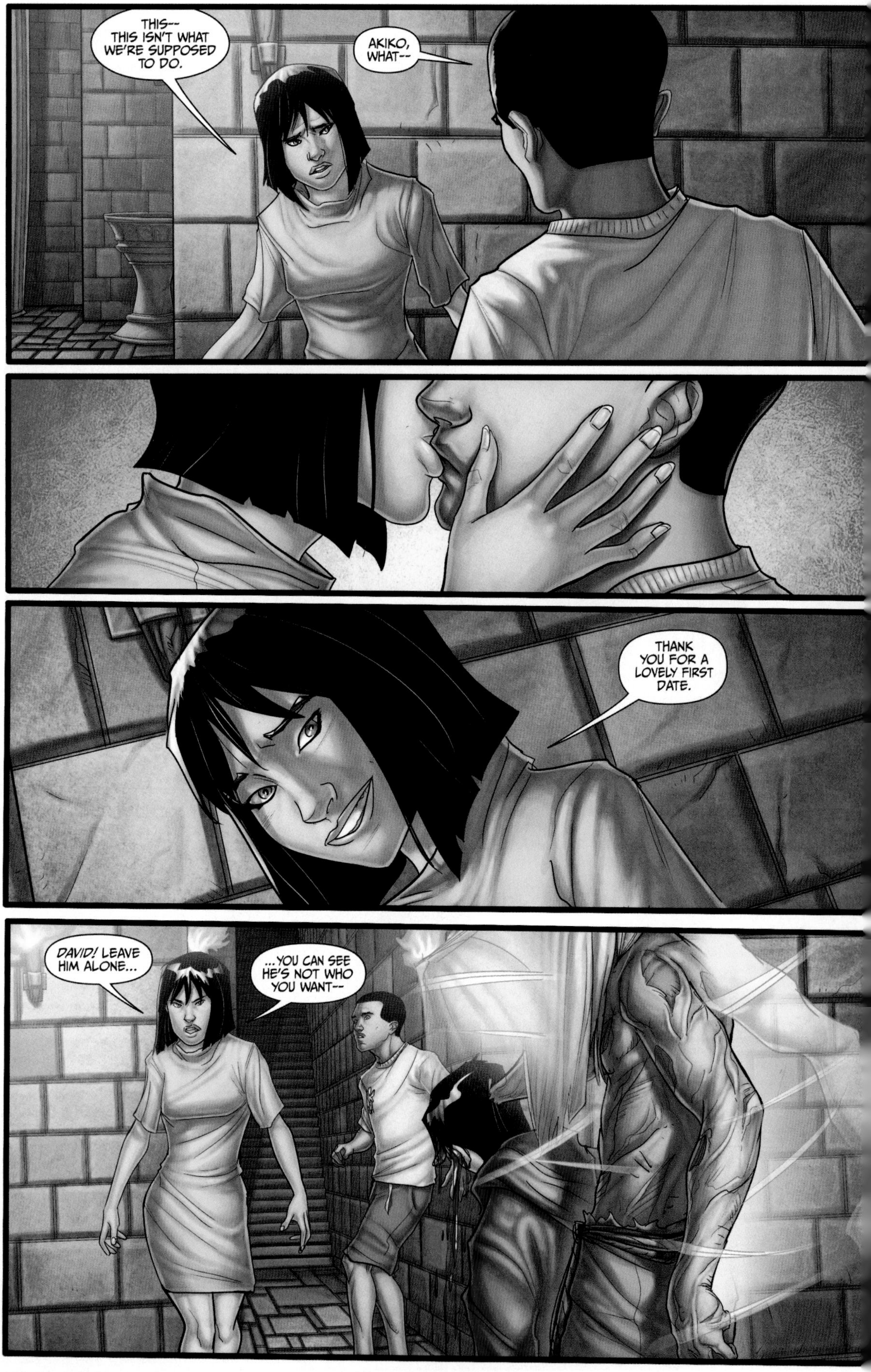
THIS-- THIS ISN'T WHAT WE'RE SUPPOSED TO DO.
AKIKO, WHAT--
THANK YOU FOR A LOVELY FIRST DATE.
DAVID! LEAVE HIM ALONE...
...YOU CAN SEE HE'S NOT WHO YOU WANT--

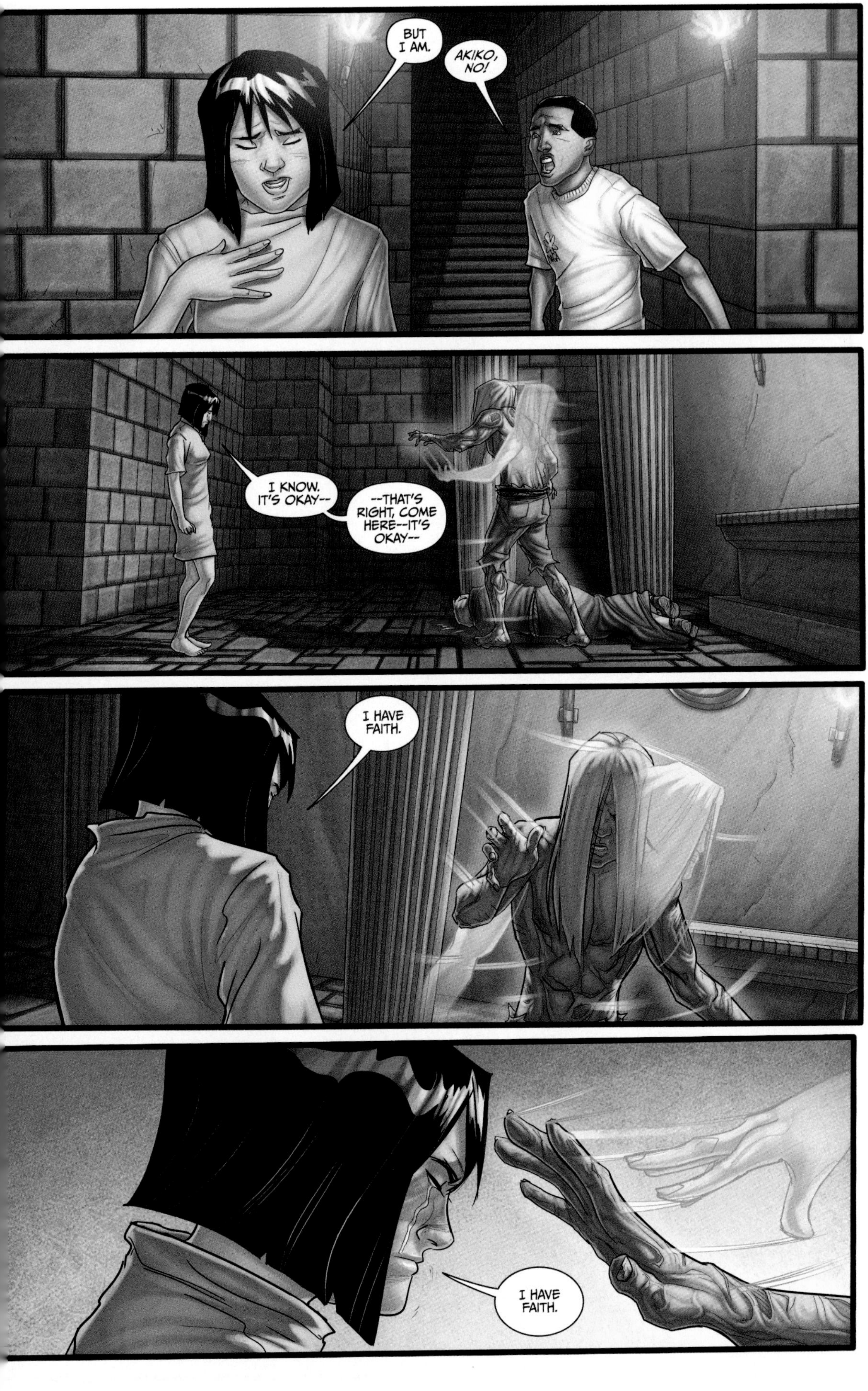
BUT I AM.
AKIKO, NO!
I KNOW. IT'S OKAY--
--THAT'S RIGHT, COME HERE--IT'S OKAY--
I HAVE FAITH.
I HAVE FAITH.

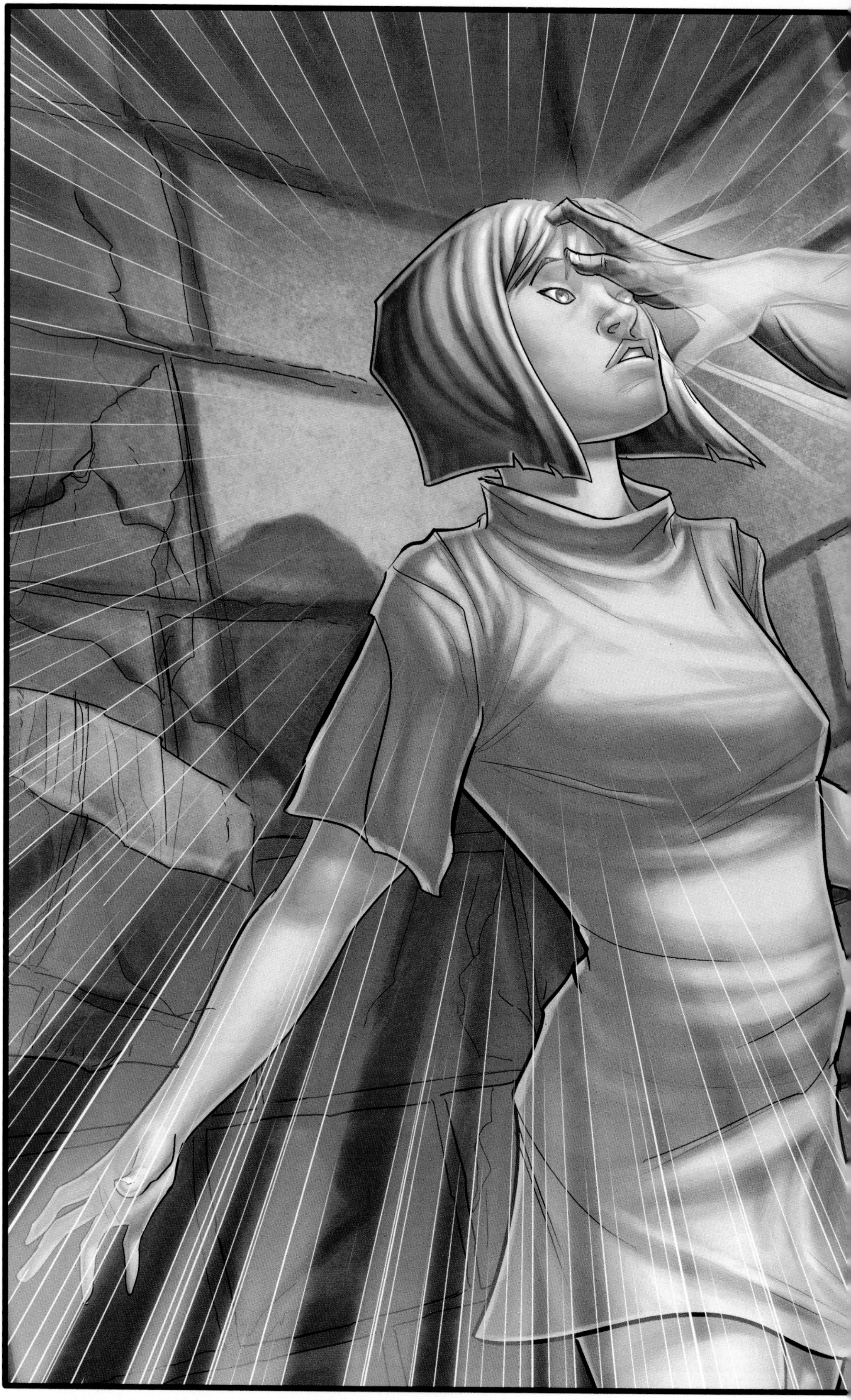

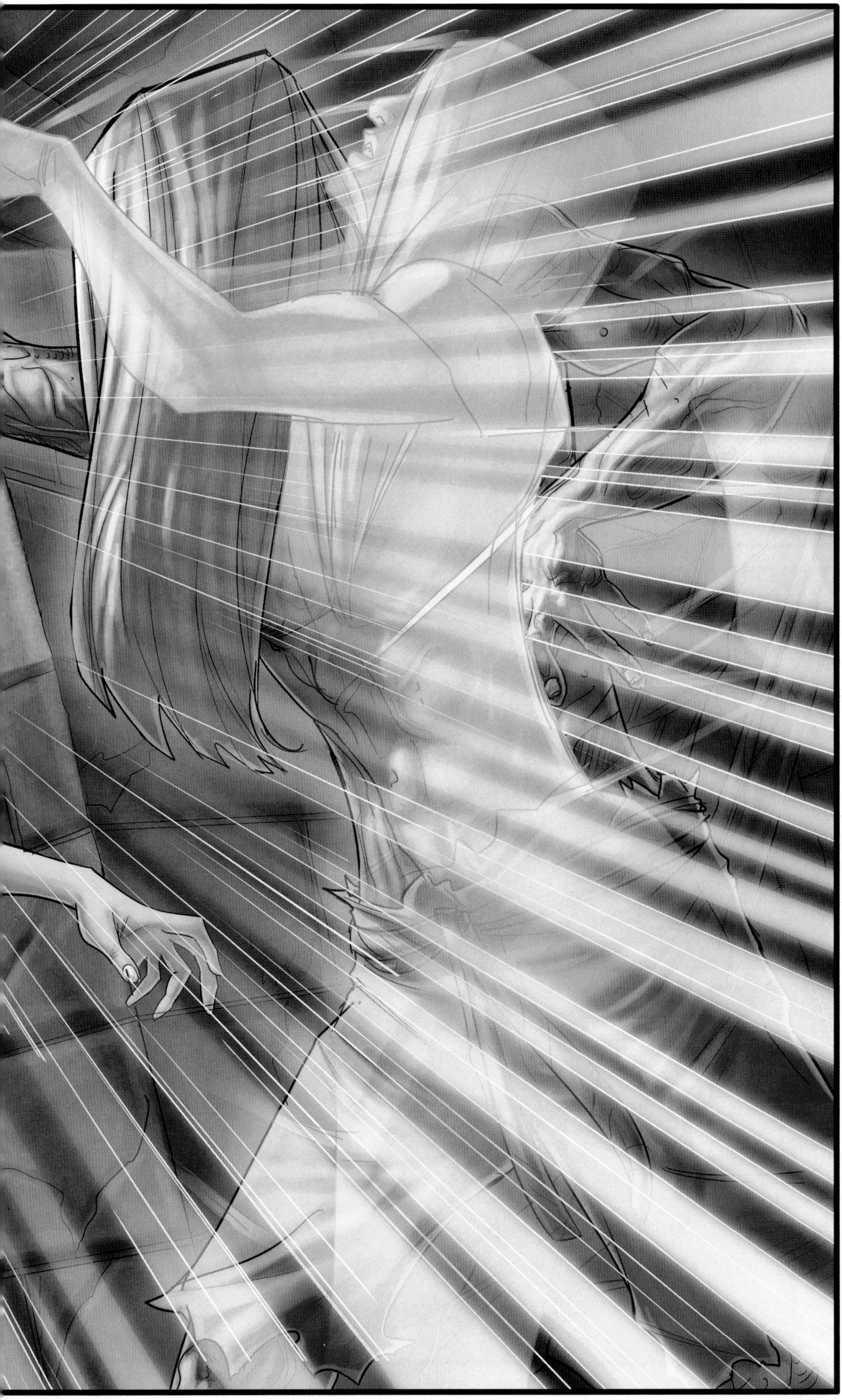

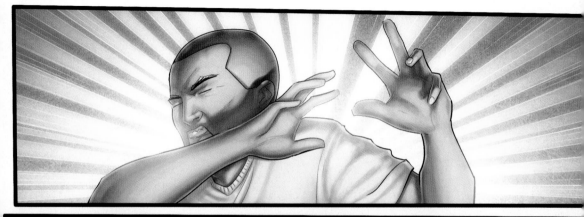

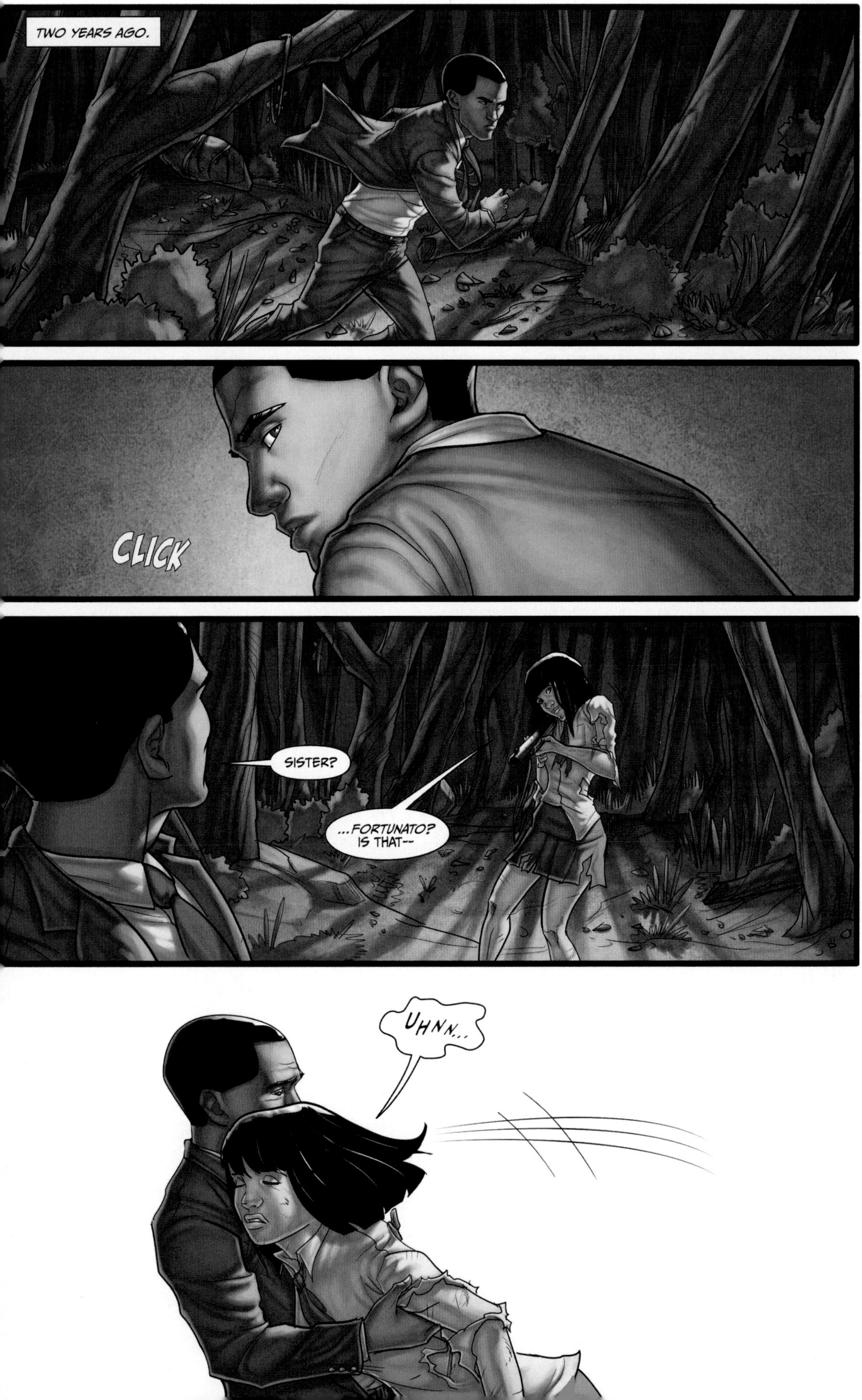
TWO YEARS AGO.
CLICK
SISTER?
...FORTUNATO? IS THAT--
UHNN...

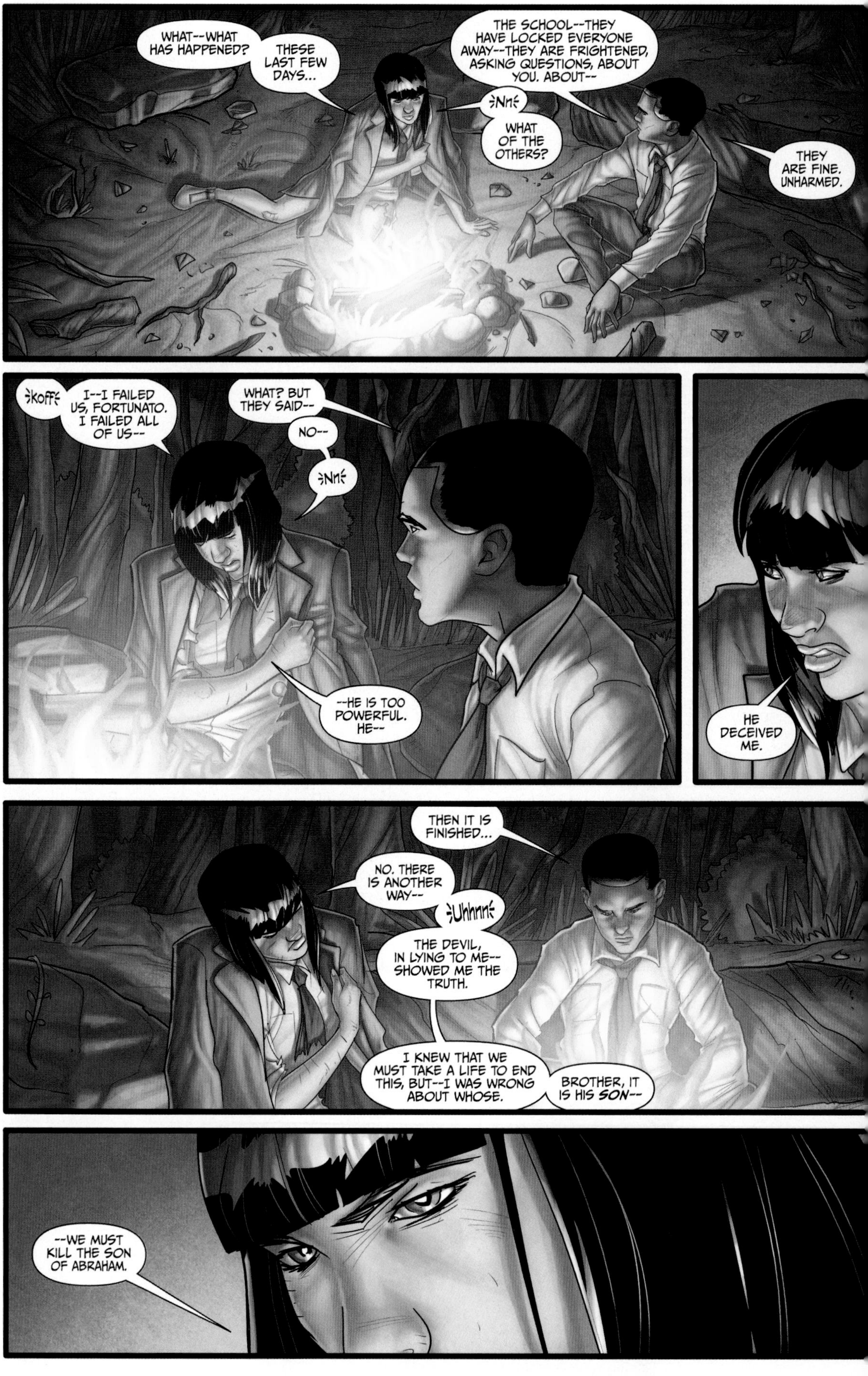
WHAT--WHAT HAS HAPPENED?
THESE LAST FEW DAYS...
THE SCHOOL--THEY HAVE LOCKED EVERYONE AWAY--THEY ARE FRIGHTENED, ASKING QUESTIONS, ABOUT YOU. ABOUT--
NN
WHAT OF THE OTHERS?
THEY ARE FINE. UNHARMED.
KOFF
I--I FAILED US, FORTUNATO. I FAILED ALL OF US--
WHAT? BUT THEY SAID--
NO--
NN
--HE IS TOO POWERFUL. HE--
HE DECEIVED ME.
THEN IT IS FINISHED...
NO. THERE IS ANOTHER WAY--
UHHNN
THE DEVIL, IN LYING TO ME--SHOWED ME THE TRUTH.
I KNEW THAT WE MUST TAKE A LIFE TO END THIS, BUT--I WAS WRONG ABOUT WHOSE.
BROTHER, IT IS HIS SON--
--WE MUST KILL THE SON OF ABRAHAM.

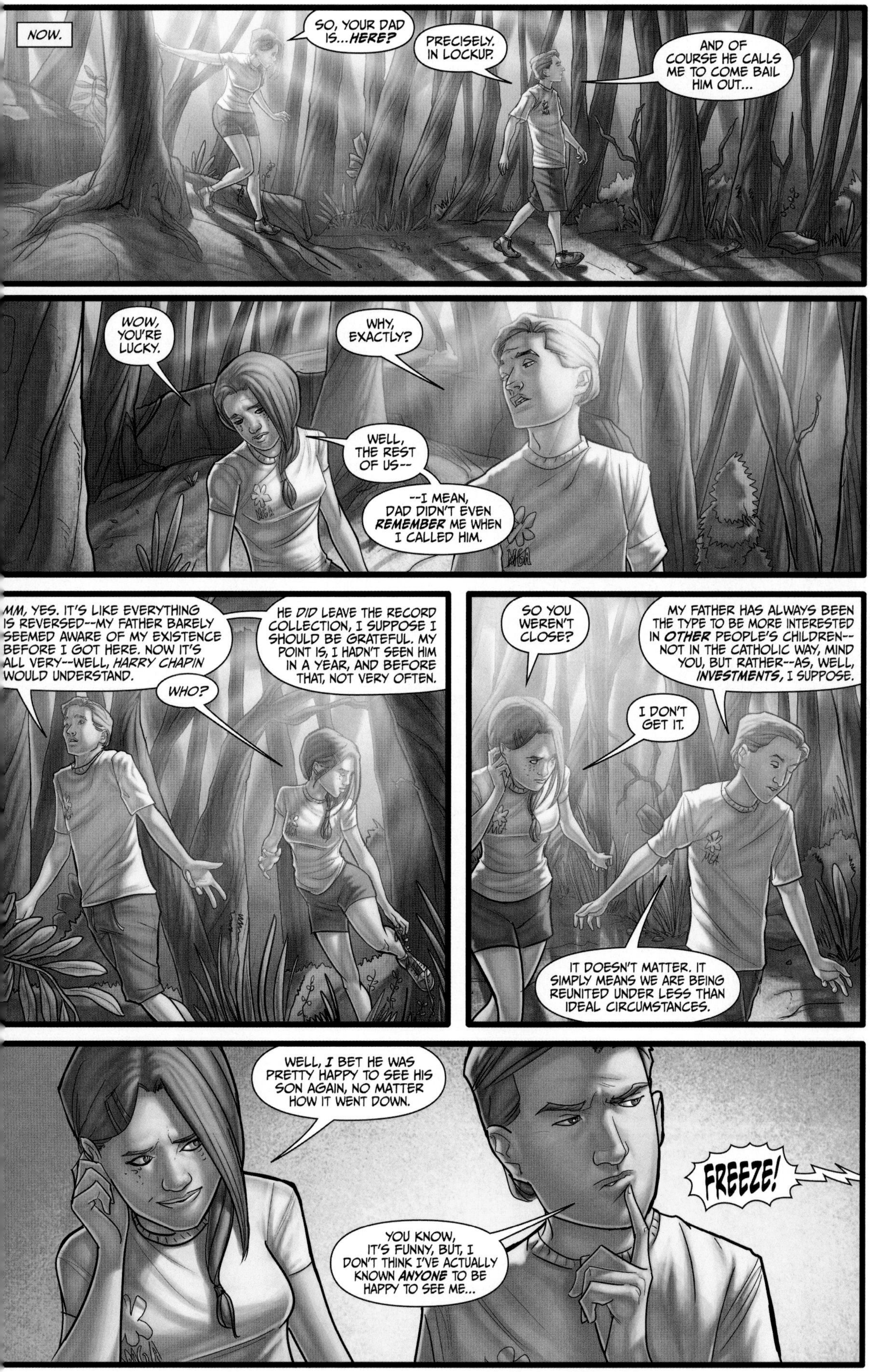
NOW.
SO, YOUR DAD IS...HERE?
PRECISELY. IN LOCKUP.
AND OF COURSE HE CALLS ME TO COME BAIL HIM OUT...
WOW, YOU'RE LUCKY.
WHY, EXACTLY?
WELL, THE REST OF US--
--I MEAN, DAD DIDN'T EVEN REMEMBER ME WHEN I CALLED HIM.
MM, YES. IT'S LIKE EVERYTHING IS REVERSED--MY FATHER BARELY SEEMED AWARE OF MY EXISTENCE BEFORE I GOT HERE. NOW IT'S ALL VERY--WELL, HARRY CHAPIN WOULD UNDERSTAND.
WHO?
HE DID LEAVE THE RECORD COLLECTION, I SUPPOSE I SHOULD BE GRATEFUL. MY POINT IS, I HADN'T SEEN HIM IN A YEAR, AND BEFORE THAT, NOT VERY OFTEN.
SO YOU WEREN'T CLOSE?
MY FATHER HAS ALWAYS BEEN THE TYPE TO BE MORE INTERESTED IN OTHER PEOPLE'S CHILDREN--NOT IN THE CATHOLIC WAY, MIND YOU, BUT RATHER--AS, WELL, INVESTMENTS, I SUPPOSE.
I DON'T GET IT.
IT DOESN'T MATTER. IT SIMPLY MEANS WE ARE BEING REUNITED UNDER LESS THAN IDEAL CIRCUMSTANCES.
WELL, I BET HE WAS PRETTY HAPPY TO SEE HIS SON AGAIN, NO MATTER HOW IT WENT DOWN.
YOU KNOW, IT'S FUNNY, BUT, I DON'T THINK I'VE ACTUALLY KNOWN ANYONE TO BE HAPPY TO SEE ME...
FREEZE!

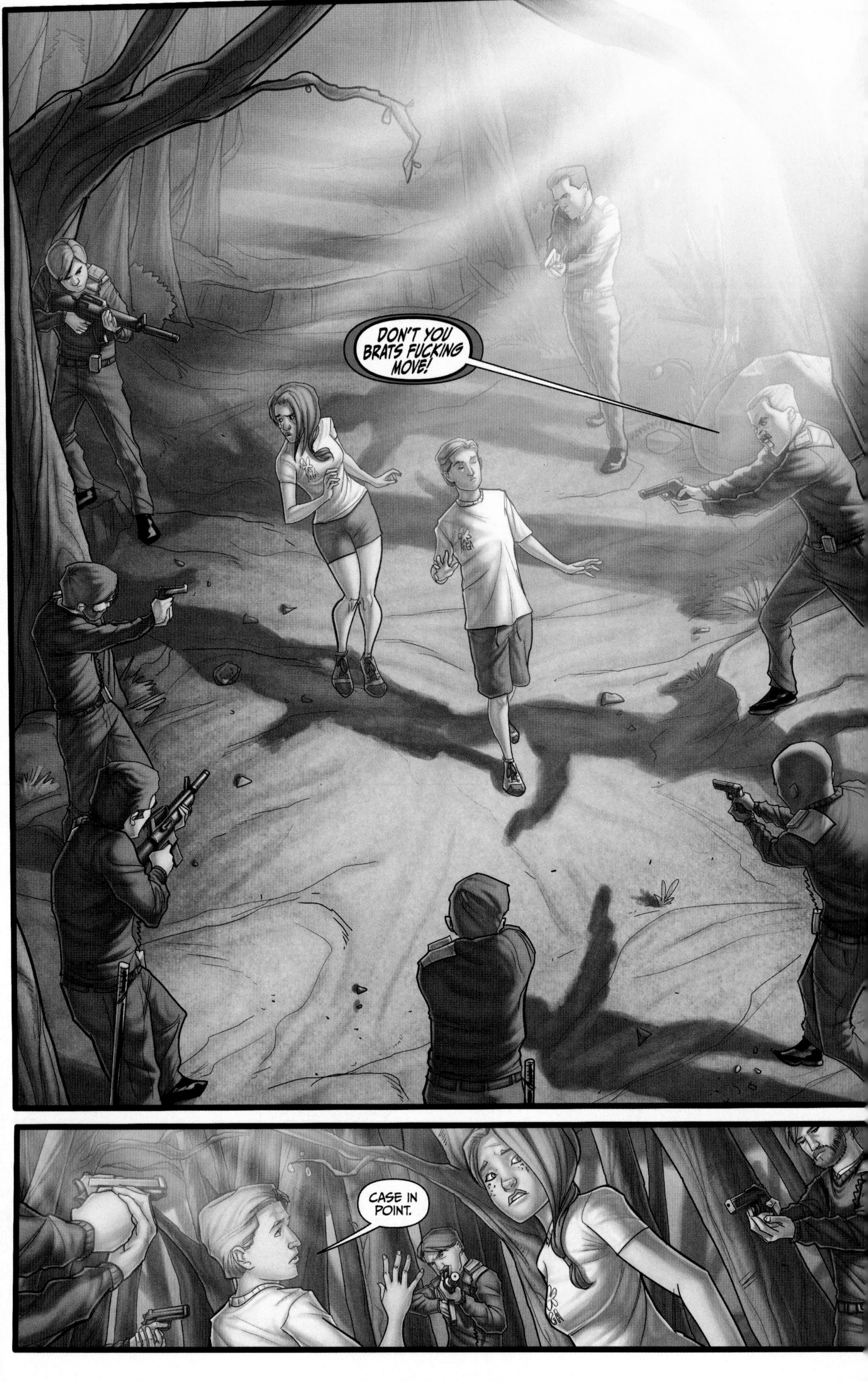
DON'T YOU BRATS FUCKING MOVE!
CASE IN POINT.

twenty**four**

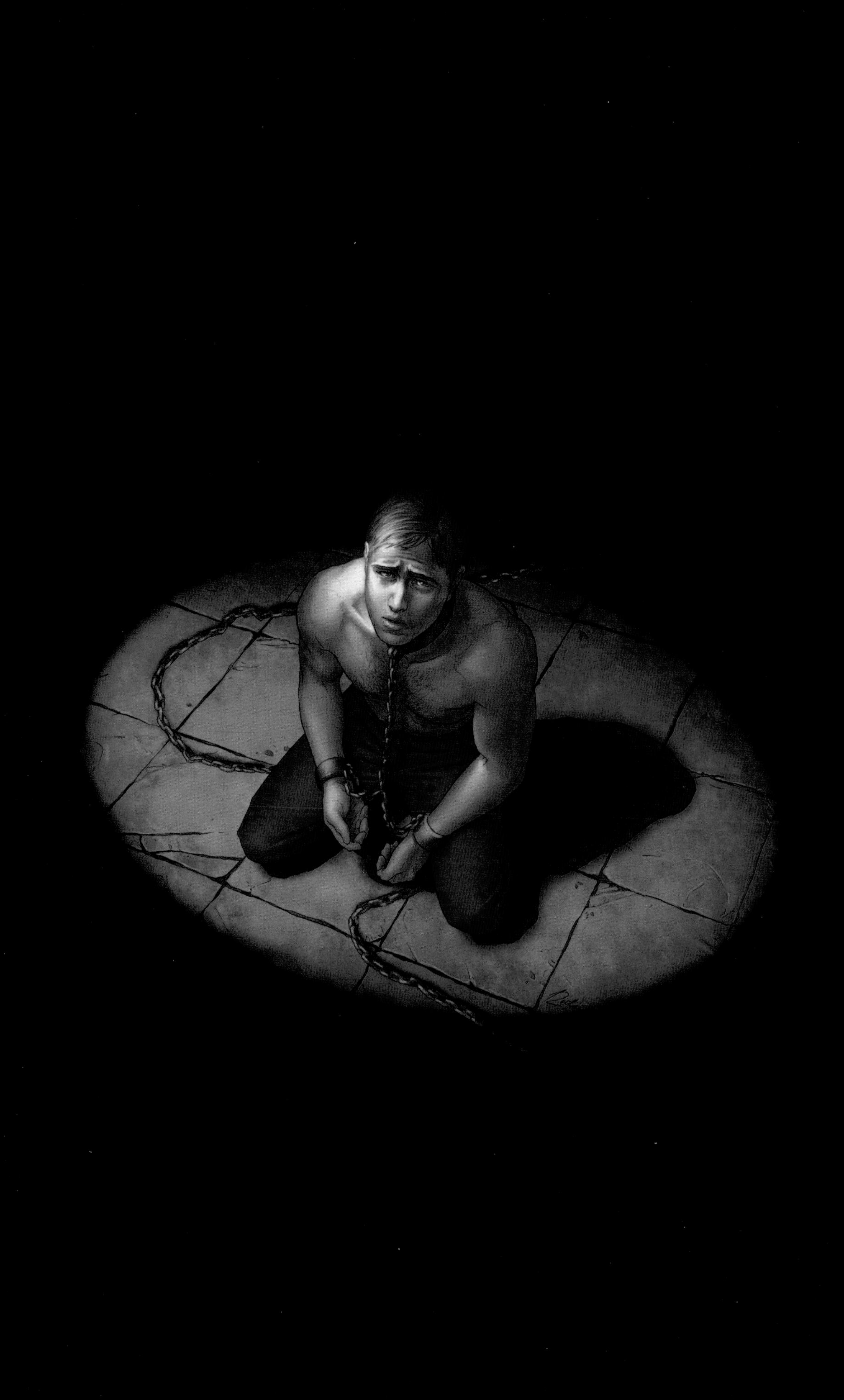

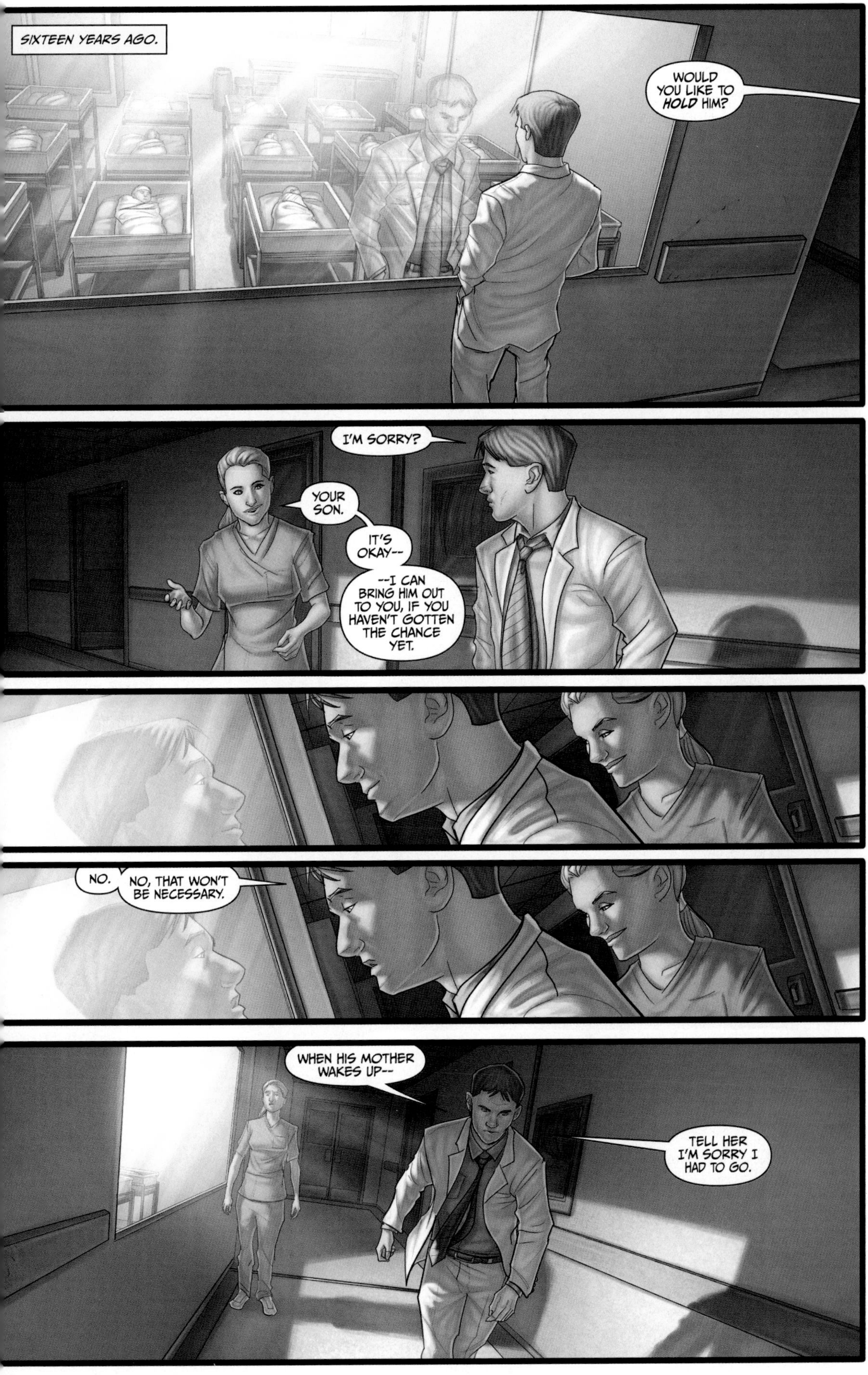
SIXTEEN YEARS AGO.
WOULD YOU LIKE TO HOLD HIM?
I'M SORRY?
YOUR SON.
IT'S OKAY--
--I CAN BRING HIM OUT TO YOU, IF YOU HAVEN'T GOTTEN THE CHANCE YET.
NO.
NO, THAT WON'T BE NECESSARY.
WHEN HIS MOTHER WAKES UP--
TELL HER I'M SORRY I HAD TO GO.

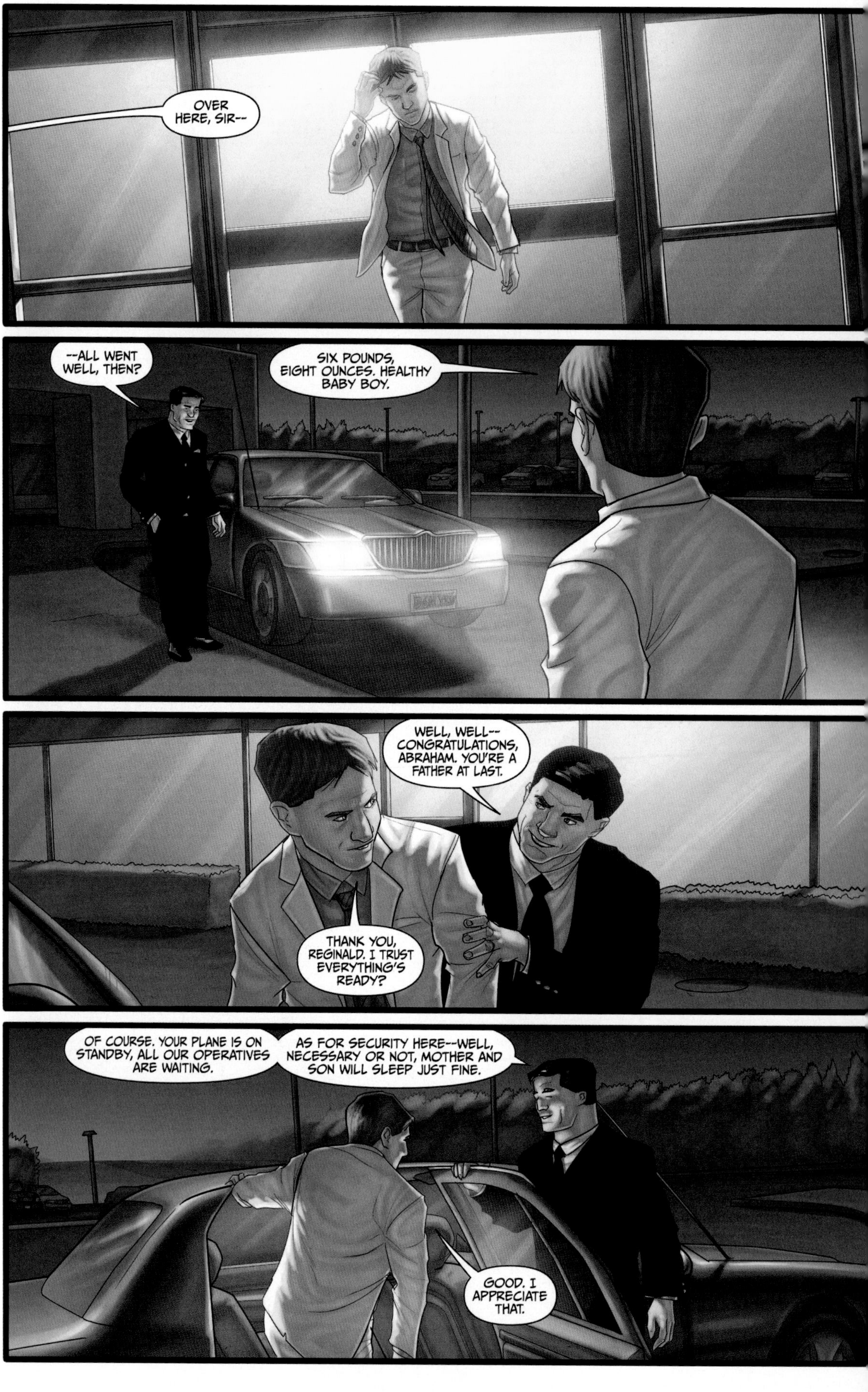
OVER HERE, SIR--
--ALL WENT WELL, THEN?
SIX POUNDS, EIGHT OUNCES. HEALTHY BABY BOY.
WELL, WELL-- CONGRATULATIONS, ABRAHAM. YOU'RE A FATHER AT LAST.
THANK YOU, REGINALD. I TRUST EVERYTHING'S READY?
OF COURSE. YOUR PLANE IS ON STANDBY, ALL OUR OPERATIVES ARE WAITING.
AS FOR SECURITY HERE--WELL, NECESSARY OR NOT, MOTHER AND SON WILL SLEEP JUST FINE.
GOOD. I APPRECIATE THAT.

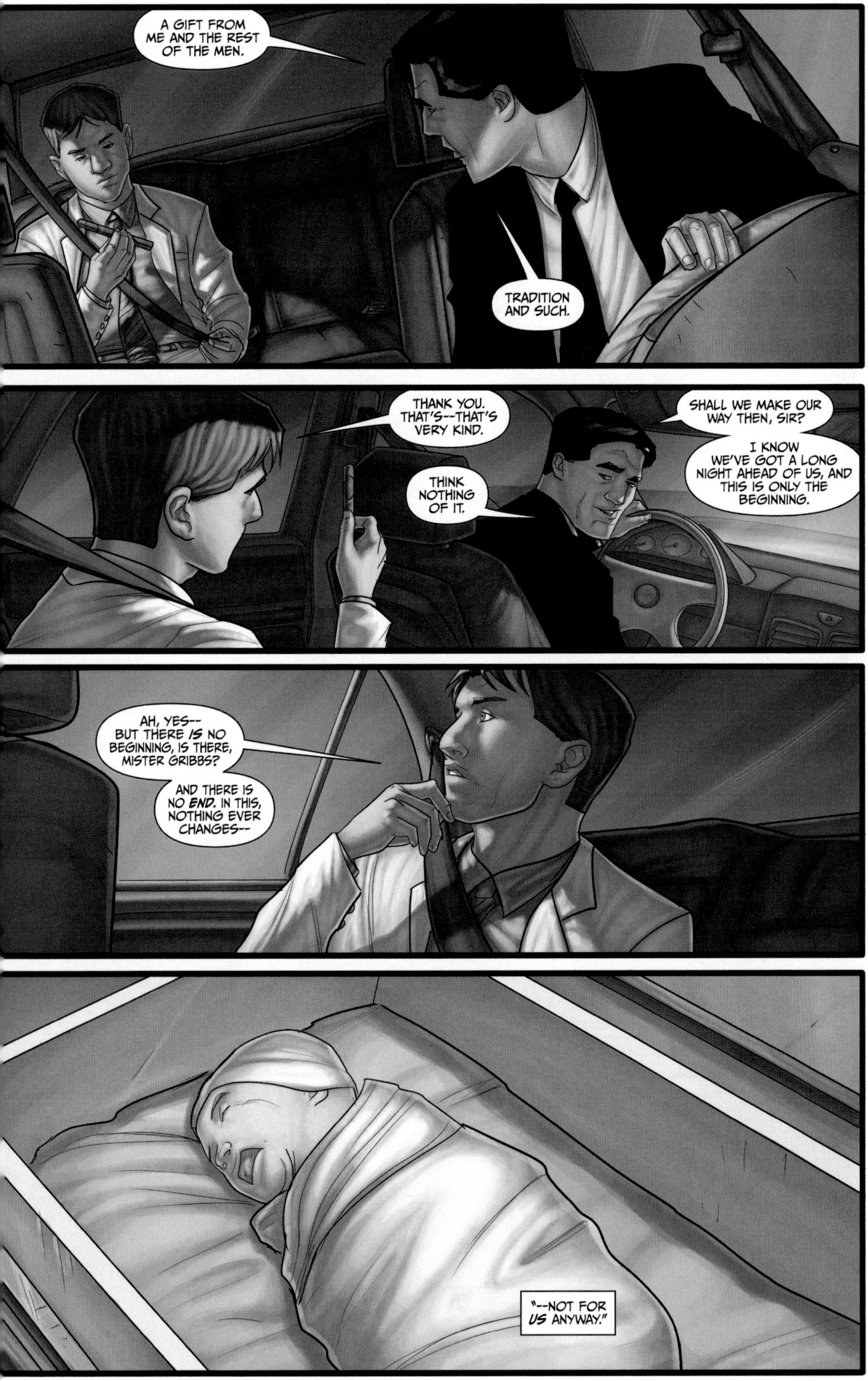
A GIFT FROM ME AND THE REST OF THE MEN.
TRADITION AND SUCH.
THANK YOU. THAT'S--THAT'S VERY KIND.
THINK NOTHING OF IT.
SHALL WE MAKE OUR WAY THEN, SIR?
I KNOW WE'VE GOT A LONG NIGHT AHEAD OF US, AND THIS IS ONLY THE BEGINNING.
AH, YES-- BUT THERE *IS* NO BEGINNING, IS THERE, MISTER GRIBBS?
AND THERE IS NO *END*. IN THIS, NOTHING EVER CHANGES--
"--NOT FOR *US* ANYWAY."

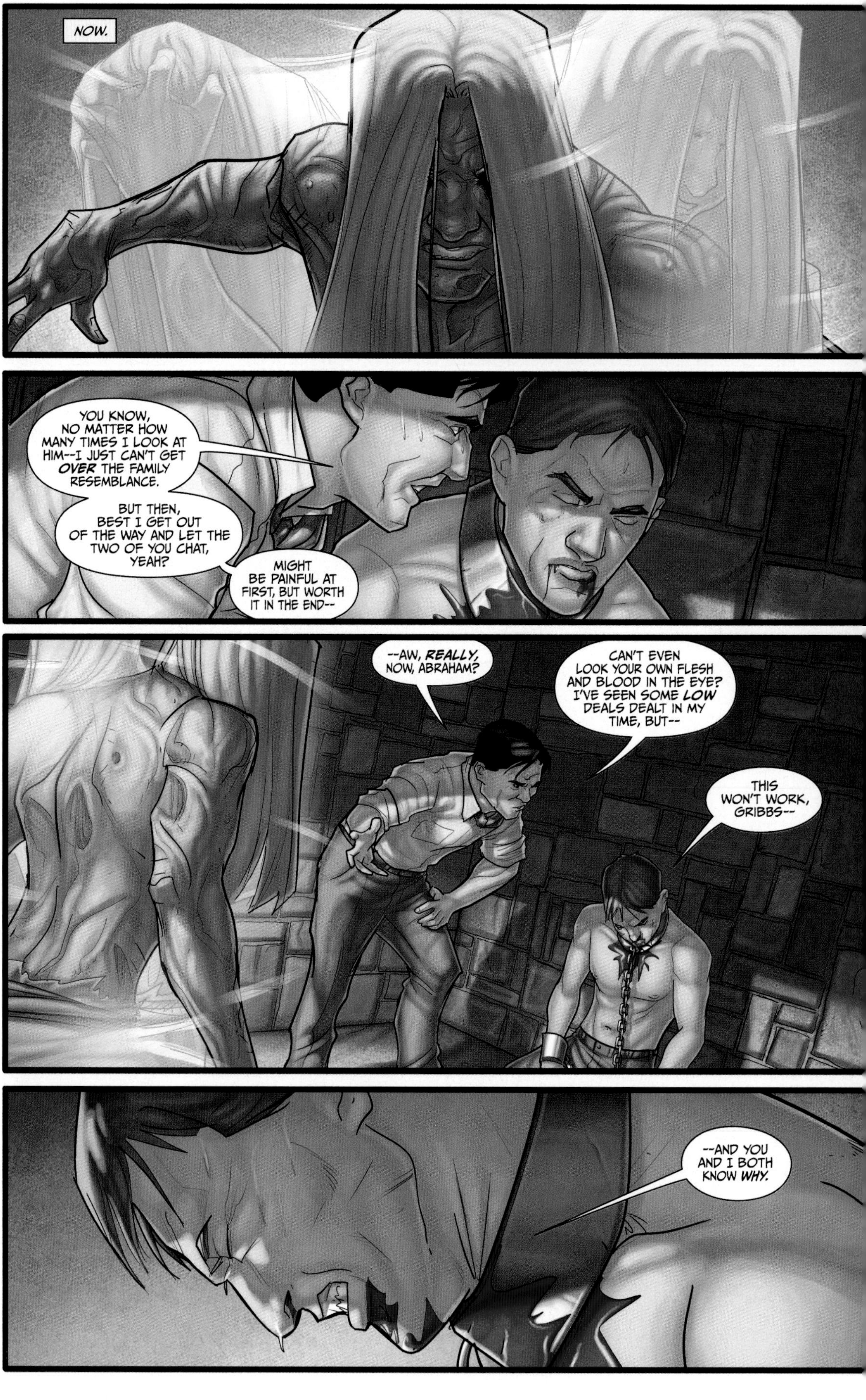
NOW.
YOU KNOW, NO MATTER HOW MANY TIMES I LOOK AT HIM--I JUST CAN'T GET OVER THE FAMILY RESEMBLANCE.
BUT THEN, BEST I GET OUT OF THE WAY AND LET THE TWO OF YOU CHAT, YEAH?
MIGHT BE PAINFUL AT FIRST, BUT WORTH IT IN THE END--
--AW, REALLY, NOW, ABRAHAM?
CAN'T EVEN LOOK YOUR OWN FLESH AND BLOOD IN THE EYE? I'VE SEEN SOME LOW DEALS DEALT IN MY TIME, BUT--
THIS WON'T WORK, GRIBBS--
--AND YOU AND I BOTH KNOW WHY.

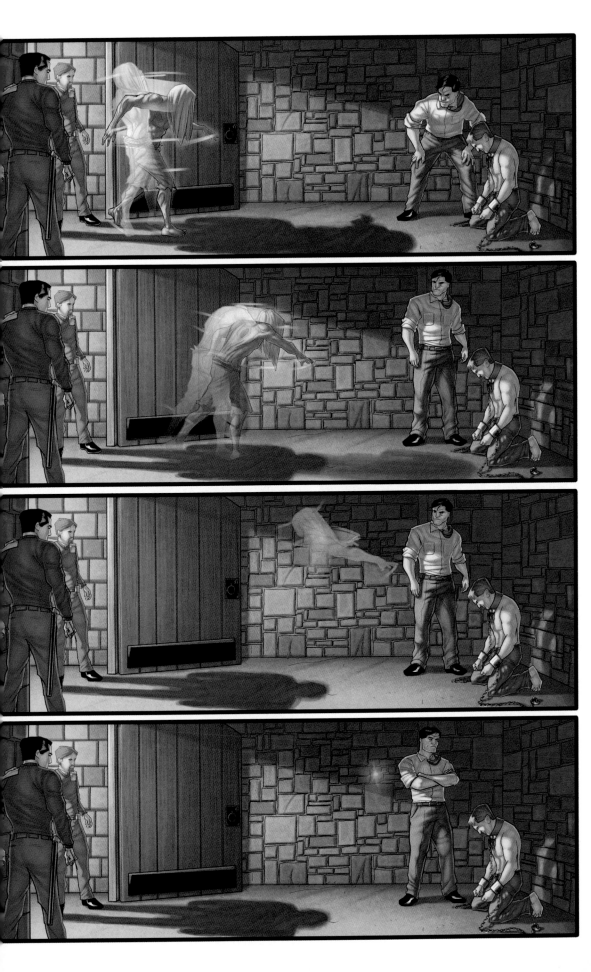

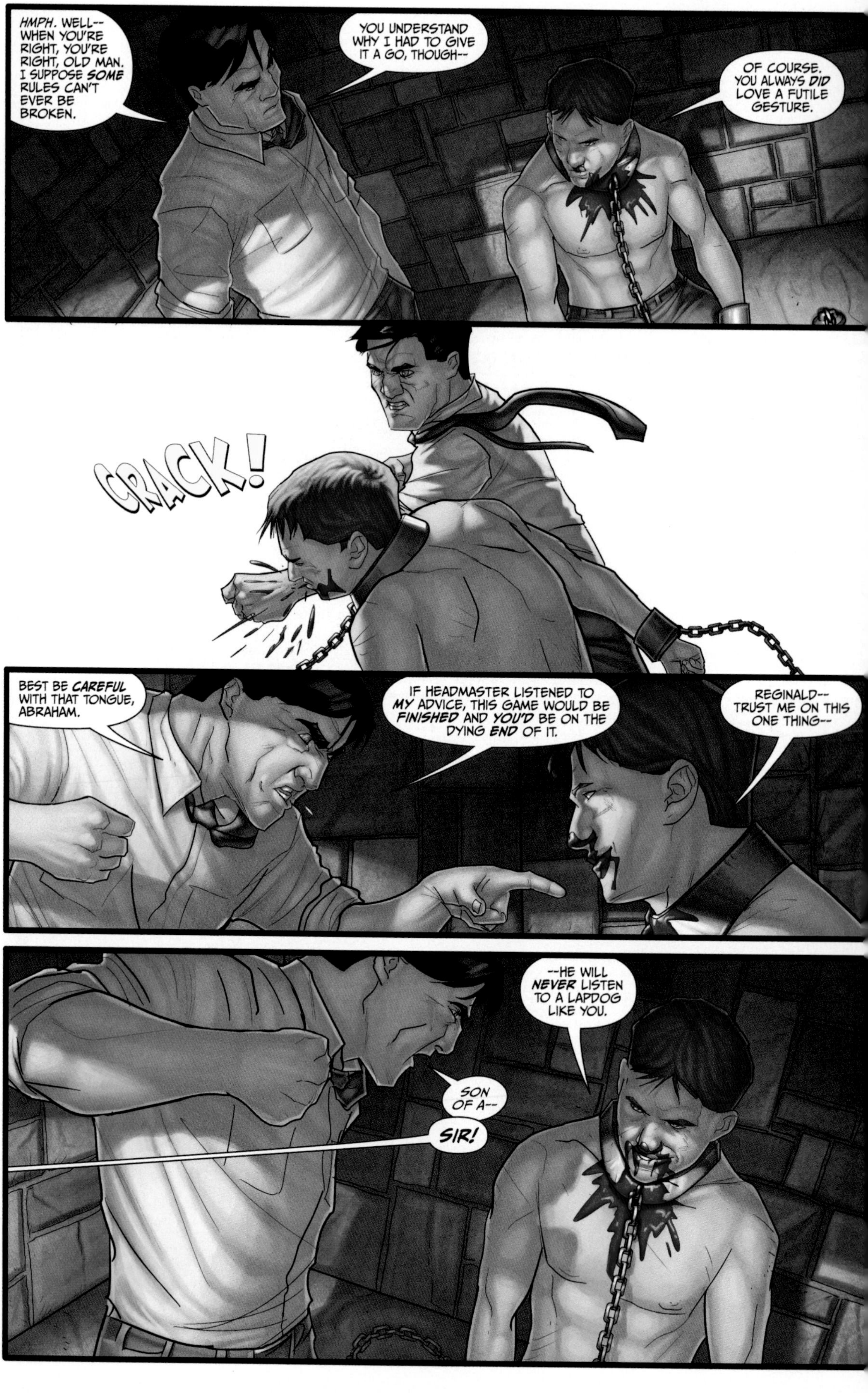
HMPH. WELL-- WHEN YOU'RE RIGHT, YOU'RE RIGHT, OLD MAN. I SUPPOSE SOME RULES CAN'T EVER BE BROKEN.
YOU UNDERSTAND WHY I HAD TO GIVE IT A GO, THOUGH--
OF COURSE. YOU ALWAYS DID LOVE A FUTILE GESTURE.
CRACK!
BEST BE CAREFUL WITH THAT TONGUE, ABRAHAM.
IF HEADMASTER LISTENED TO MY ADVICE, THIS GAME WOULD BE FINISHED AND YOU'D BE ON THE DYING END OF IT.
REGINALD-- TRUST ME ON THIS ONE THING--
--HE WILL NEVER LISTEN TO A LAPDOG LIKE YOU.
SON OF A--
SIR!

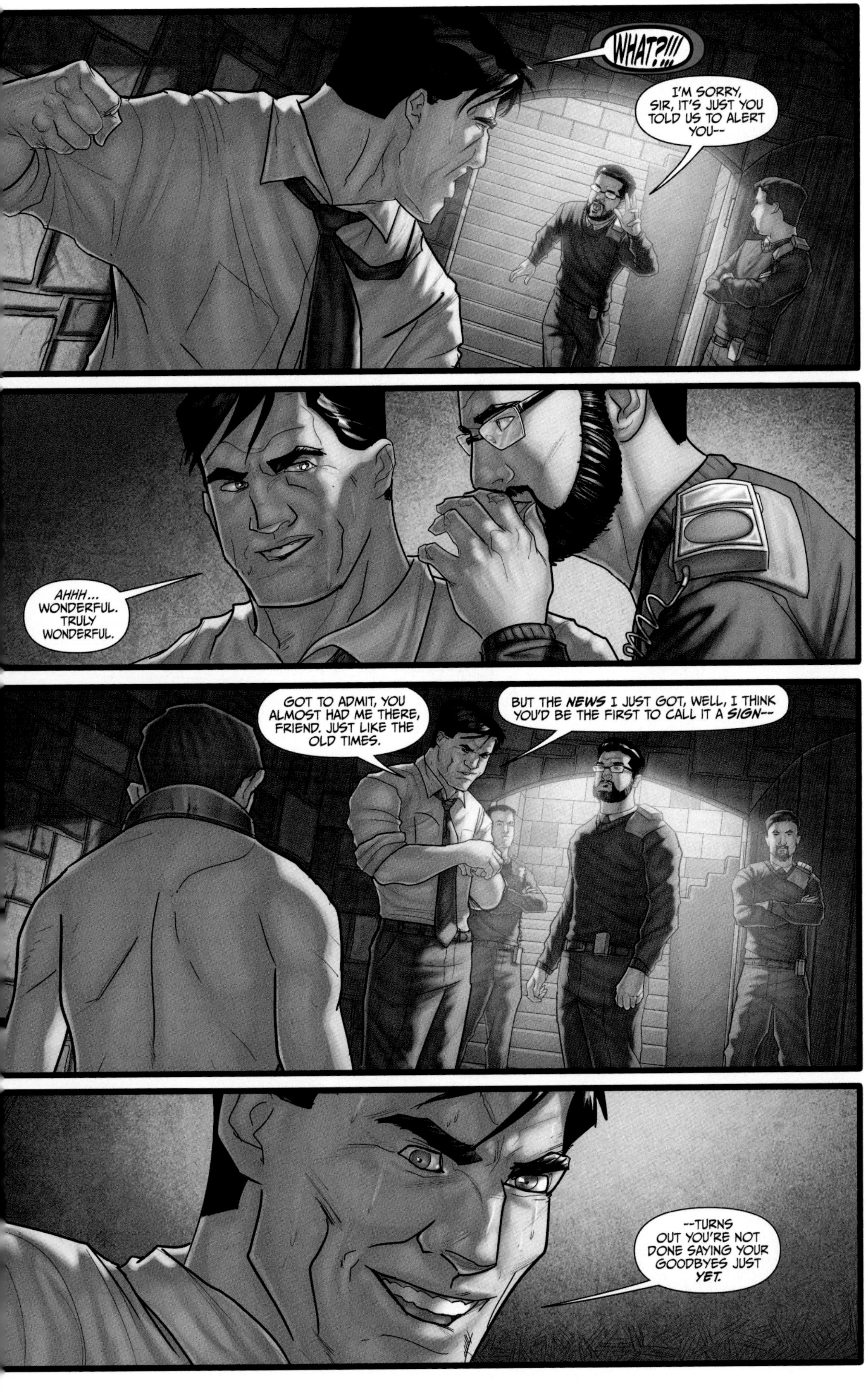
WHAT?!!!
I'M SORRY, SIR, IT'S JUST YOU TOLD US TO ALERT YOU--
AHHH... WONDERFUL. TRULY WONDERFUL.
GOT TO ADMIT, YOU ALMOST HAD ME THERE, FRIEND. JUST LIKE THE OLD TIMES.
BUT THE NEWS I JUST GOT, WELL, I THINK YOU'D BE THE FIRST TO CALL IT A SIGN--
--TURNS OUT YOU'RE NOT DONE SAYING YOUR GOODBYES JUST YET.

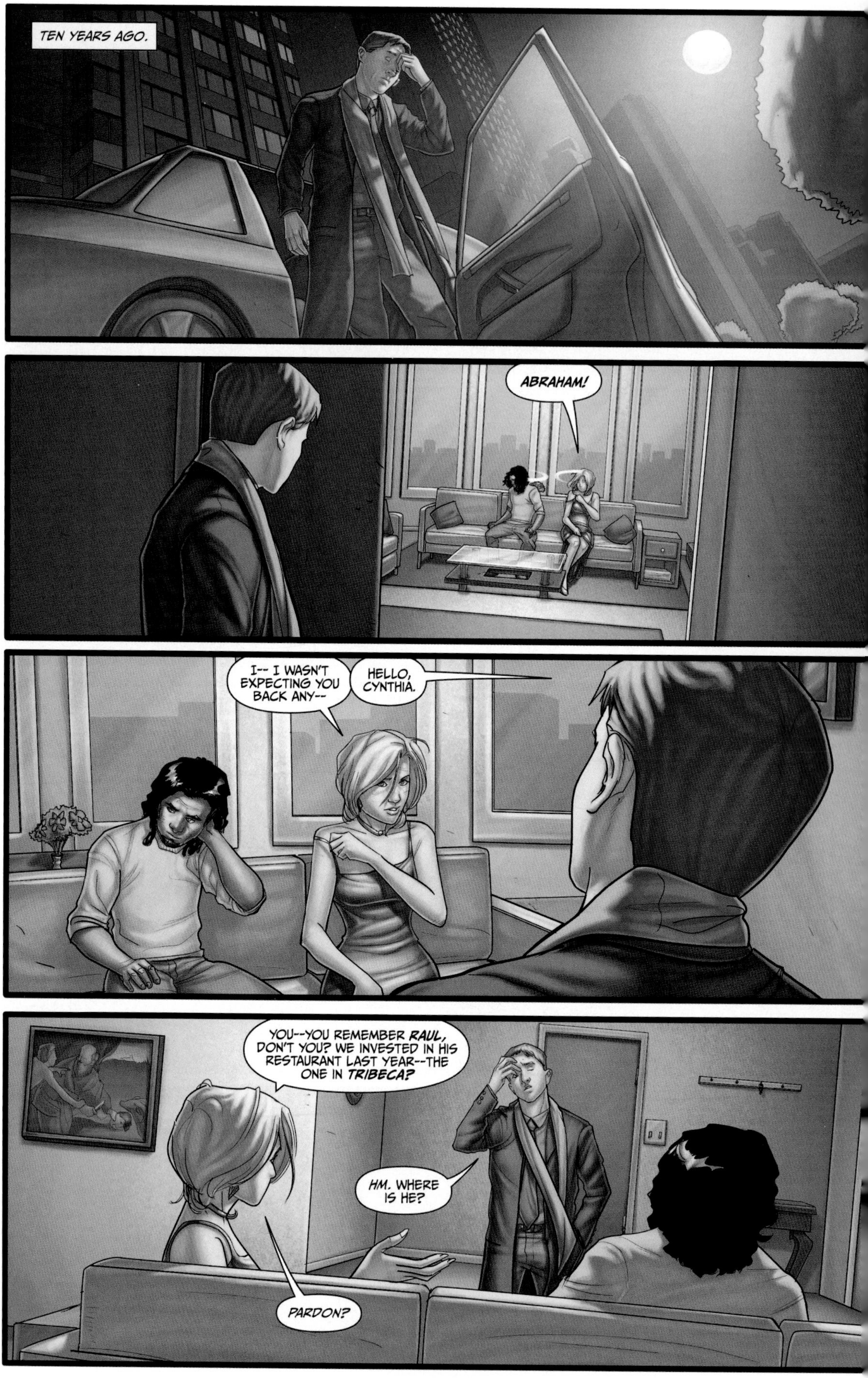

TEN YEARS AGO.
ABRAHAM!
I-- I WASN'T EXPECTING YOU BACK ANY--
HELLO, CYNTHIA.
YOU--YOU REMEMBER RAUL, DON'T YOU? WE INVESTED IN HIS RESTAURANT LAST YEAR--THE ONE IN TRIBECA?
HM. WHERE IS HE?
PARDON?

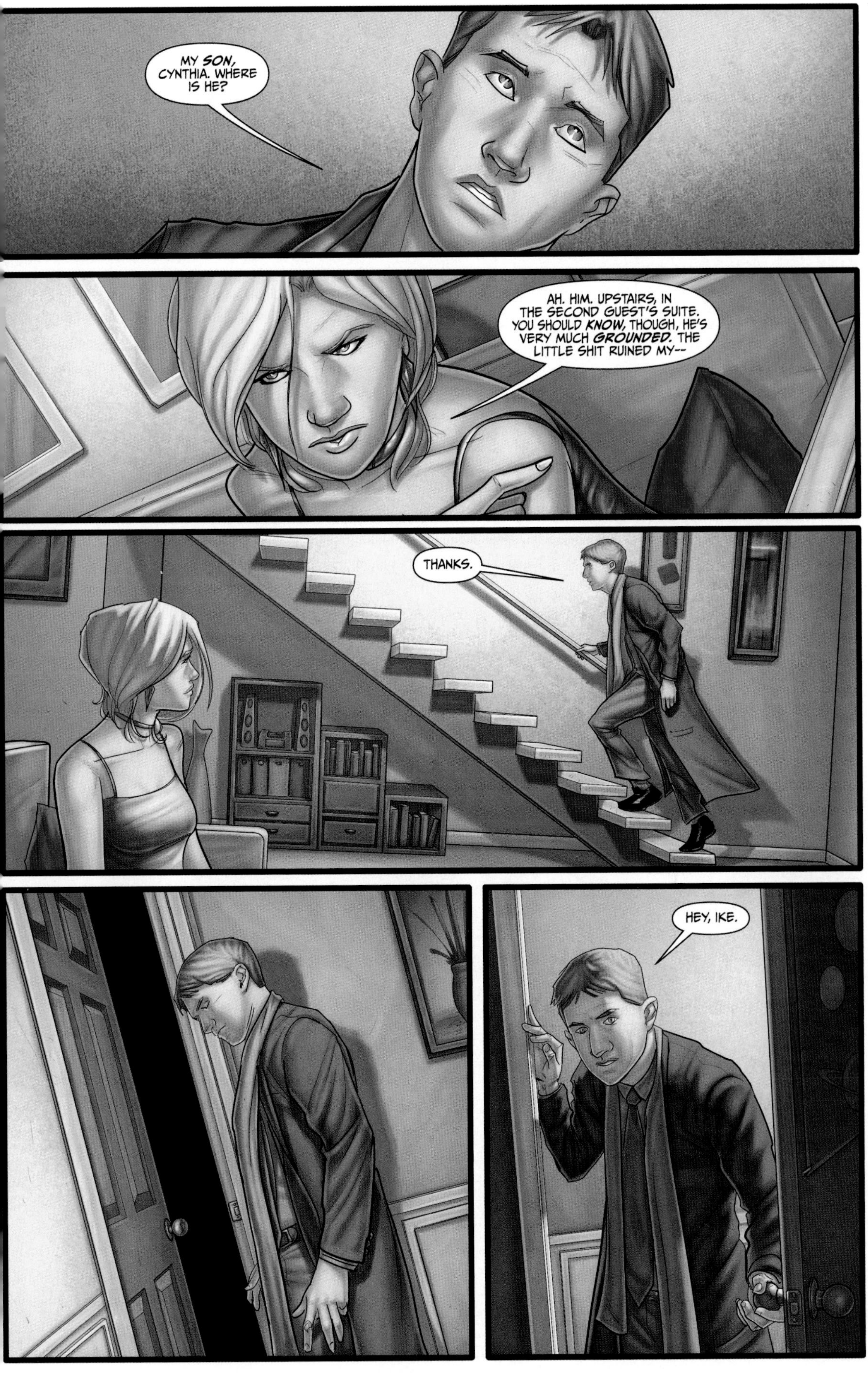

MY SON, CYNTHIA. WHERE IS HE?
AH. HIM. UPSTAIRS, IN THE SECOND GUEST'S SUITE. YOU SHOULD KNOW, THOUGH, HE'S VERY MUCH GROUNDED. THE LITTLE SHIT RUINED MY--
THANKS.
HEY, IKE.

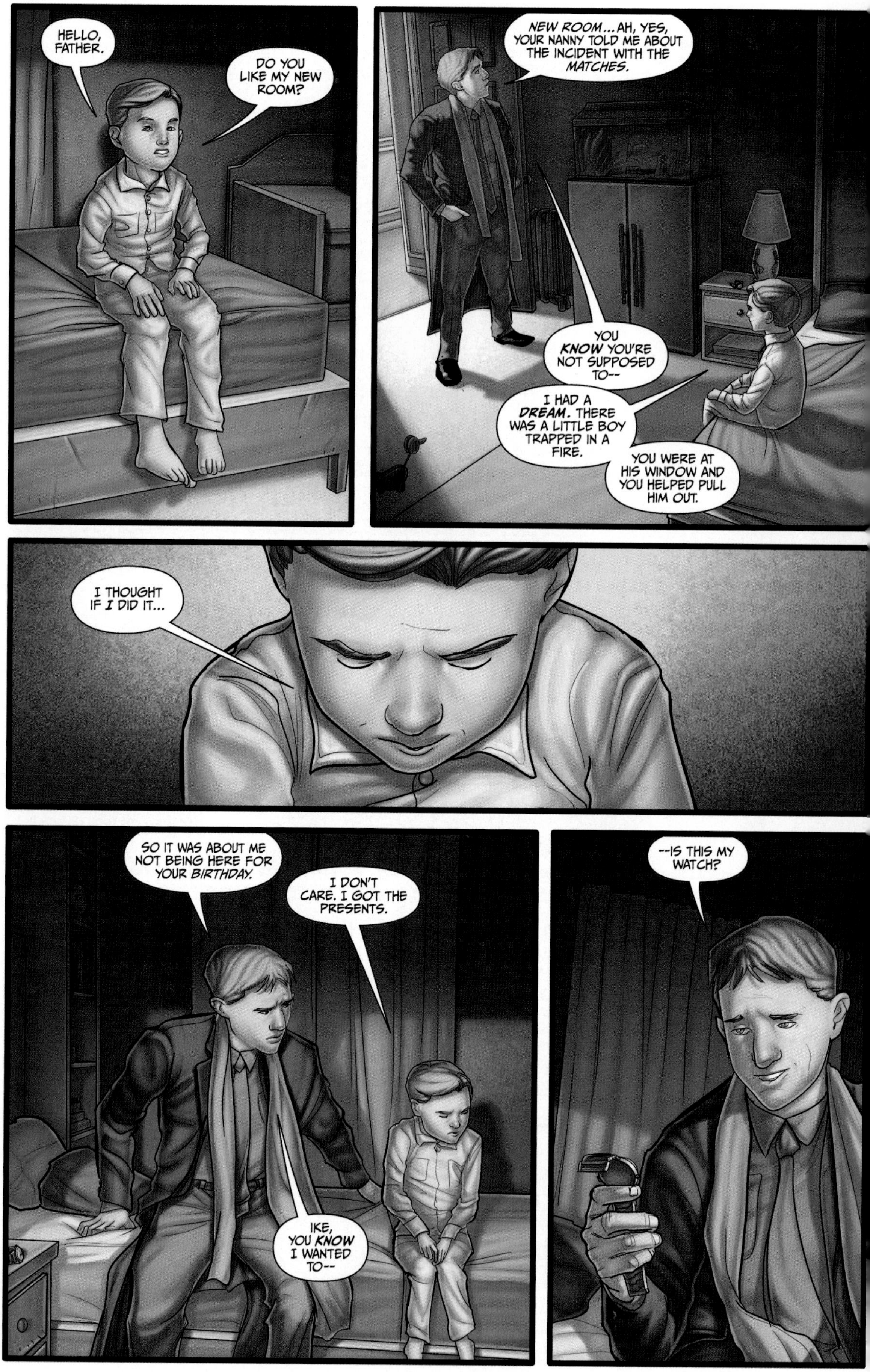

HELLO, FATHER.
DO YOU LIKE MY NEW ROOM?
NEW ROOM... AH, YES, YOUR NANNY TOLD ME ABOUT THE INCIDENT WITH THE MATCHES.
YOU KNOW YOU'RE NOT SUPPOSED TO--
I HAD A DREAM. THERE WAS A LITTLE BOY TRAPPED IN A FIRE.
YOU WERE AT HIS WINDOW AND YOU HELPED PULL HIM OUT.
I THOUGHT IF I DID IT...
SO IT WAS ABOUT ME NOT BEING HERE FOR YOUR BIRTHDAY.
I DON'T CARE. I GOT THE PRESENTS.
IKE, YOU KNOW I WANTED TO--
--IS THIS MY WATCH?

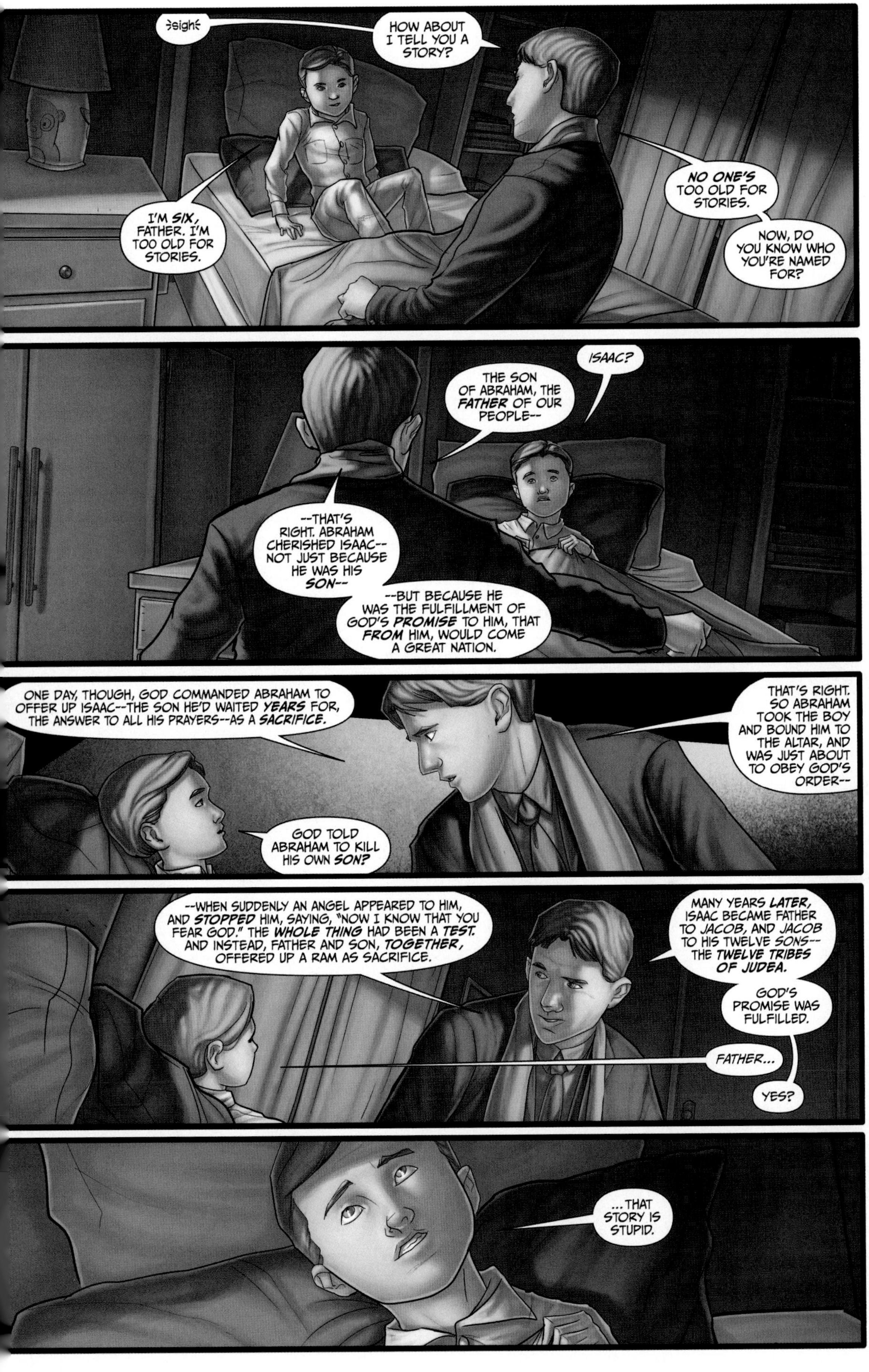

sigh
HOW ABOUT I TELL YOU A STORY?
I'M SIX, FATHER. I'M TOO OLD FOR STORIES.
NO ONE'S TOO OLD FOR STORIES.
NOW, DO YOU KNOW WHO YOU'RE NAMED FOR?
ISAAC?
THE SON OF ABRAHAM, THE FATHER OF OUR PEOPLE--
--THAT'S RIGHT. ABRAHAM CHERISHED ISAAC--NOT JUST BECAUSE HE WAS HIS SON--
--BUT BECAUSE HE WAS THE FULFILLMENT OF GOD'S PROMISE TO HIM, THAT FROM HIM, WOULD COME A GREAT NATION.
ONE DAY, THOUGH, GOD COMMANDED ABRAHAM TO OFFER UP ISAAC--THE SON HE'D WAITED YEARS FOR, THE ANSWER TO ALL HIS PRAYERS--AS A SACRIFICE.
GOD TOLD ABRAHAM TO KILL HIS OWN SON?
THAT'S RIGHT. SO ABRAHAM TOOK THE BOY AND BOUND HIM TO THE ALTAR, AND WAS JUST ABOUT TO OBEY GOD'S ORDER--
--WHEN SUDDENLY AN ANGEL APPEARED TO HIM, AND STOPPED HIM, SAYING, "NOW I KNOW THAT YOU FEAR GOD." THE WHOLE THING HAD BEEN A TEST. AND INSTEAD, FATHER AND SON, TOGETHER, OFFERED UP A RAM AS SACRIFICE.
MANY YEARS LATER, ISAAC BECAME FATHER TO JACOB, AND JACOB TO HIS TWELVE SONS--THE TWELVE TRIBES OF JUDEA.
GOD'S PROMISE WAS FULFILLED.
FATHER...
YES?
...THAT STORY IS STUPID.

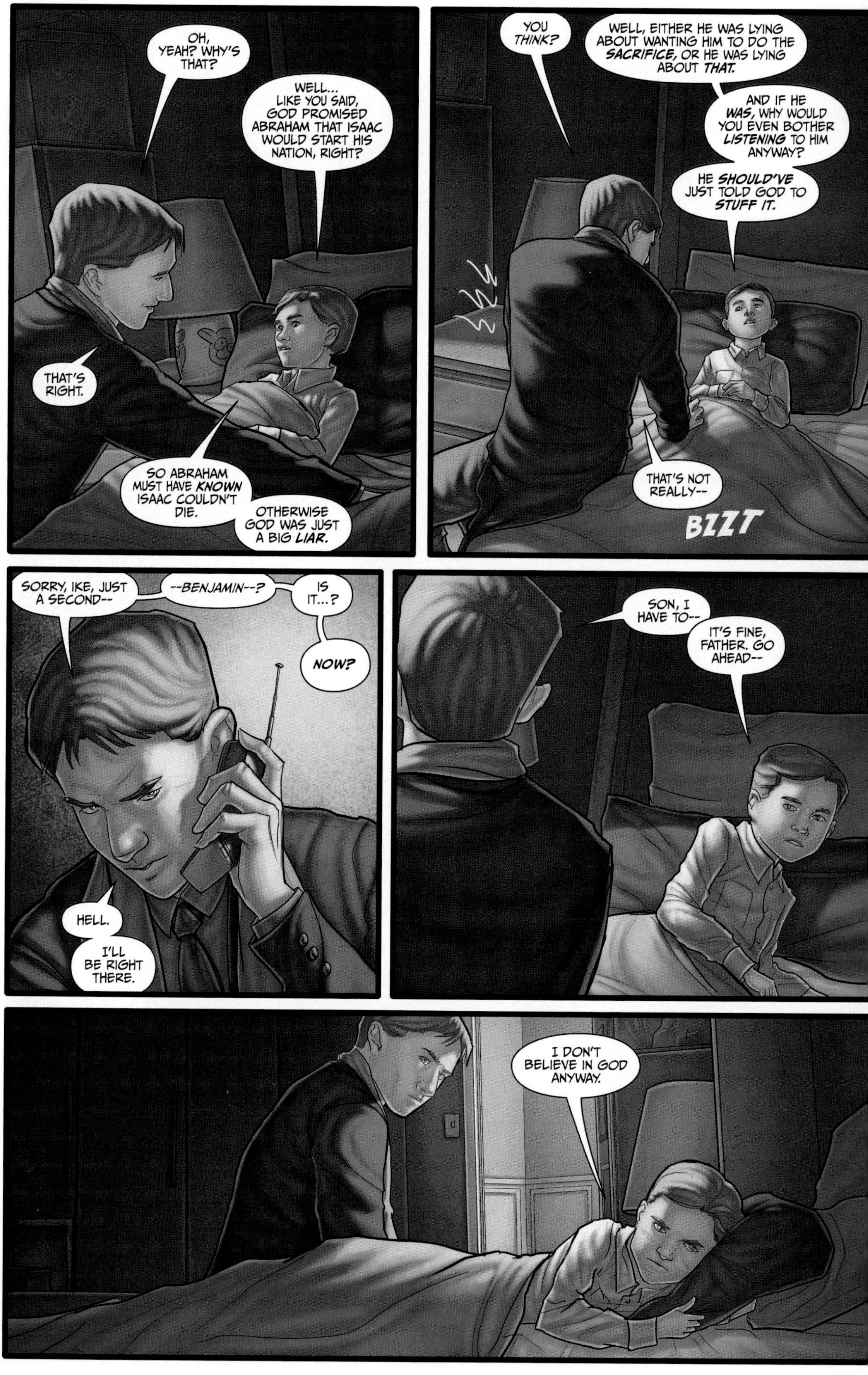
OH, YEAH? WHY'S THAT?
WELL... LIKE YOU SAID, GOD PROMISED ABRAHAM THAT ISAAC WOULD START HIS NATION, RIGHT?
THAT'S RIGHT.
SO ABRAHAM MUST HAVE KNOWN ISAAC COULDN'T DIE.
OTHERWISE GOD WAS JUST A BIG LIAR.
YOU THINK?
WELL, EITHER HE WAS LYING ABOUT WANTING HIM TO DO THE SACRIFICE, OR HE WAS LYING ABOUT THAT.
AND IF HE WAS, WHY WOULD YOU EVEN BOTHER LISTENING TO HIM ANYWAY?
HE SHOULD'VE JUST TOLD GOD TO STUFF IT.
THAT'S NOT REALLY--
BZZT
SORRY, IKE, JUST A SECOND--
--BENJAMIN--?
IS IT...?
NOW?
HELL.
I'LL BE RIGHT THERE.
SON, I HAVE TO--
IT'S FINE, FATHER. GO AHEAD--
I DON'T BELIEVE IN GOD ANYWAY.

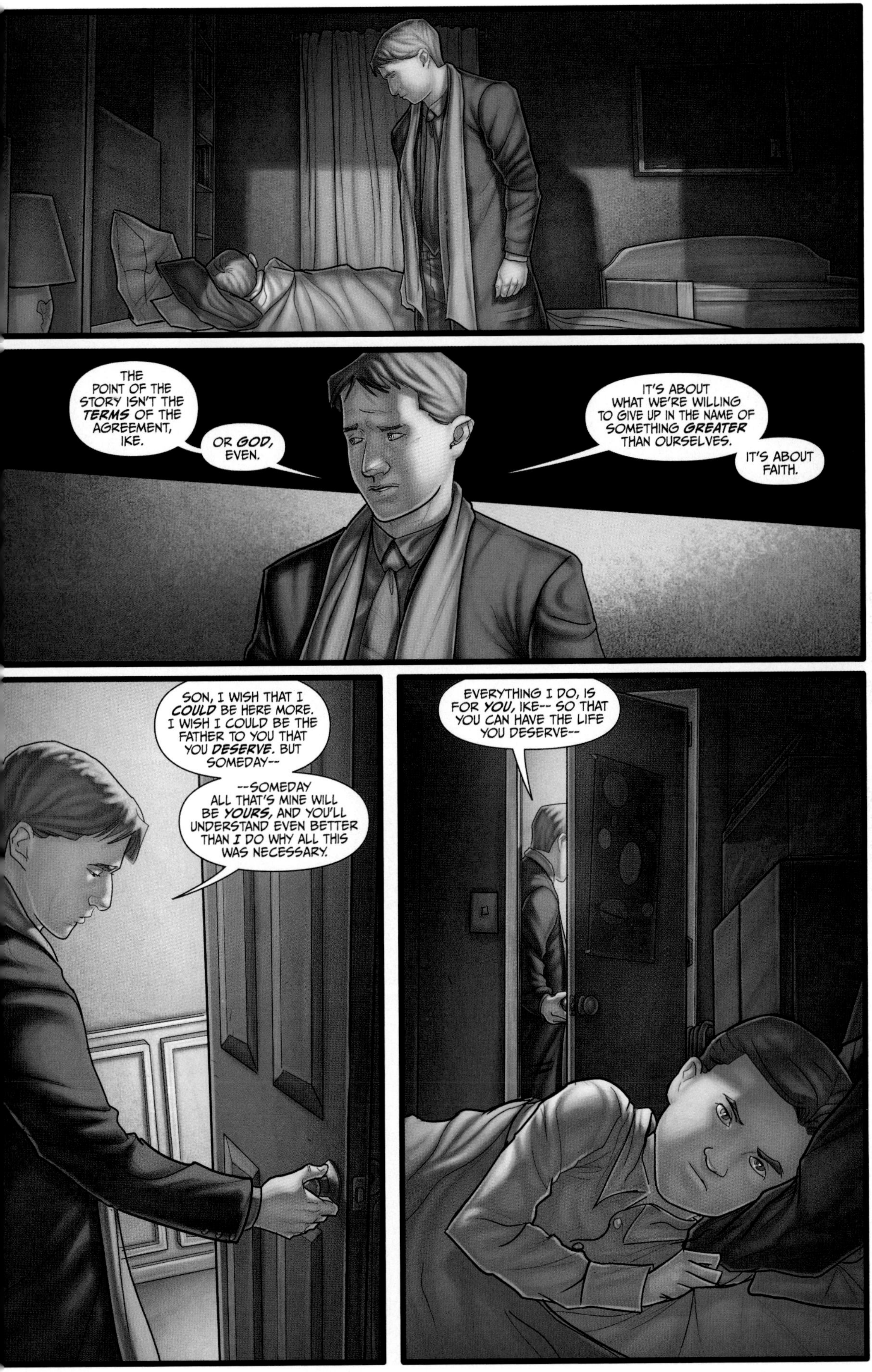
THE POINT OF THE STORY ISN'T THE TERMS OF THE AGREEMENT, IKE.
OR GOD, EVEN.
IT'S ABOUT WHAT WE'RE WILLING TO GIVE UP IN THE NAME OF SOMETHING GREATER THAN OURSELVES.
IT'S ABOUT FAITH.
SON, I WISH THAT I COULD BE HERE MORE. I WISH I COULD BE THE FATHER TO YOU THAT YOU DESERVE. BUT SOMEDAY--
--SOMEDAY ALL THAT'S MINE WILL BE YOURS, AND YOU'LL UNDERSTAND EVEN BETTER THAN I DO WHY ALL THIS WAS NECESSARY.
EVERYTHING I DO, IS FOR YOU, IKE-- SO THAT YOU CAN HAVE THE LIFE YOU DESERVE--

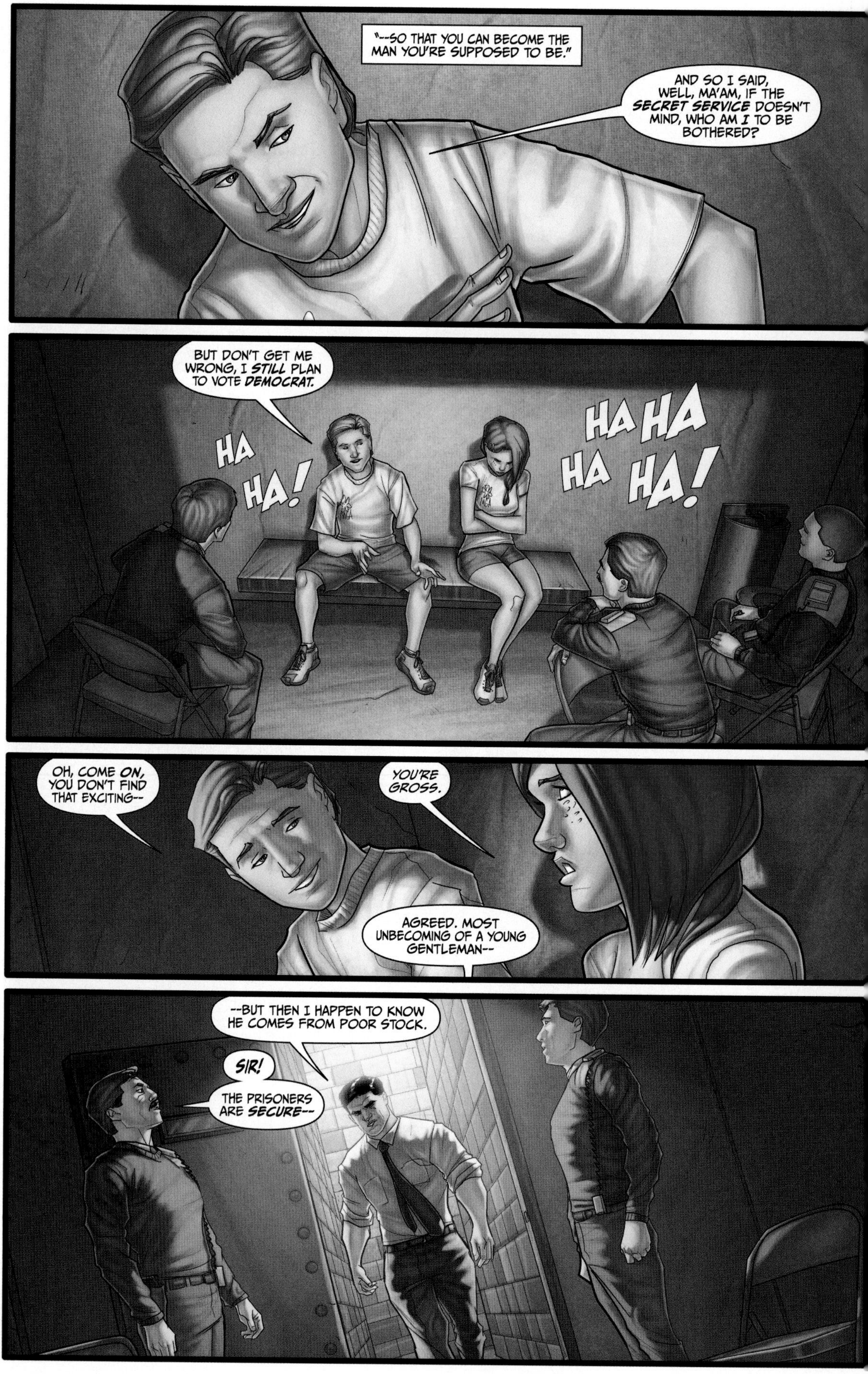
"--SO THAT YOU CAN BECOME THE MAN YOU'RE SUPPOSED TO BE."
AND SO I SAID, WELL, MA'AM, IF THE SECRET SERVICE DOESN'T MIND, WHO AM I TO BE BOTHERED?
BUT DON'T GET ME WRONG, I STILL PLAN TO VOTE DEMOCRAT.
HA HA!
HA HA HA HA!
OH, COME ON, YOU DON'T FIND THAT EXCITING--
YOU'RE GROSS.
AGREED. MOST UNBECOMING OF A YOUNG GENTLEMAN--
--BUT THEN I HAPPEN TO KNOW HE COMES FROM POOR STOCK.
SIR!
THE PRISONERS ARE SECURE--

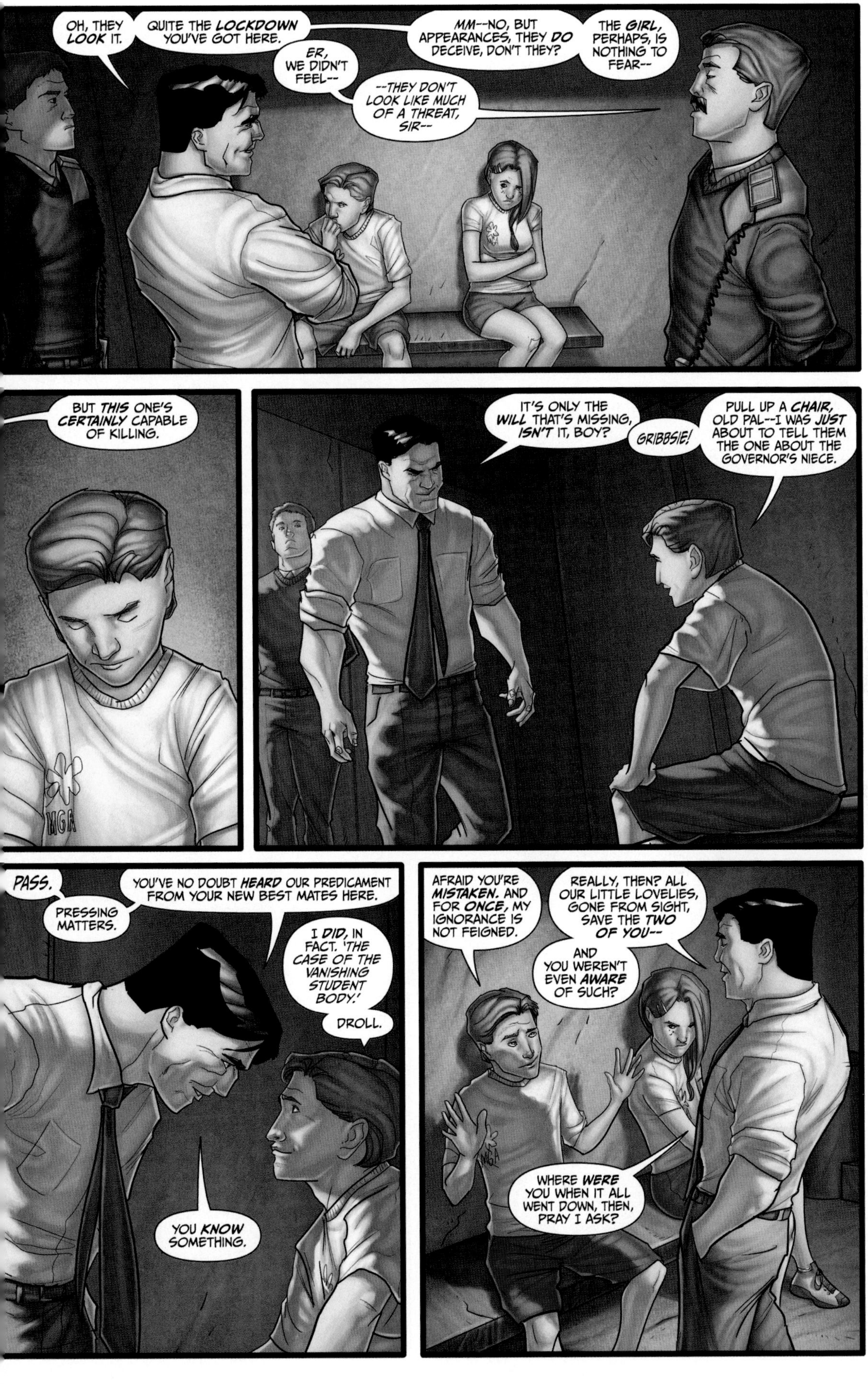

OH, THEY LOOK IT.
QUITE THE LOCKDOWN YOU'VE GOT HERE.
ER, WE DIDN'T FEEL--
--THEY DON'T LOOK LIKE MUCH OF A THREAT, SIR--
MM--NO, BUT APPEARANCES, THEY DO DECEIVE, DON'T THEY?
THE GIRL, PERHAPS, IS NOTHING TO FEAR--
BUT THIS ONE'S CERTAINLY CAPABLE OF KILLING.
MGA
IT'S ONLY THE WILL THAT'S MISSING, ISN'T IT, BOY?
GRIBBSIE!
PULL UP A CHAIR, OLD PAL--I WAS JUST ABOUT TO TELL THEM THE ONE ABOUT THE GOVERNOR'S NIECE.
PASS.
PRESSING MATTERS.
YOU'VE NO DOUBT HEARD OUR PREDICAMENT FROM YOUR NEW BEST MATES HERE.
I DID, IN FACT. 'THE CASE OF THE VANISHING STUDENT BODY.'
DROLL.
YOU KNOW SOMETHING.
AFRAID YOU'RE MISTAKEN. AND FOR ONCE, MY IGNORANCE IS NOT FEIGNED.
REALLY, THEN? ALL OUR LITTLE LOVELIES, GONE FROM SIGHT, SAVE THE TWO OF YOU--
AND YOU WEREN'T EVEN AWARE OF SUCH?
MGA
WHERE WERE YOU WHEN IT ALL WENT DOWN, THEN, PRAY I ASK?

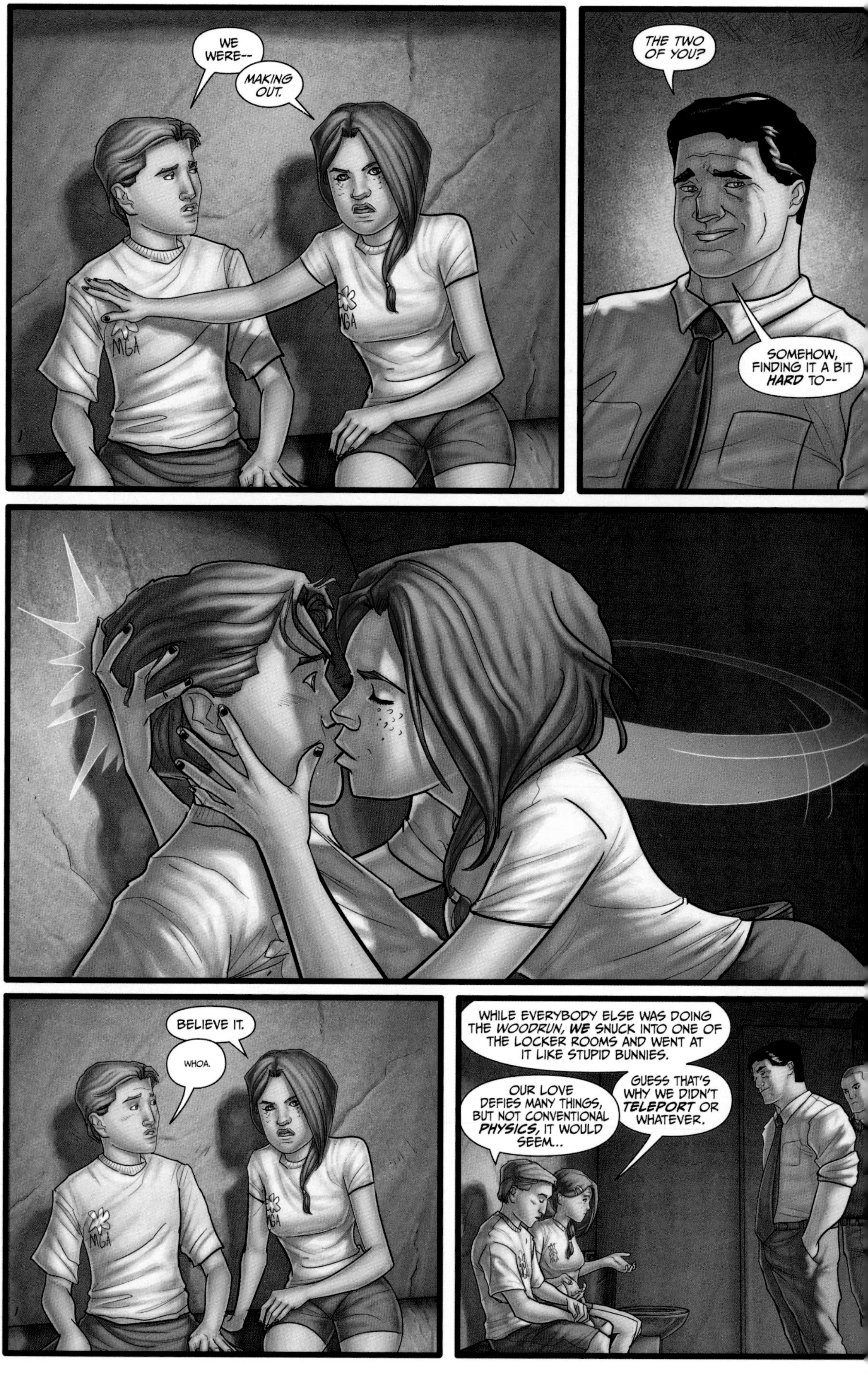
WE WERE--
MAKING OUT.
THE TWO OF YOU?
SOMEHOW, FINDING IT A BIT HARD TO--
BELIEVE IT.
WHOA.
WHILE EVERYBODY ELSE WAS DOING THE WOODRUN, WE SNUCK INTO ONE OF THE LOCKER ROOMS AND WENT AT IT LIKE STUPID BUNNIES.
OUR LOVE DEFIES MANY THINGS, BUT NOT CONVENTIONAL PHYSICS, IT WOULD SEEM...
GUESS THAT'S WHY WE DIDN'T TELEPORT OR WHATEVER.

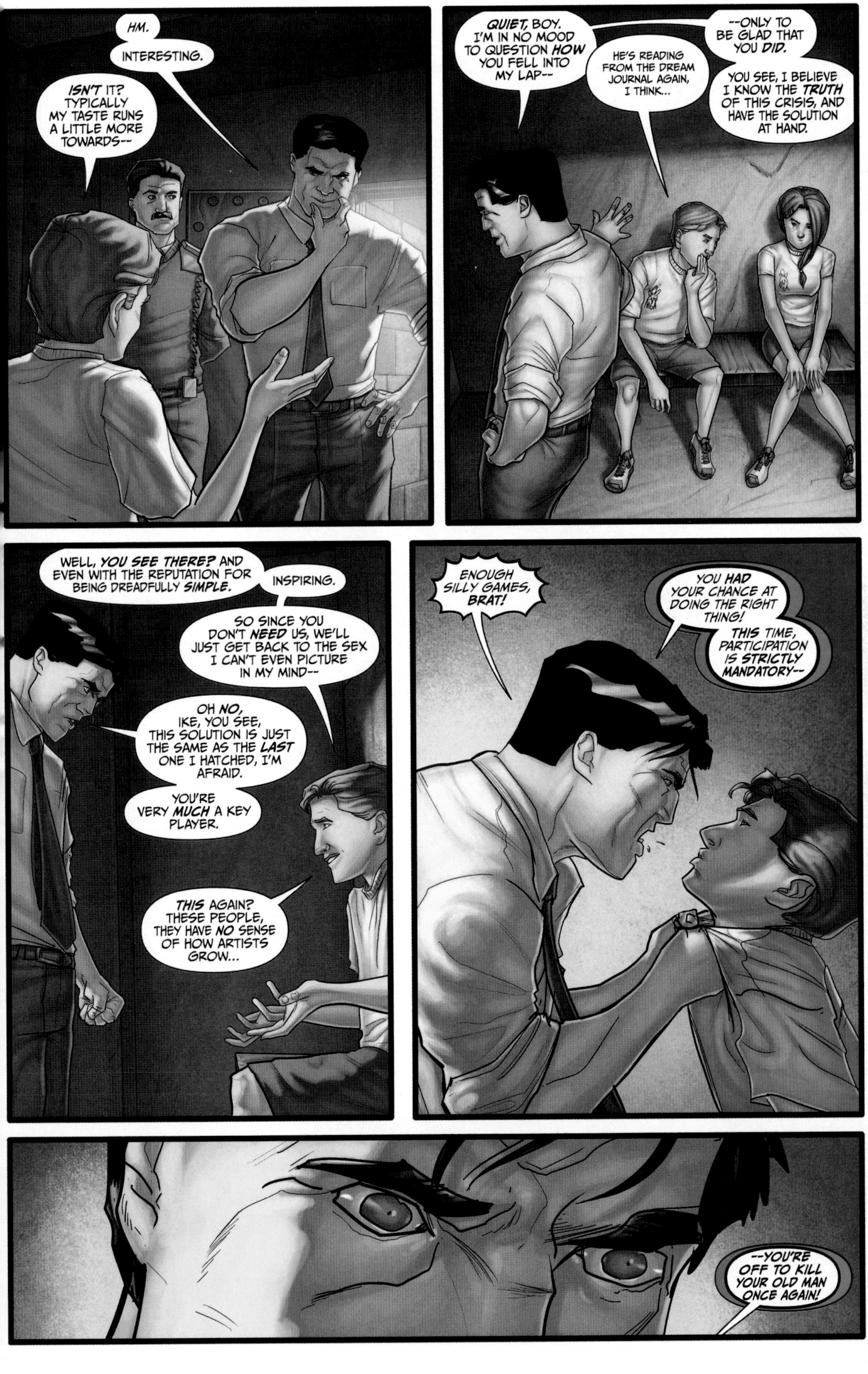
HM.
INTERESTING.
ISN'T IT? TYPICALLY MY TASTE RUNS A LITTLE MORE TOWARDS--
QUIET, BOY. I'M IN NO MOOD TO QUESTION HOW YOU FELL INTO MY LAP--
--ONLY TO BE GLAD THAT YOU DID.
HE'S READING FROM THE DREAM JOURNAL AGAIN, I THINK...
YOU SEE, I BELIEVE I KNOW THE TRUTH OF THIS CRISIS, AND HAVE THE SOLUTION AT HAND.
WELL, YOU SEE THERE? AND EVEN WITH THE REPUTATION FOR BEING DREADFULLY SIMPLE.
INSPIRING.
SO SINCE YOU DON'T NEED US, WE'LL JUST GET BACK TO THE SEX I CAN'T EVEN PICTURE IN MY MIND--
OH NO, IKE, YOU SEE, THIS SOLUTION IS JUST THE SAME AS THE LAST ONE I HATCHED, I'M AFRAID.
YOU'RE VERY MUCH A KEY PLAYER.
THIS AGAIN? THESE PEOPLE, THEY HAVE NO SENSE OF HOW ARTISTS GROW...
ENOUGH SILLY GAMES, BRAT!
YOU HAD YOUR CHANCE AT DOING THE RIGHT THING!
THIS TIME, PARTICIPATION IS STRICTLY MANDATORY--
--YOU'RE OFF TO KILL YOUR OLD MAN ONCE AGAIN!

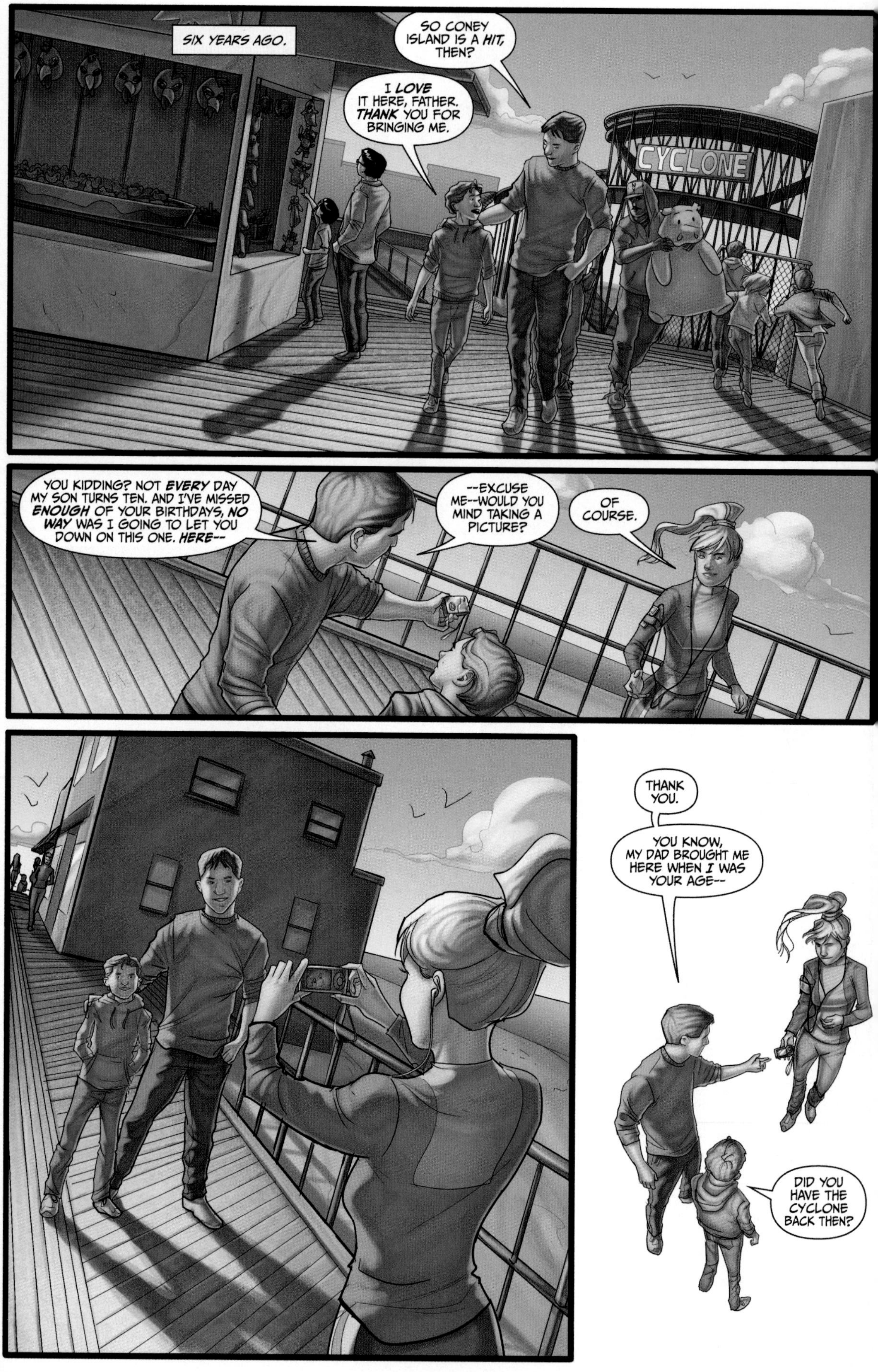

SIX YEARS AGO.
SO CONEY ISLAND IS A HIT, THEN?
I LOVE IT HERE, FATHER. THANK YOU FOR BRINGING ME.
CYCLONE
YOU KIDDING? NOT EVERY DAY MY SON TURNS TEN. AND I'VE MISSED ENOUGH OF YOUR BIRTHDAYS, NO WAY WAS I GOING TO LET YOU DOWN ON THIS ONE. HERE--
--EXCUSE ME--WOULD YOU MIND TAKING A PICTURE?
OF COURSE.
THANK YOU.
YOU KNOW, MY DAD BROUGHT ME HERE WHEN I WAS YOUR AGE--
DID YOU HAVE THE CYCLONE BACK THEN?

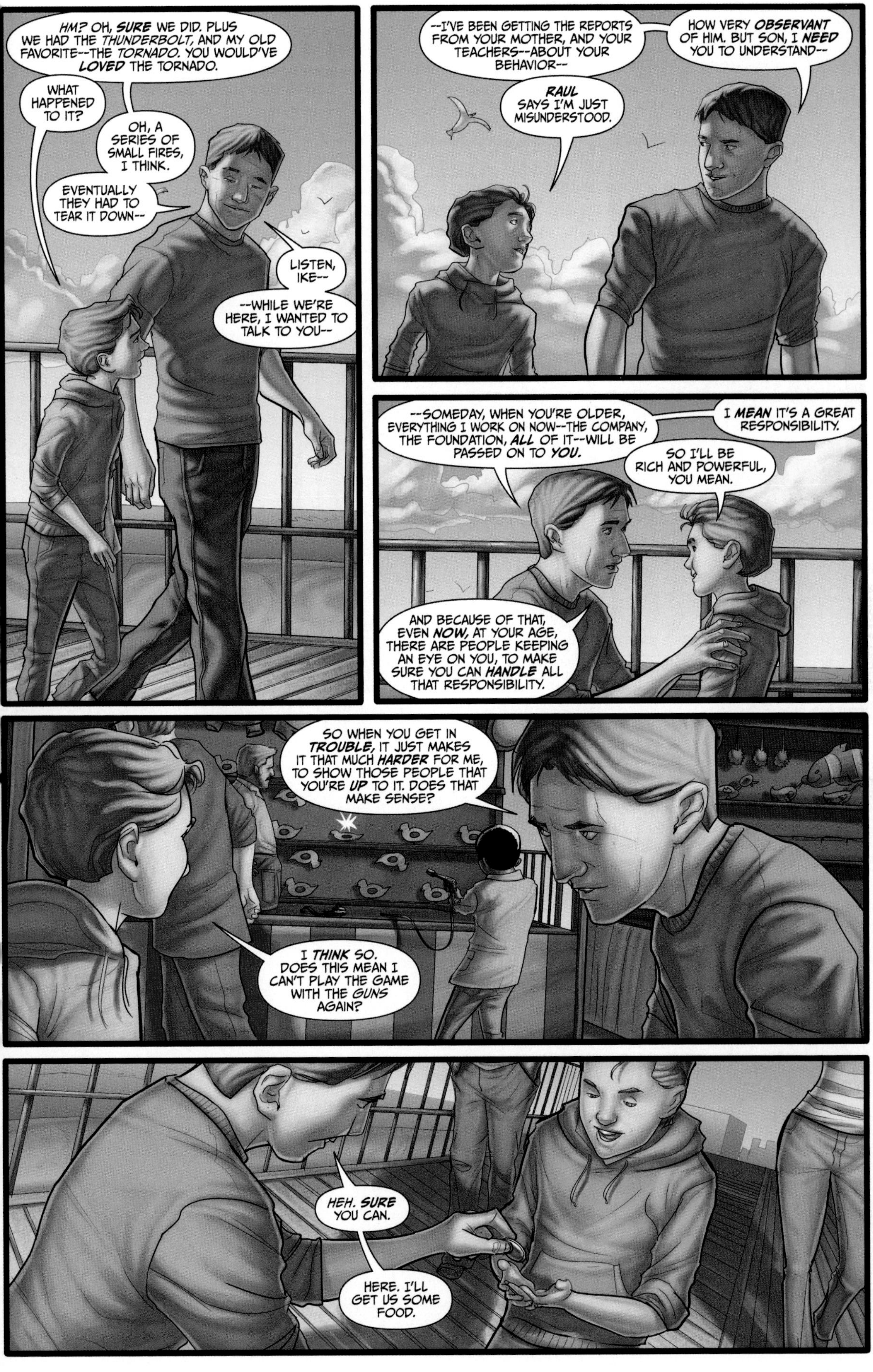
HM? OH, SURE WE DID. PLUS WE HAD THE THUNDERBOLT, AND MY OLD FAVORITE--THE TORNADO. YOU WOULD'VE LOVED THE TORNADO.
WHAT HAPPENED TO IT?
OH, A SERIES OF SMALL FIRES, I THINK.
EVENTUALLY THEY HAD TO TEAR IT DOWN--
LISTEN, IKE--
--WHILE WE'RE HERE, I WANTED TO TALK TO YOU--
--I'VE BEEN GETTING THE REPORTS FROM YOUR MOTHER, AND YOUR TEACHERS--ABOUT YOUR BEHAVIOR--
RAUL SAYS I'M JUST MISUNDERSTOOD.
HOW VERY OBSERVANT OF HIM. BUT SON, I NEED YOU TO UNDERSTAND--
--SOMEDAY, WHEN YOU'RE OLDER, EVERYTHING I WORK ON NOW--THE COMPANY, THE FOUNDATION, ALL OF IT--WILL BE PASSED ON TO YOU.
SO I'LL BE RICH AND POWERFUL, YOU MEAN.
I MEAN IT'S A GREAT RESPONSIBILITY.
AND BECAUSE OF THAT, EVEN NOW, AT YOUR AGE, THERE ARE PEOPLE KEEPING AN EYE ON YOU, TO MAKE SURE YOU CAN HANDLE ALL THAT RESPONSIBILITY.
SO WHEN YOU GET IN TROUBLE, IT JUST MAKES IT THAT MUCH HARDER FOR ME, TO SHOW THOSE PEOPLE THAT YOU'RE UP TO IT. DOES THAT MAKE SENSE?
I THINK SO. DOES THIS MEAN I CAN'T PLAY THE GAME WITH THE GUNS AGAIN?
HEH. SURE YOU CAN.
HERE. I'LL GET US SOME FOOD.

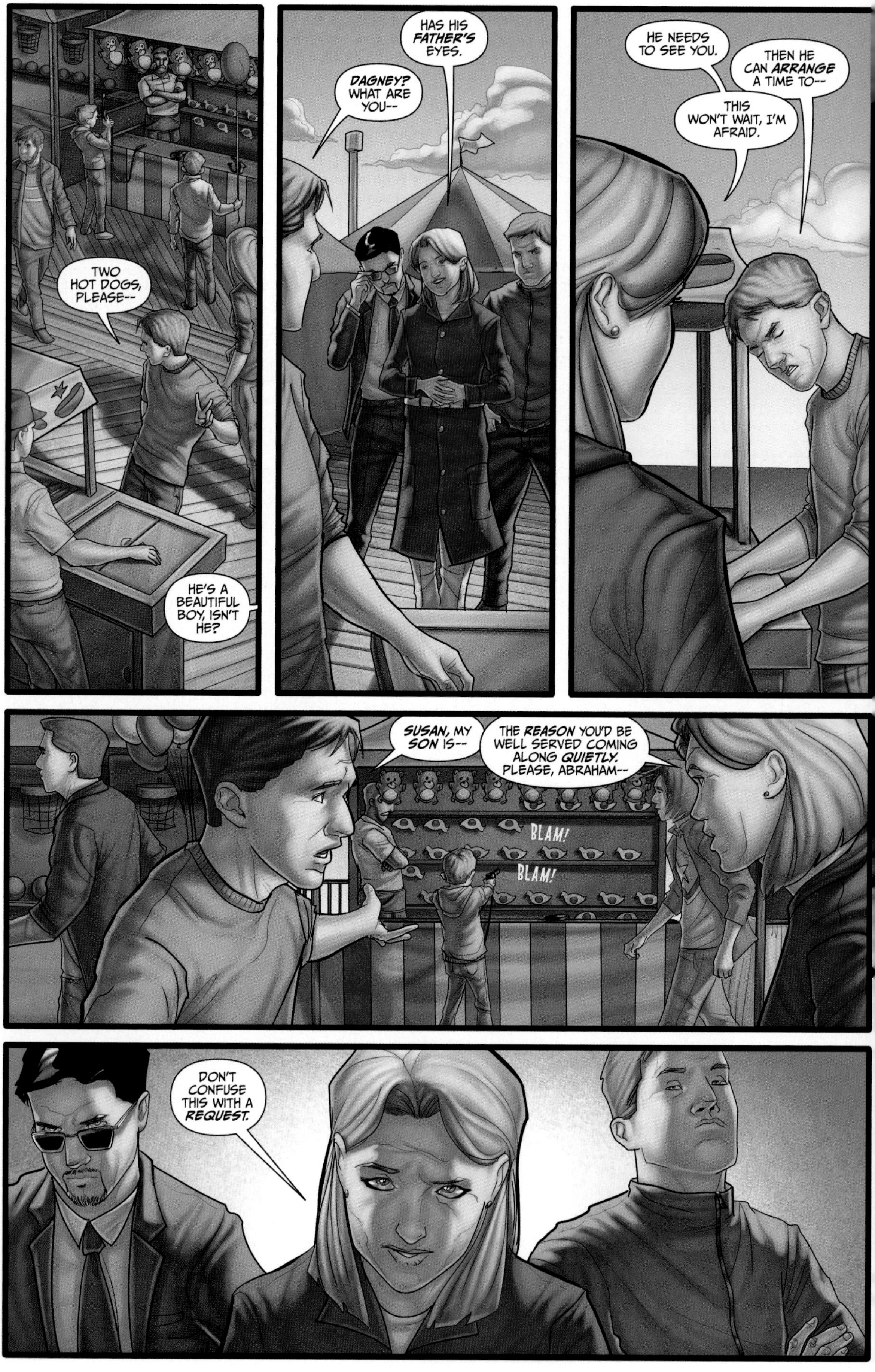
TWO HOT DOGS, PLEASE--
HE'S A BEAUTIFUL BOY, ISN'T HE?
DAGNEY? WHAT ARE YOU--
HAS HIS FATHER'S EYES.
HE NEEDS TO SEE YOU.
THEN HE CAN ARRANGE A TIME TO--
THIS WON'T WAIT, I'M AFRAID.
SUSAN, MY SON IS--
THE REASON YOU'D BE WELL SERVED COMING ALONG QUIETLY. PLEASE, ABRAHAM--
BLAM!
BLAM!
DON'T CONFUSE THIS WITH A REQUEST.

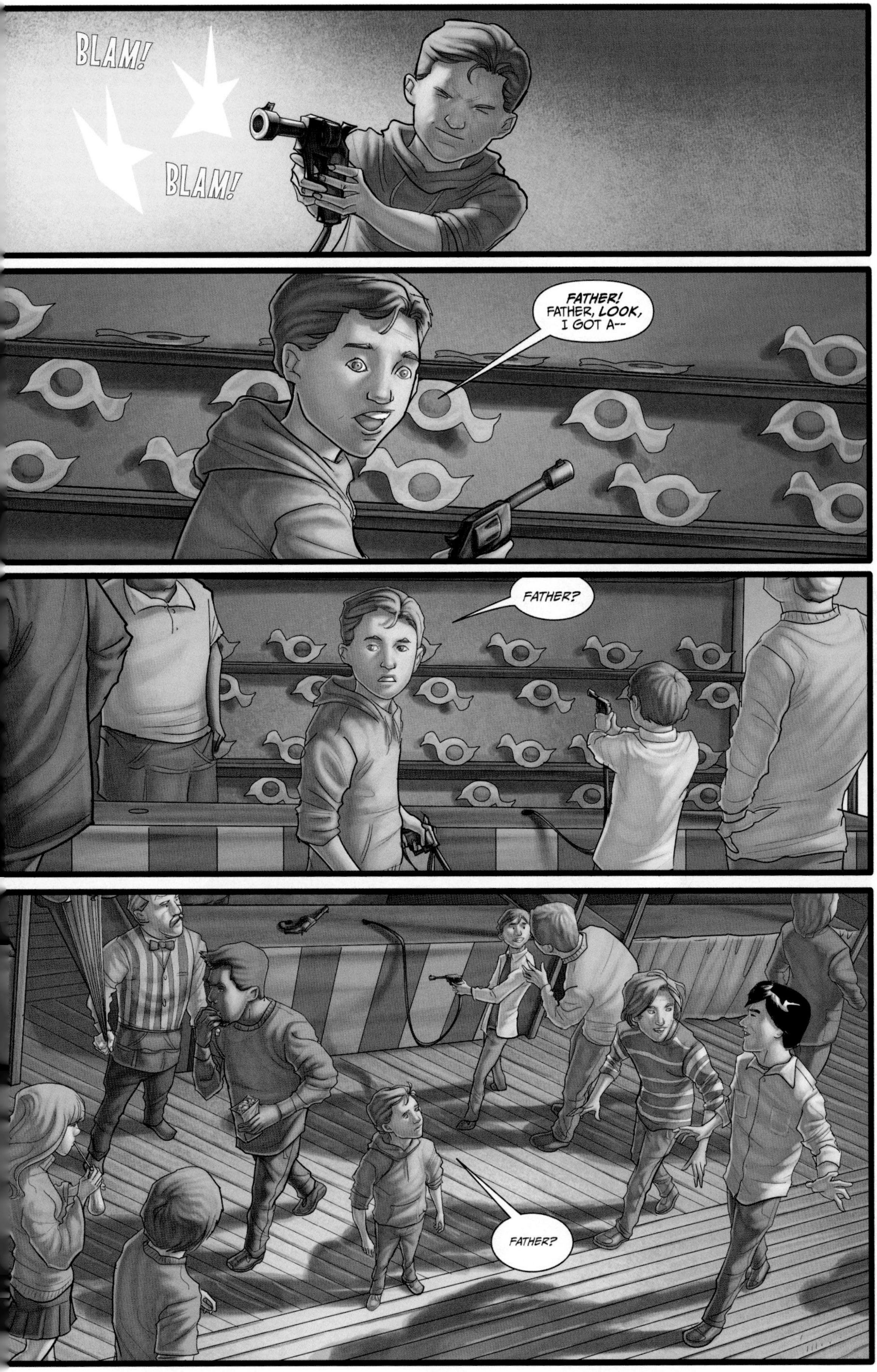
BLAM!
BLAM!
FATHER! FATHER, LOOK, I GOT A--
FATHER?
FATHER?

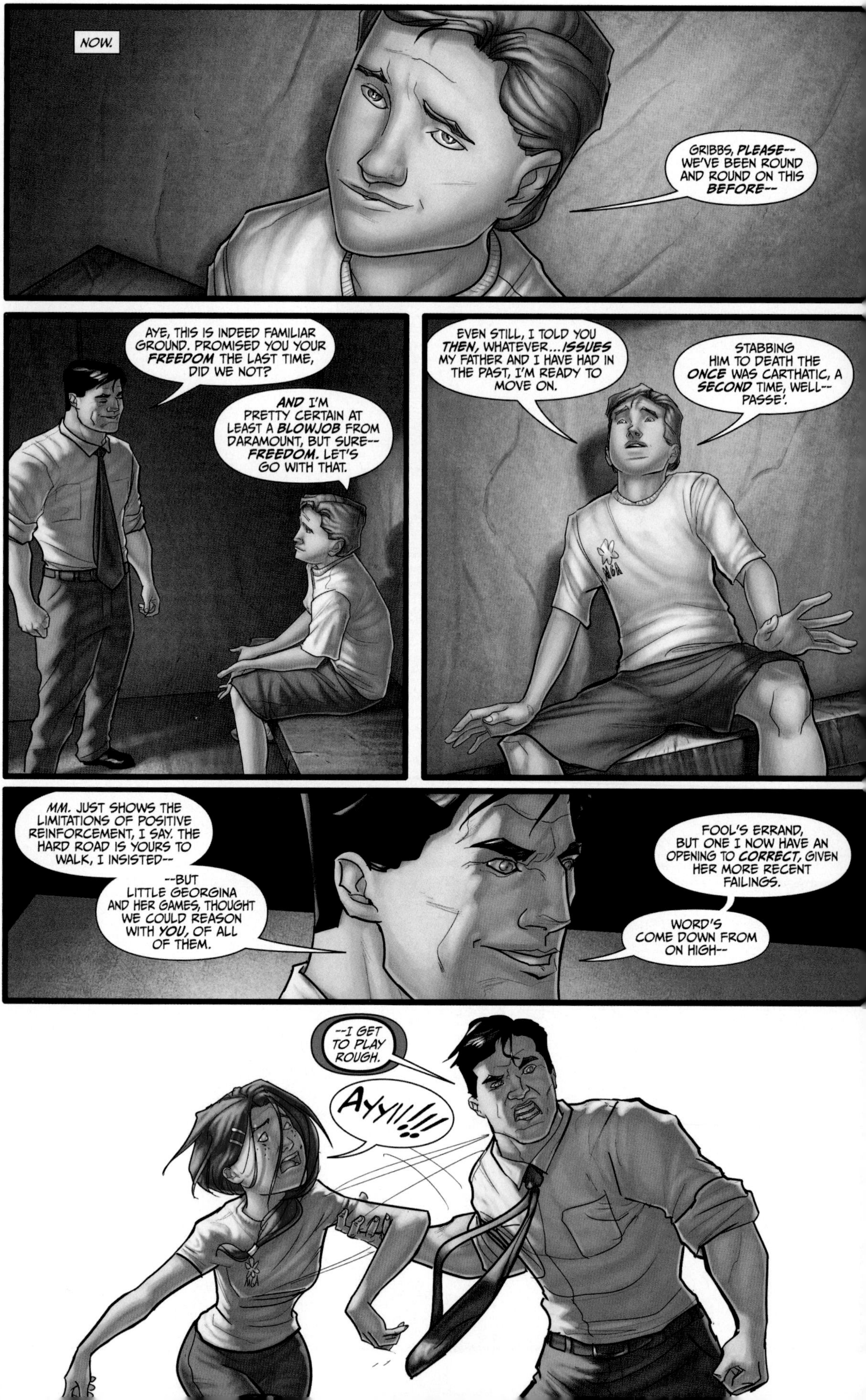
NOW.
GRIBBS, PLEASE-- WE'VE BEEN ROUND AND ROUND ON THIS BEFORE--
AYE, THIS IS INDEED FAMILIAR GROUND. PROMISED YOU YOUR FREEDOM THE LAST TIME, DID WE NOT?
AND I'M PRETTY CERTAIN AT LEAST A BLOWJOB FROM DARAMOUNT, BUT SURE-- FREEDOM. LET'S GO WITH THAT.
EVEN STILL, I TOLD YOU THEN, WHATEVER...ISSUES MY FATHER AND I HAVE HAD IN THE PAST, I'M READY TO MOVE ON.
STABBING HIM TO DEATH THE ONCE WAS CARTHATIC, A SECOND TIME, WELL-- PASSE'.
MM. JUST SHOWS THE LIMITATIONS OF POSITIVE REINFORCEMENT, I SAY. THE HARD ROAD IS YOURS TO WALK, I INSISTED--
--BUT LITTLE GEORGINA AND HER GAMES, THOUGHT WE COULD REASON WITH YOU, OF ALL OF THEM.
FOOL'S ERRAND, BUT ONE I NOW HAVE AN OPENING TO CORRECT, GIVEN HER MORE RECENT FAILINGS.
WORD'S COME DOWN FROM ON HIGH--
--I GET TO PLAY ROUGH.
AYY!!!!!!

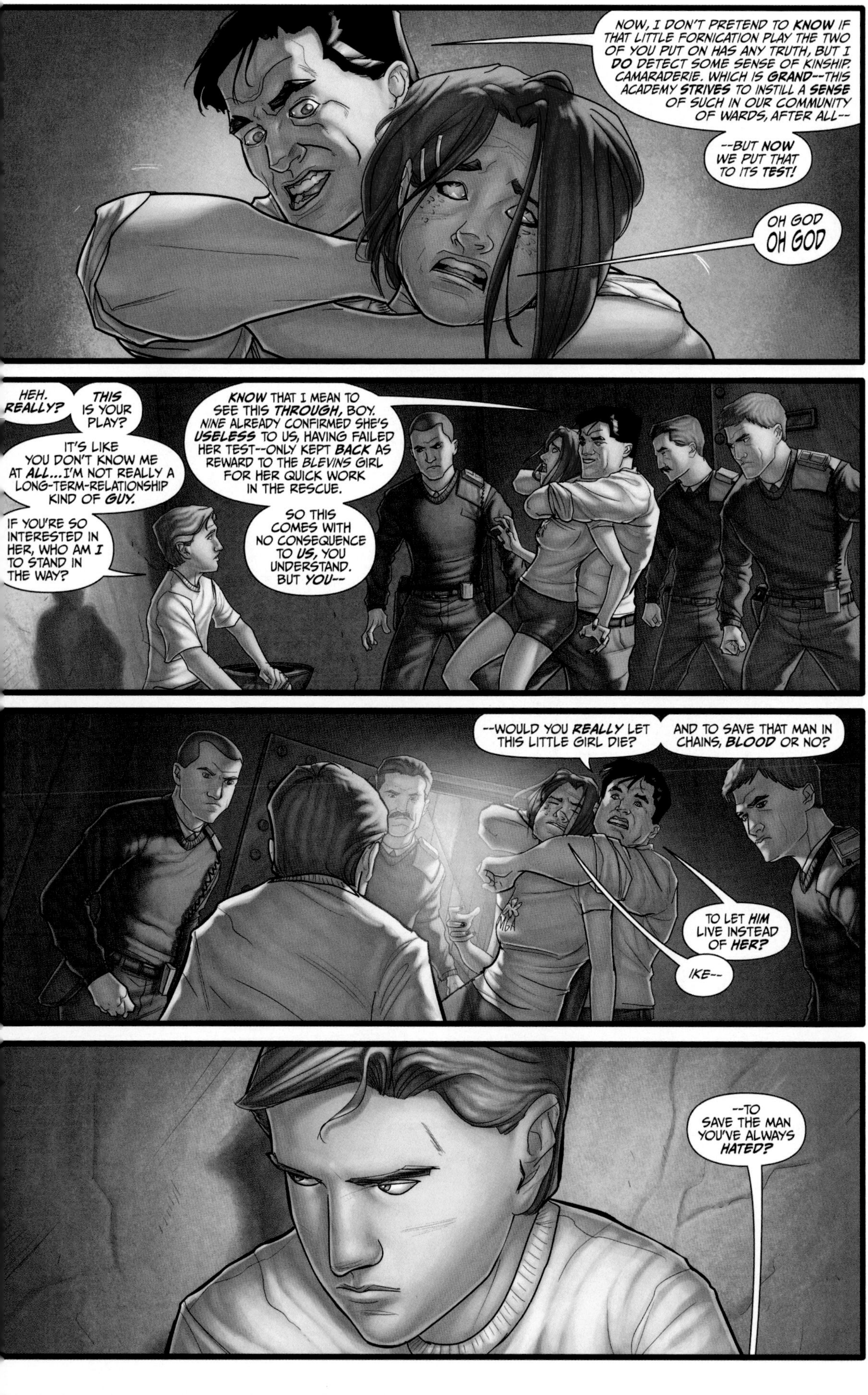
NOW, I DON'T PRETEND TO KNOW IF THAT LITTLE FORNICATION PLAY THE TWO OF YOU PUT ON HAS ANY TRUTH, BUT I DO DETECT SOME SENSE OF KINSHIP. CAMARADERIE. WHICH IS GRAND--THIS ACADEMY STRIVES TO INSTILL A SENSE OF SUCH IN OUR COMMUNITY OF WARDS, AFTER ALL--
--BUT NOW WE PUT THAT TO ITS TEST!
OH GOD OH GOD
HEH. REALLY?
THIS IS YOUR PLAY?
IT'S LIKE YOU DON'T KNOW ME AT ALL... I'M NOT REALLY A LONG-TERM-RELATIONSHIP KIND OF GUY.
IF YOU'RE SO INTERESTED IN HER, WHO AM I TO STAND IN THE WAY?
KNOW THAT I MEAN TO SEE THIS THROUGH, BOY. NINE ALREADY CONFIRMED SHE'S USELESS TO US, HAVING FAILED HER TEST--ONLY KEPT BACK AS REWARD TO THE BLEVINS GIRL FOR HER QUICK WORK IN THE RESCUE.
SO THIS COMES WITH NO CONSEQUENCE TO US, YOU UNDERSTAND. BUT YOU--
--WOULD YOU REALLY LET THIS LITTLE GIRL DIE?
AND TO SAVE THAT MAN IN CHAINS, BLOOD OR NO?
TO LET HIM LIVE INSTEAD OF HER?
IKE--
--TO SAVE THE MAN YOU'VE ALWAYS HATED?

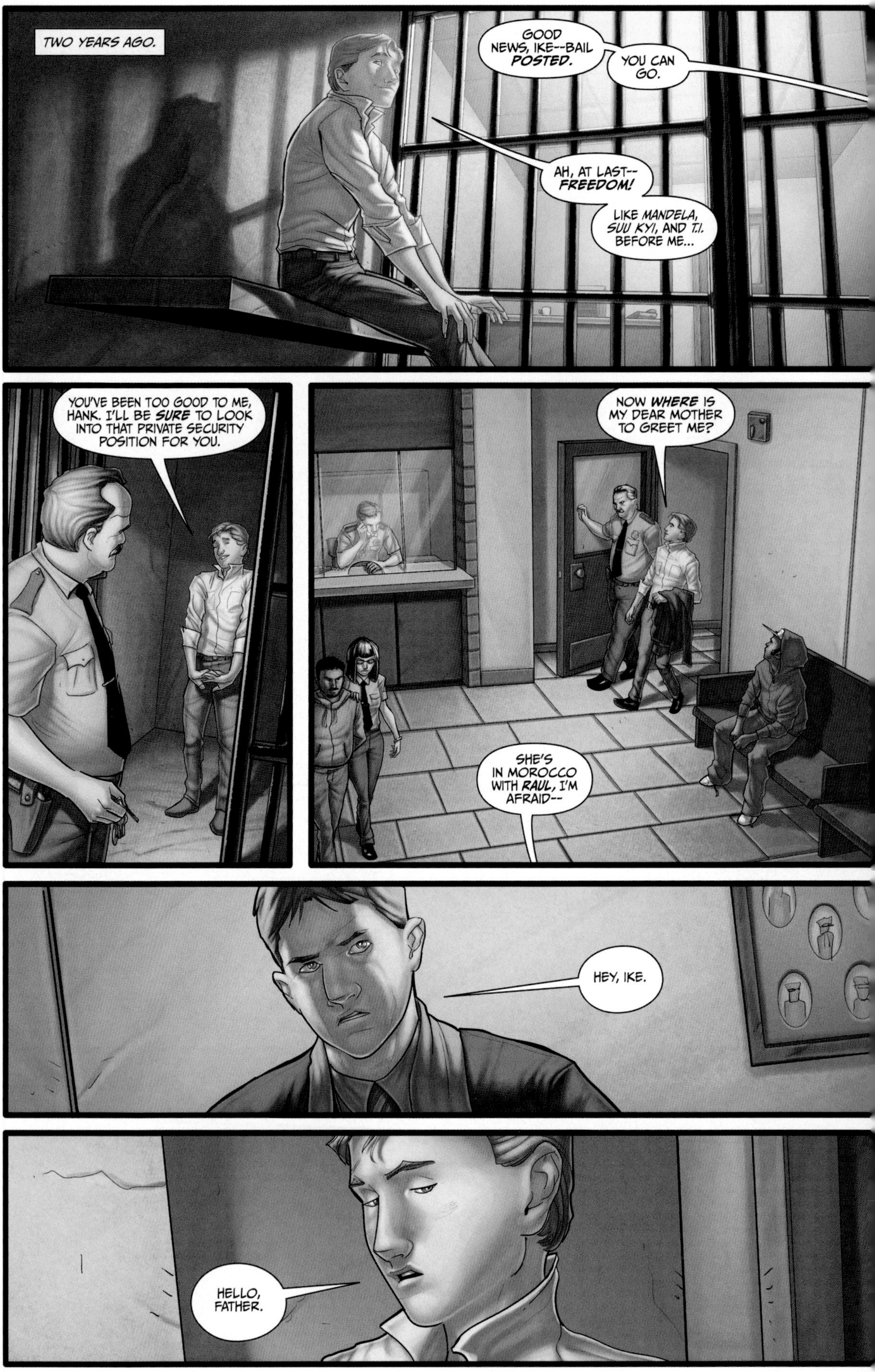

TWO YEARS AGO.
GOOD NEWS, IKE--BAIL POSTED.
YOU CAN GO.
AH, AT LAST-- FREEDOM!
LIKE MANDELA, SUU KYI, AND T.I. BEFORE ME...
YOU'VE BEEN TOO GOOD TO ME, HANK. I'LL BE SURE TO LOOK INTO THAT PRIVATE SECURITY POSITION FOR YOU.
NOW WHERE IS MY DEAR MOTHER TO GREET ME?
SHE'S IN MOROCCO WITH RAUL, I'M AFRAID--
HEY, IKE.
HELLO, FATHER.

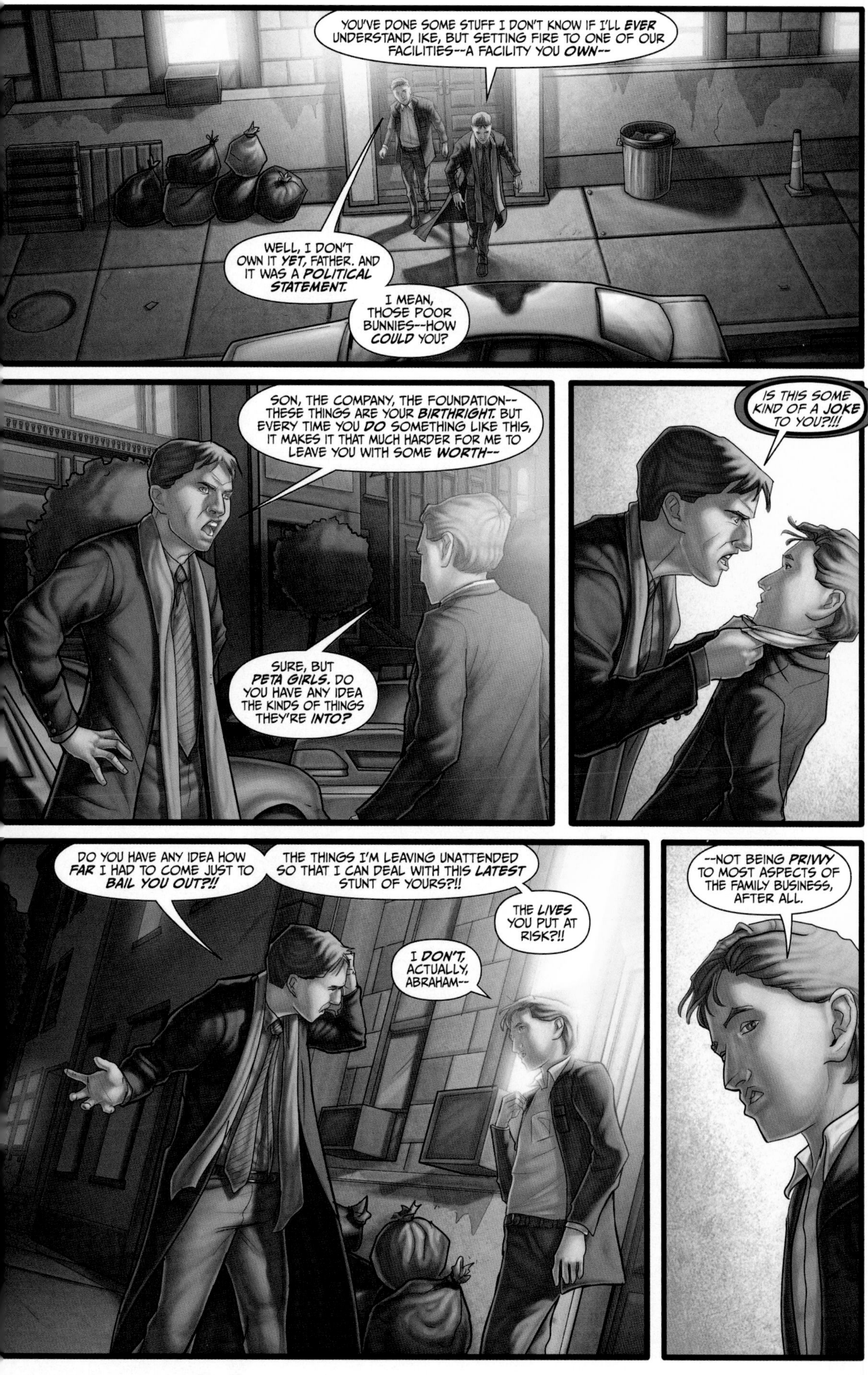
YOU'VE DONE SOME STUFF I DON'T KNOW IF I'LL EVER UNDERSTAND, IKE, BUT SETTING FIRE TO ONE OF OUR FACILITIES--A FACILITY YOU OWN--
WELL, I DON'T OWN IT YET, FATHER. AND IT WAS A POLITICAL STATEMENT.
I MEAN, THOSE POOR BUNNIES--HOW COULD YOU?
SON, THE COMPANY, THE FOUNDATION--THESE THINGS ARE YOUR BIRTHRIGHT. BUT EVERY TIME YOU DO SOMETHING LIKE THIS, IT MAKES IT THAT MUCH HARDER FOR ME TO LEAVE YOU WITH SOME WORTH--
SURE, BUT PETA GIRLS. DO YOU HAVE ANY IDEA THE KINDS OF THINGS THEY'RE INTO?
IS THIS SOME KIND OF A JOKE TO YOU?!!!
DO YOU HAVE ANY IDEA HOW FAR I HAD TO COME JUST TO BAIL YOU OUT?!!
THE THINGS I'M LEAVING UNATTENDED SO THAT I CAN DEAL WITH THIS LATEST STUNT OF YOURS?!!
THE LIVES YOU PUT AT RISK?!!
I DON'T, ACTUALLY, ABRAHAM--
--NOT BEING PRIVVY TO MOST ASPECTS OF THE FAMILY BUSINESS, AFTER ALL.

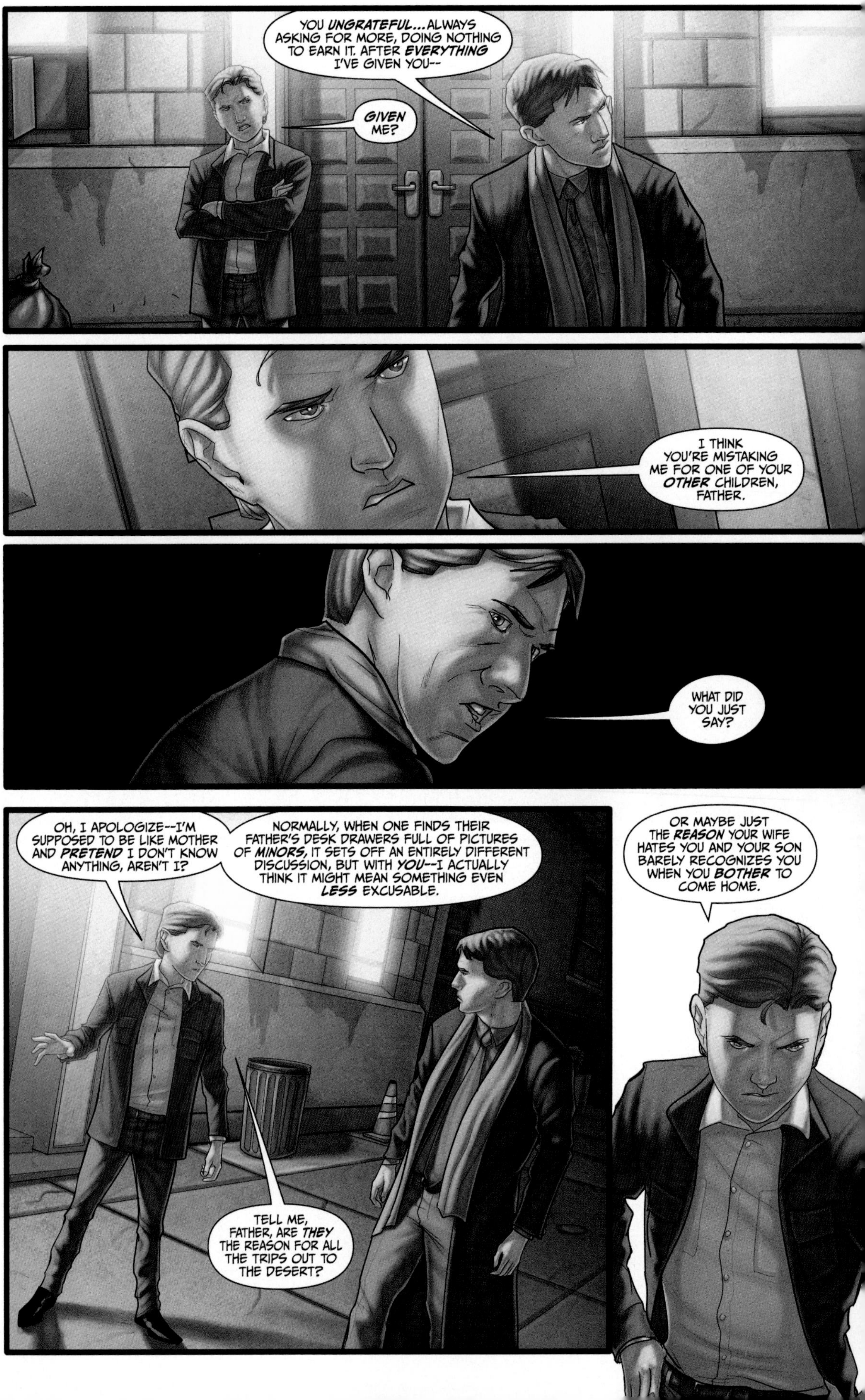

YOU UNGRATEFUL... ALWAYS ASKING FOR MORE, DOING NOTHING TO EARN IT. AFTER EVERYTHING I'VE GIVEN YOU--
GIVEN ME?
I THINK YOU'RE MISTAKING ME FOR ONE OF YOUR OTHER CHILDREN, FATHER.
WHAT DID YOU JUST SAY?
OH, I APOLOGIZE--I'M SUPPOSED TO BE LIKE MOTHER AND PRETEND I DON'T KNOW ANYTHING, AREN'T I?
NORMALLY, WHEN ONE FINDS THEIR FATHER'S DESK DRAWERS FULL OF PICTURES OF MINORS, IT SETS OFF AN ENTIRELY DIFFERENT DISCUSSION, BUT WITH YOU--I ACTUALLY THINK IT MIGHT MEAN SOMETHING EVEN LESS EXCUSABLE.
TELL ME, FATHER, ARE THEY THE REASON FOR ALL THE TRIPS OUT TO THE DESERT?
OR MAYBE JUST THE REASON YOUR WIFE HATES YOU AND YOUR SON BARELY RECOGNIZES YOU WHEN YOU BOTHER TO COME HOME.

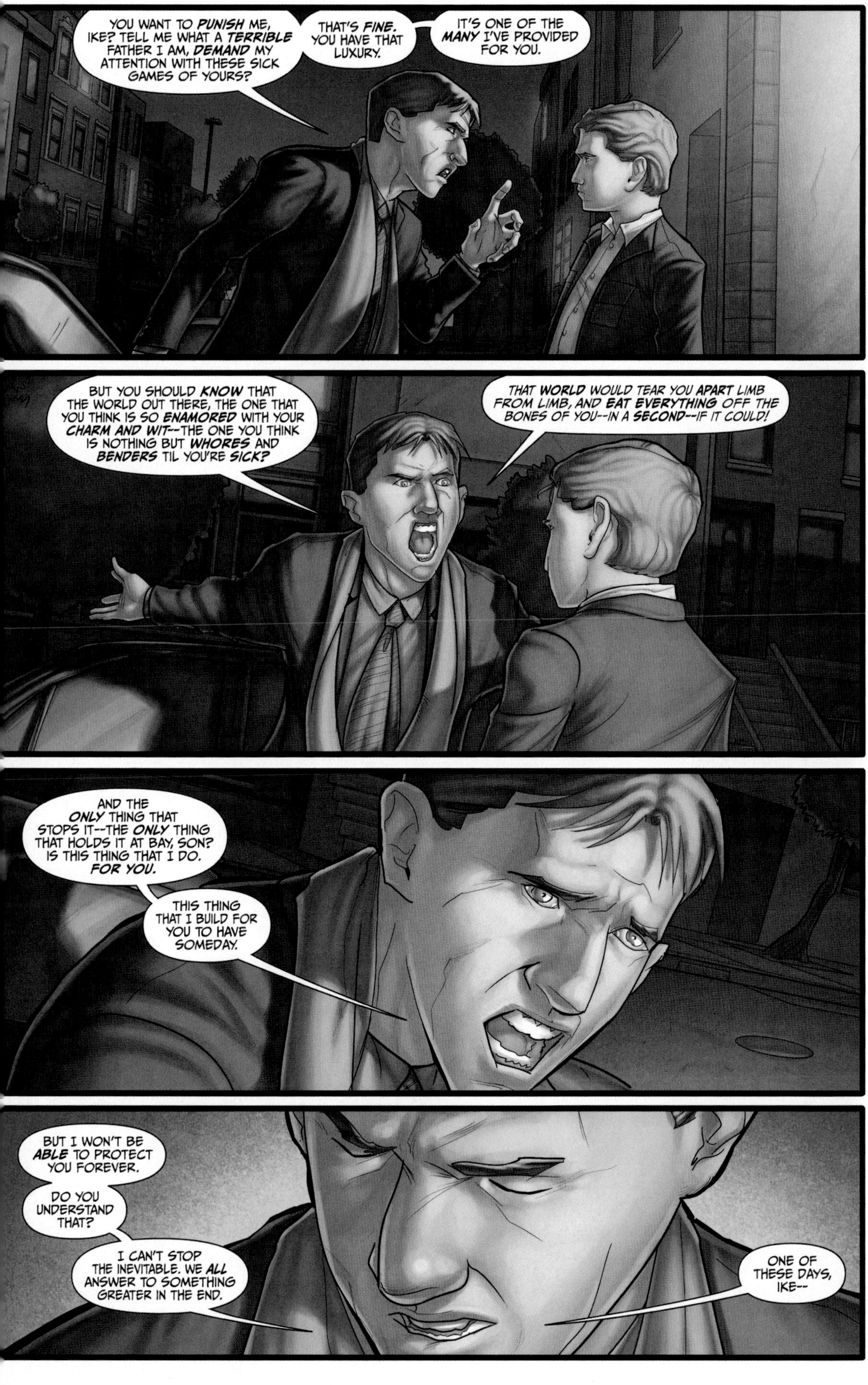
YOU WANT TO PUNISH ME, IKE? TELL ME WHAT A TERRIBLE FATHER I AM, DEMAND MY ATTENTION WITH THESE SICK GAMES OF YOURS?
THAT'S FINE. YOU HAVE THAT LUXURY.
IT'S ONE OF THE MANY I'VE PROVIDED FOR YOU.
BUT YOU SHOULD KNOW THAT THE WORLD OUT THERE, THE ONE THAT YOU THINK IS SO ENAMORED WITH YOUR CHARM AND WIT--THE ONE YOU THINK IS NOTHING BUT WHORES AND BENDERS TIL YOU'RE SICK?
THAT WORLD WOULD TEAR YOU APART LIMB FROM LIMB, AND EAT EVERYTHING OFF THE BONES OF YOU--IN A SECOND--IF IT COULD!
AND THE ONLY THING THAT STOPS IT--THE ONLY THING THAT HOLDS IT AT BAY, SON? IS THIS THING THAT I DO. FOR YOU.
THIS THING THAT I BUILD FOR YOU TO HAVE SOMEDAY.
BUT I WON'T BE ABLE TO PROTECT YOU FOREVER.
DO YOU UNDERSTAND THAT?
I CAN'T STOP THE INEVITABLE. WE ALL ANSWER TO SOMETHING GREATER IN THE END.
ONE OF THESE DAYS, IKE--

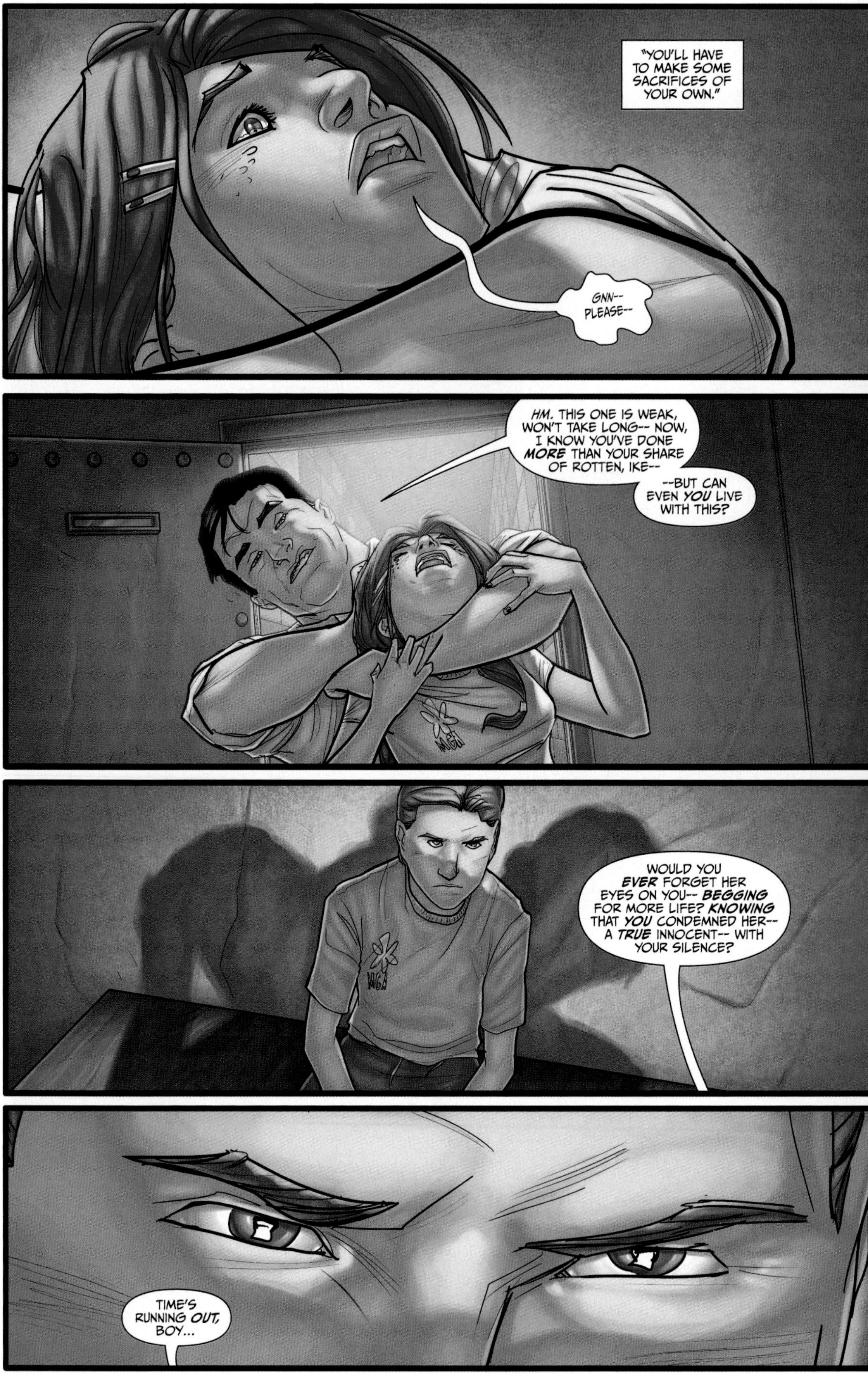
"YOU'LL HAVE TO MAKE SOME SACRIFICES OF YOUR OWN."
GNN-- PLEASE--
HM. THIS ONE IS WEAK, WON'T TAKE LONG-- NOW, I KNOW YOU'VE DONE ***MORE*** THAN YOUR SHARE OF ROTTEN, IKE--
--BUT CAN EVEN ***YOU*** LIVE WITH THIS?
WOULD YOU ***EVER*** FORGET HER EYES ON YOU-- ***BEGGING*** FOR MORE LIFE? ***KNOWING*** THAT ***YOU*** CONDEMNED HER-- A ***TRUE*** INNOCENT-- WITH YOUR SILENCE?
TIME'S RUNNING ***OUT,*** BOY...

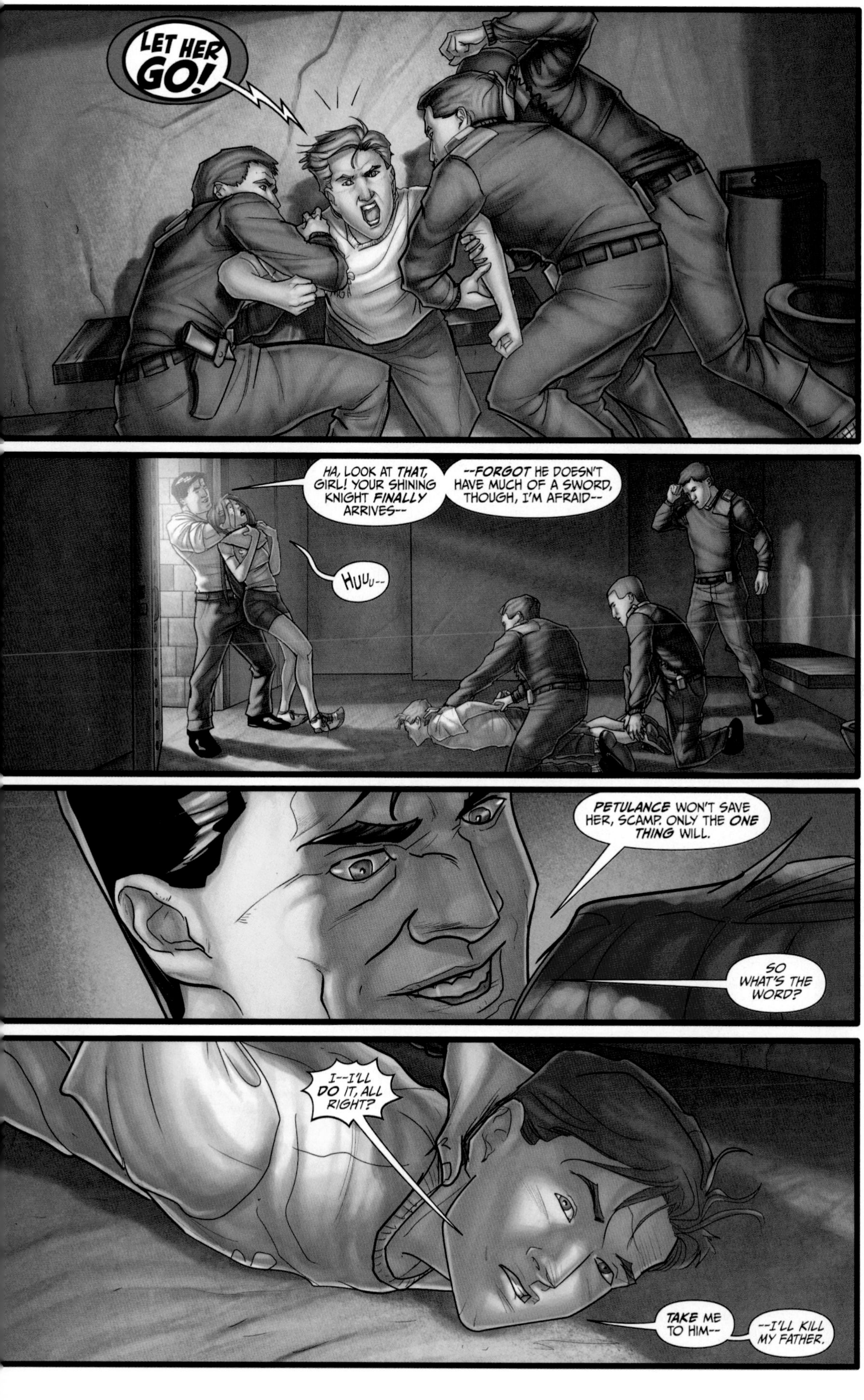
LET HER GO!
HA, LOOK AT THAT, GIRL! YOUR SHINING KNIGHT FINALLY ARRIVES--
--FORGOT HE DOESN'T HAVE MUCH OF A SWORD, THOUGH, I'M AFRAID--
HUUU--
PETULANCE WON'T SAVE HER, SCAMP. ONLY THE ONE THING WILL.
SO WHAT'S THE WORD?
I--I'LL DO IT, ALL RIGHT?
TAKE ME TO HIM--
--I'LL KILL MY FATHER.

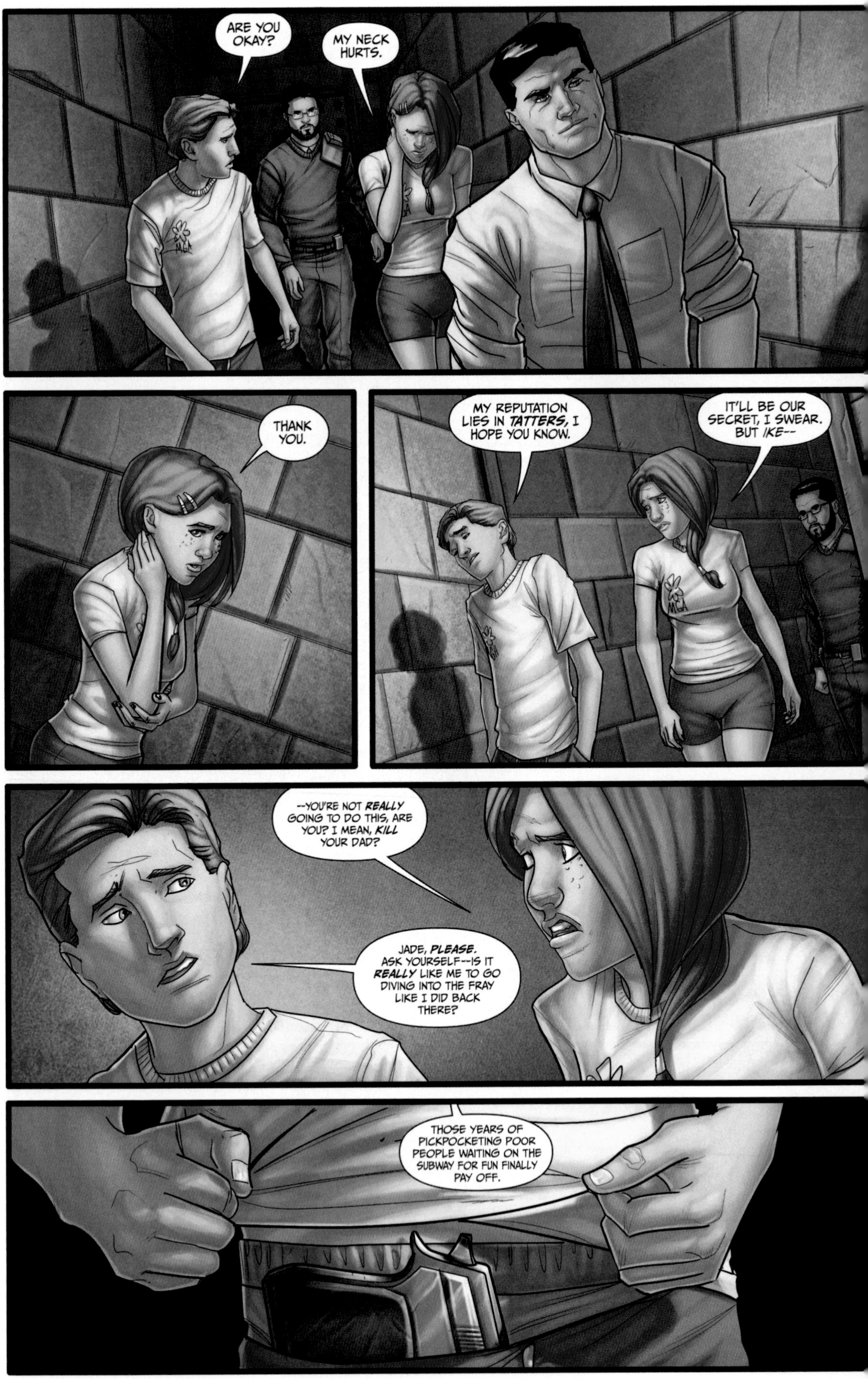
ARE YOU OKAY?
MY NECK HURTS.
THANK YOU.
MY REPUTATION LIES IN TATTERS, I HOPE YOU KNOW.
IT'LL BE OUR SECRET, I SWEAR. BUT IKE--
--YOU'RE NOT REALLY GOING TO DO THIS, ARE YOU? I MEAN, KILL YOUR DAD?
JADE, PLEASE. ASK YOURSELF--IS IT REALLY LIKE ME TO GO DIVING INTO THE FRAY LIKE I DID BACK THERE?
THOSE YEARS OF PICKPOCKETING POOR PEOPLE WAITING ON THE SUBWAY FOR FUN FINALLY PAY OFF.

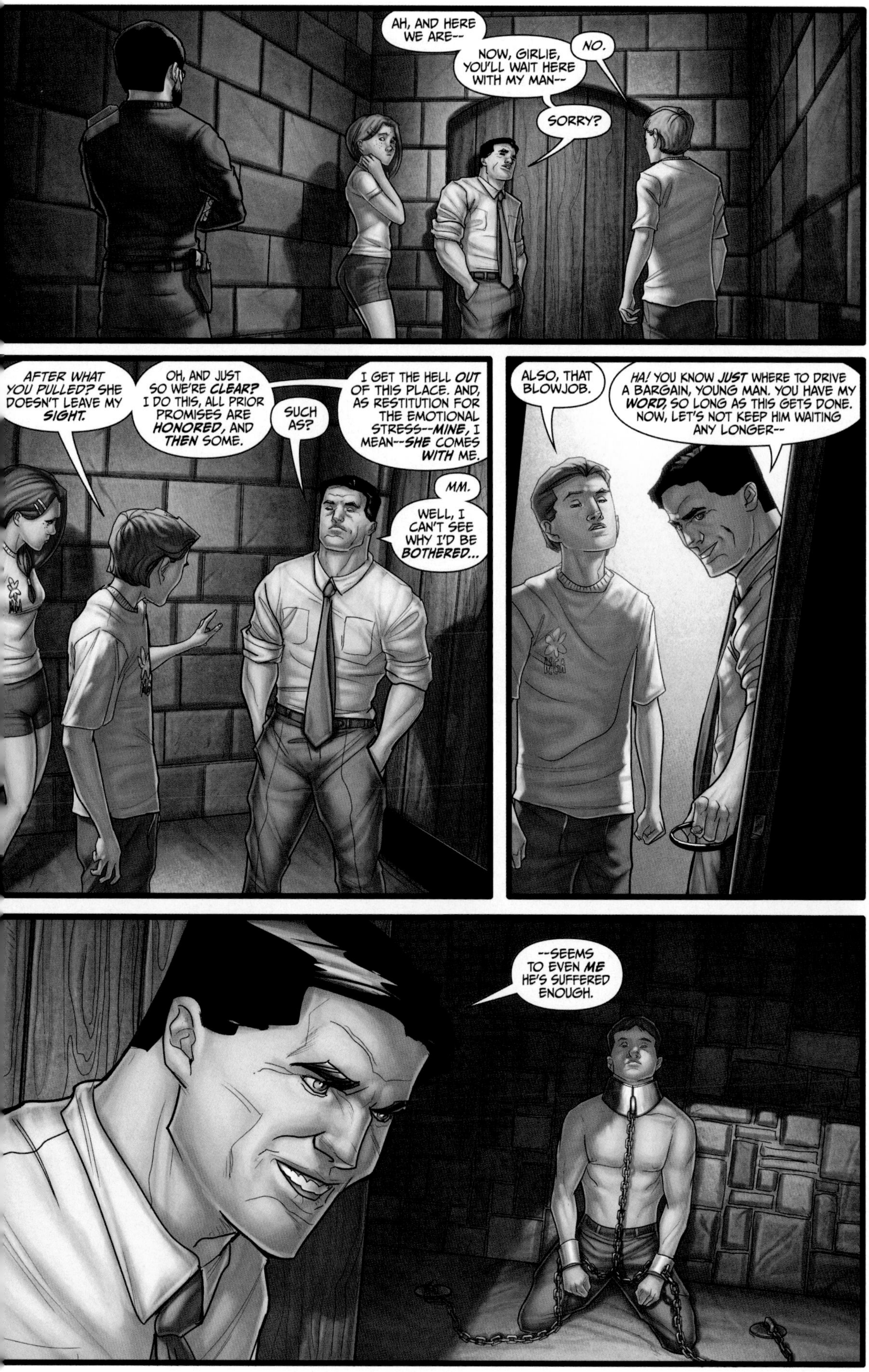
AH, AND HERE WE ARE--
NOW, GIRLIE, YOU'LL WAIT HERE WITH MY MAN--
NO.
SORRY?
AFTER WHAT YOU PULLED? SHE DOESN'T LEAVE MY SIGHT.
OH, AND JUST SO WE'RE CLEAR? I DO THIS, ALL PRIOR PROMISES ARE HONORED, AND THEN SOME.
SUCH AS?
I GET THE HELL OUT OF THIS PLACE. AND, AS RESTITUTION FOR THE EMOTIONAL STRESS--MINE, I MEAN--SHE COMES WITH ME.
MM.
WELL, I CAN'T SEE WHY I'D BE BOTHERED...
ALSO, THAT BLOWJOB.
HA! YOU KNOW JUST WHERE TO DRIVE A BARGAIN, YOUNG MAN. YOU HAVE MY WORD, SO LONG AS THIS GETS DONE. NOW, LET'S NOT KEEP HIM WAITING ANY LONGER--
--SEEMS TO EVEN ME HE'S SUFFERED ENOUGH.

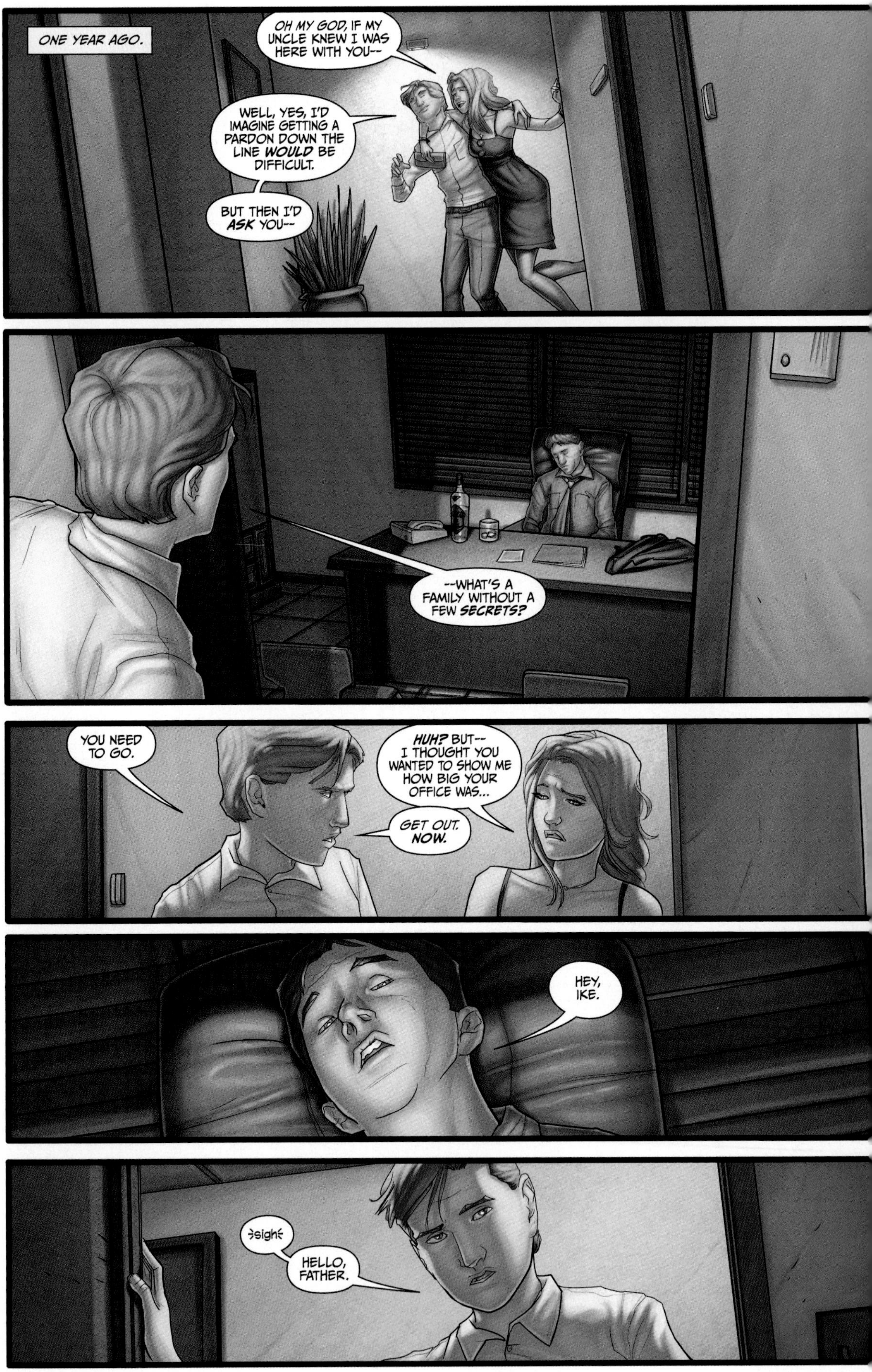
ONE YEAR AGO.
OH MY GOD, IF MY UNCLE KNEW I WAS HERE WITH YOU--
WELL, YES, I'D IMAGINE GETTING A PARDON DOWN THE LINE WOULD BE DIFFICULT.
BUT THEN I'D ASK YOU--
--WHAT'S A FAMILY WITHOUT A FEW SECRETS?
YOU NEED TO GO.
HUH? BUT-- I THOUGHT YOU WANTED TO SHOW ME HOW BIG YOUR OFFICE WAS...
GET OUT. NOW.
HEY, IKE.
sigh
HELLO, FATHER.

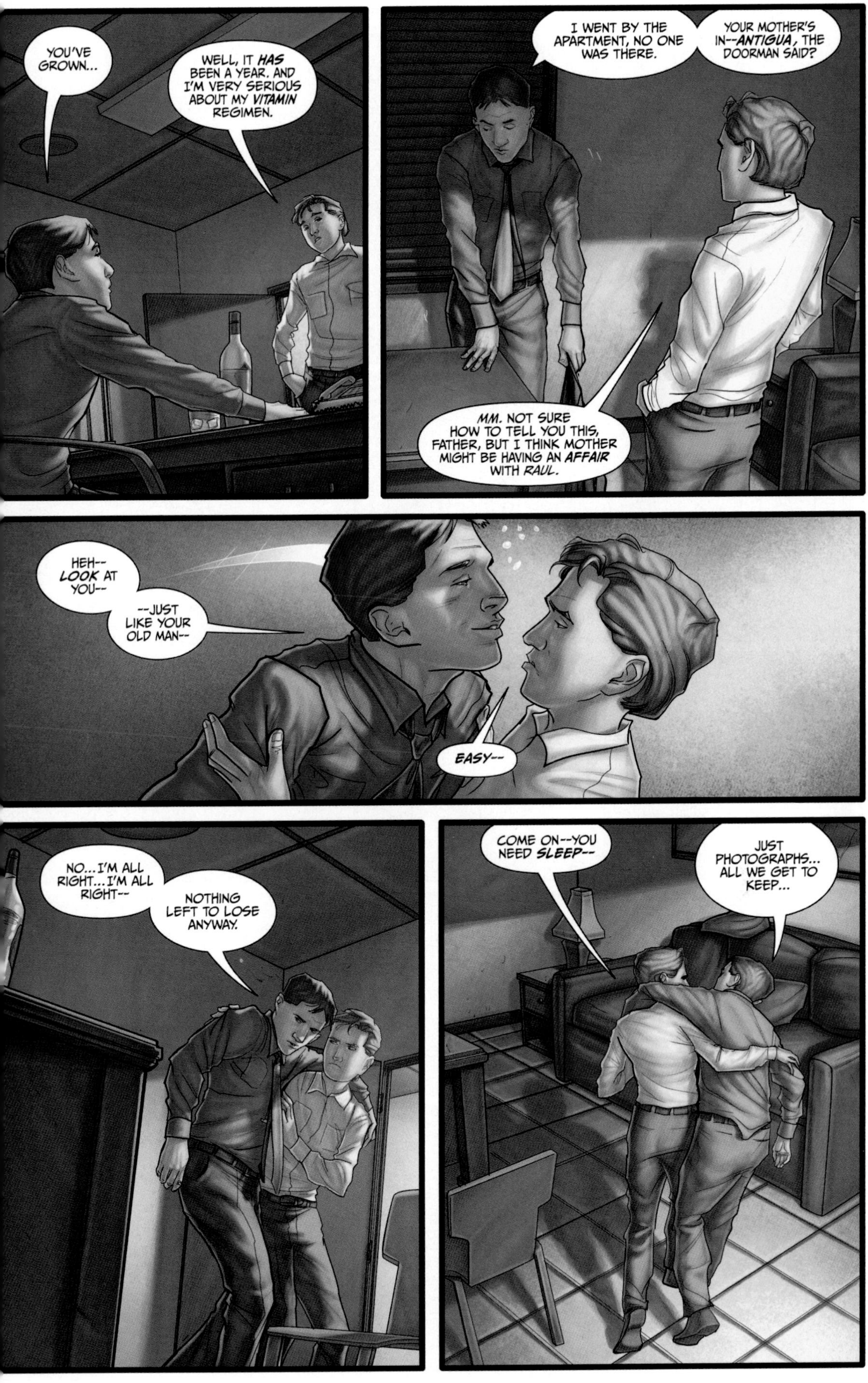
YOU'VE GROWN...
WELL, IT HAS BEEN A YEAR. AND I'M VERY SERIOUS ABOUT MY VITAMIN REGIMEN.
I WENT BY THE APARTMENT, NO ONE WAS THERE.
YOUR MOTHER'S IN--ANTIGUA, THE DOORMAN SAID?
MM. NOT SURE HOW TO TELL YOU THIS, FATHER, BUT I THINK MOTHER MIGHT BE HAVING AN AFFAIR WITH RAUL.
HEH-- LOOK AT YOU--
--JUST LIKE YOUR OLD MAN--
EASY--
NO...I'M ALL RIGHT...I'M ALL RIGHT--
NOTHING LEFT TO LOSE ANYWAY.
COME ON--YOU NEED SLEEP--
JUST PHOTOGRAPHS... ALL WE GET TO KEEP...

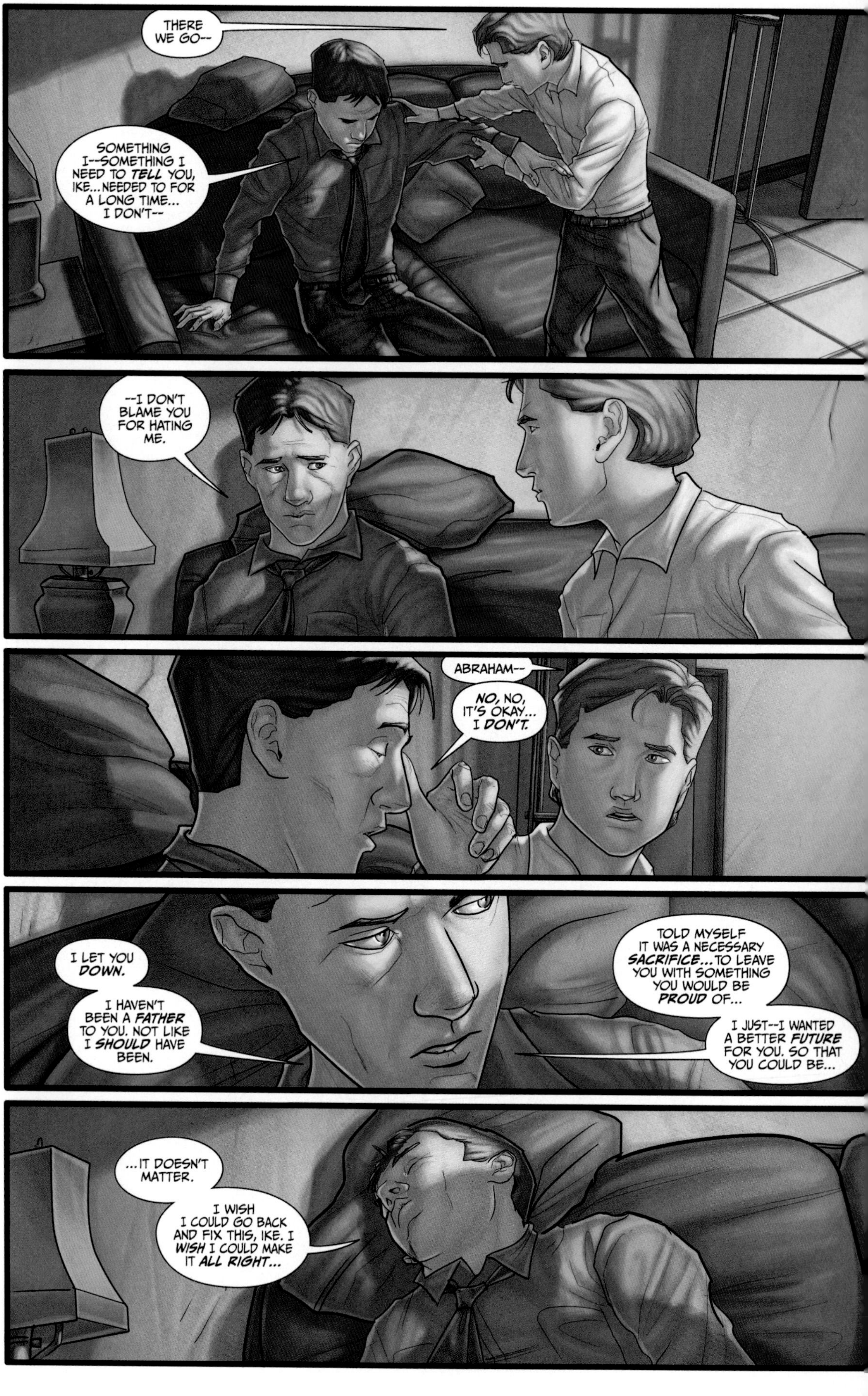
THERE WE GO--
SOMETHING I--SOMETHING I NEED TO TELL YOU, IKE...NEEDED TO FOR A LONG TIME... I DON'T--
--I DON'T BLAME YOU FOR HATING ME.
ABRAHAM--
NO, NO, IT'S OKAY... I DON'T.
I LET YOU DOWN.
I HAVEN'T BEEN A FATHER TO YOU. NOT LIKE I SHOULD HAVE BEEN.
TOLD MYSELF IT WAS A NECESSARY SACRIFICE...TO LEAVE YOU WITH SOMETHING YOU WOULD BE PROUD OF...
I JUST--I WANTED A BETTER FUTURE FOR YOU. SO THAT YOU COULD BE...
...IT DOESN'T MATTER.
I WISH I COULD GO BACK AND FIX THIS, IKE. I WISH I COULD MAKE IT ALL RIGHT...

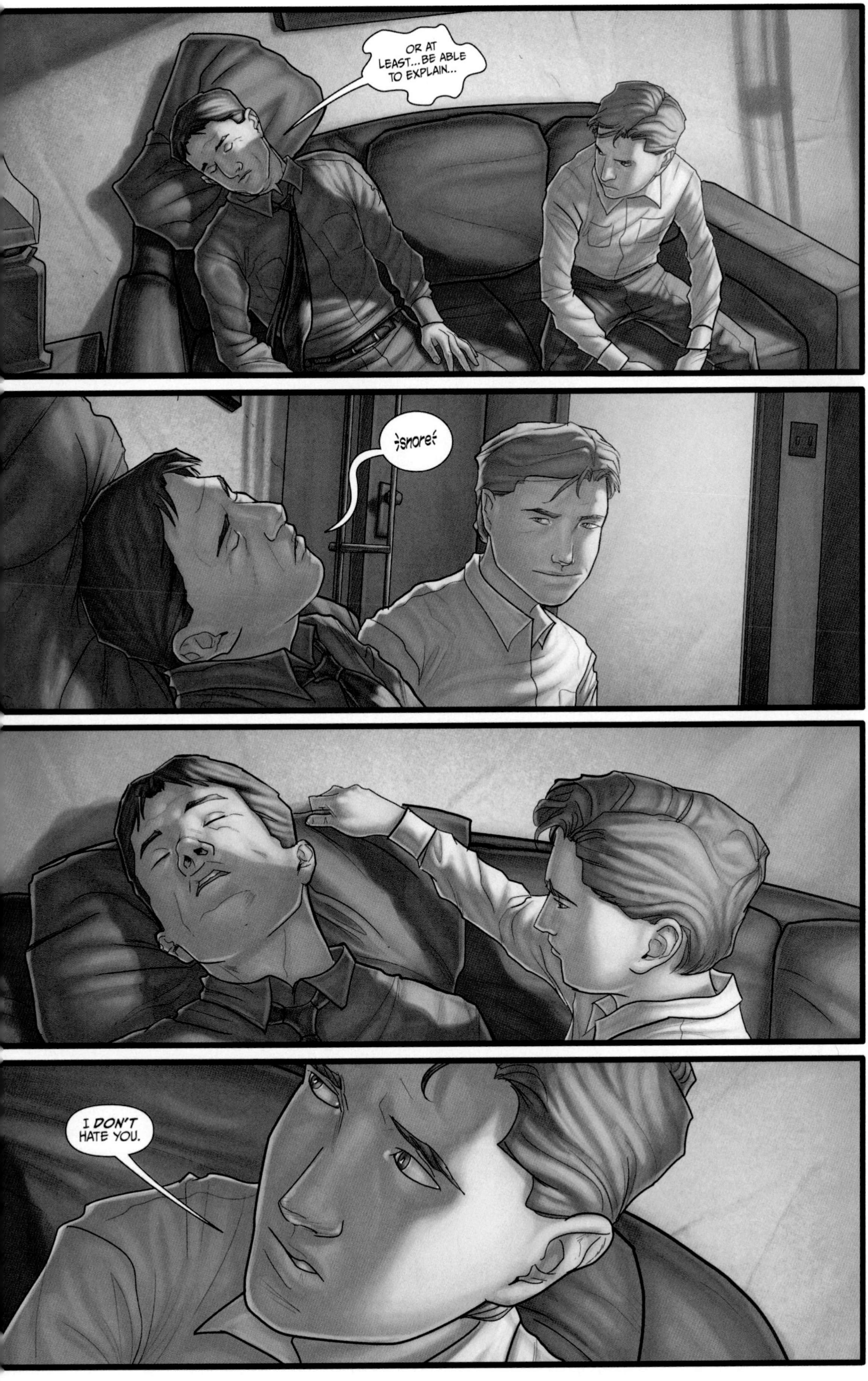
OR AT LEAST...BE ABLE TO EXPLAIN...
snore
I DON'T HATE YOU.

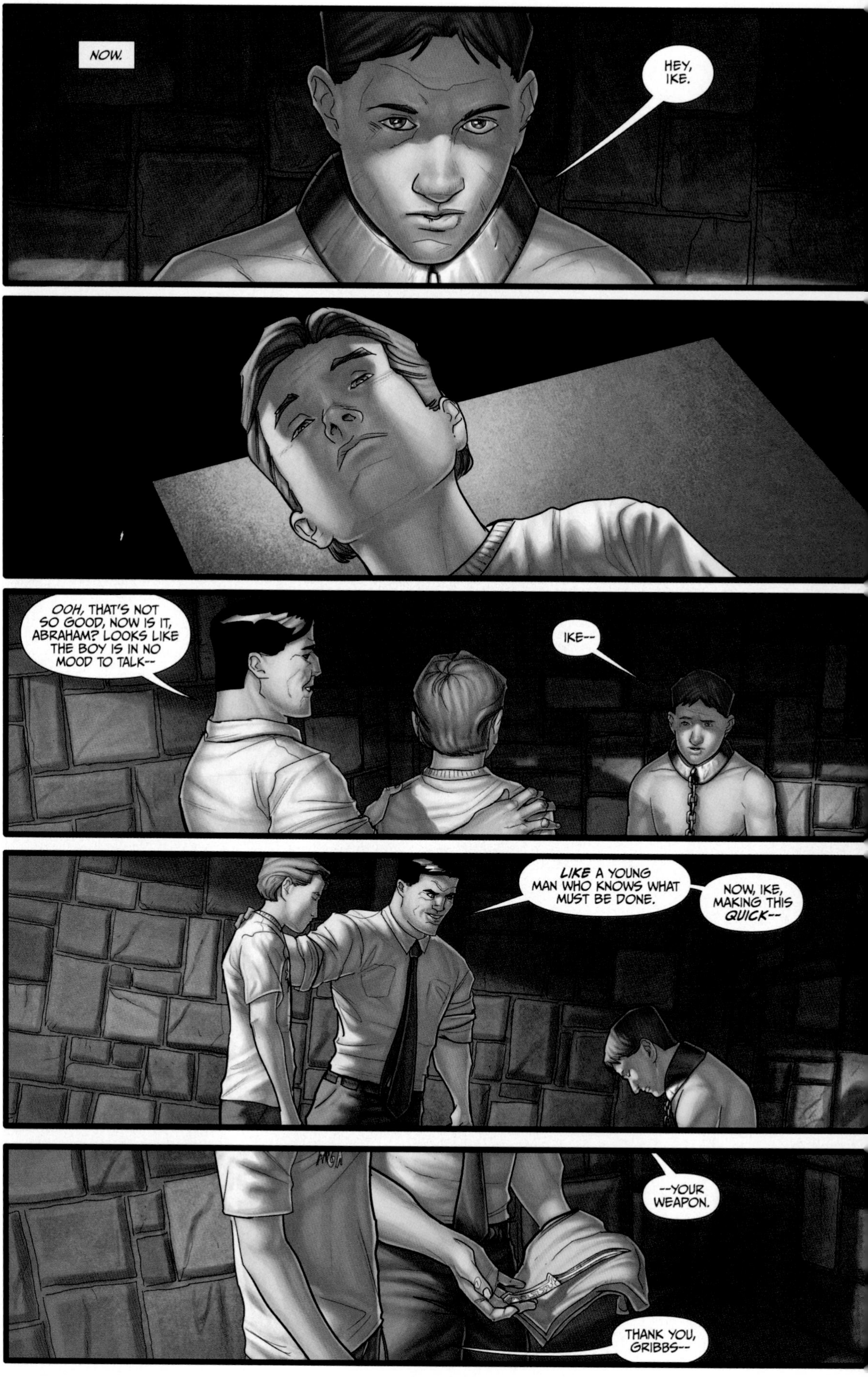
NOW.
HEY, IKE.
OOH, THAT'S NOT SO GOOD, NOW IS IT, ABRAHAM? LOOKS LIKE THE BOY IS IN NO MOOD TO TALK--
IKE--
LIKE A YOUNG MAN WHO KNOWS WHAT MUST BE DONE.
NOW, IKE, MAKING THIS QUICK--
--YOUR WEAPON.
THANK YOU, GRIBBS--

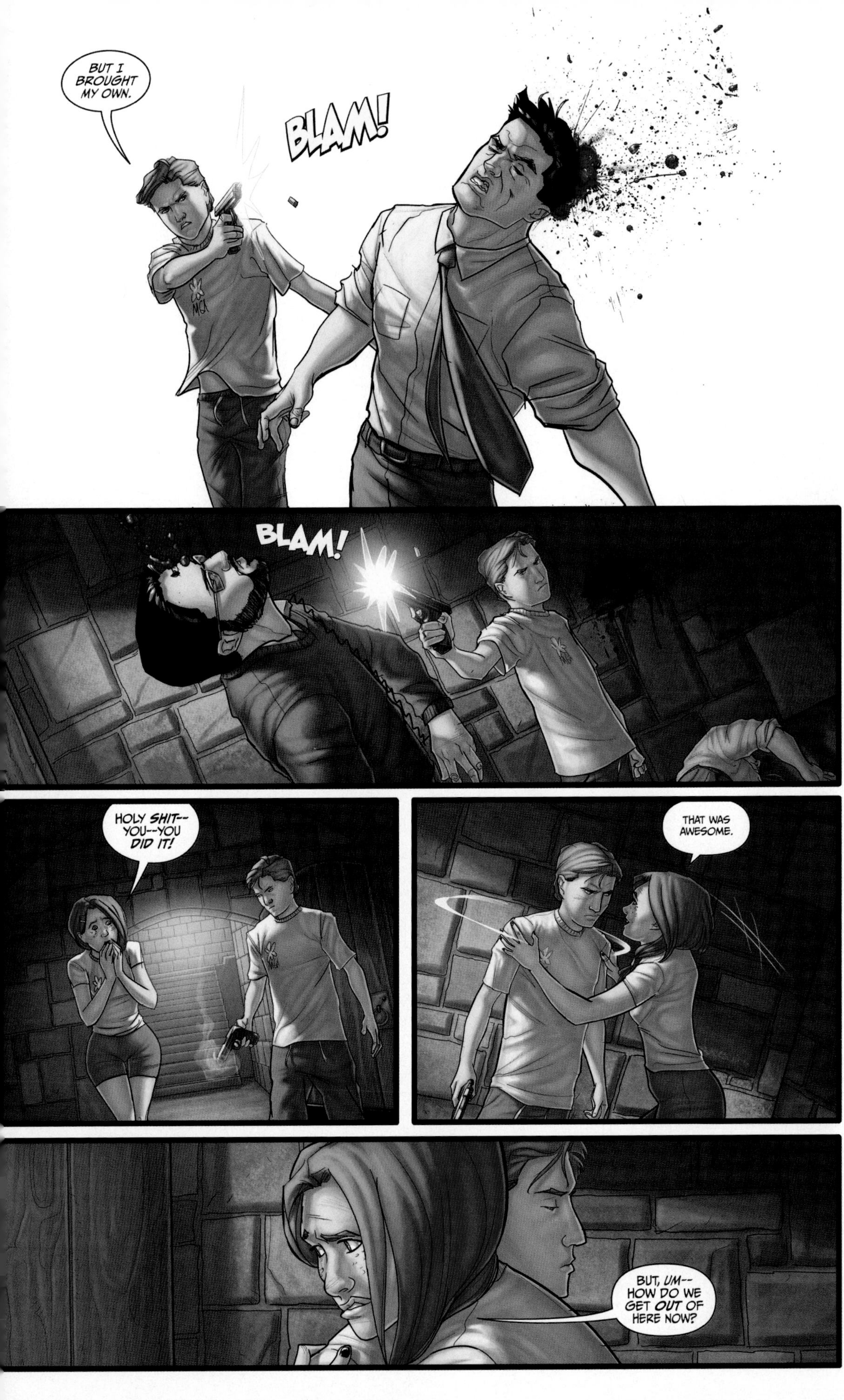
BUT I BROUGHT MY OWN.
BLAM!
BLAM!
HOLY SHIT--YOU--YOU DID IT!
THAT WAS AWESOME.
BUT, UM--HOW DO WE GET OUT OF HERE NOW?

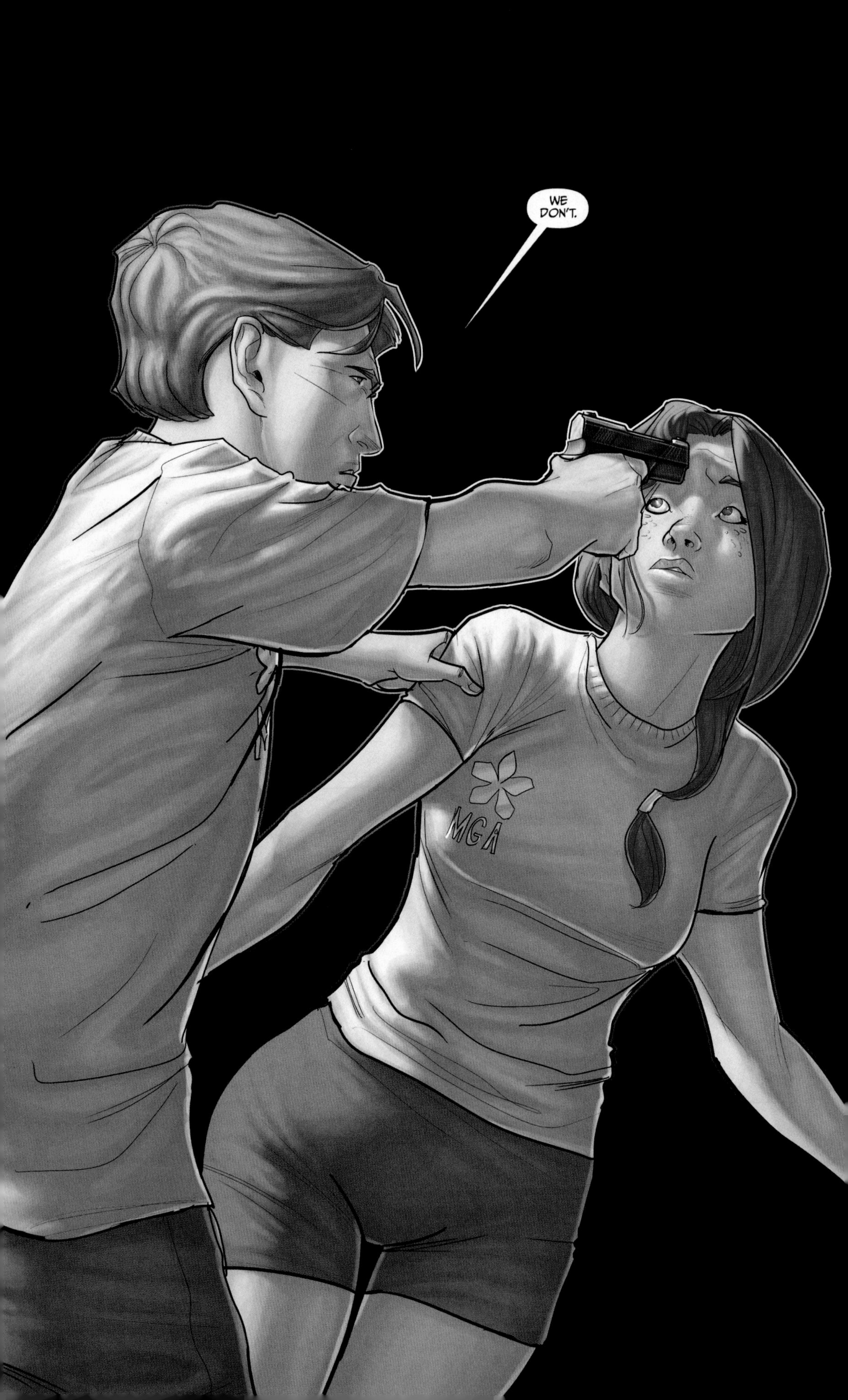
WE DON'T.

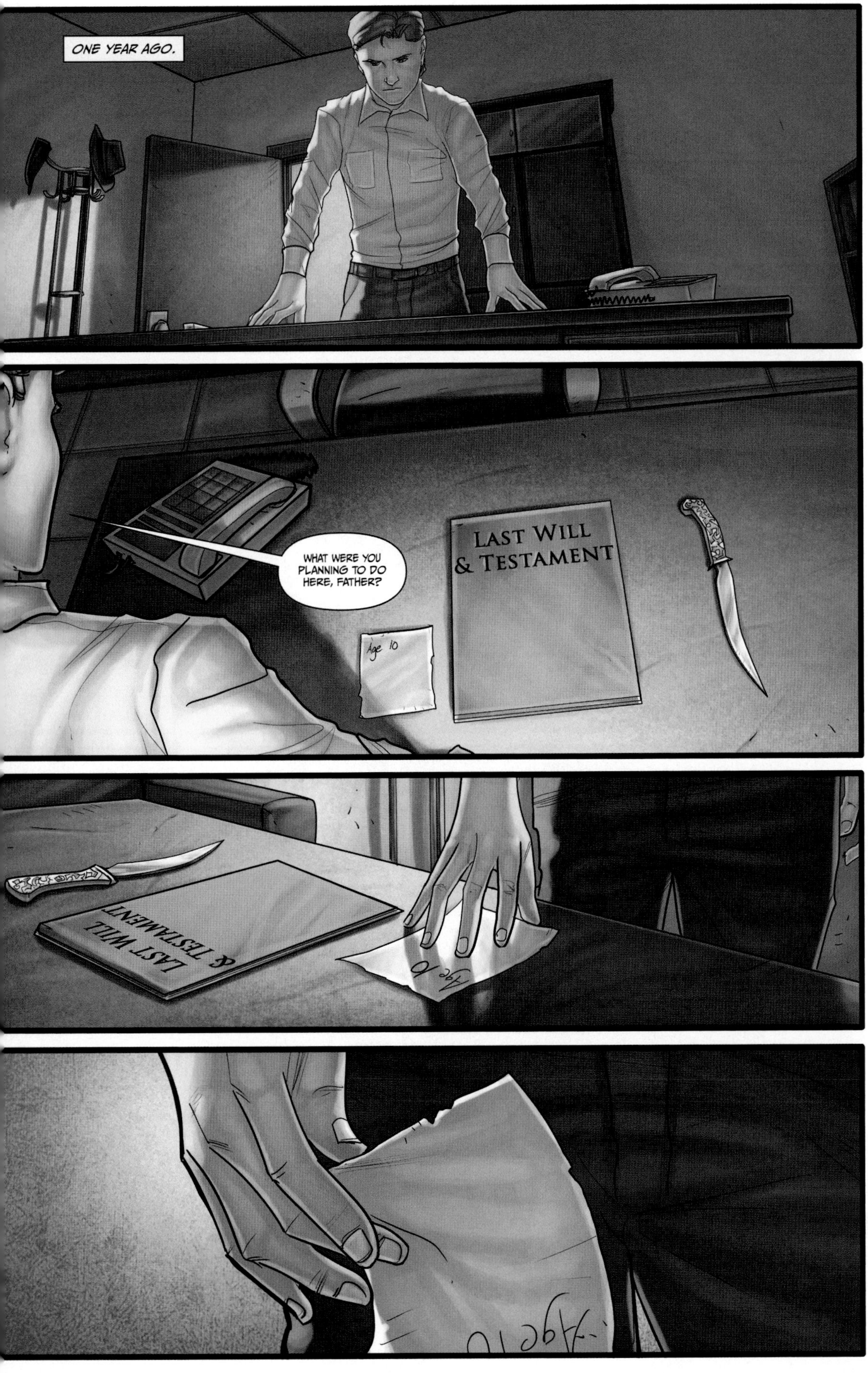
ONE YEAR AGO.
WHAT WERE YOU PLANNING TO DO HERE, FATHER?
LAST WILL & TESTAMENT
Age 10

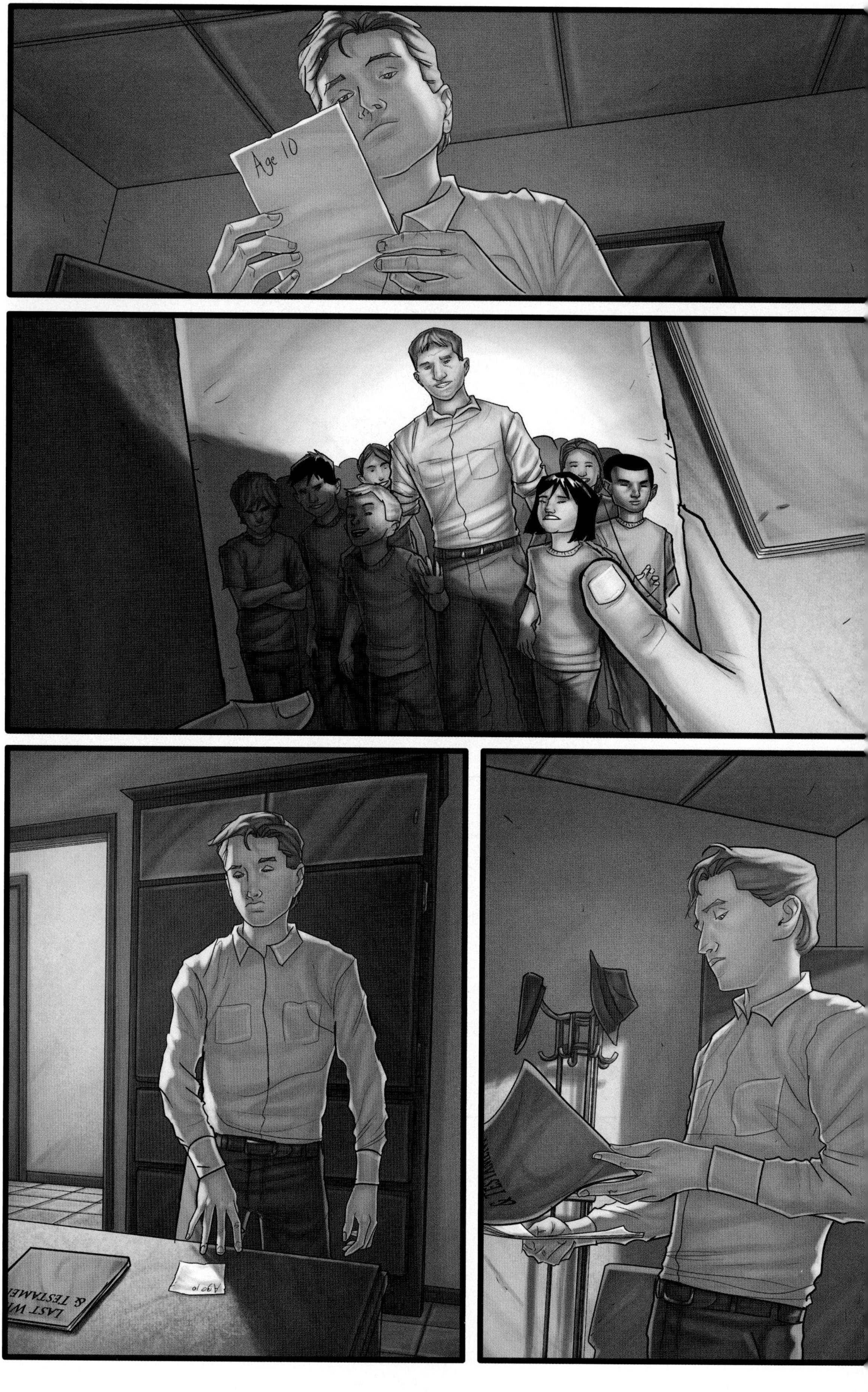
Age 10

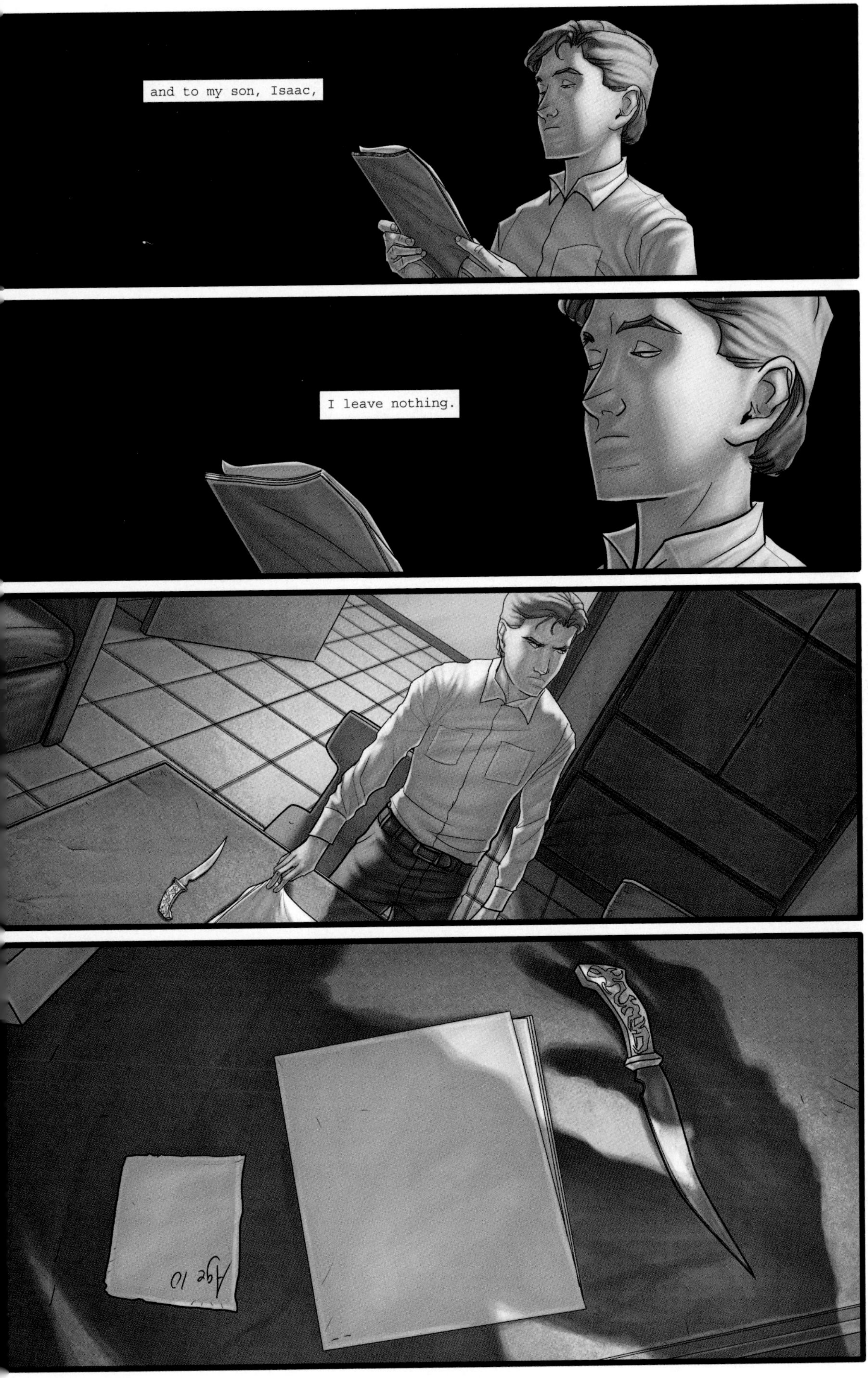

and to my son, Isaac,
I leave nothing.
Age 10

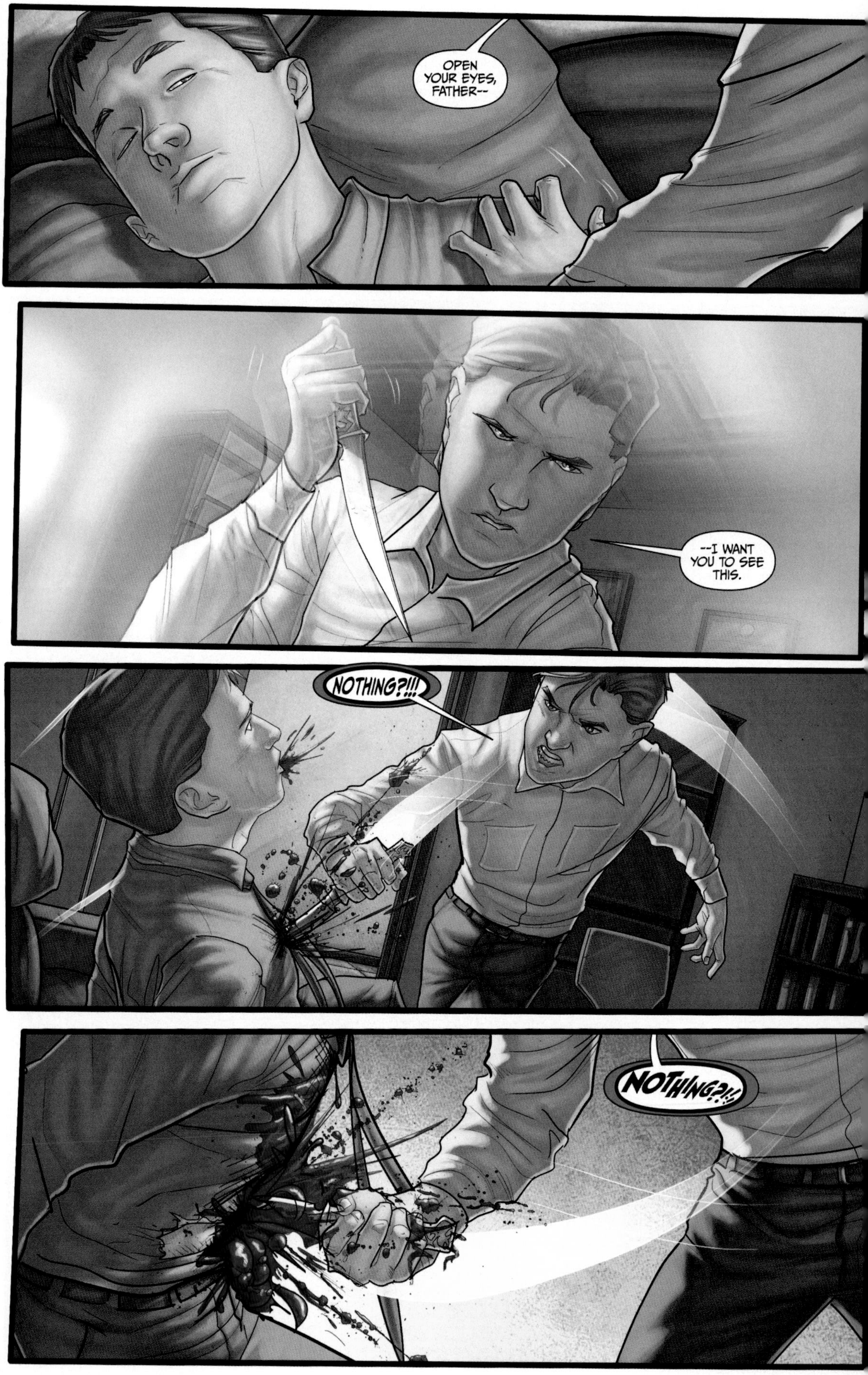
OPEN YOUR EYES, FATHER--
--I WANT YOU TO SEE THIS.
NOTHING?!!!
NOTHING?!!!

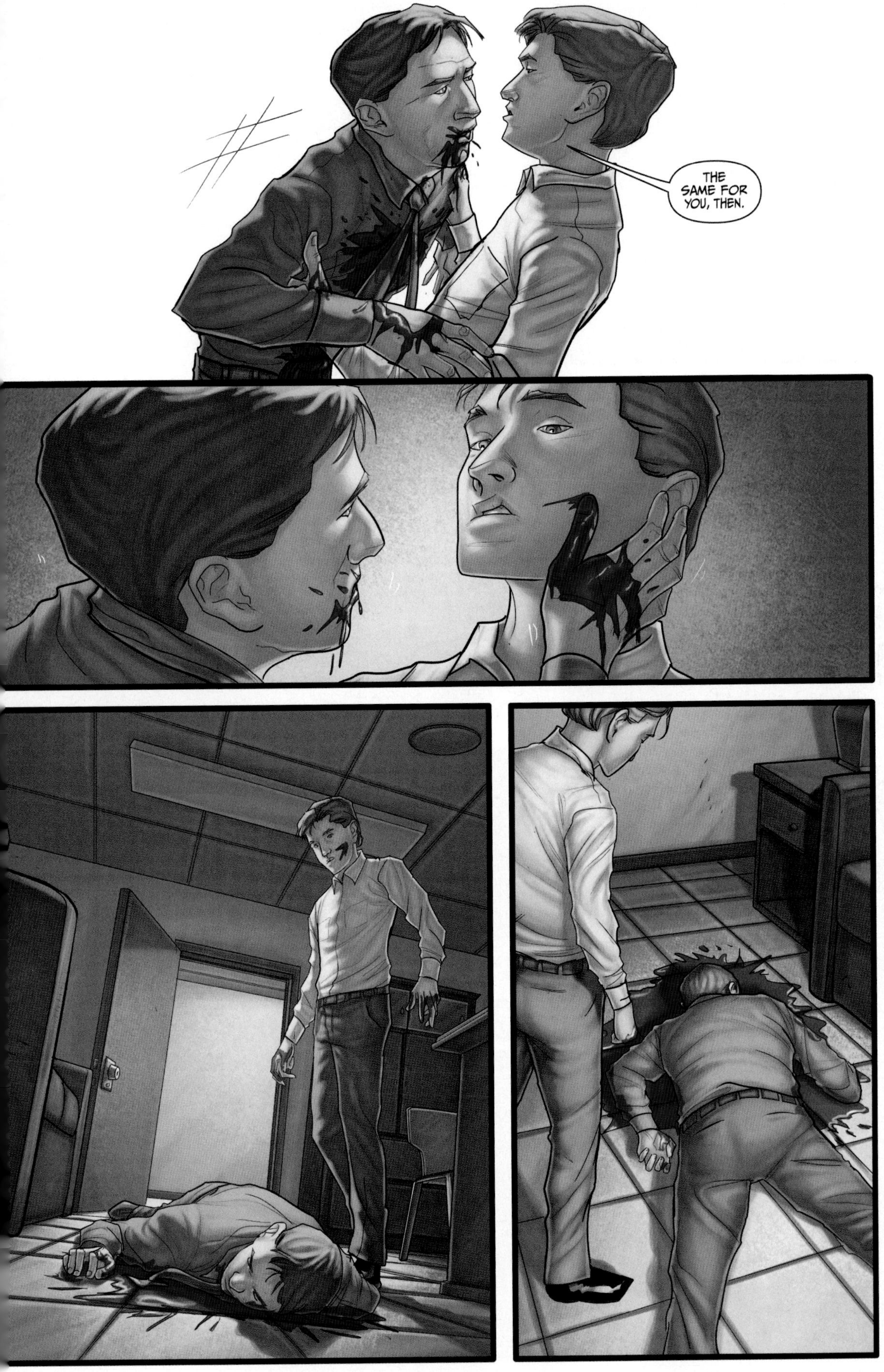
THE SAME FOR YOU, THEN.

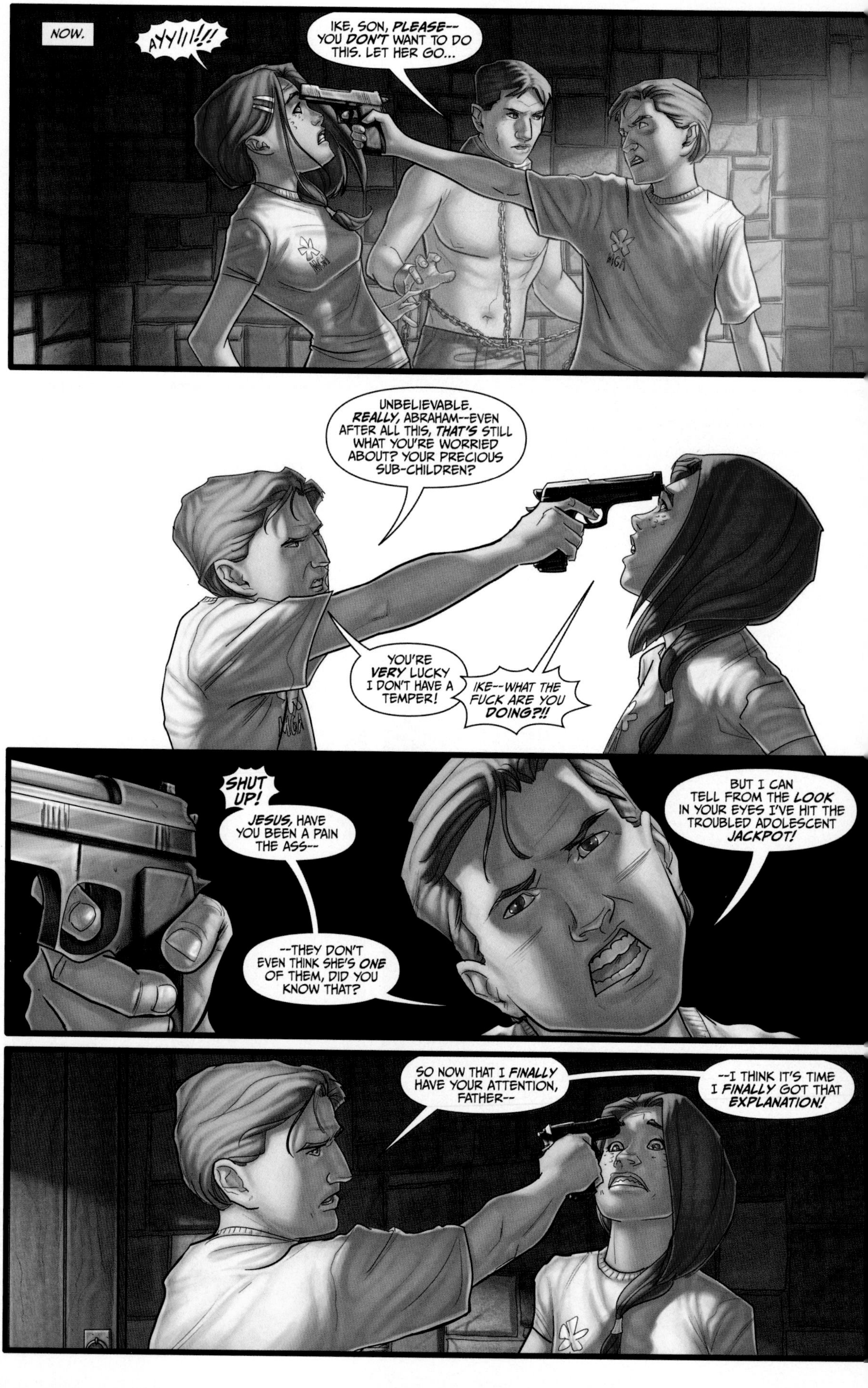
NOW.
AYY!!!!!!
IKE, SON, PLEASE-- YOU DON'T WANT TO DO THIS. LET HER GO...
UNBELIEVABLE. REALLY, ABRAHAM--EVEN AFTER ALL THIS, THAT'S STILL WHAT YOU'RE WORRIED ABOUT? YOUR PRECIOUS SUB-CHILDREN?
YOU'RE VERY LUCKY I DON'T HAVE A TEMPER!
IKE--WHAT THE FUCK ARE YOU DOING?!!
SHUT UP!
JESUS, HAVE YOU BEEN A PAIN THE ASS--
--THEY DON'T EVEN THINK SHE'S ONE OF THEM, DID YOU KNOW THAT?
BUT I CAN TELL FROM THE LOOK IN YOUR EYES I'VE HIT THE TROUBLED ADOLESCENT JACKPOT!
SO NOW THAT I FINALLY HAVE YOUR ATTENTION, FATHER--
--I THINK IT'S TIME I FINALLY GOT THAT EXPLANATION!

twenty**five**

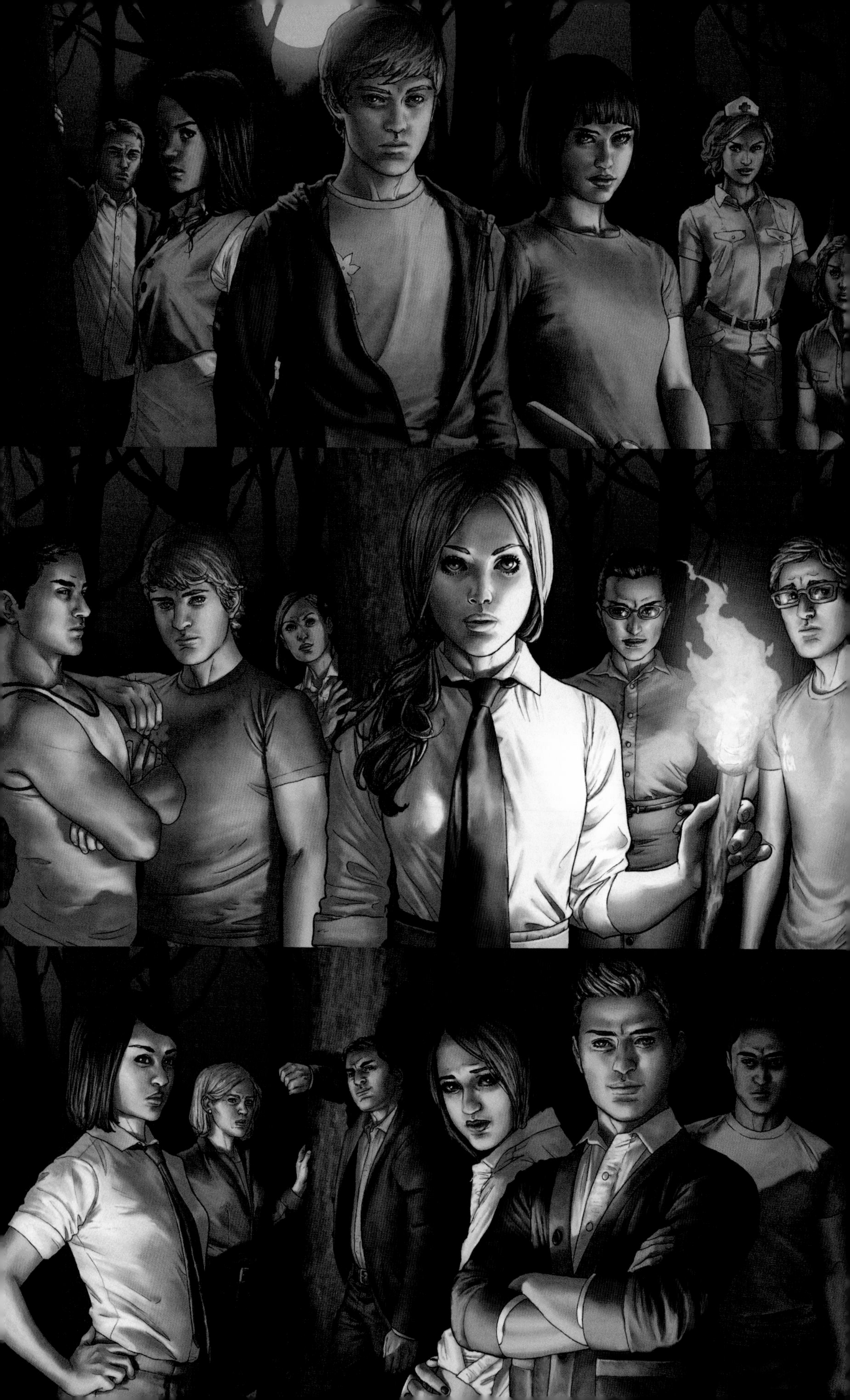

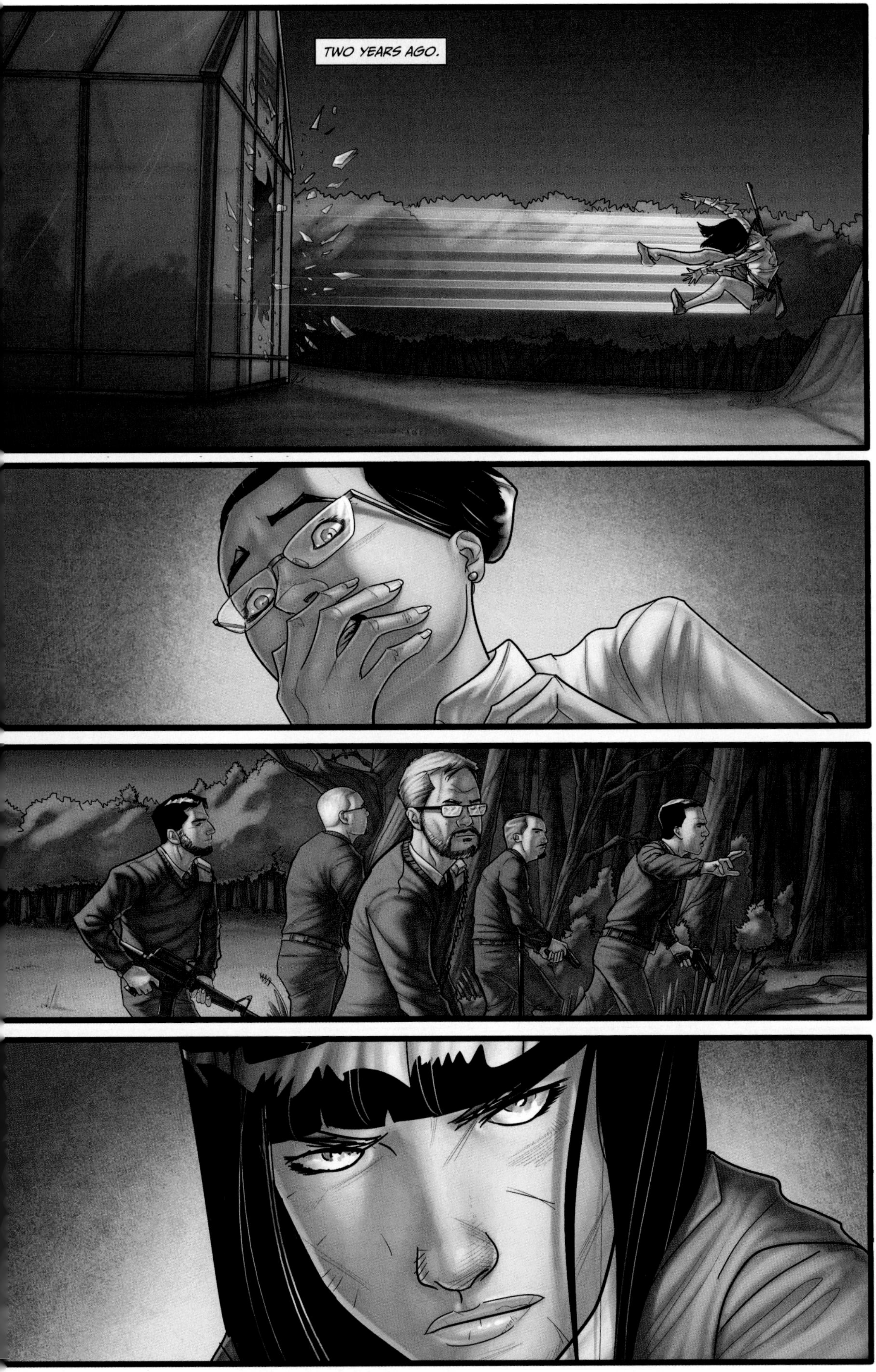
TWO YEARS AGO.

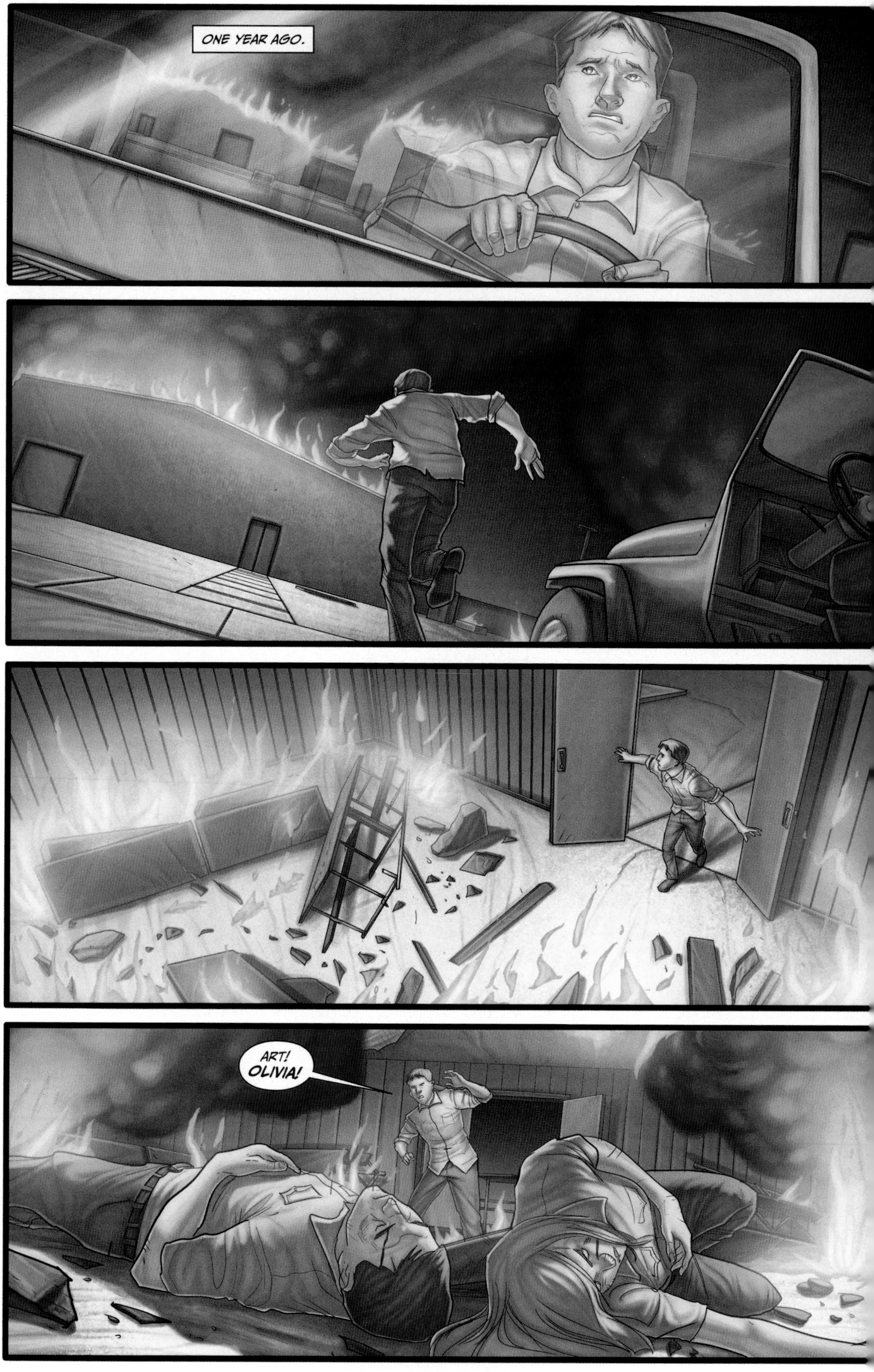
ONE YEAR AGO.
ART!
OLIVIA!

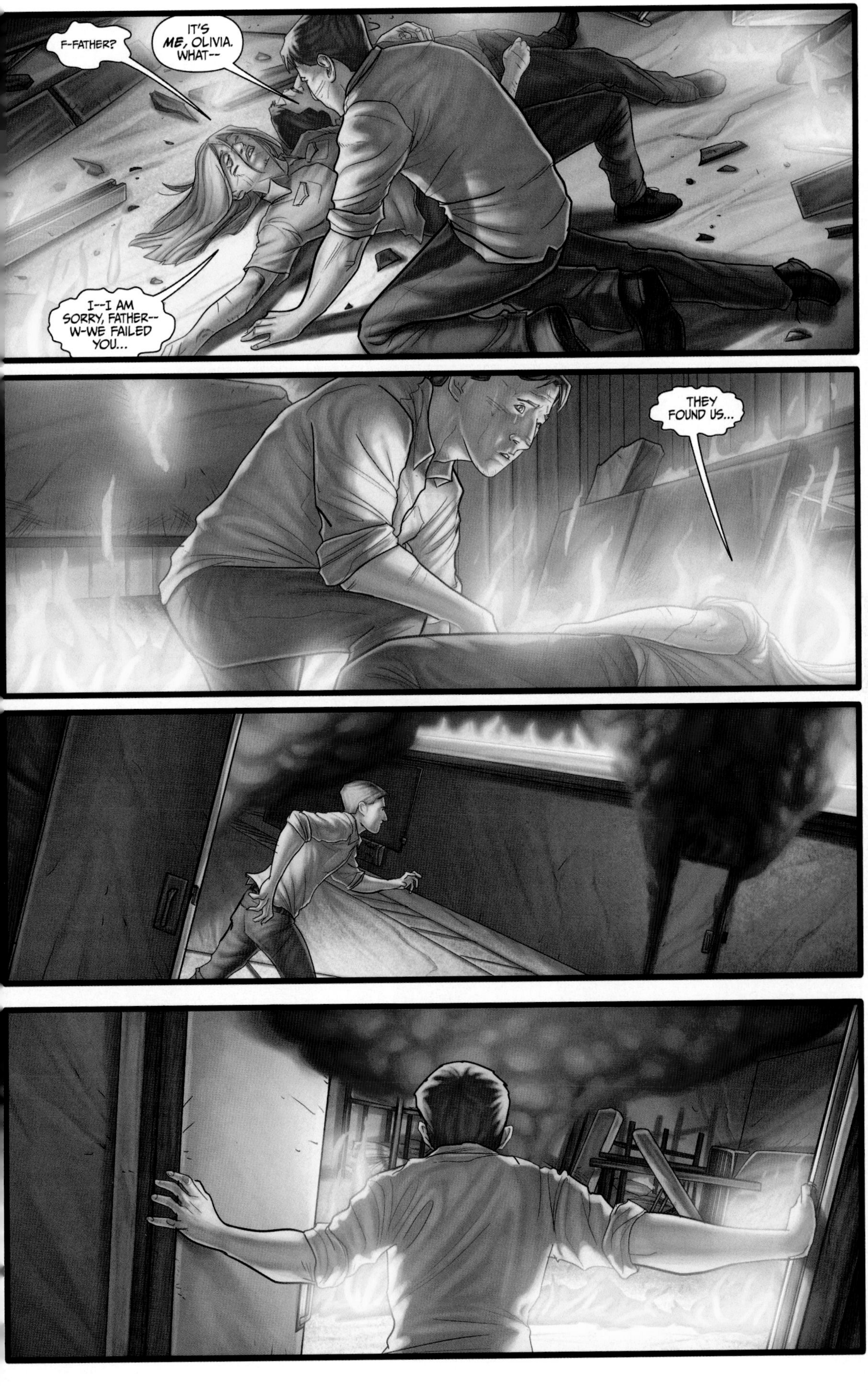
F-FATHER?
IT'S ME, OLIVIA. WHAT--
I--I AM SORRY, FATHER-- W-WE FAILED YOU...
THEY FOUND US...

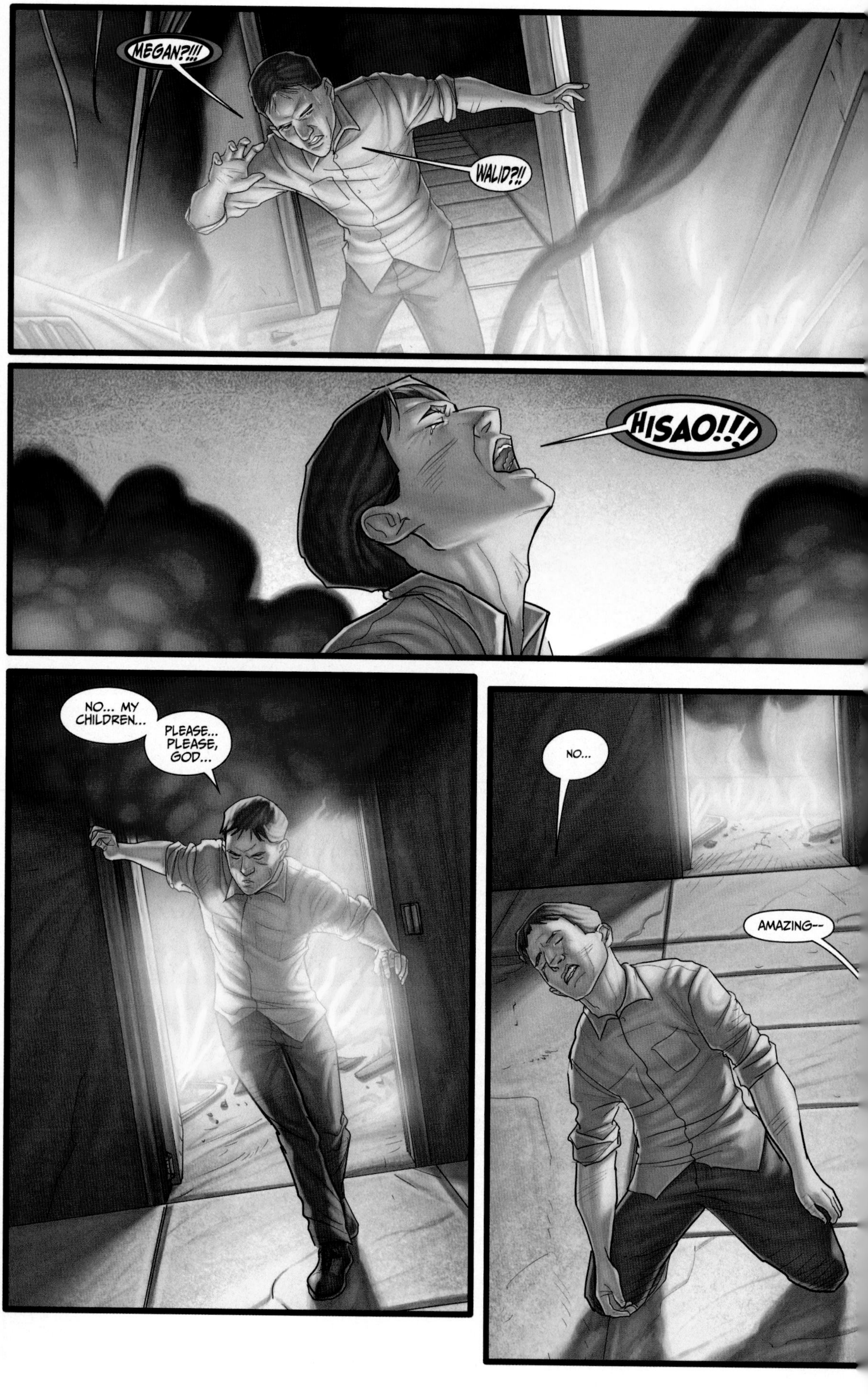

MEGAN?!!!
WALID?!!
HISAO!!!
NO... MY CHILDREN...
PLEASE... PLEASE, GOD...
NO...
AMAZING--

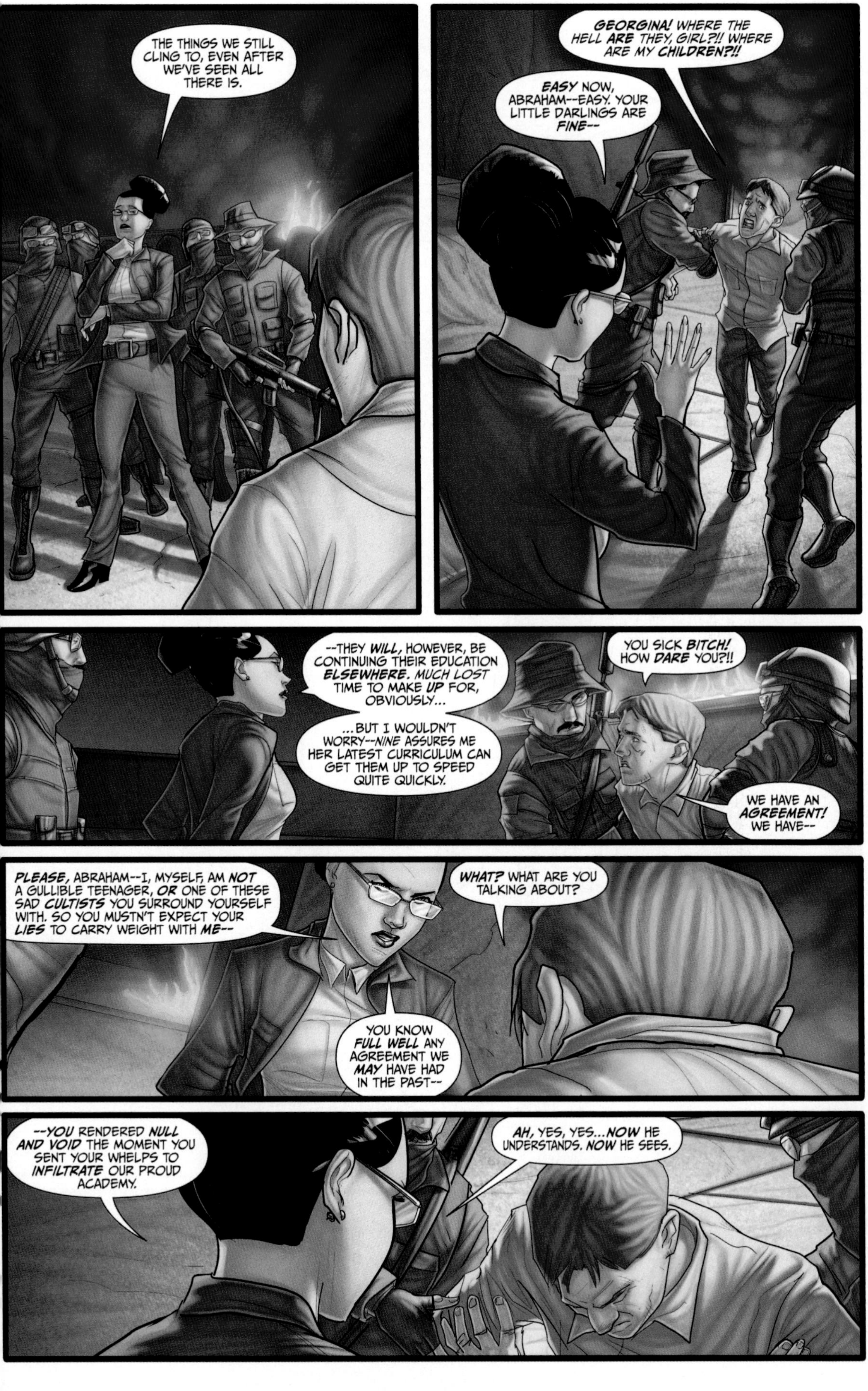
THE THINGS WE STILL CLING TO, EVEN AFTER WE'VE SEEN ALL THERE IS.
GEORGINA! WHERE THE HELL ARE THEY, GIRL?!! WHERE ARE MY CHILDREN?!!
EASY NOW, ABRAHAM--EASY. YOUR LITTLE DARLINGS ARE FINE--
--THEY WILL, HOWEVER, BE CONTINUING THEIR EDUCATION ELSEWHERE. MUCH LOST TIME TO MAKE UP FOR, OBVIOUSLY...
...BUT I WOULDN'T WORRY--NINE ASSURES ME HER LATEST CURRICULUM CAN GET THEM UP TO SPEED QUITE QUICKLY.
YOU SICK BITCH! HOW DARE YOU?!!
WE HAVE AN AGREEMENT! WE HAVE--
PLEASE, ABRAHAM--I, MYSELF, AM NOT A GULLIBLE TEENAGER, OR ONE OF THESE SAD CULTISTS YOU SURROUND YOURSELF WITH. SO YOU MUSTN'T EXPECT YOUR LIES TO CARRY WEIGHT WITH ME--
YOU KNOW FULL WELL ANY AGREEMENT WE MAY HAVE HAD IN THE PAST--
WHAT? WHAT ARE YOU TALKING ABOUT?
--YOU RENDERED NULL AND VOID THE MOMENT YOU SENT YOUR WHELPS TO INFILTRATE OUR PROUD ACADEMY.
AH, YES, YES...NOW HE UNDERSTANDS. NOW HE SEES.

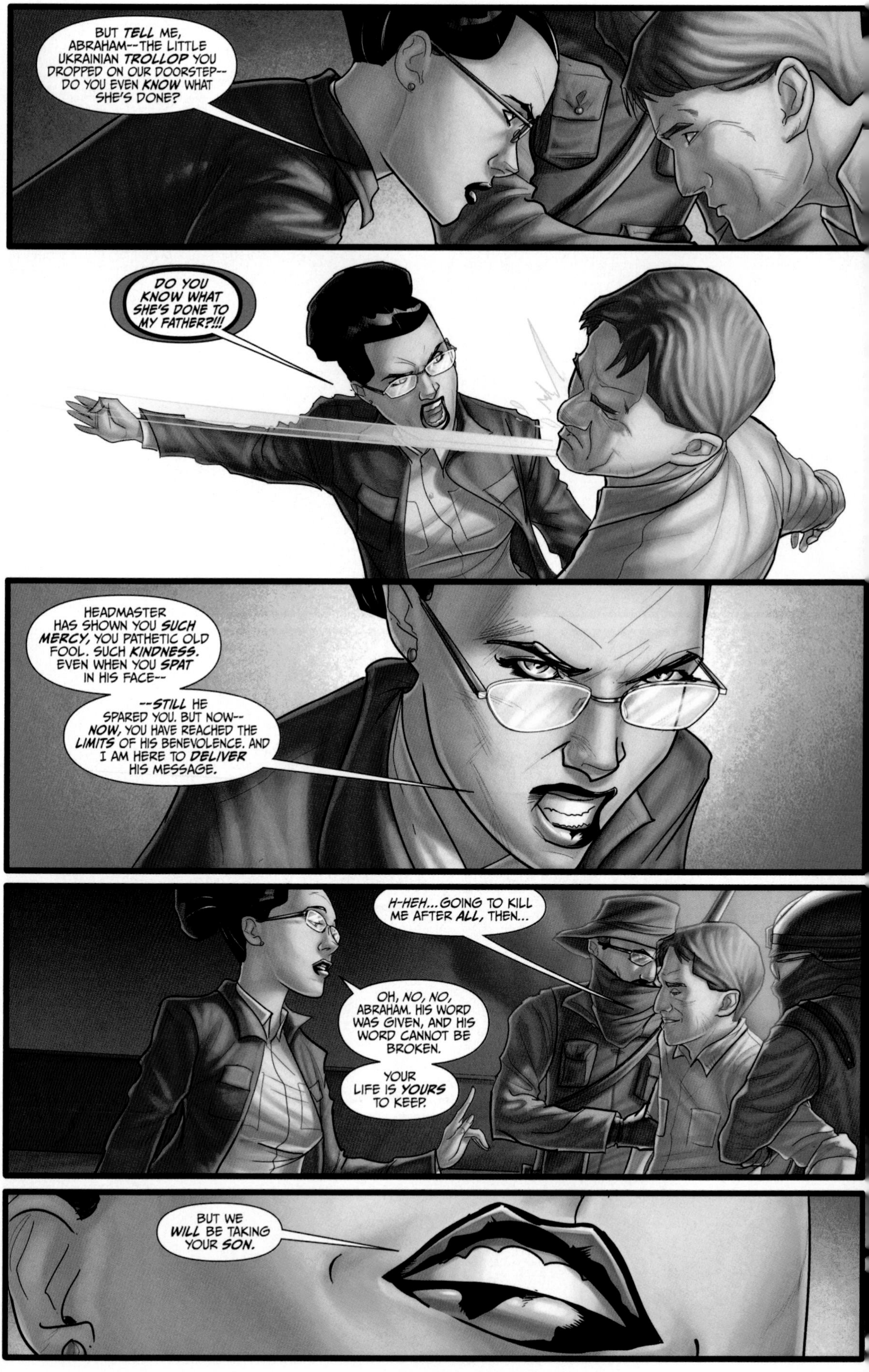
BUT TELL ME, ABRAHAM--THE LITTLE UKRAINIAN TROLLOP YOU DROPPED ON OUR DOORSTEP--DO YOU EVEN KNOW WHAT SHE'S DONE?
DO YOU KNOW WHAT SHE'S DONE TO MY FATHER?!!!
HEADMASTER HAS SHOWN YOU SUCH MERCY, YOU PATHETIC OLD FOOL. SUCH KINDNESS. EVEN WHEN YOU SPAT IN HIS FACE--
--STILL HE SPARED YOU. BUT NOW--NOW, YOU HAVE REACHED THE LIMITS OF HIS BENEVOLENCE. AND I AM HERE TO DELIVER HIS MESSAGE.
H-HEH...GOING TO KILL ME AFTER ALL, THEN...
OH, NO, NO, ABRAHAM. HIS WORD WAS GIVEN, AND HIS WORD CANNOT BE BROKEN.
YOUR LIFE IS YOURS TO KEEP.
BUT WE WILL BE TAKING YOUR SON.

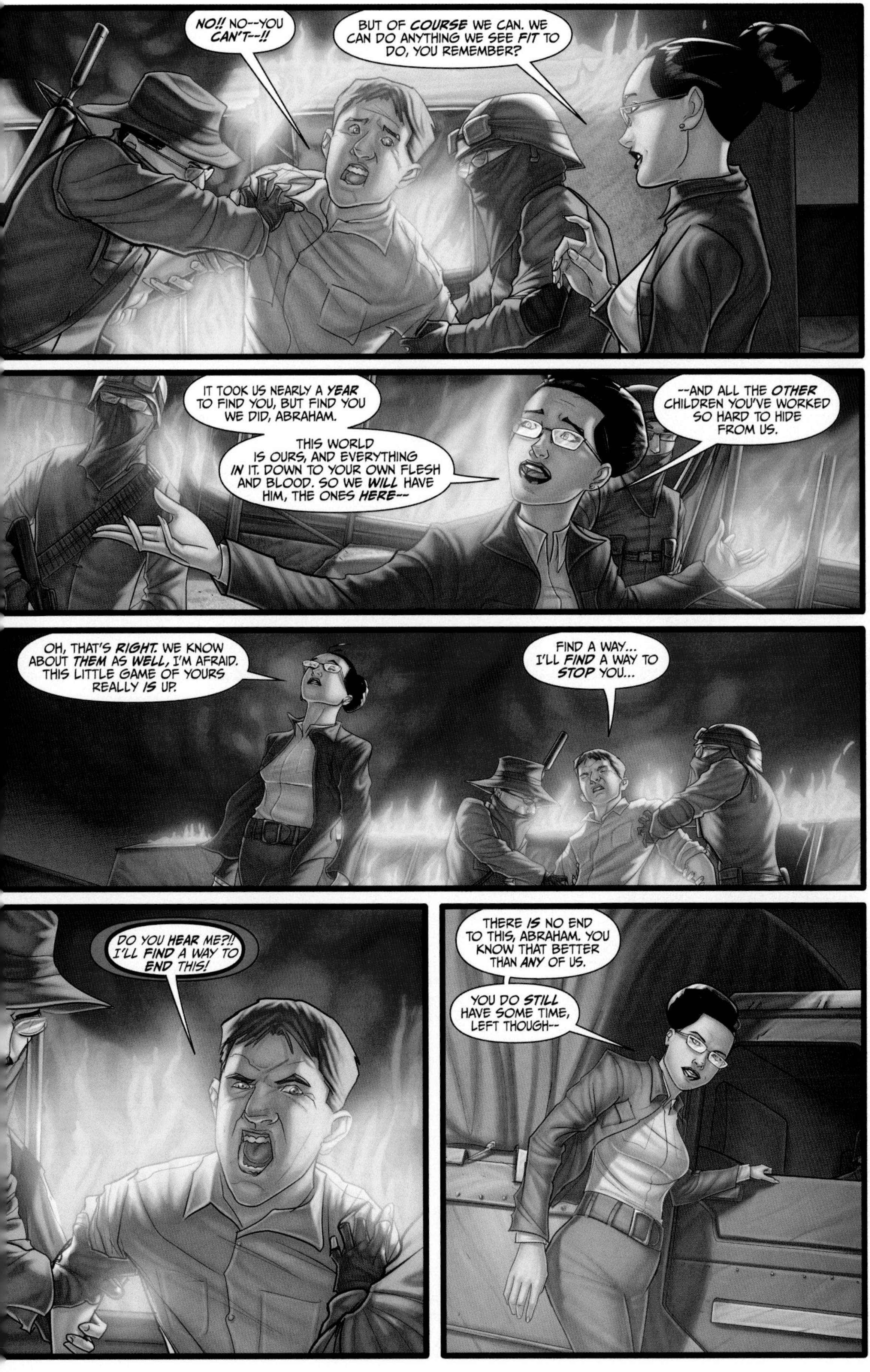
NO!! NO--YOU CAN'T--!!
BUT OF COURSE WE CAN. WE CAN DO ANYTHING WE SEE FIT TO DO, YOU REMEMBER?
IT TOOK US NEARLY A YEAR TO FIND YOU, BUT FIND YOU WE DID, ABRAHAM.
THIS WORLD IS OURS, AND EVERYTHING IN IT. DOWN TO YOUR OWN FLESH AND BLOOD. SO WE WILL HAVE HIM, THE ONES HERE--
--AND ALL THE OTHER CHILDREN YOU'VE WORKED SO HARD TO HIDE FROM US.
OH, THAT'S RIGHT. WE KNOW ABOUT THEM AS WELL, I'M AFRAID. THIS LITTLE GAME OF YOURS REALLY IS UP.
FIND A WAY... I'LL FIND A WAY TO STOP YOU...
DO YOU HEAR ME?!! I'LL FIND A WAY TO END THIS!
THERE IS NO END TO THIS, ABRAHAM. YOU KNOW THAT BETTER THAN ANY OF US.
YOU DO STILL HAVE SOME TIME, LEFT THOUGH--

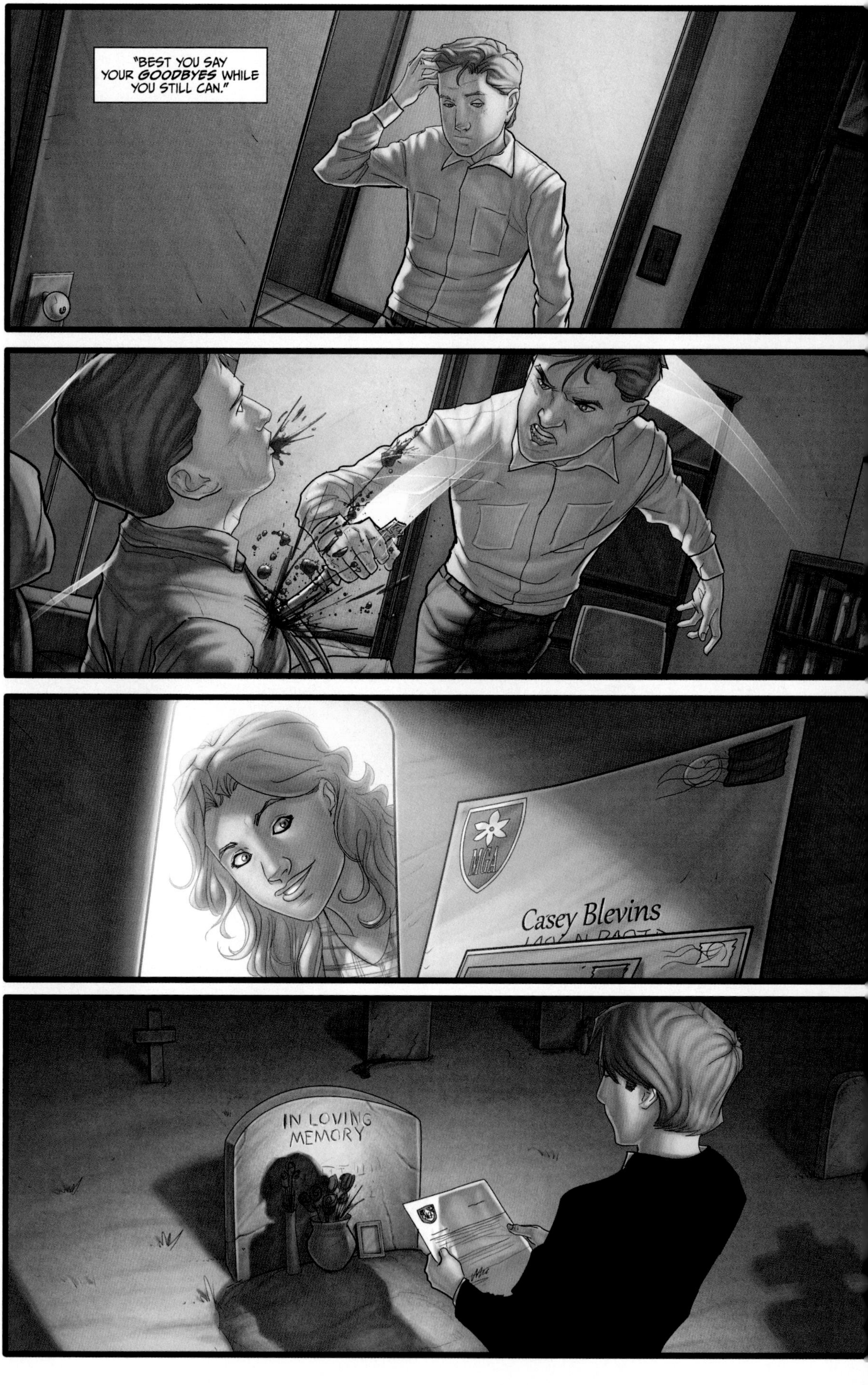
"BEST YOU SAY YOUR GOODBYES WHILE YOU STILL CAN."
MGA
Casey Blevins
IN LOVING MEMORY

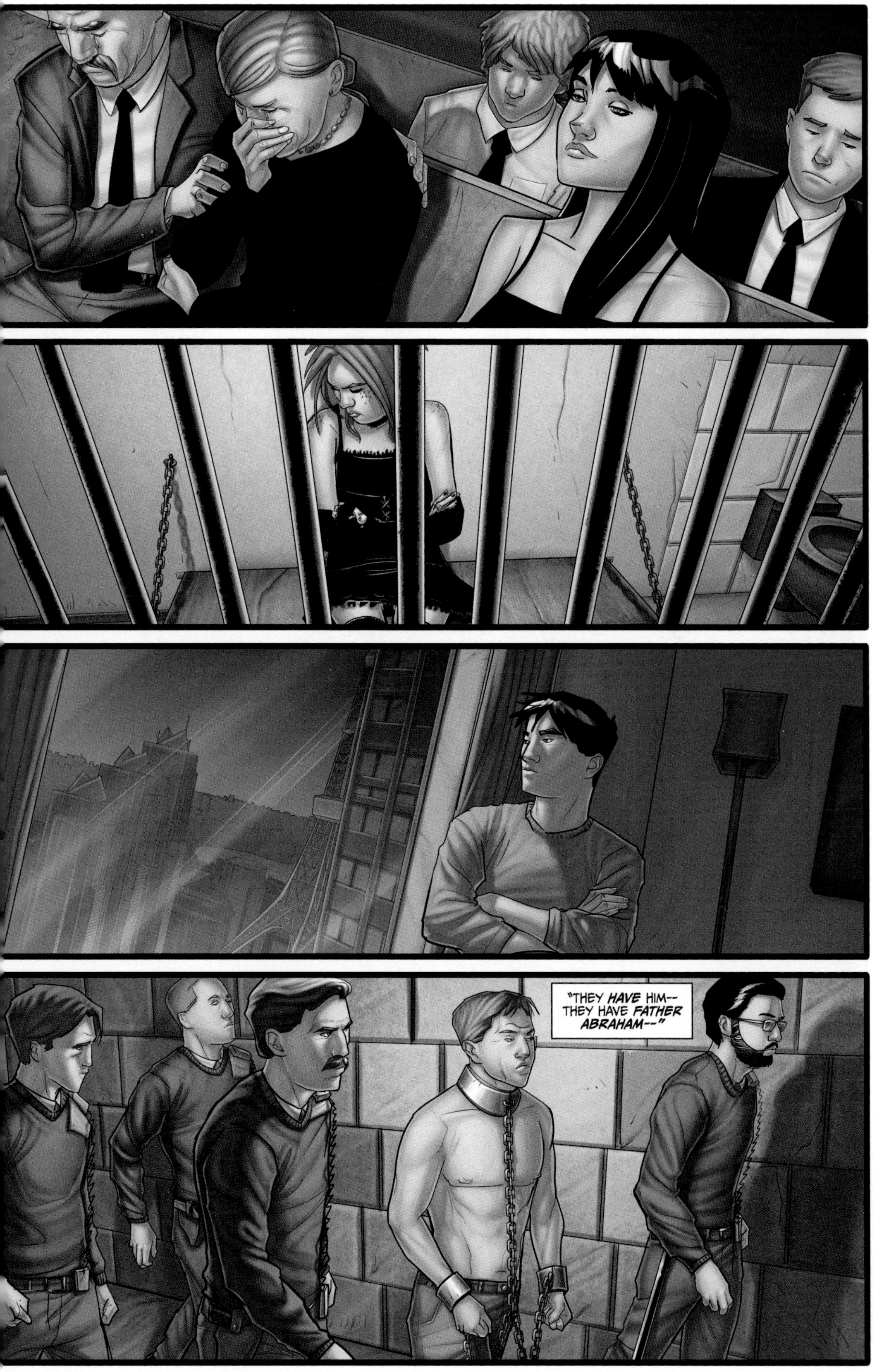
"THEY HAVE HIM--
THEY HAVE FATHER
ABRAHAM--"

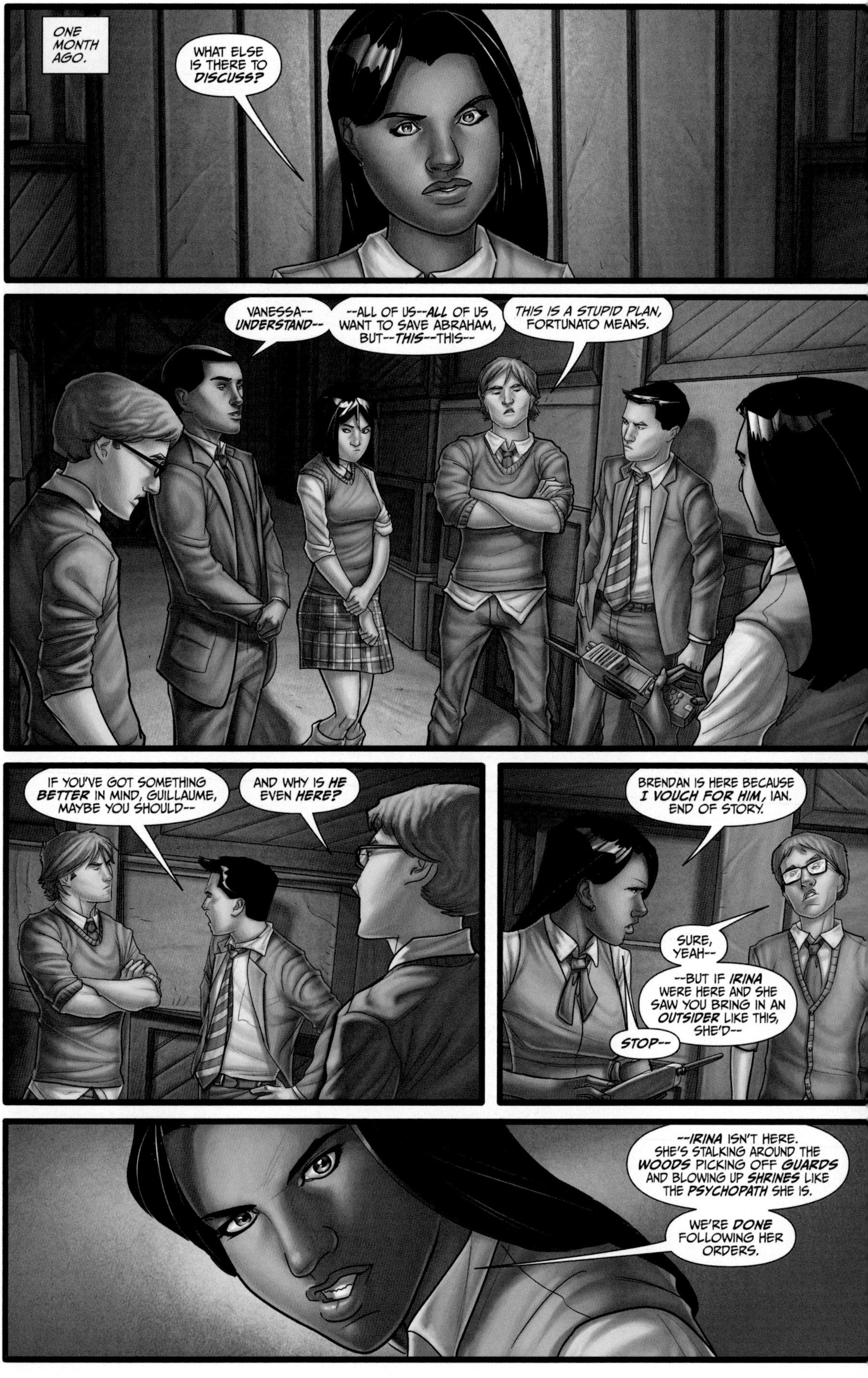
ONE MONTH AGO.
WHAT ELSE IS THERE TO DISCUSS?
VANESSA-- UNDERSTAND--
--ALL OF US--ALL OF US WANT TO SAVE ABRAHAM, BUT--THIS--THIS--
THIS IS A STUPID PLAN, FORTUNATO MEANS.
IF YOU'VE GOT SOMETHING BETTER IN MIND, GUILLAUME, MAYBE YOU SHOULD--
AND WHY IS HE EVEN HERE?
BRENDAN IS HERE BECAUSE I VOUCH FOR HIM, IAN. END OF STORY.
SURE, YEAH--
--BUT IF IRINA WERE HERE AND SHE SAW YOU BRING IN AN OUTSIDER LIKE THIS, SHE'D--
STOP--
--IRINA ISN'T HERE. SHE'S STALKING AROUND THE WOODS PICKING OFF GUARDS AND BLOWING UP SHRINES LIKE THE PSYCHOPATH SHE IS.
WE'RE DONE FOLLOWING HER ORDERS.

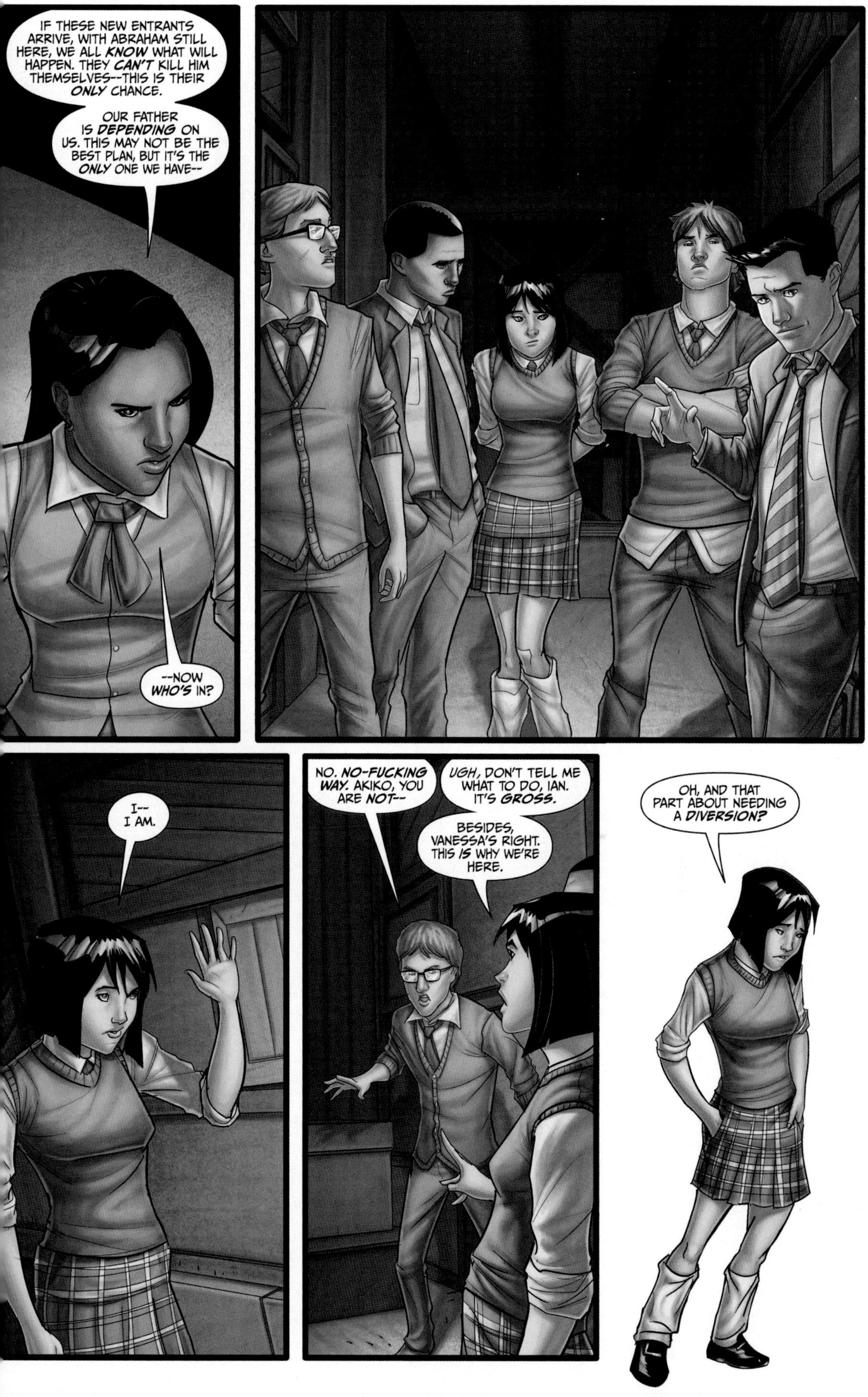
IF THESE NEW ENTRANTS ARRIVE, WITH ABRAHAM STILL HERE, WE ALL KNOW WHAT WILL HAPPEN. THEY CAN'T KILL HIM THEMSELVES--THIS IS THEIR ONLY CHANCE.
OUR FATHER IS DEPENDING ON US. THIS MAY NOT BE THE BEST PLAN, BUT IT'S THE ONLY ONE WE HAVE--
--NOW WHO'S IN?
I-- I AM.
NO. NO-FUCKING WAY. AKIKO, YOU ARE NOT--
UGH, DON'T TELL ME WHAT TO DO, IAN. IT'S GROSS.
BESIDES, VANESSA'S RIGHT. THIS IS WHY WE'RE HERE.
OH, AND THAT PART ABOUT NEEDING A DIVERSION?

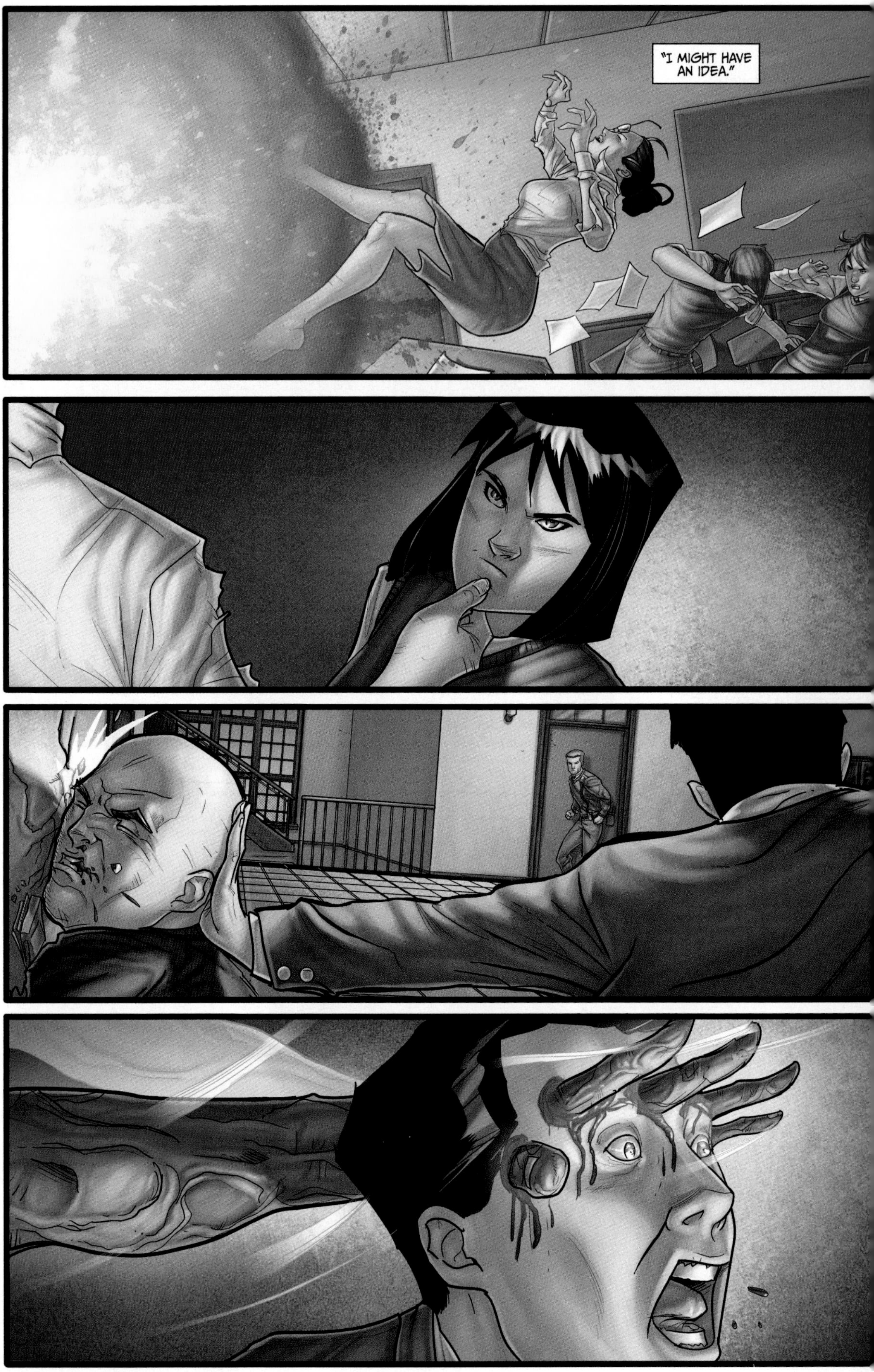
"I MIGHT HAVE AN IDEA."

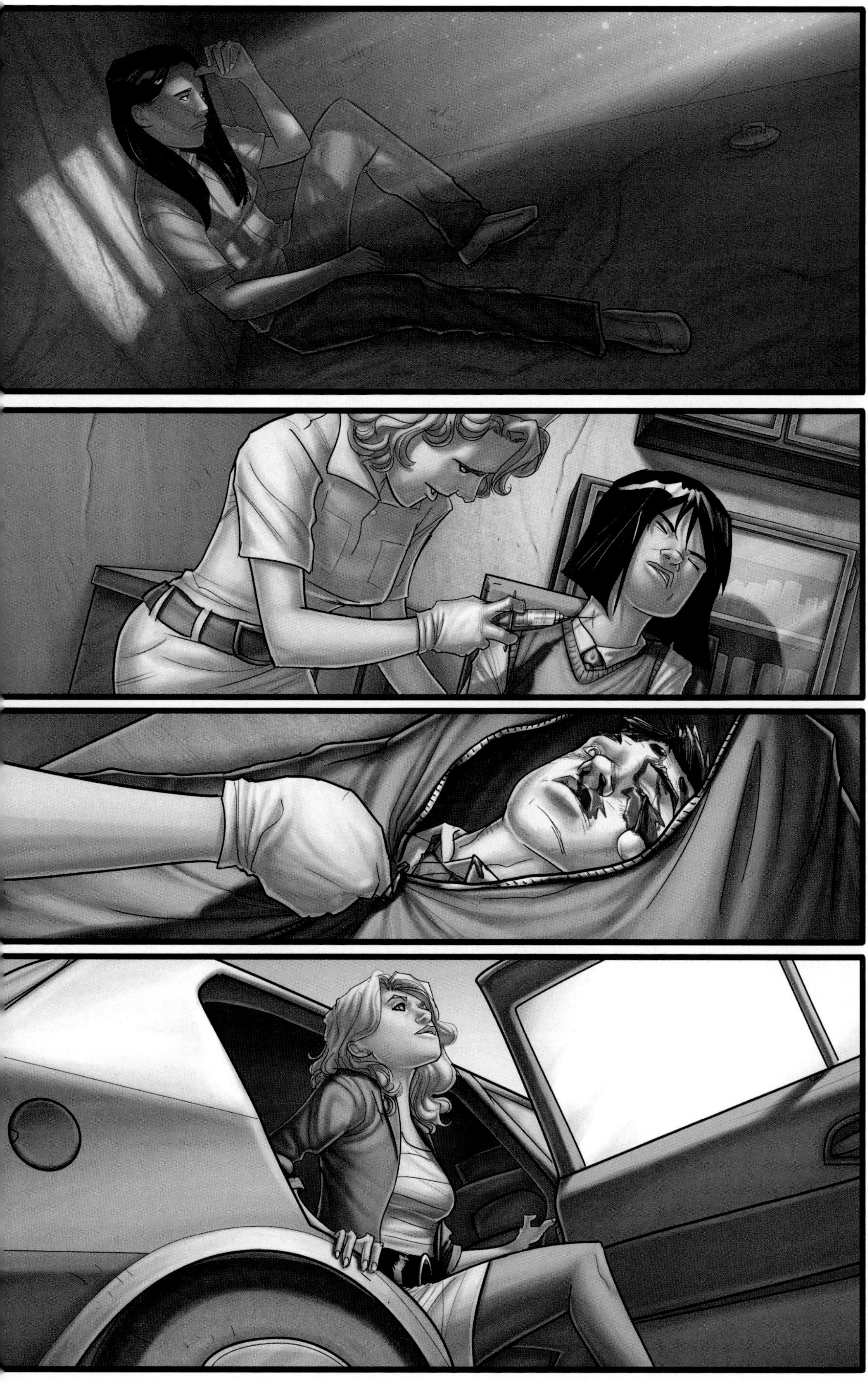

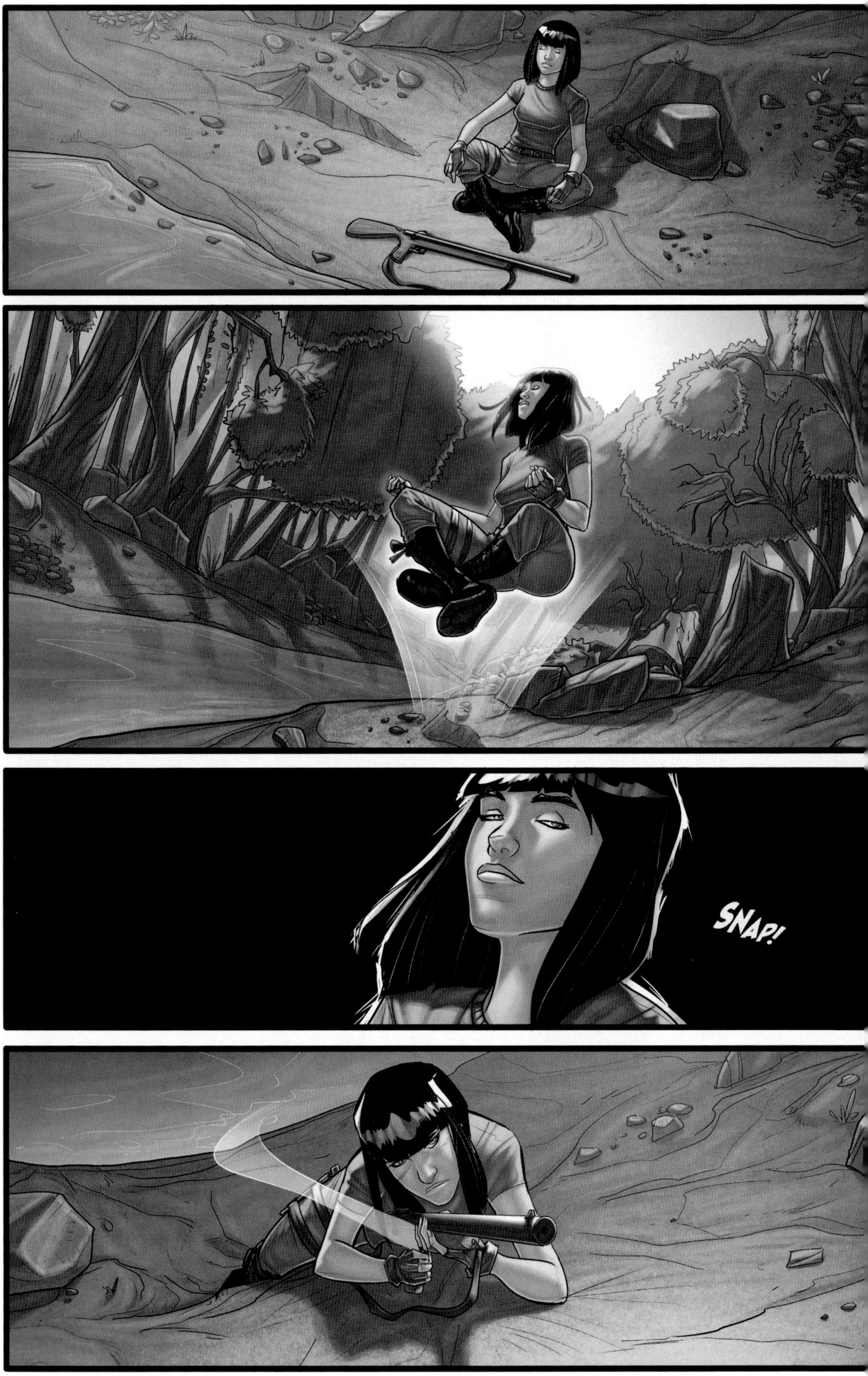
SNAP!

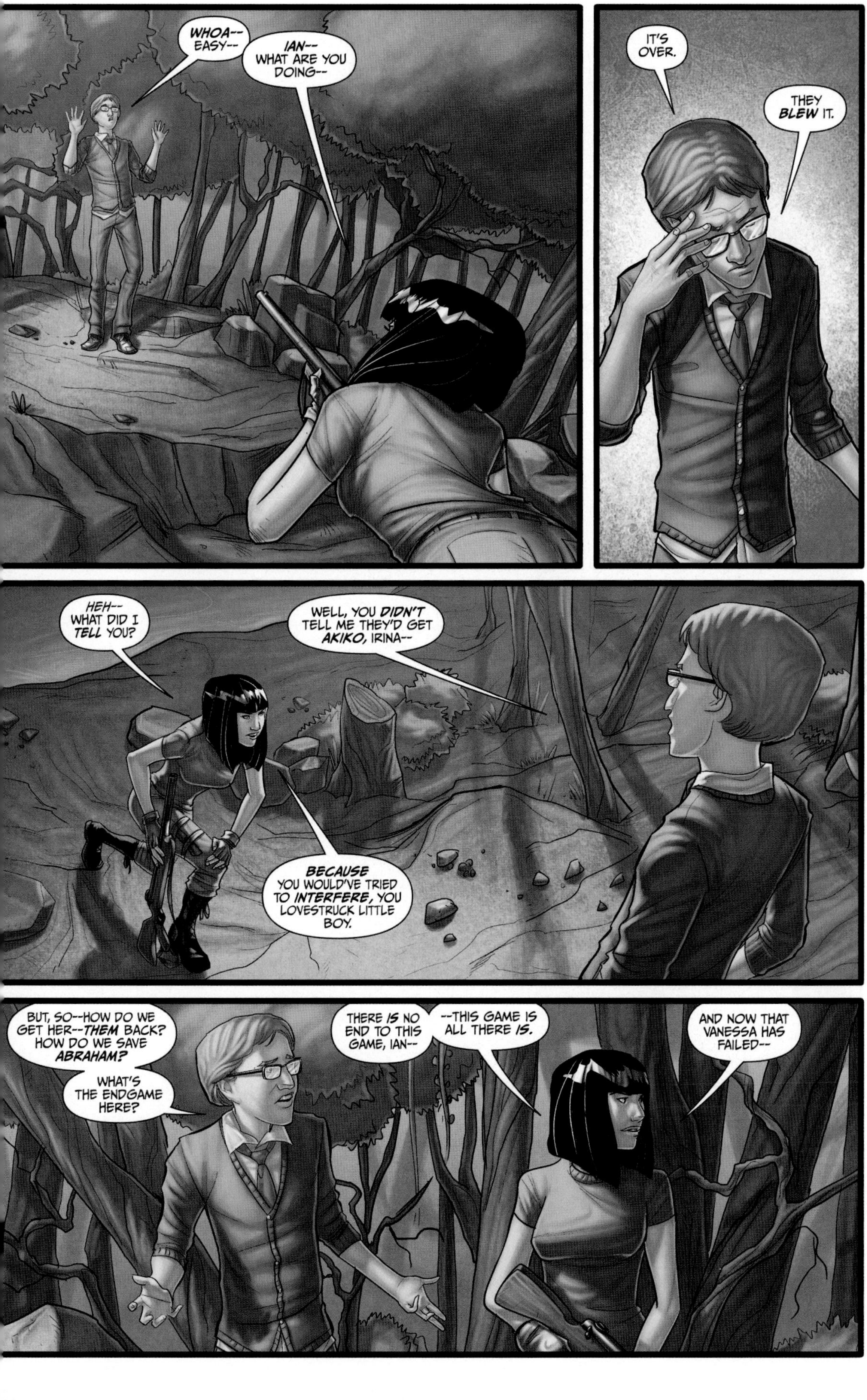
WHOA--
EASY--
IAN--
WHAT ARE YOU DOING--
IT'S OVER.
THEY BLEW IT.
HEH--
WHAT DID I TELL YOU?
WELL, YOU DIDN'T TELL ME THEY'D GET AKIKO, IRINA--
BECAUSE YOU WOULD'VE TRIED TO INTERFERE, YOU LOVESTRUCK LITTLE BOY.
BUT, SO--HOW DO WE GET HER--THEM BACK? HOW DO WE SAVE ABRAHAM?
WHAT'S THE ENDGAME HERE?
THERE IS NO END TO THIS GAME, IAN--
--THIS GAME IS ALL THERE IS.
AND NOW THAT VANESSA HAS FAILED--

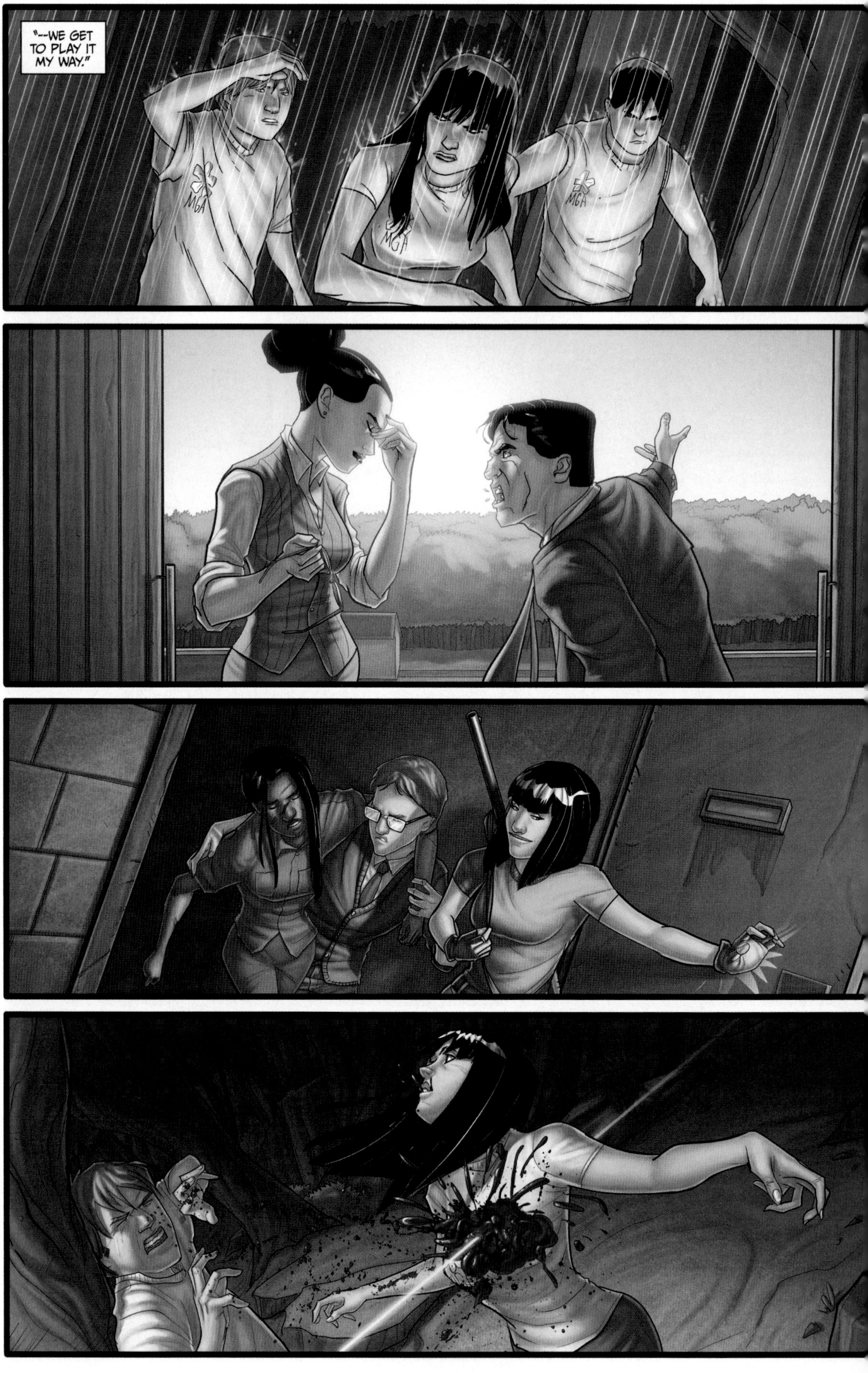
"--WE GET TO PLAY IT MY WAY."
MGA
MGA
MGA

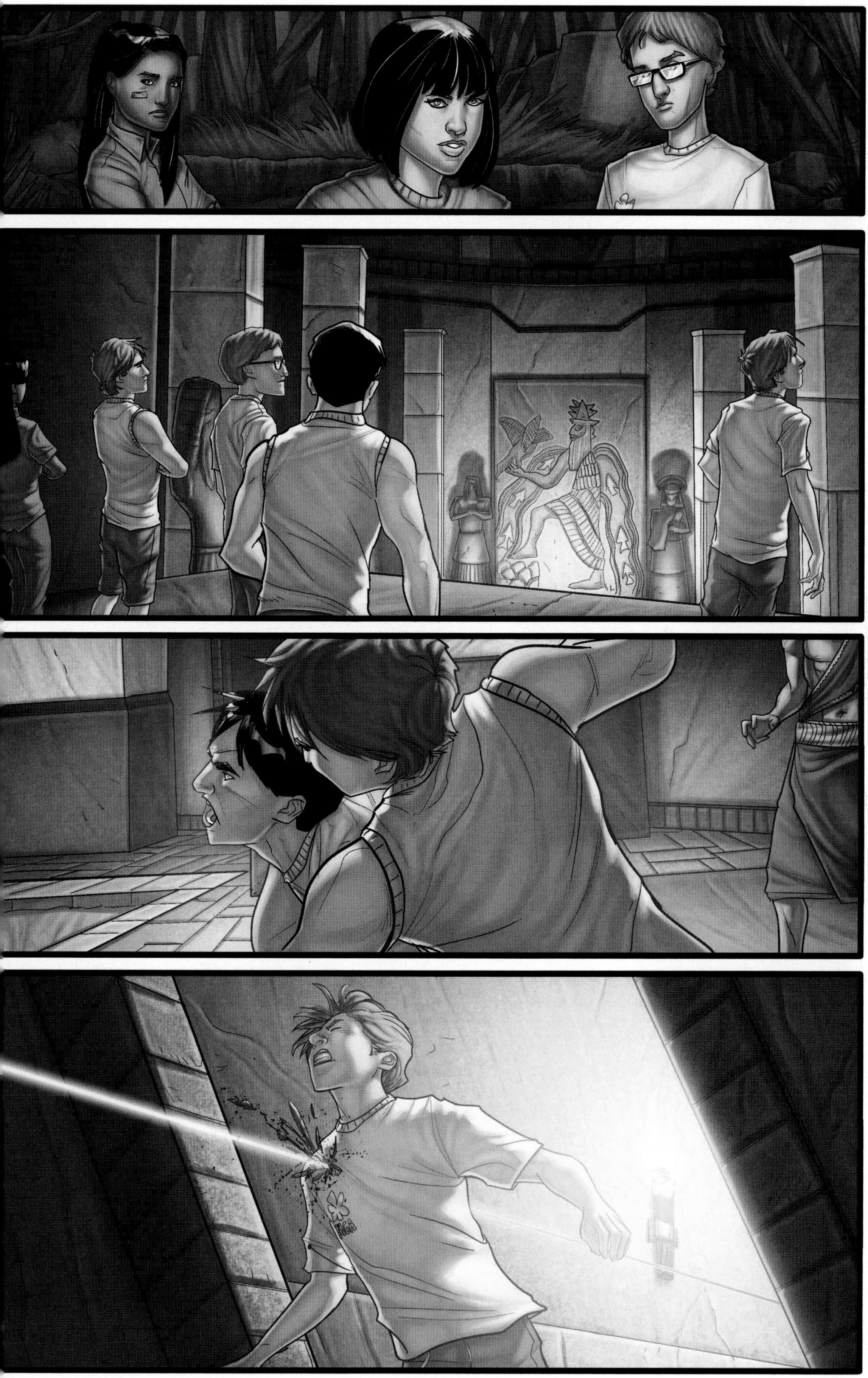

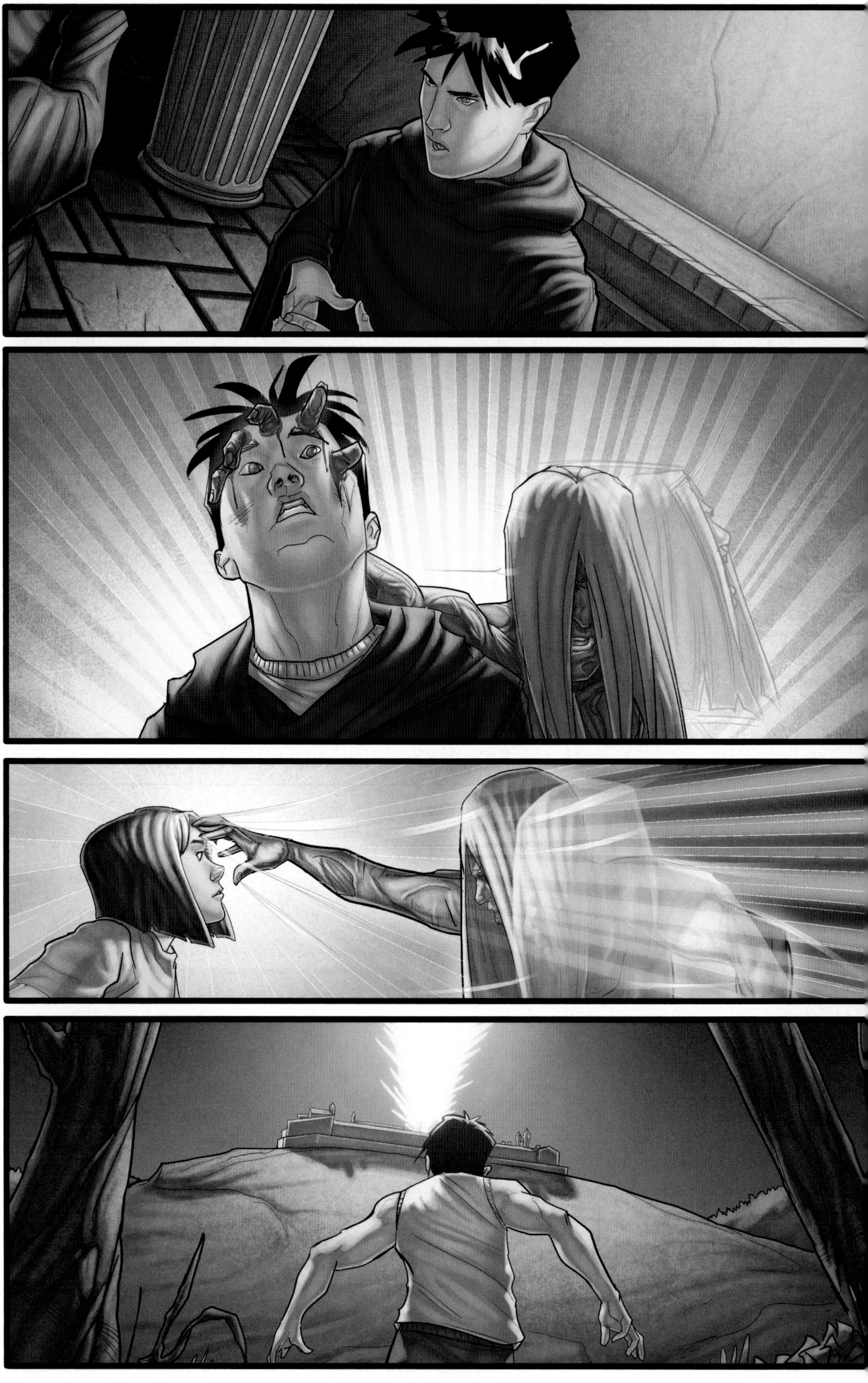

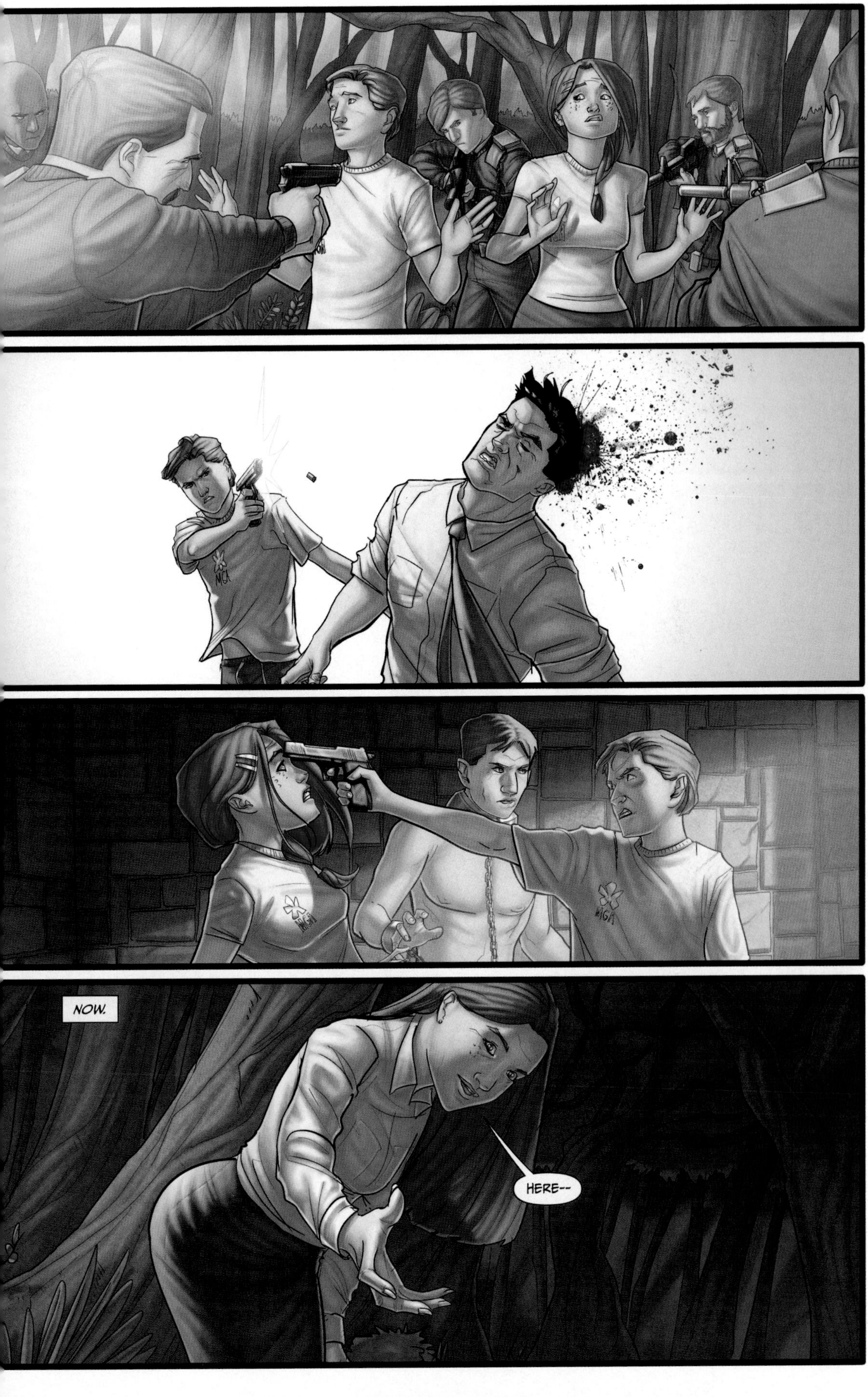
NOW.
HERE--

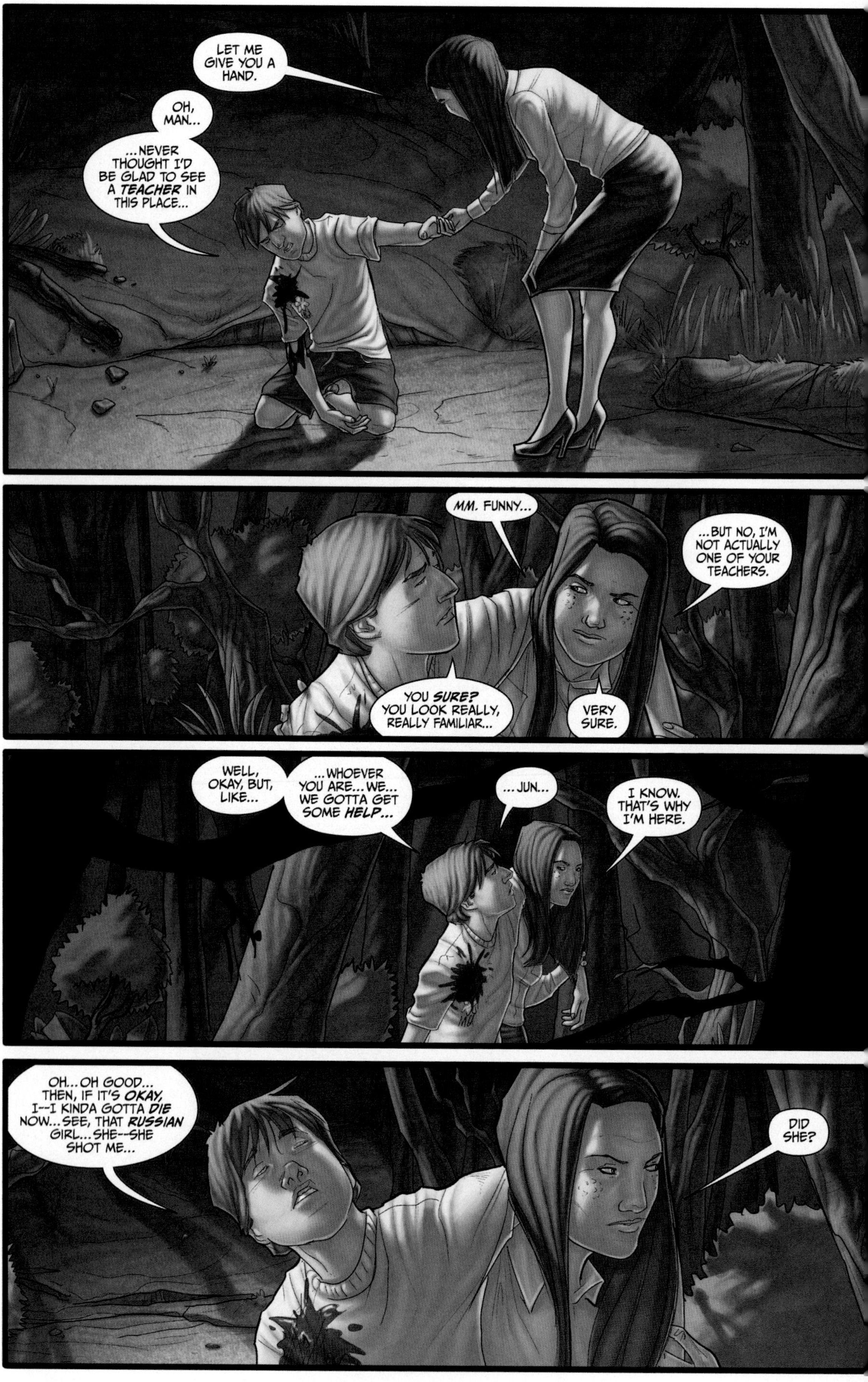
LET ME GIVE YOU A HAND.
OH, MAN...
...NEVER THOUGHT I'D BE GLAD TO SEE A TEACHER IN THIS PLACE...
MM. FUNNY...
...BUT NO, I'M NOT ACTUALLY ONE OF YOUR TEACHERS.
YOU SURE? YOU LOOK REALLY, REALLY FAMILIAR...
VERY SURE.
WELL, OKAY, BUT, LIKE...
...WHOEVER YOU ARE...WE... WE GOTTA GET SOME HELP...
...JUN...
I KNOW. THAT'S WHY I'M HERE.
OH...OH GOOD... THEN, IF IT'S OKAY, I--I KINDA GOTTA DIE NOW...SEE, THAT RUSSIAN GIRL...SHE--SHE SHOT ME...
DID SHE?

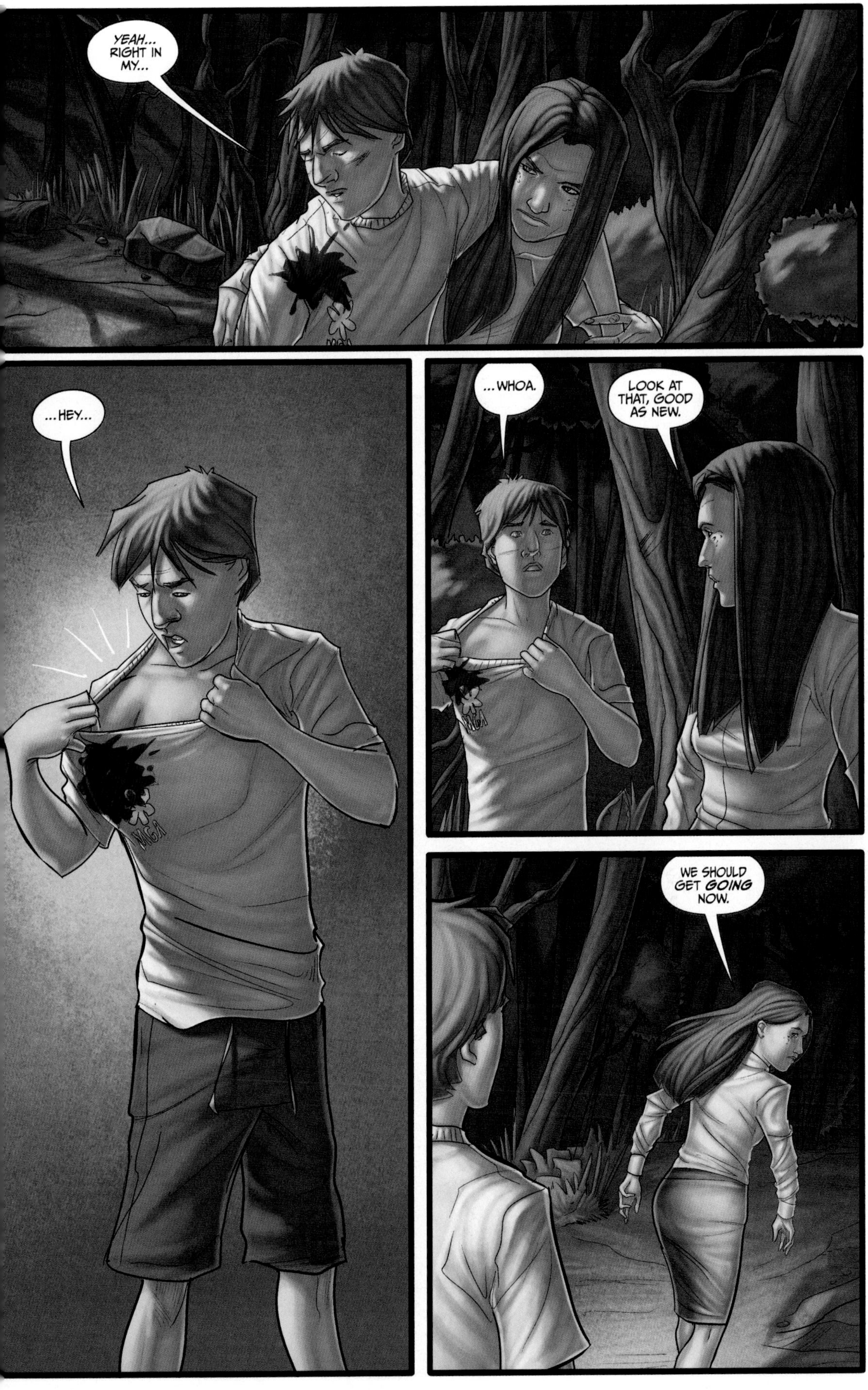
YEAH... RIGHT IN MY...
...HEY...
...WHOA.
LOOK AT THAT, GOOD AS NEW.
WE SHOULD GET GOING NOW.

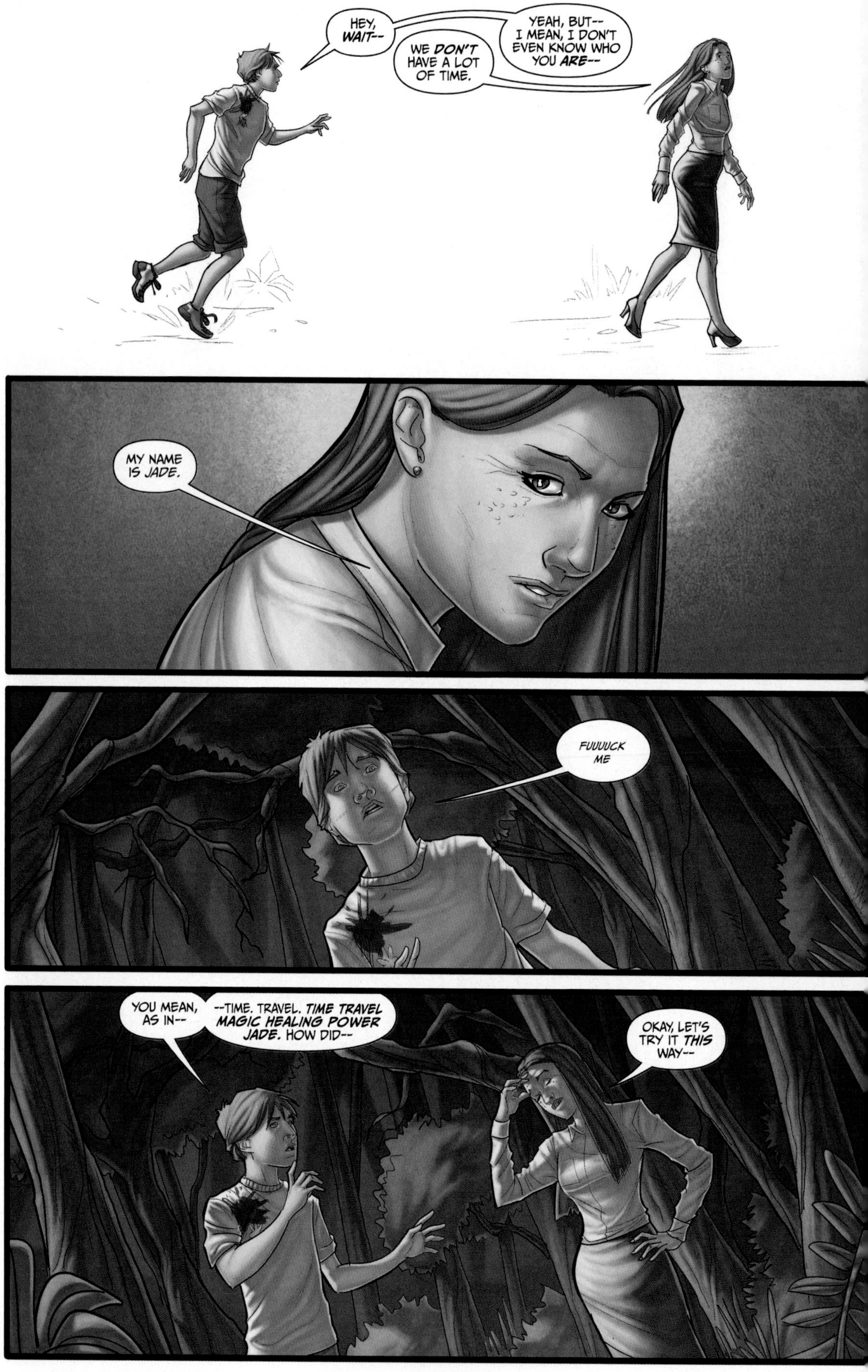
HEY, WAIT--
YEAH, BUT-- I MEAN, I DON'T EVEN KNOW WHO YOU ARE--
WE DON'T HAVE A LOT OF TIME.
MY NAME IS JADE.
FUUUUCK ME
YOU MEAN, AS IN--
--TIME. TRAVEL. TIME TRAVEL MAGIC HEALING POWER JADE. HOW DID--
OKAY, LET'S TRY IT THIS WAY--

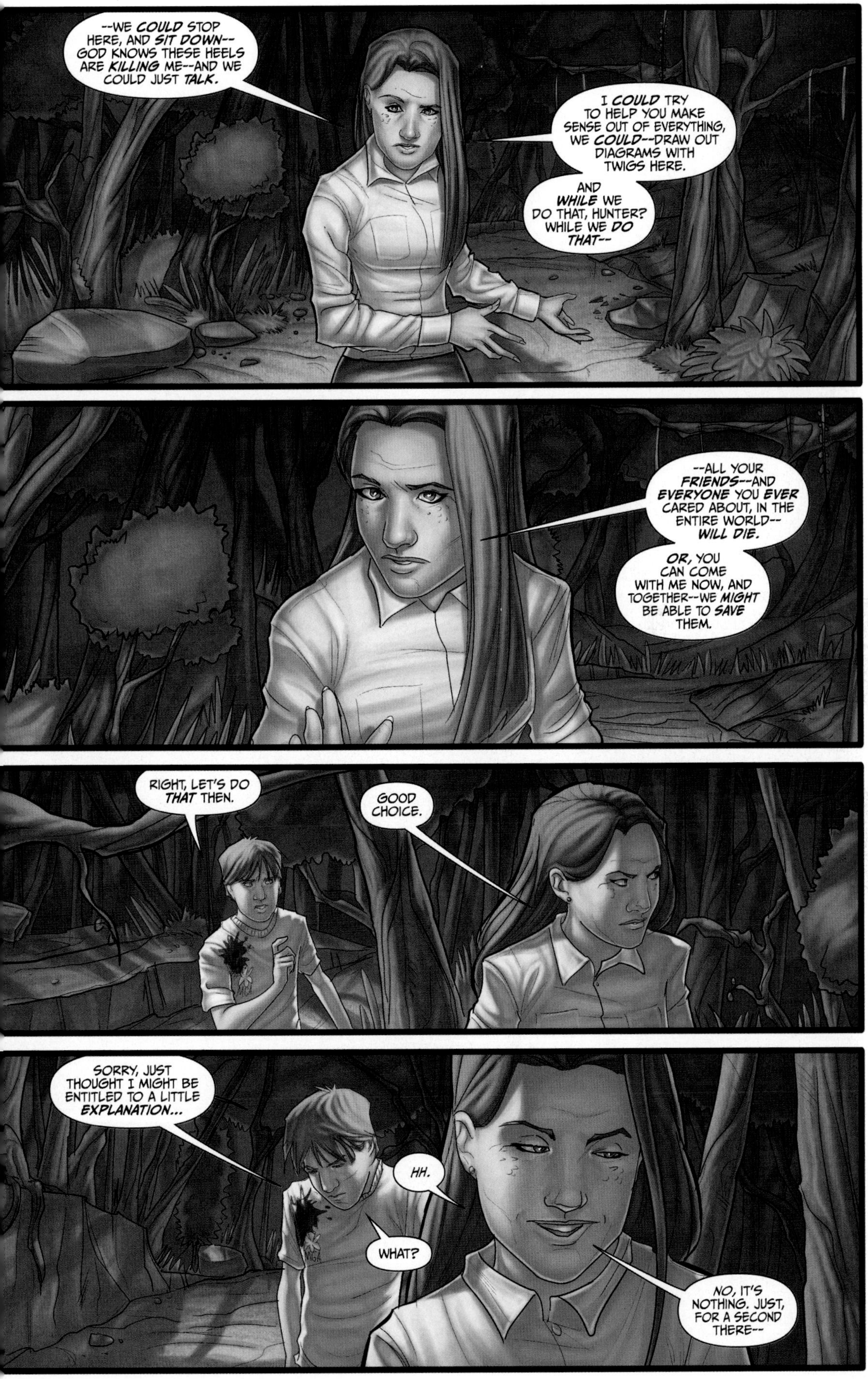
--WE COULD STOP HERE, AND SIT DOWN--GOD KNOWS THESE HEELS ARE KILLING ME--AND WE COULD JUST TALK.
I COULD TRY TO HELP YOU MAKE SENSE OUT OF EVERYTHING, WE COULD--DRAW OUT DIAGRAMS WITH TWIGS HERE.
AND WHILE WE DO THAT, HUNTER? WHILE WE DO THAT--
--ALL YOUR FRIENDS--AND EVERYONE YOU EVER CARED ABOUT, IN THE ENTIRE WORLD--WILL DIE.
OR, YOU CAN COME WITH ME NOW, AND TOGETHER--WE MIGHT BE ABLE TO SAVE THEM.
RIGHT, LET'S DO THAT THEN.
GOOD CHOICE.
SORRY, JUST THOUGHT I MIGHT BE ENTITLED TO A LITTLE EXPLANATION...
HH.
WHAT?
NO, IT'S NOTHING. JUST, FOR A SECOND THERE--

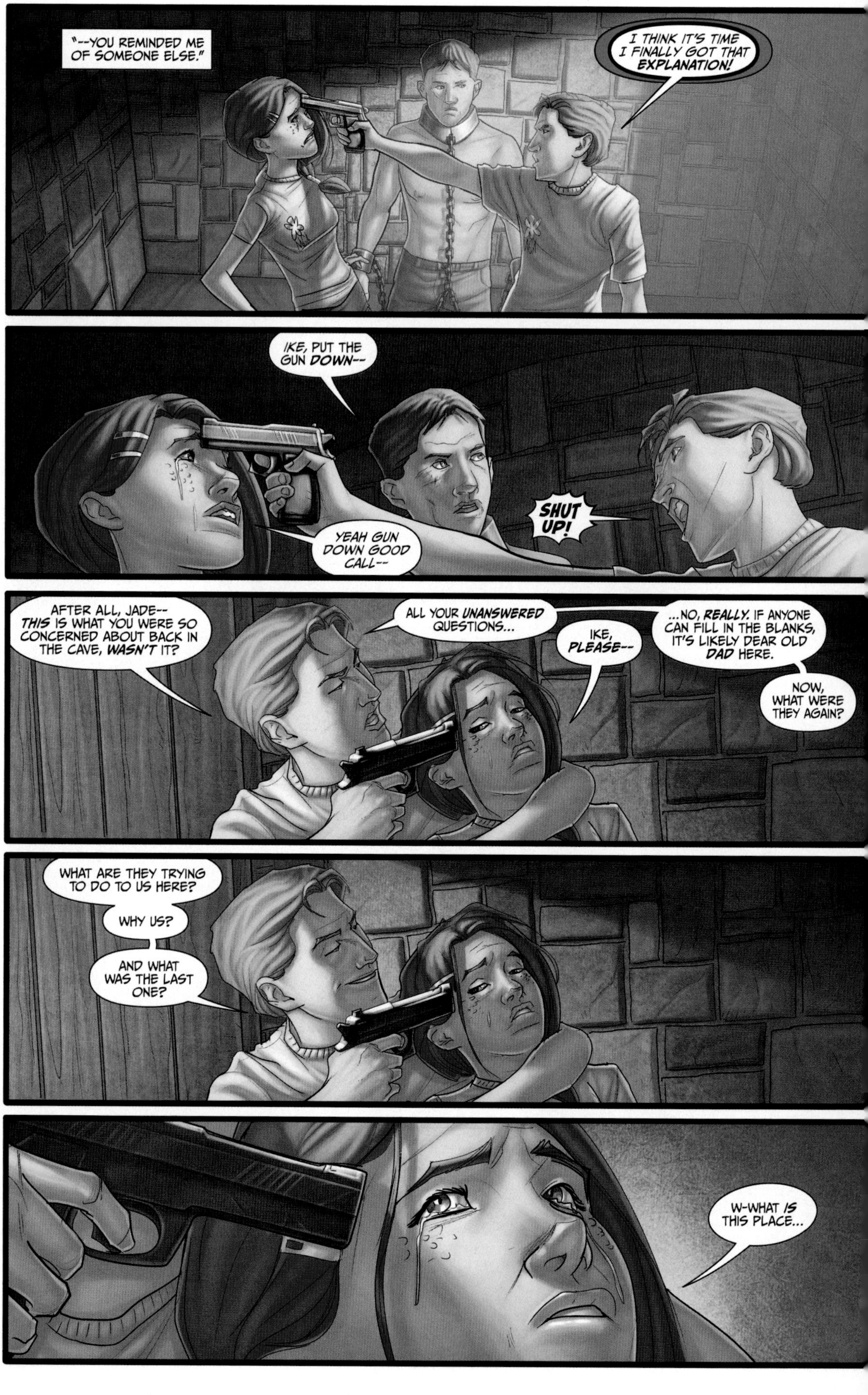
"--YOU REMINDED ME OF SOMEONE ELSE."
I THINK IT'S TIME I FINALLY GOT THAT EXPLANATION!
IKE, PUT THE GUN DOWN--
YEAH GUN DOWN GOOD CALL--
SHUT UP!
AFTER ALL, JADE-- THIS IS WHAT YOU WERE SO CONCERNED ABOUT BACK IN THE CAVE, WASN'T IT?
ALL YOUR UNANSWERED QUESTIONS...
IKE, PLEASE--
...NO, REALLY. IF ANYONE CAN FILL IN THE BLANKS, IT'S LIKELY DEAR OLD DAD HERE.
NOW, WHAT WERE THEY AGAIN?
WHAT ARE THEY TRYING TO DO TO US HERE?
WHY US?
AND WHAT WAS THE LAST ONE?
W-WHAT IS THIS PLACE...

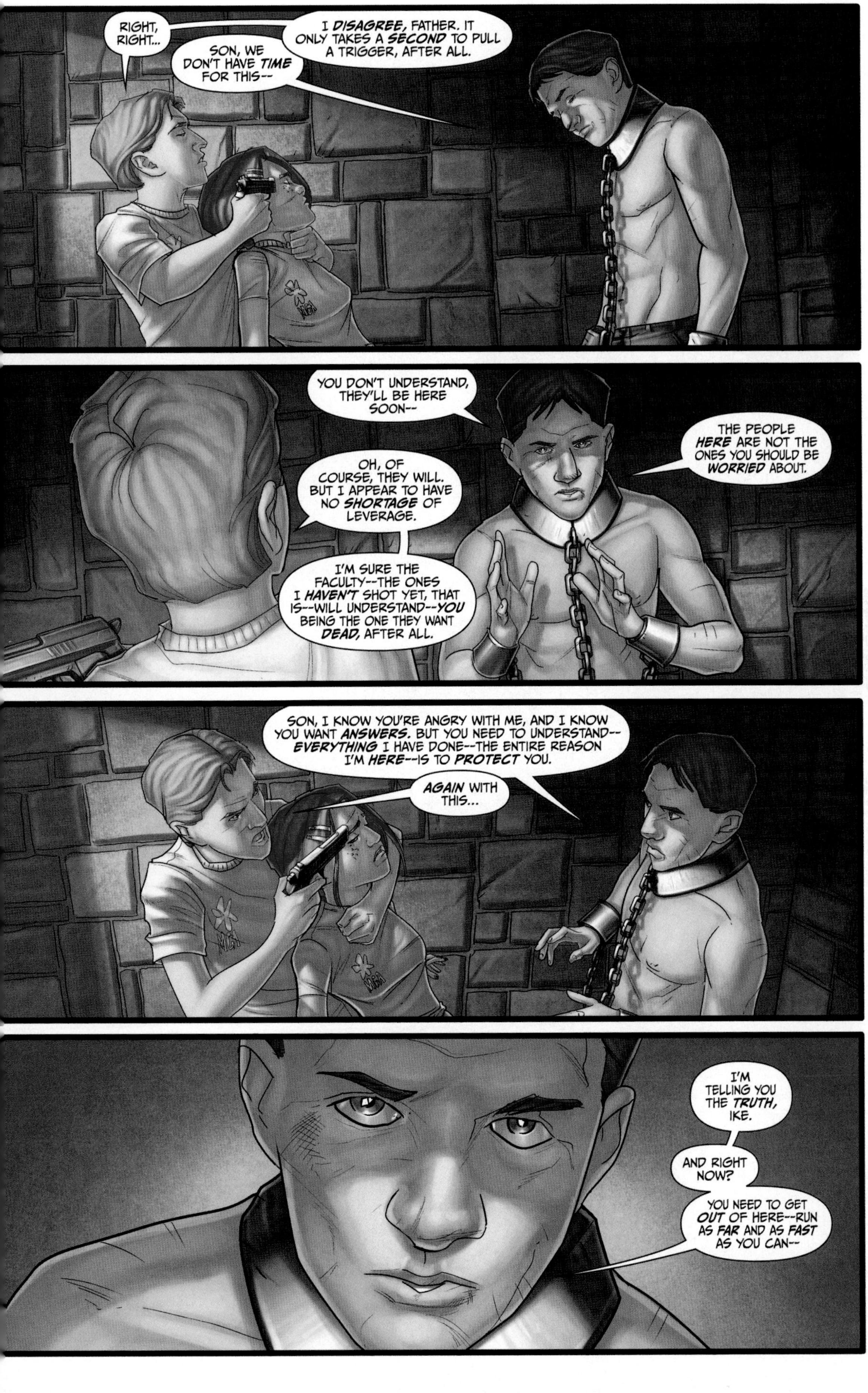
RIGHT, RIGHT...
SON, WE DON'T HAVE TIME FOR THIS--
I DISAGREE, FATHER. IT ONLY TAKES A SECOND TO PULL A TRIGGER, AFTER ALL.
YOU DON'T UNDERSTAND, THEY'LL BE HERE SOON--
THE PEOPLE HERE ARE NOT THE ONES YOU SHOULD BE WORRIED ABOUT.
OH, OF COURSE, THEY WILL. BUT I APPEAR TO HAVE NO SHORTAGE OF LEVERAGE.
I'M SURE THE FACULTY--THE ONES I HAVEN'T SHOT YET, THAT IS--WILL UNDERSTAND--YOU BEING THE ONE THEY WANT DEAD, AFTER ALL.
SON, I KNOW YOU'RE ANGRY WITH ME, AND I KNOW YOU WANT ANSWERS. BUT YOU NEED TO UNDERSTAND--EVERYTHING I HAVE DONE--THE ENTIRE REASON I'M HERE--IS TO PROTECT YOU.
AGAIN WITH THIS...
I'M TELLING YOU THE TRUTH, IKE.
AND RIGHT NOW?
YOU NEED TO GET OUT OF HERE--RUN AS FAR AND AS FAST AS YOU CAN--

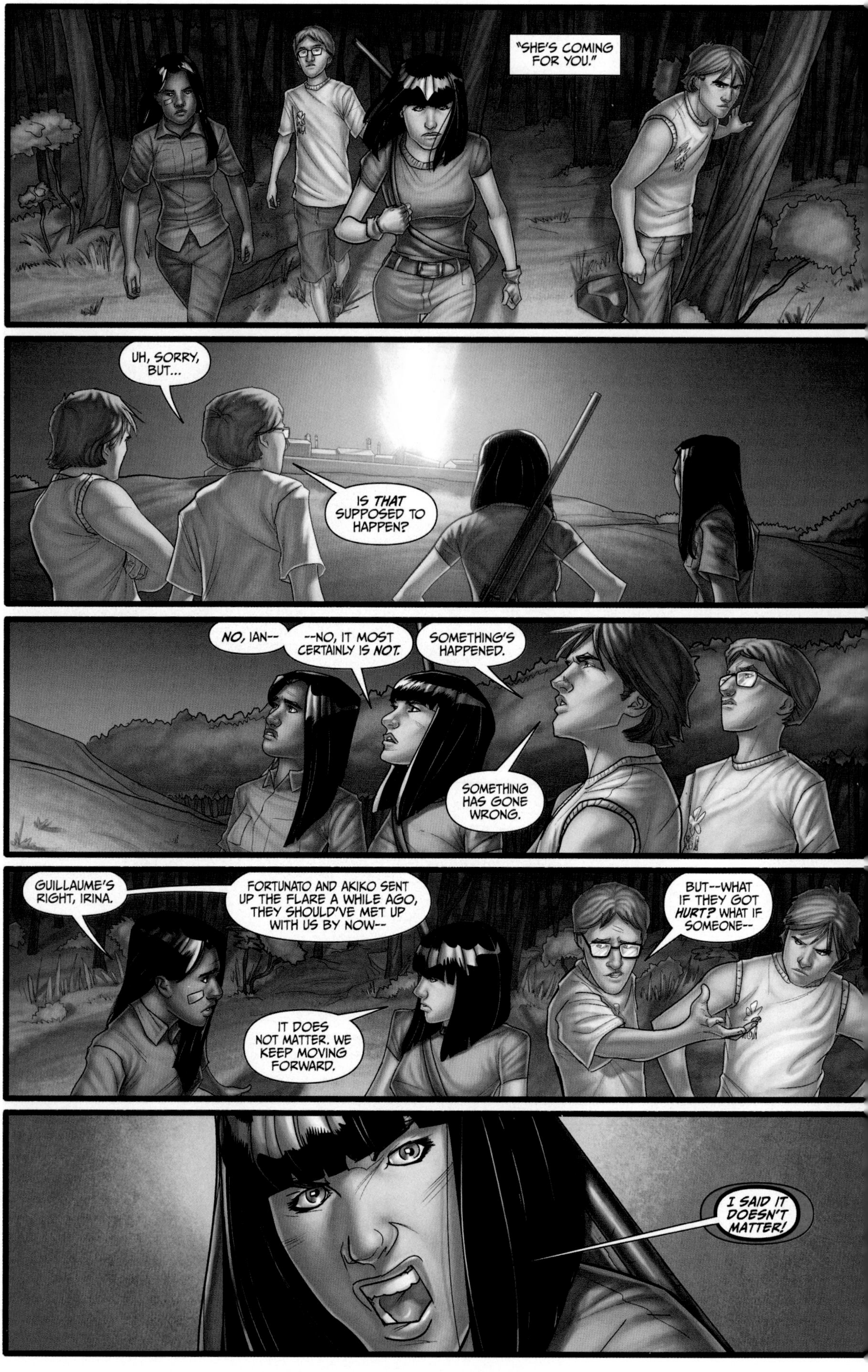
"SHE'S COMING FOR YOU."
UH, SORRY, BUT...
IS *THAT* SUPPOSED TO HAPPEN?
NO, IAN--
--NO, IT MOST CERTAINLY IS *NOT.*
SOMETHING'S HAPPENED.
SOMETHING HAS GONE WRONG.
GUILLAUME'S RIGHT, IRINA.
FORTUNATO AND AKIKO SENT UP THE FLARE A WHILE AGO, THEY SHOULD'VE MET UP WITH US BY NOW--
BUT--WHAT IF THEY GOT *HURT?* WHAT IF SOMEONE--
IT DOES NOT MATTER. WE KEEP MOVING FORWARD.
I SAID IT DOESN'T MATTER!

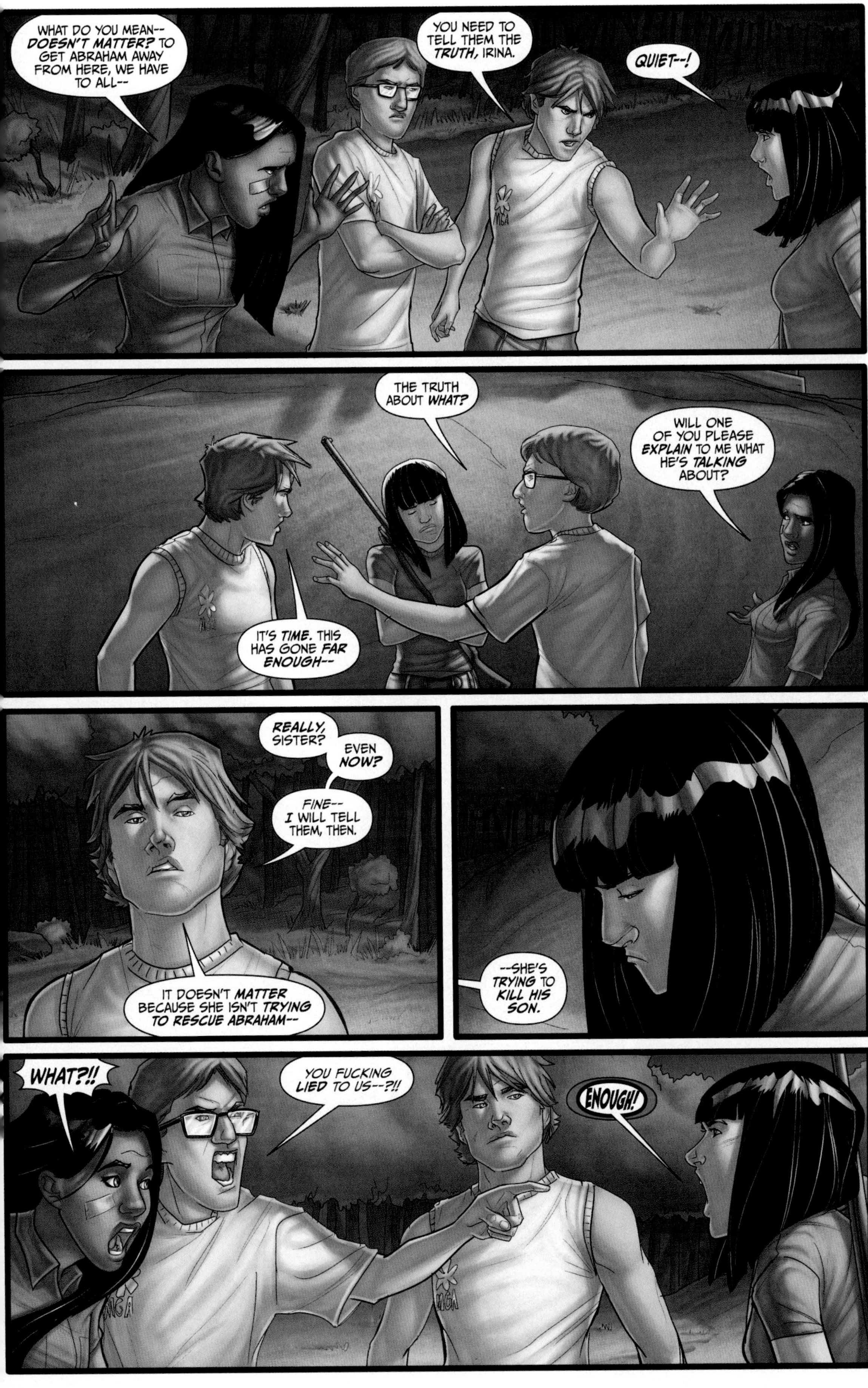

WHAT DO YOU MEAN-- DOESN'T MATTER? TO GET ABRAHAM AWAY FROM HERE, WE HAVE TO ALL--
YOU NEED TO TELL THEM THE TRUTH, IRINA.
QUIET--!
THE TRUTH ABOUT WHAT?
WILL ONE OF YOU PLEASE EXPLAIN TO ME WHAT HE'S TALKING ABOUT?
IT'S TIME. THIS HAS GONE FAR ENOUGH--
REALLY, SISTER?
EVEN NOW?
FINE-- I WILL TELL THEM, THEN.
IT DOESN'T MATTER BECAUSE SHE ISN'T TRYING TO RESCUE ABRAHAM--
--SHE'S TRYING TO KILL HIS SON.
WHAT?!!
YOU FUCKING LIED TO US--?!!
ENOUGH!

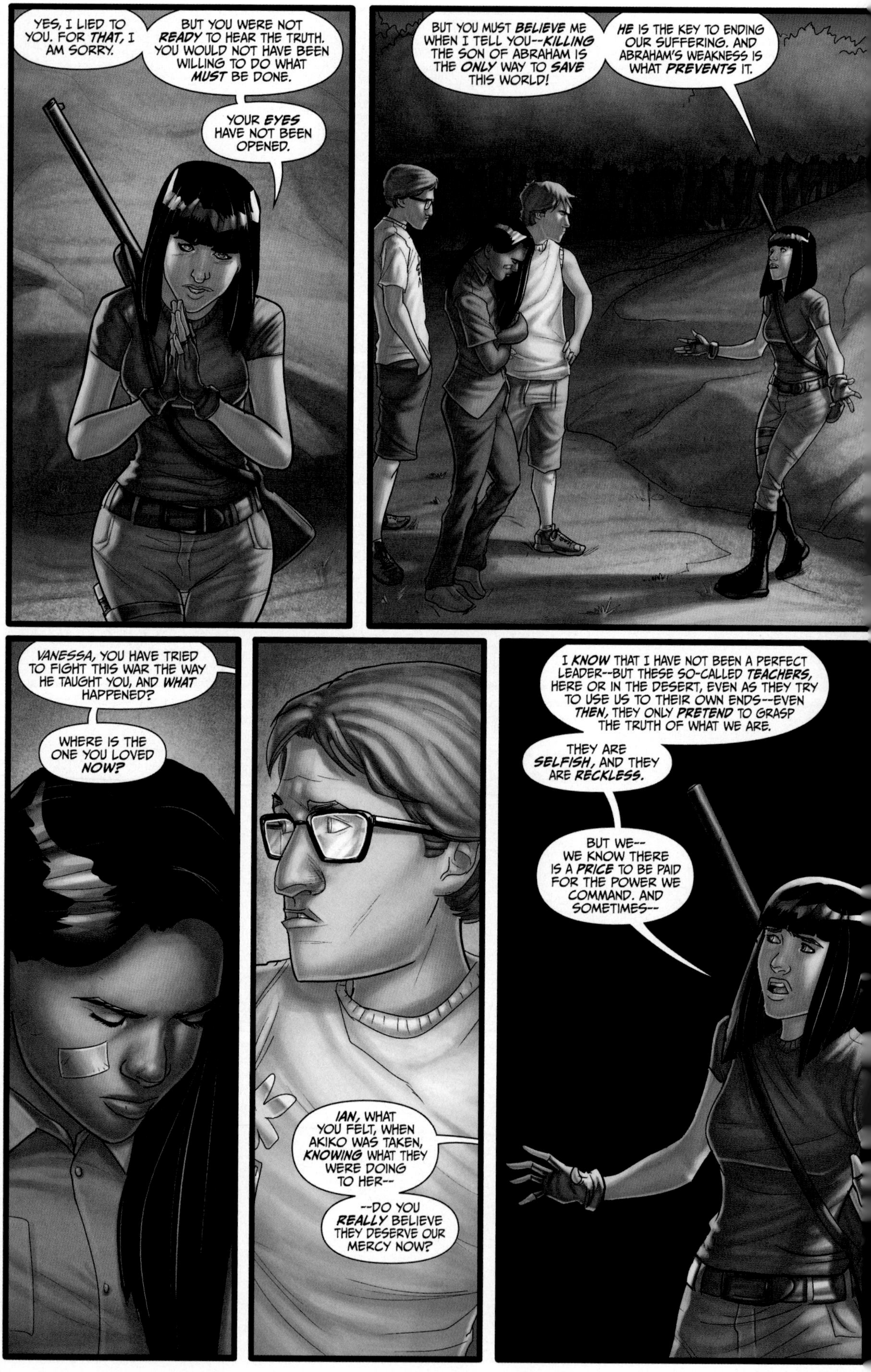
YES, I LIED TO YOU. FOR THAT, I AM SORRY.
BUT YOU WERE NOT READY TO HEAR THE TRUTH. YOU WOULD NOT HAVE BEEN WILLING TO DO WHAT MUST BE DONE.
YOUR EYES HAVE NOT BEEN OPENED.
BUT YOU MUST BELIEVE ME WHEN I TELL YOU--KILLING THE SON OF ABRAHAM IS THE ONLY WAY TO SAVE THIS WORLD!
HE IS THE KEY TO ENDING OUR SUFFERING. AND ABRAHAM'S WEAKNESS IS WHAT PREVENTS IT.
VANESSA, YOU HAVE TRIED TO FIGHT THIS WAR THE WAY HE TAUGHT YOU, AND WHAT HAPPENED?
WHERE IS THE ONE YOU LOVED NOW?
IAN, WHAT YOU FELT, WHEN AKIKO WAS TAKEN, KNOWING WHAT THEY WERE DOING TO HER--
--DO YOU REALLY BELIEVE THEY DESERVE OUR MERCY NOW?
I KNOW THAT I HAVE NOT BEEN A PERFECT LEADER--BUT THESE SO-CALLED TEACHERS, HERE OR IN THE DESERT, EVEN AS THEY TRY TO USE US TO THEIR OWN ENDS--EVEN THEN, THEY ONLY PRETEND TO GRASP THE TRUTH OF WHAT WE ARE.
THEY ARE SELFISH, AND THEY ARE RECKLESS.
BUT WE-- WE KNOW THERE IS A PRICE TO BE PAID FOR THE POWER WE COMMAND. AND SOMETIMES--

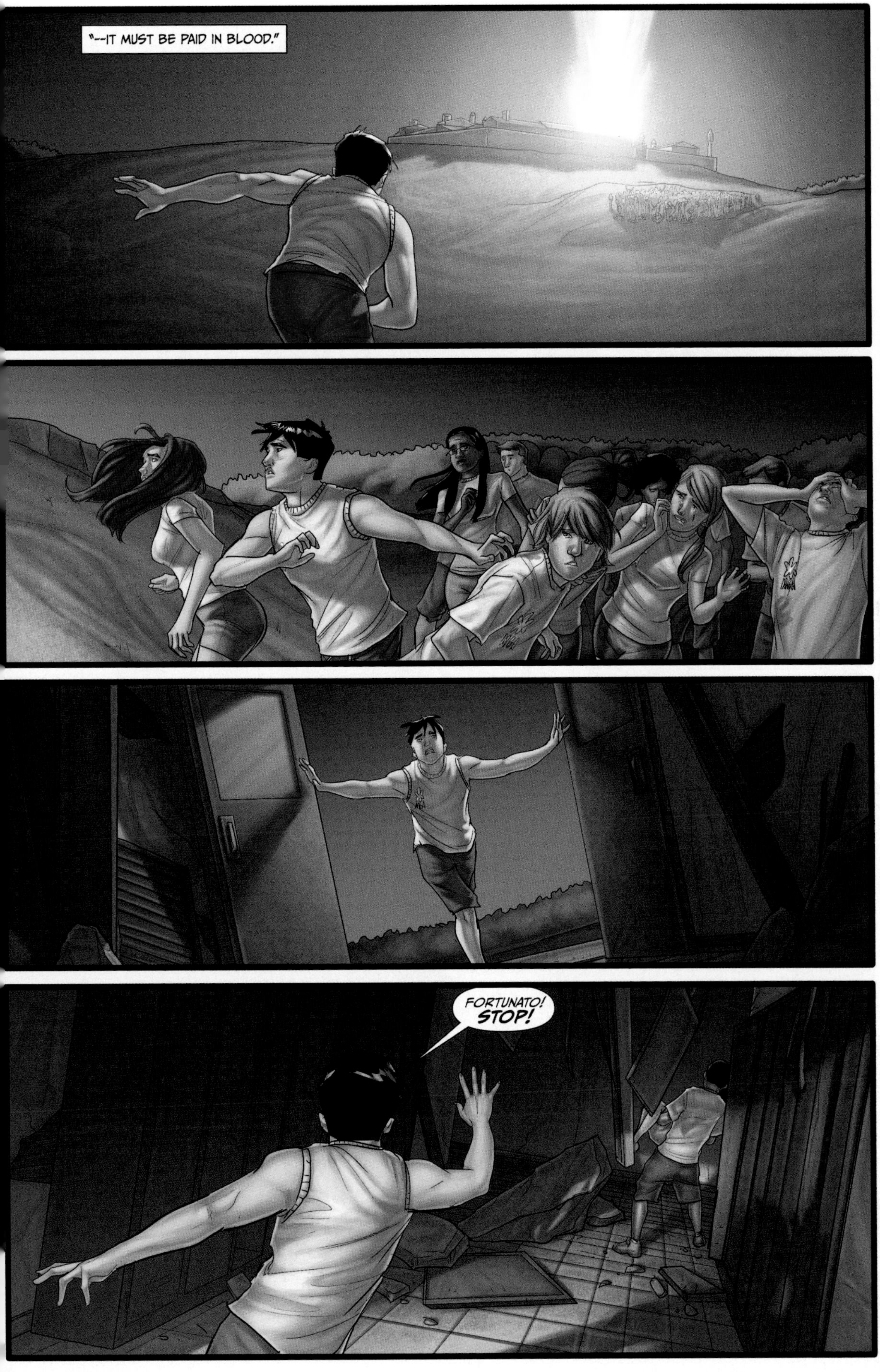
"--IT MUST BE PAID IN BLOOD."
FORTUNATO! STOP!

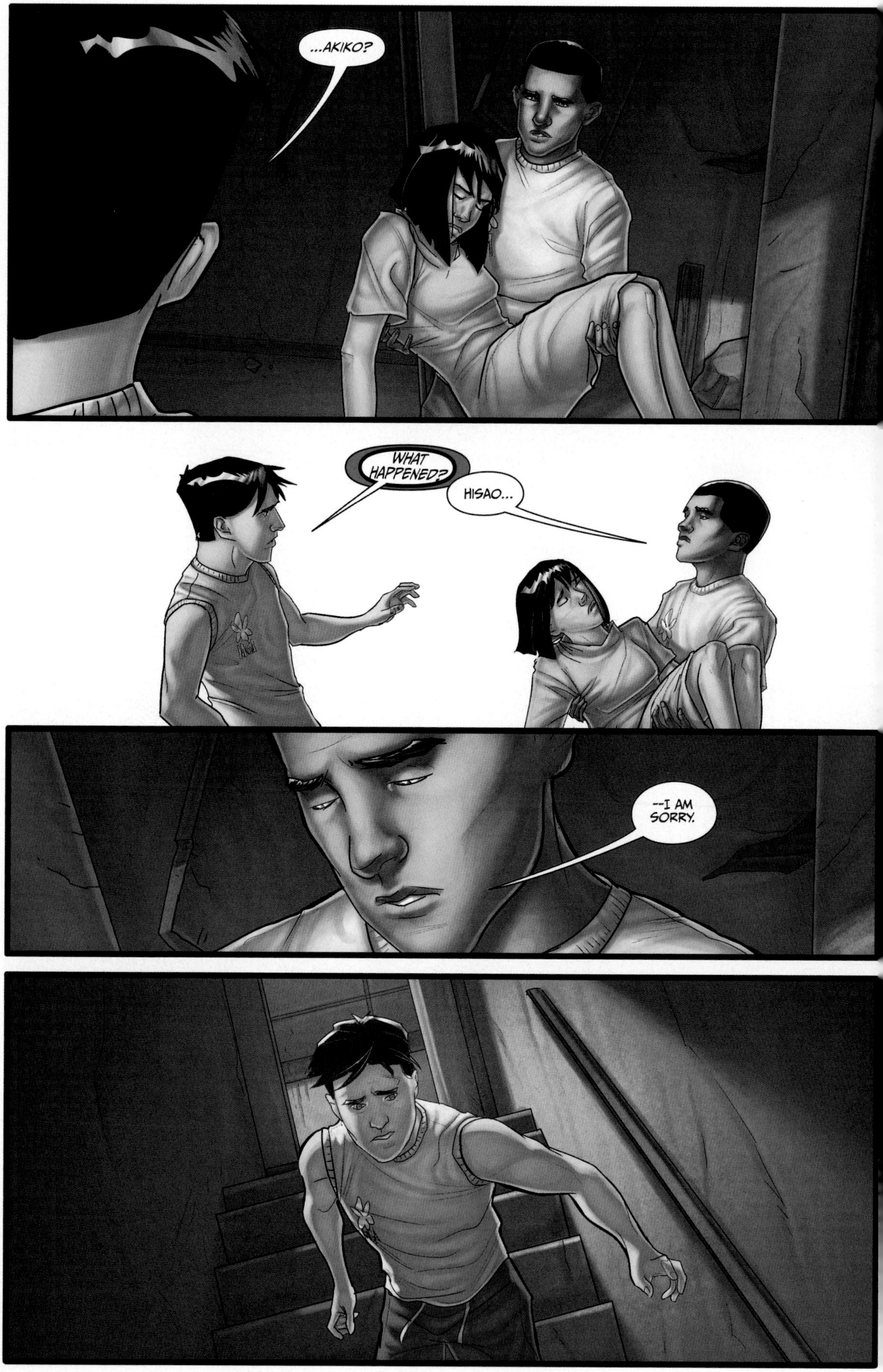
...AKIKO?
WHAT HAPPENED?
HISAO...
--I AM SORRY.

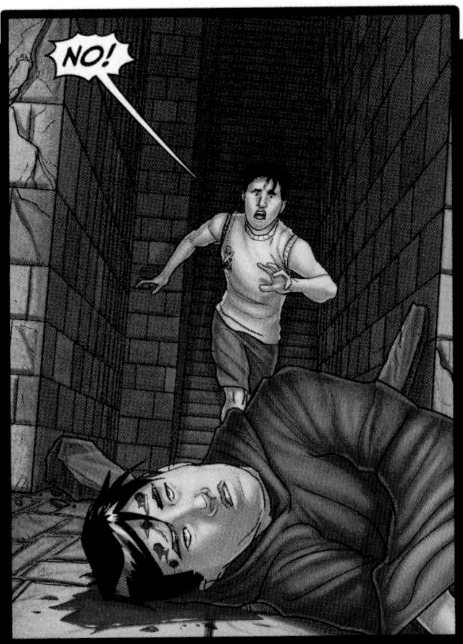
NO!

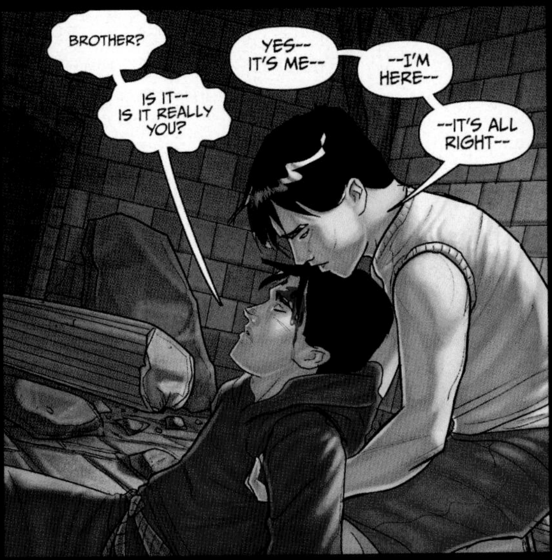
BROTHER?
IS IT-- IS IT REALLY YOU?
YES-- IT'S ME--
--I'M HERE--
--IT'S ALL RIGHT--

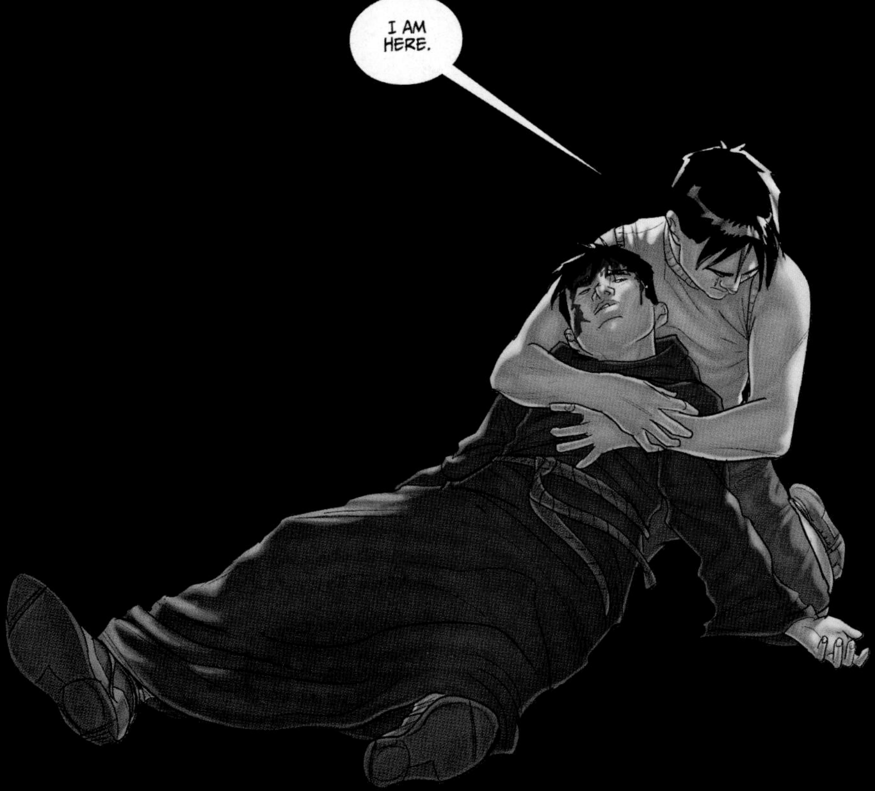
I AM HERE.

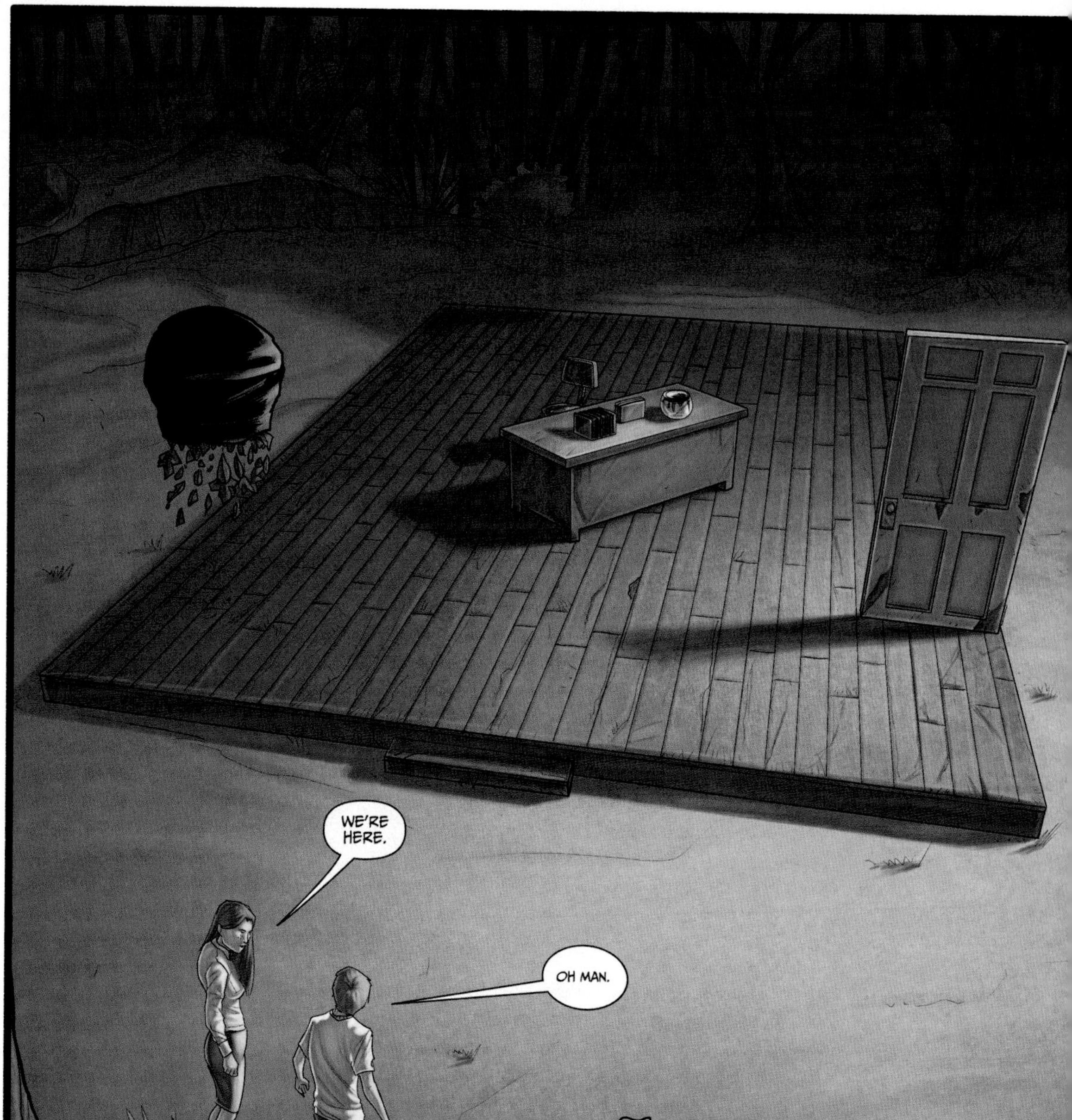
WE'RE HERE.
OH MAN.

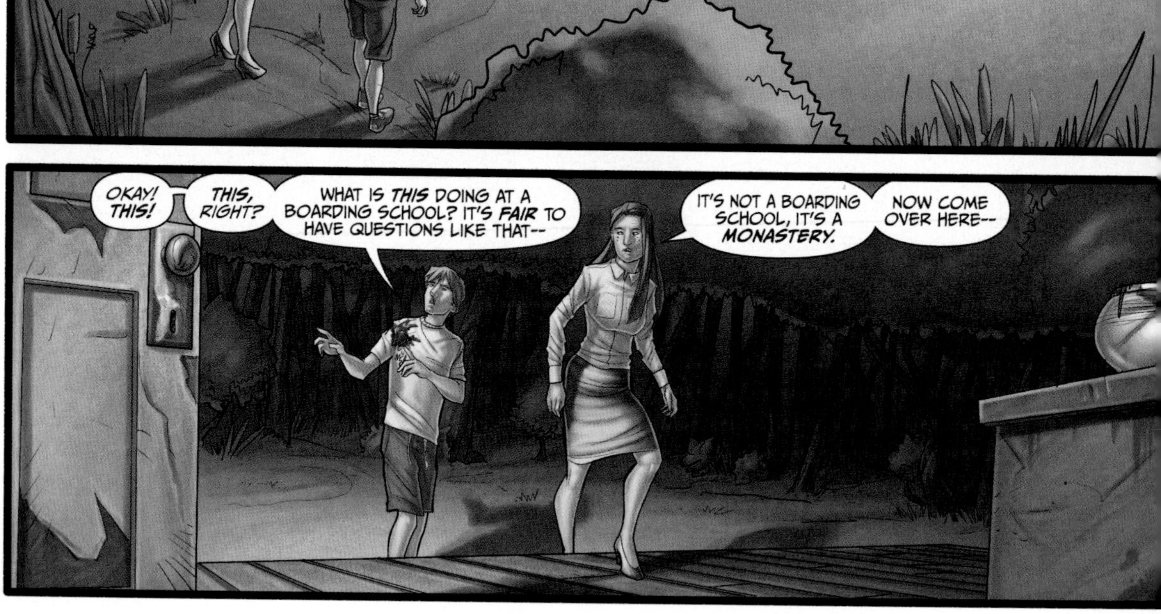
OKAY! THIS!
THIS, RIGHT?
WHAT IS THIS DOING AT A BOARDING SCHOOL? IT'S FAIR TO HAVE QUESTIONS LIKE THAT--
IT'S NOT A BOARDING SCHOOL, IT'S A MONASTERY.
NOW COME OVER HERE--

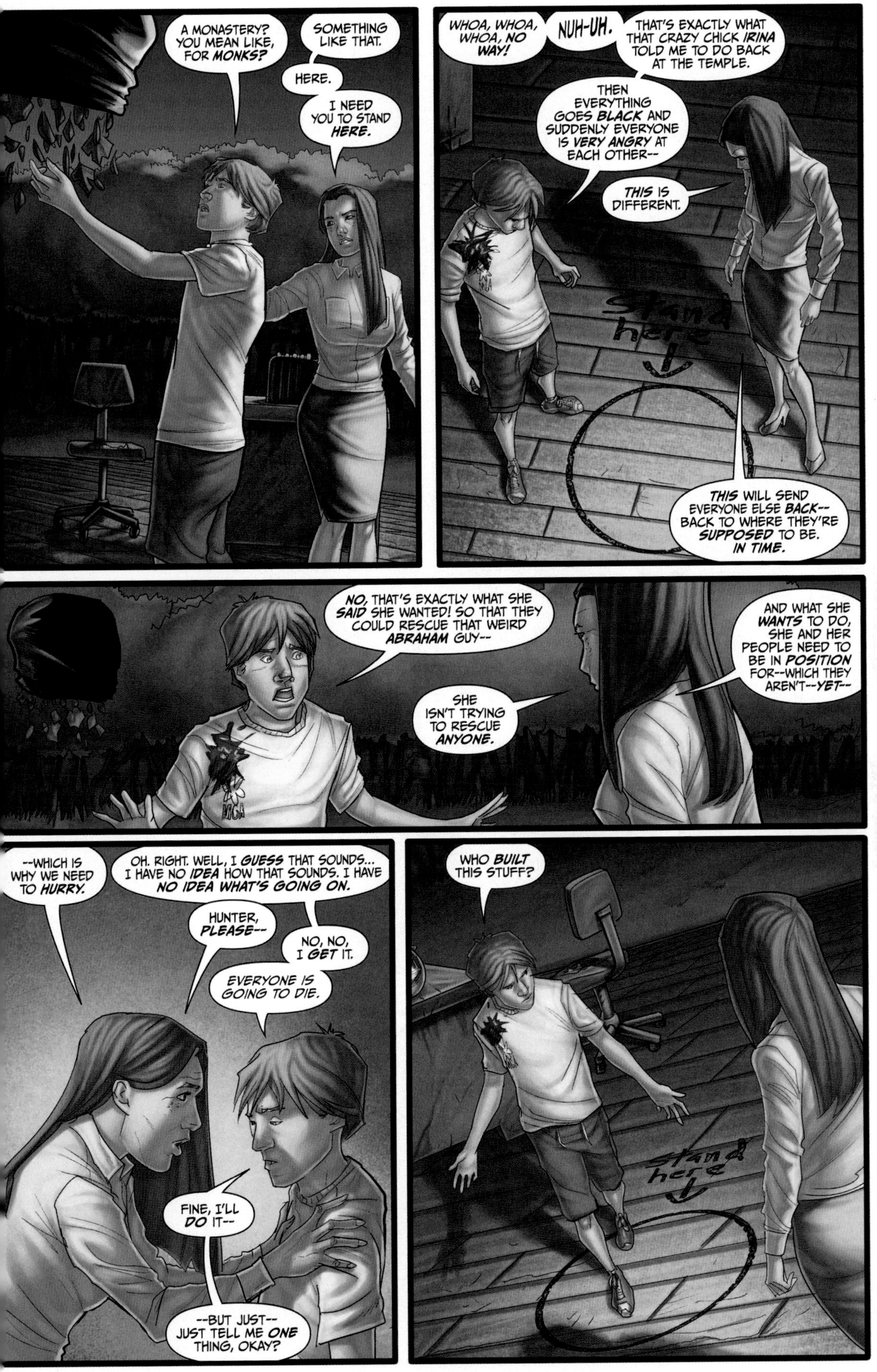
A MONASTERY? YOU MEAN LIKE, FOR MONKS?
SOMETHING LIKE THAT.
HERE.
I NEED YOU TO STAND HERE.
WHOA, WHOA, WHOA, NO WAY!
NUH-UH.
THAT'S EXACTLY WHAT THAT CRAZY CHICK IRINA TOLD ME TO DO BACK AT THE TEMPLE.
THEN EVERYTHING GOES BLACK AND SUDDENLY EVERYONE IS VERY ANGRY AT EACH OTHER--
THIS IS DIFFERENT.
Stand here
THIS WILL SEND EVERYONE ELSE BACK--BACK TO WHERE THEY'RE SUPPOSED TO BE. IN TIME.
NO, THAT'S EXACTLY WHAT SHE SAID SHE WANTED! SO THAT THEY COULD RESCUE THAT WEIRD ABRAHAM GUY--
SHE ISN'T TRYING TO RESCUE ANYONE.
AND WHAT SHE WANTS TO DO, SHE AND HER PEOPLE NEED TO BE IN POSITION FOR--WHICH THEY AREN'T--YET--
--WHICH IS WHY WE NEED TO HURRY.
OH. RIGHT. WELL, I GUESS THAT SOUNDS... I HAVE NO IDEA HOW THAT SOUNDS. I HAVE NO IDEA WHAT'S GOING ON.
HUNTER, PLEASE--
NO, NO, I GET IT.
EVERYONE IS GOING TO DIE.
FINE, I'LL DO IT--
--BUT JUST--JUST TELL ME ONE THING, OKAY?
WHO BUILT THIS STUFF?
Stand here

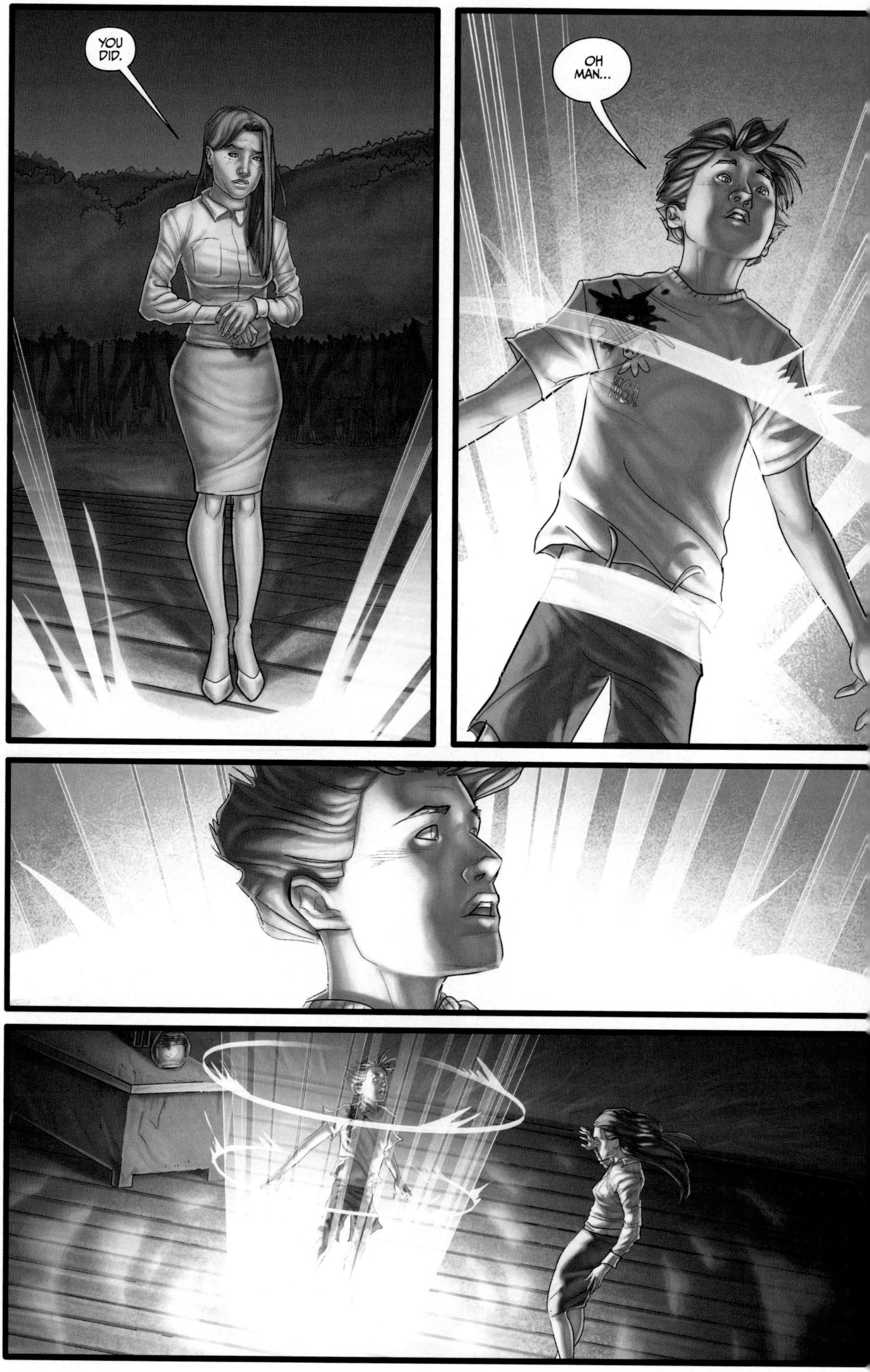
YOU DID.
OH MAN...

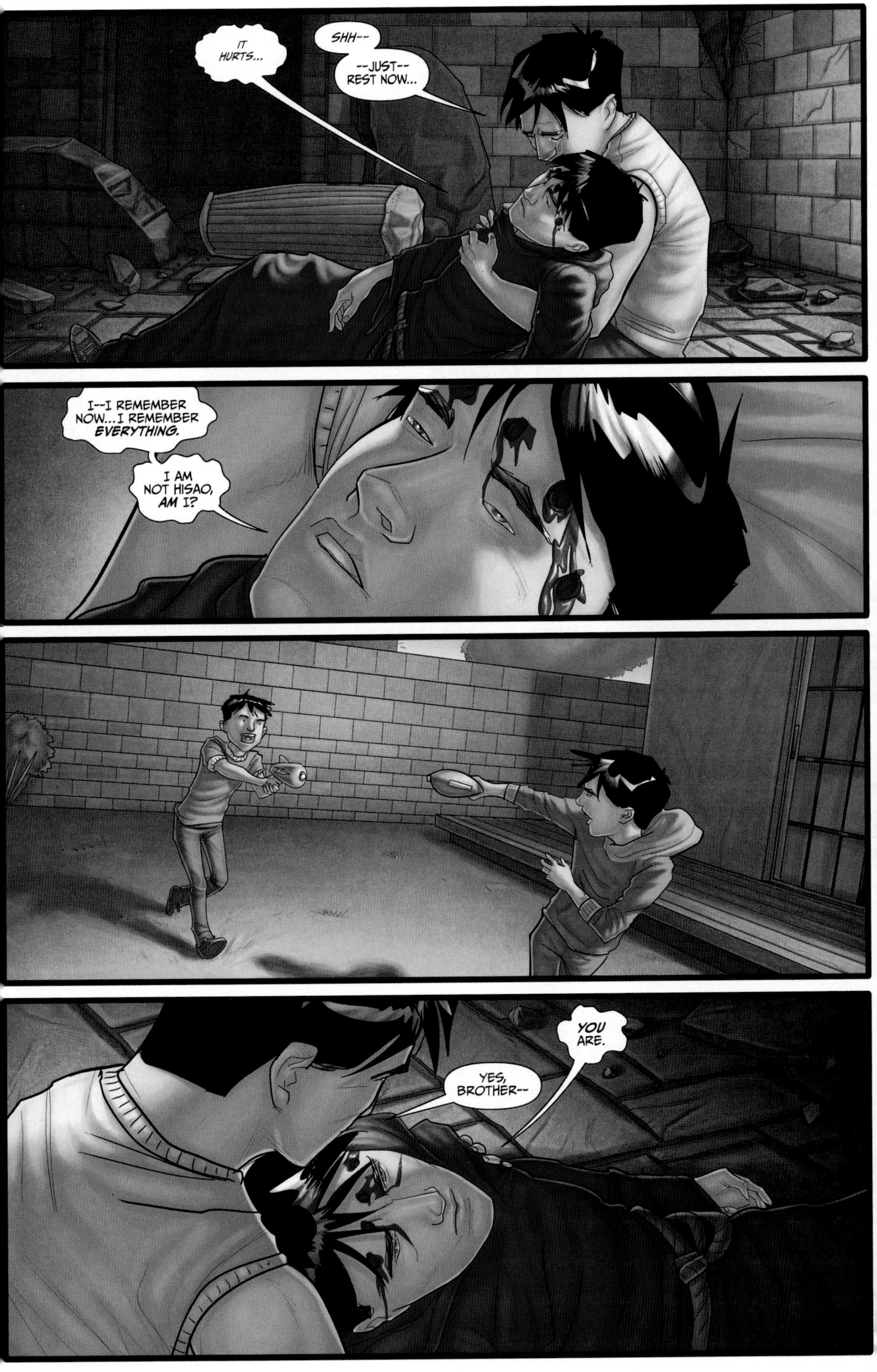
IT HURTS...
SHH--
--JUST-- REST NOW...
I--I REMEMBER NOW...I REMEMBER EVERYTHING.
I AM NOT HISAO, AM I?
YOU ARE.
YES, BROTHER--

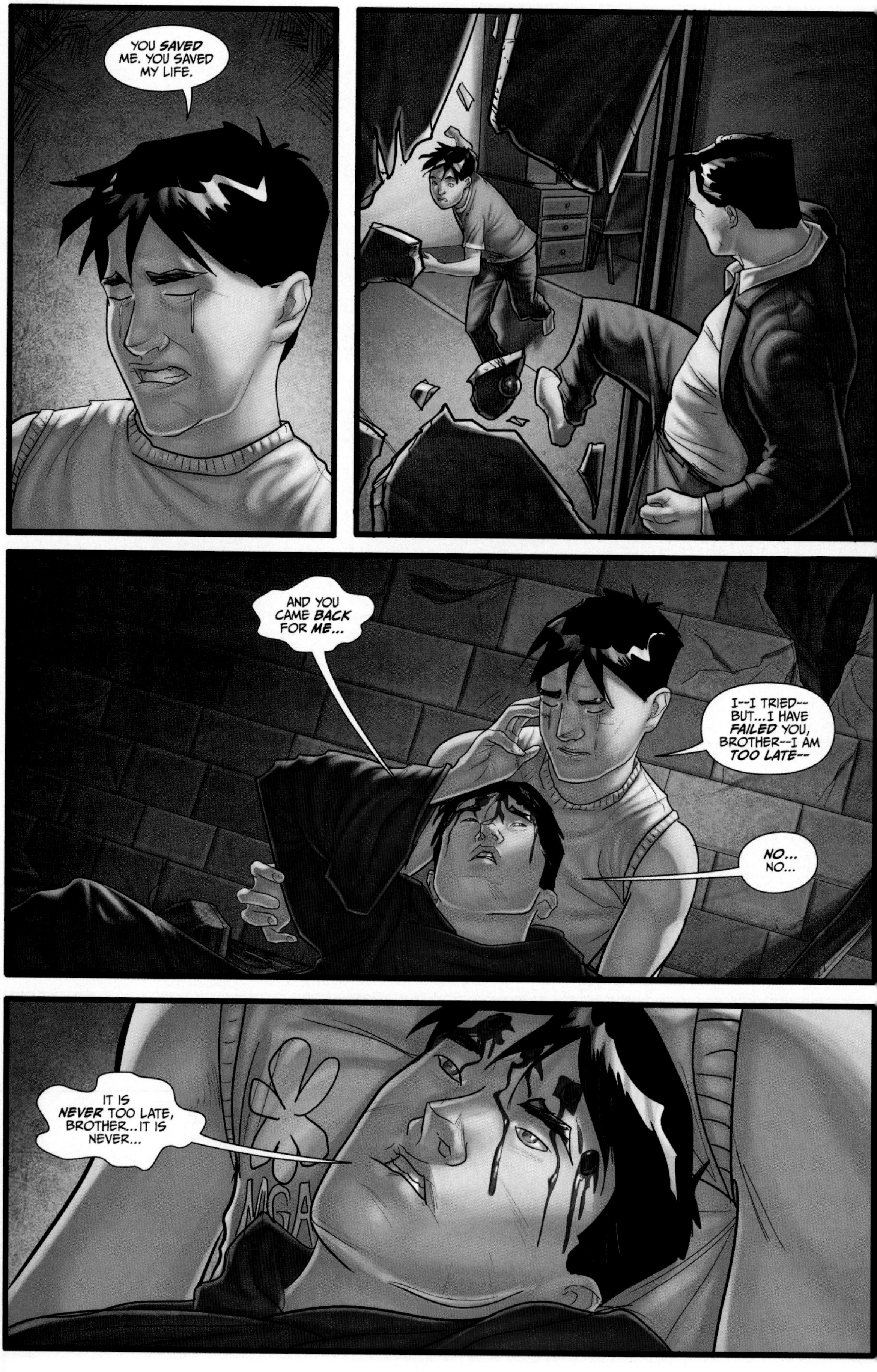
YOU SAVED ME. YOU SAVED MY LIFE.
AND YOU CAME BACK FOR ME...
I--I TRIED-- BUT...I HAVE FAILED YOU, BROTHER--I AM TOO LATE--
NO... NO...
IT IS NEVER TOO LATE, BROTHER...IT IS NEVER...

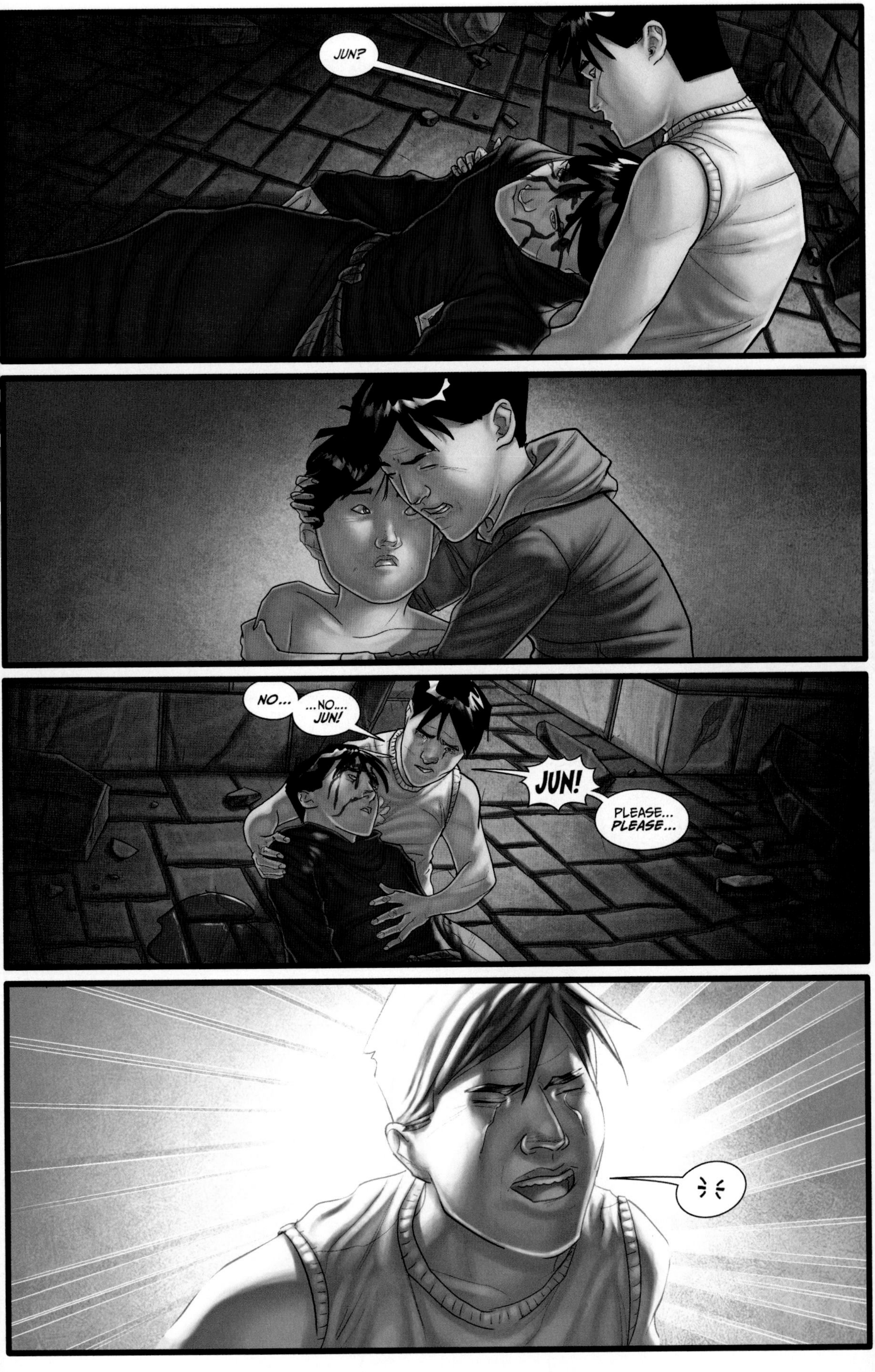
JUN?
NO...
...NO.... JUN!
JUN!
PLEASE... PLEASE...

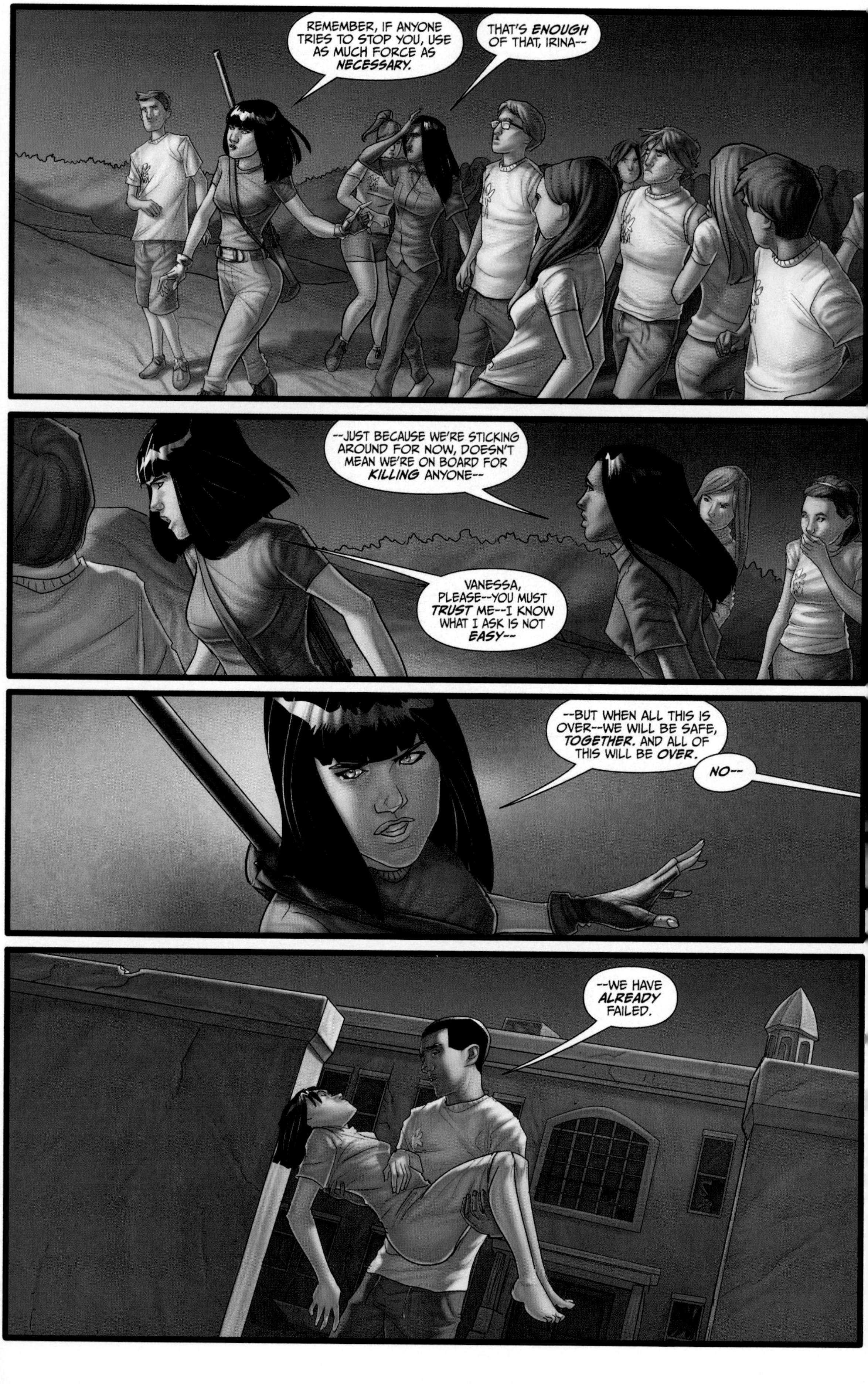
REMEMBER, IF ANYONE TRIES TO STOP YOU, USE AS MUCH FORCE AS NECESSARY.
THAT'S ENOUGH OF THAT, IRINA--
--JUST BECAUSE WE'RE STICKING AROUND FOR NOW, DOESN'T MEAN WE'RE ON BOARD FOR KILLING ANYONE--
VANESSA, PLEASE--YOU MUST TRUST ME--I KNOW WHAT I ASK IS NOT EASY--
--BUT WHEN ALL THIS IS OVER--WE WILL BE SAFE, TOGETHER. AND ALL OF THIS WILL BE OVER.
NO--
--WE HAVE ALREADY FAILED.

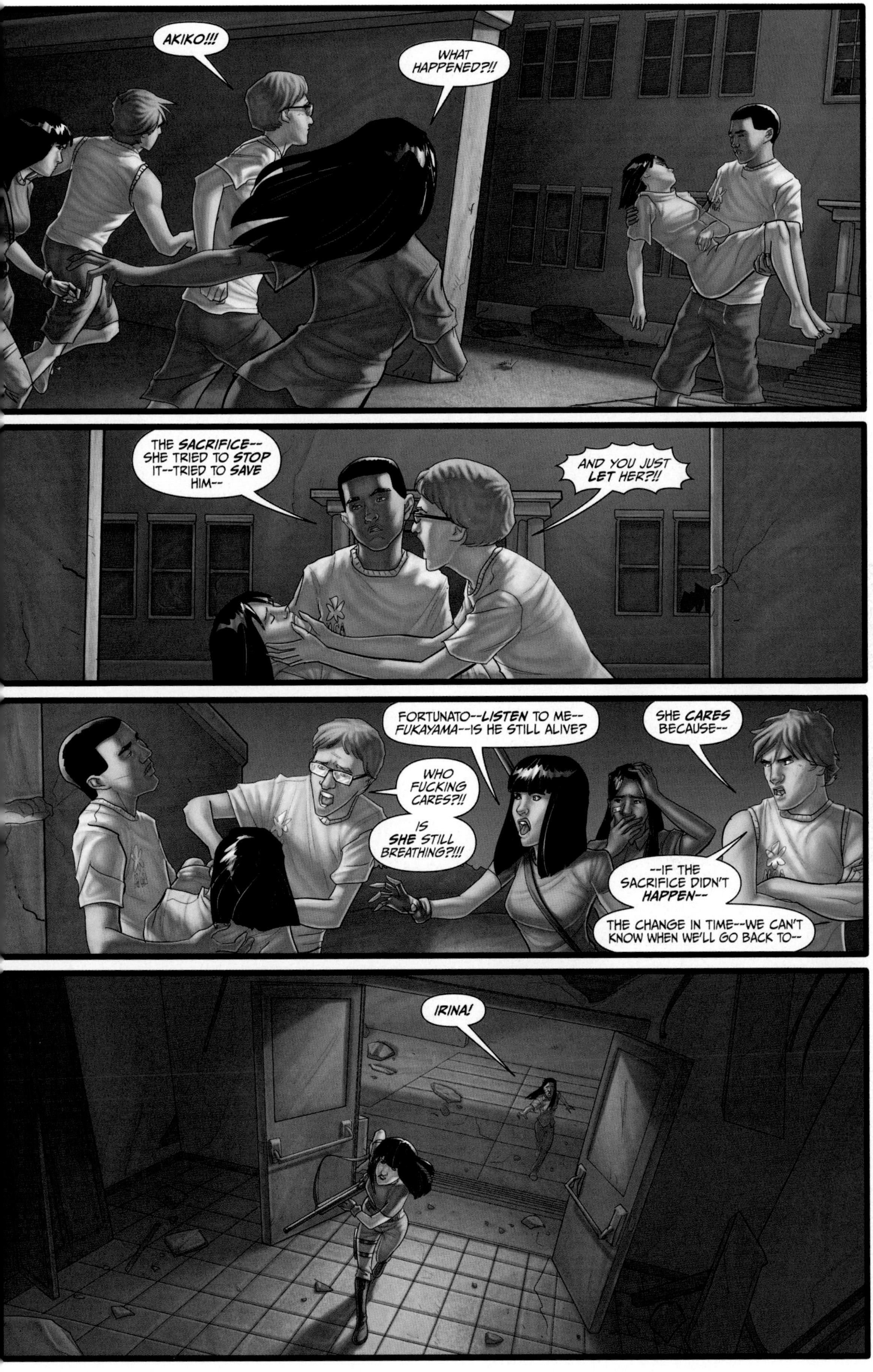

AKIKO!!!
WHAT HAPPENED?!!
THE SACRIFICE-- SHE TRIED TO STOP IT--TRIED TO SAVE HIM--
AND YOU JUST LET HER?!!
WHO FUCKING CARES?!!
IS SHE STILL BREATHING?!!!
FORTUNATO--LISTEN TO ME-- FUKAYAMA--IS HE STILL ALIVE?
SHE CARES BECAUSE--
--IF THE SACRIFICE DIDN'T HAPPEN--
THE CHANGE IN TIME--WE CAN'T KNOW WHEN WE'LL GO BACK TO--
IRINA!

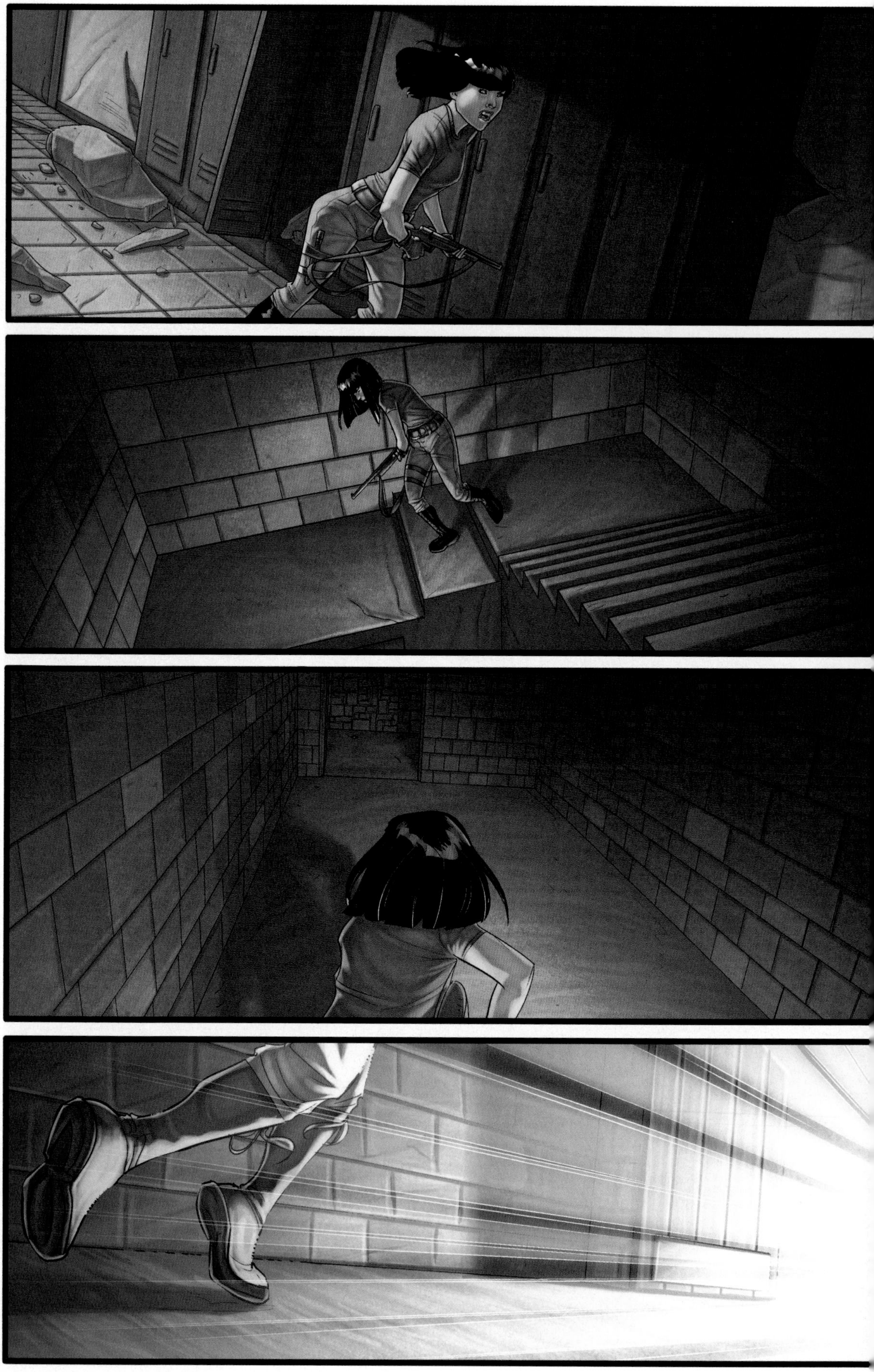

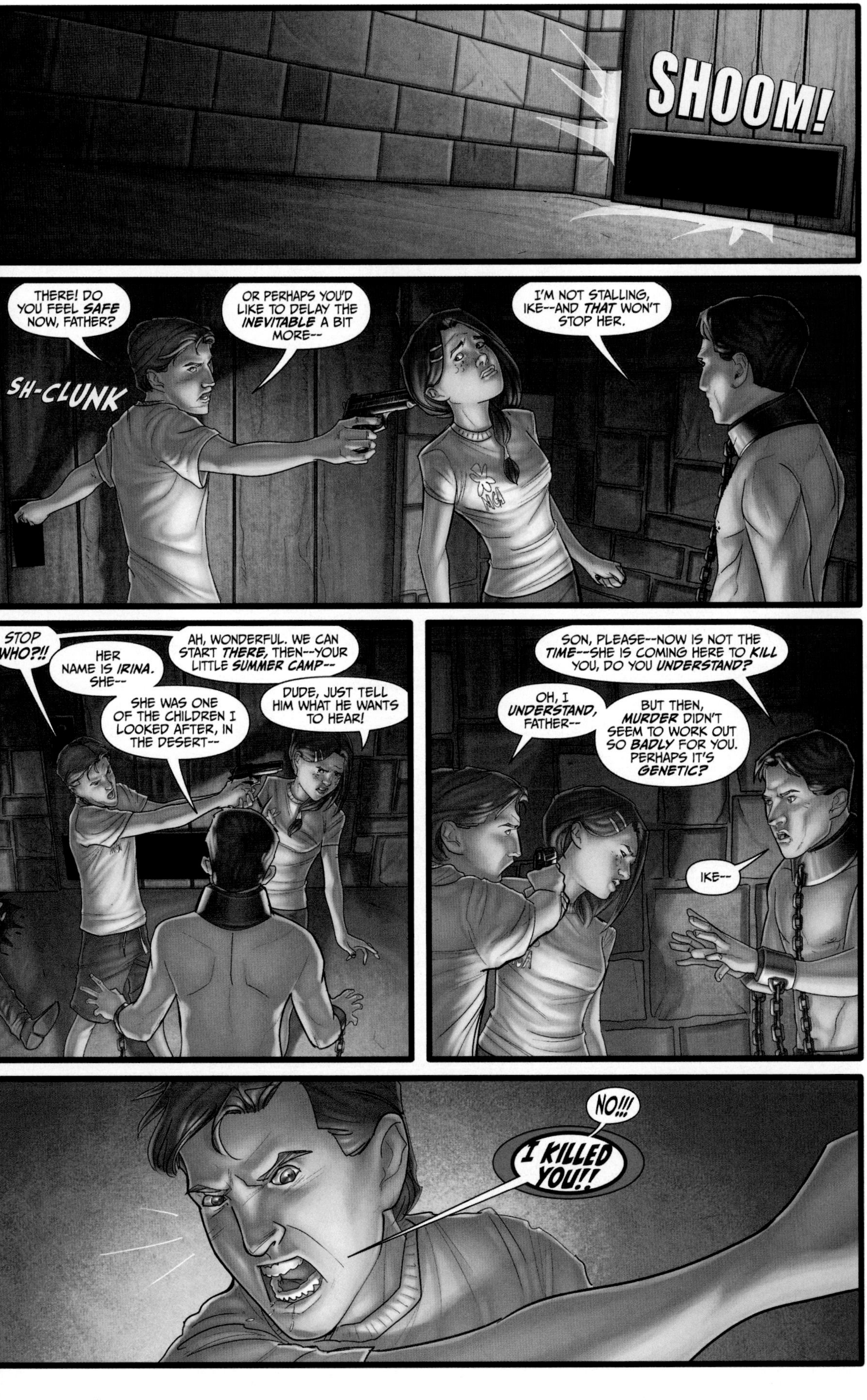
SHOOM!
THERE! DO YOU FEEL SAFE NOW, FATHER?
SH-CLUNK
OR PERHAPS YOU'D LIKE TO DELAY THE INEVITABLE A BIT MORE--
I'M NOT STALLING, IKE--AND THAT WON'T STOP HER.
STOP WHO?!!
AH, WONDERFUL. WE CAN START THERE, THEN--YOUR LITTLE SUMMER CAMP--
HER NAME IS IRINA. SHE--
SHE WAS ONE OF THE CHILDREN I LOOKED AFTER, IN THE DESERT--
DUDE, JUST TELL HIM WHAT HE WANTS TO HEAR!
SON, PLEASE--NOW IS NOT THE TIME--SHE IS COMING HERE TO KILL YOU, DO YOU UNDERSTAND?
OH, I UNDERSTAND, FATHER--
BUT THEN, MURDER DIDN'T SEEM TO WORK OUT SO BADLY FOR YOU. PERHAPS IT'S GENETIC?
IKE--
NO!!!
I KILLED YOU!!

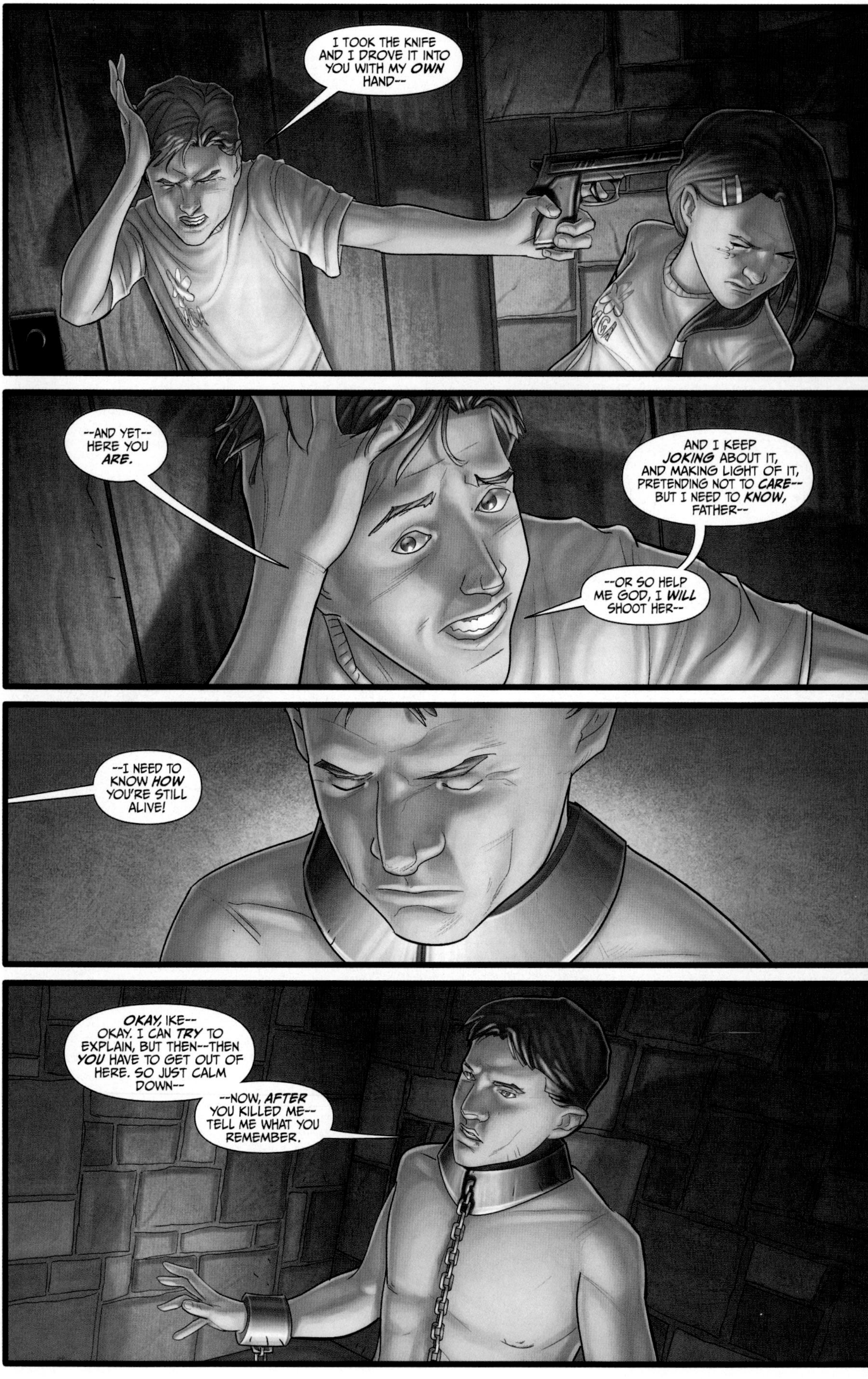
I TOOK THE KNIFE AND I DROVE IT INTO YOU WITH MY OWN HAND--
--AND YET-- HERE YOU ARE.
AND I KEEP JOKING ABOUT IT, AND MAKING LIGHT OF IT, PRETENDING NOT TO CARE-- BUT I NEED TO KNOW, FATHER--
--OR SO HELP ME GOD, I WILL SHOOT HER--
--I NEED TO KNOW HOW YOU'RE STILL ALIVE!
OKAY, IKE-- OKAY. I CAN TRY TO EXPLAIN, BUT THEN--THEN YOU HAVE TO GET OUT OF HERE. SO JUST CALM DOWN--
--NOW, AFTER YOU KILLED ME-- TELL ME WHAT YOU REMEMBER.

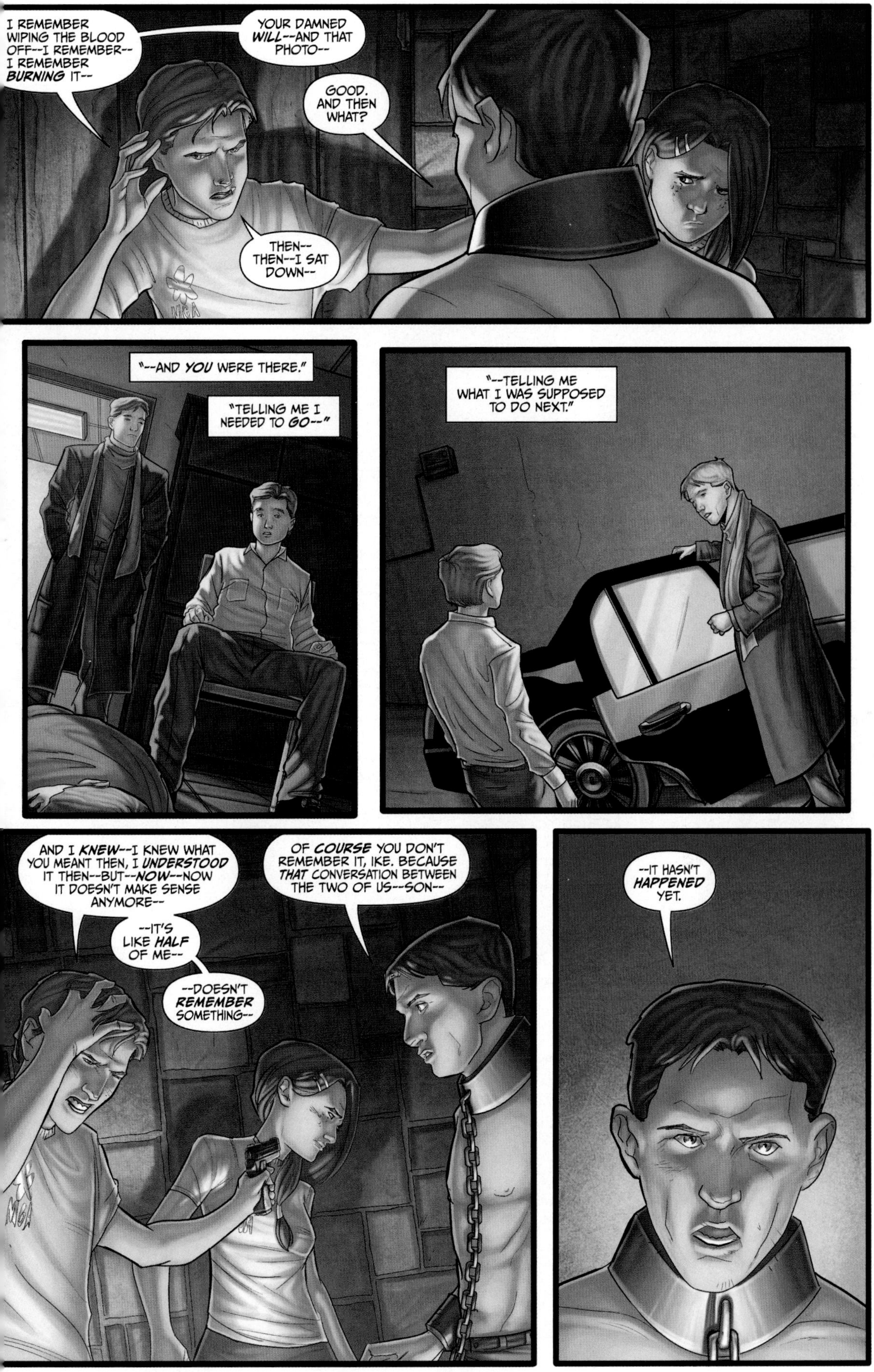
I REMEMBER WIPING THE BLOOD OFF--I REMEMBER--I REMEMBER BURNING IT--
YOUR DAMNED WILL--AND THAT PHOTO--
GOOD. AND THEN WHAT?
THEN--THEN--I SAT DOWN--
"--AND YOU WERE THERE."
"TELLING ME I NEEDED TO GO--"
"--TELLING ME WHAT I WAS SUPPOSED TO DO NEXT."
AND I KNEW--I KNEW WHAT YOU MEANT THEN, I UNDERSTOOD IT THEN--BUT--NOW--NOW IT DOESN'T MAKE SENSE ANYMORE--
--IT'S LIKE HALF OF ME--
--DOESN'T REMEMBER SOMETHING--
OF COURSE YOU DON'T REMEMBER IT, IKE. BECAUSE THAT CONVERSATION BETWEEN THE TWO OF US--SON--
--IT HASN'T HAPPENED YET.

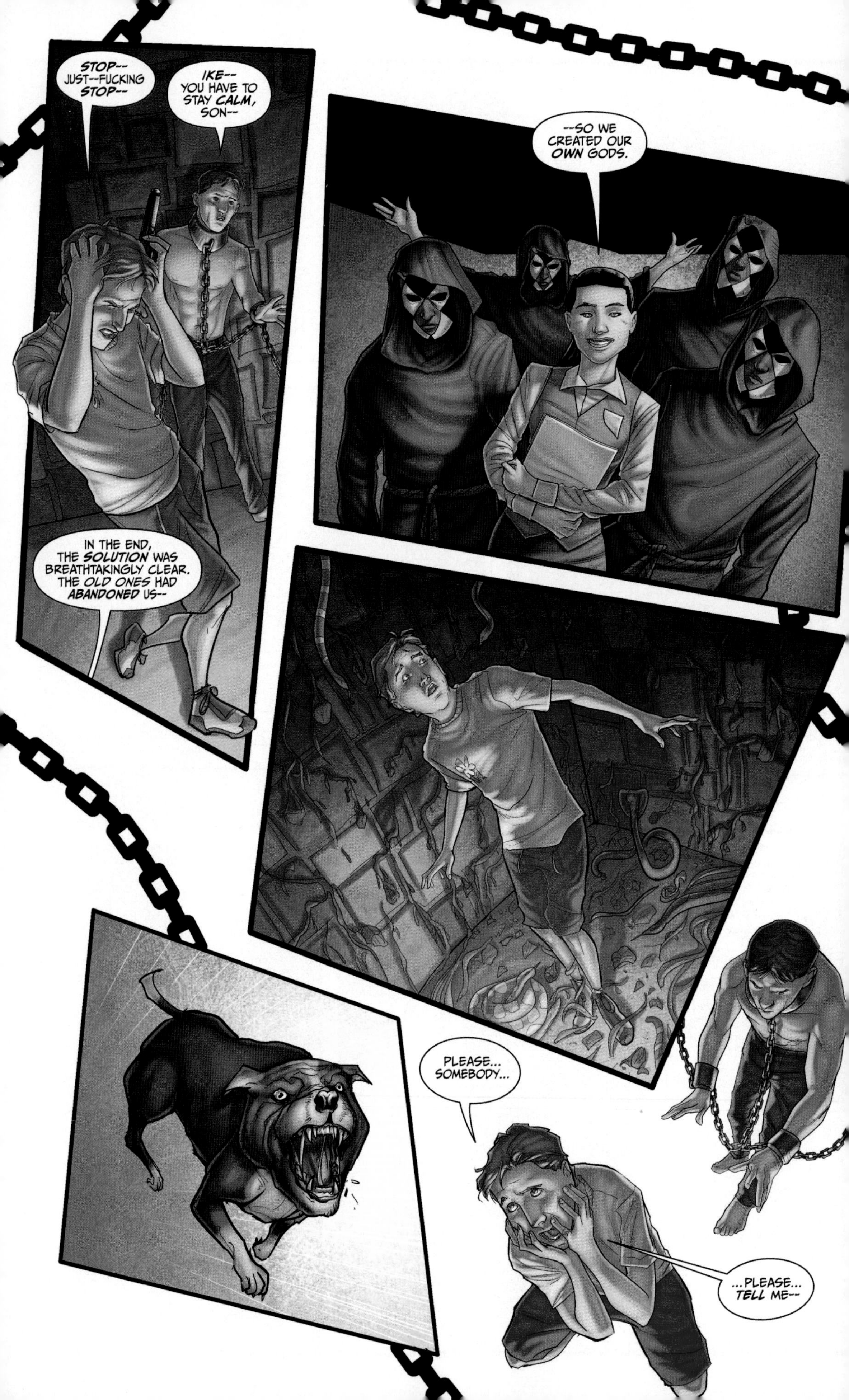
STOP--
JUST--FUCKING
STOP--
IKE--
YOU HAVE TO
STAY CALM,
SON--
IN THE END,
THE SOLUTION WAS
BREATHTAKINGLY CLEAR.
THE OLD ONES HAD
ABANDONED US--
--SO WE
CREATED OUR
OWN GODS.
PLEASE...
SOMEBODY...
...PLEASE...
TELL ME--

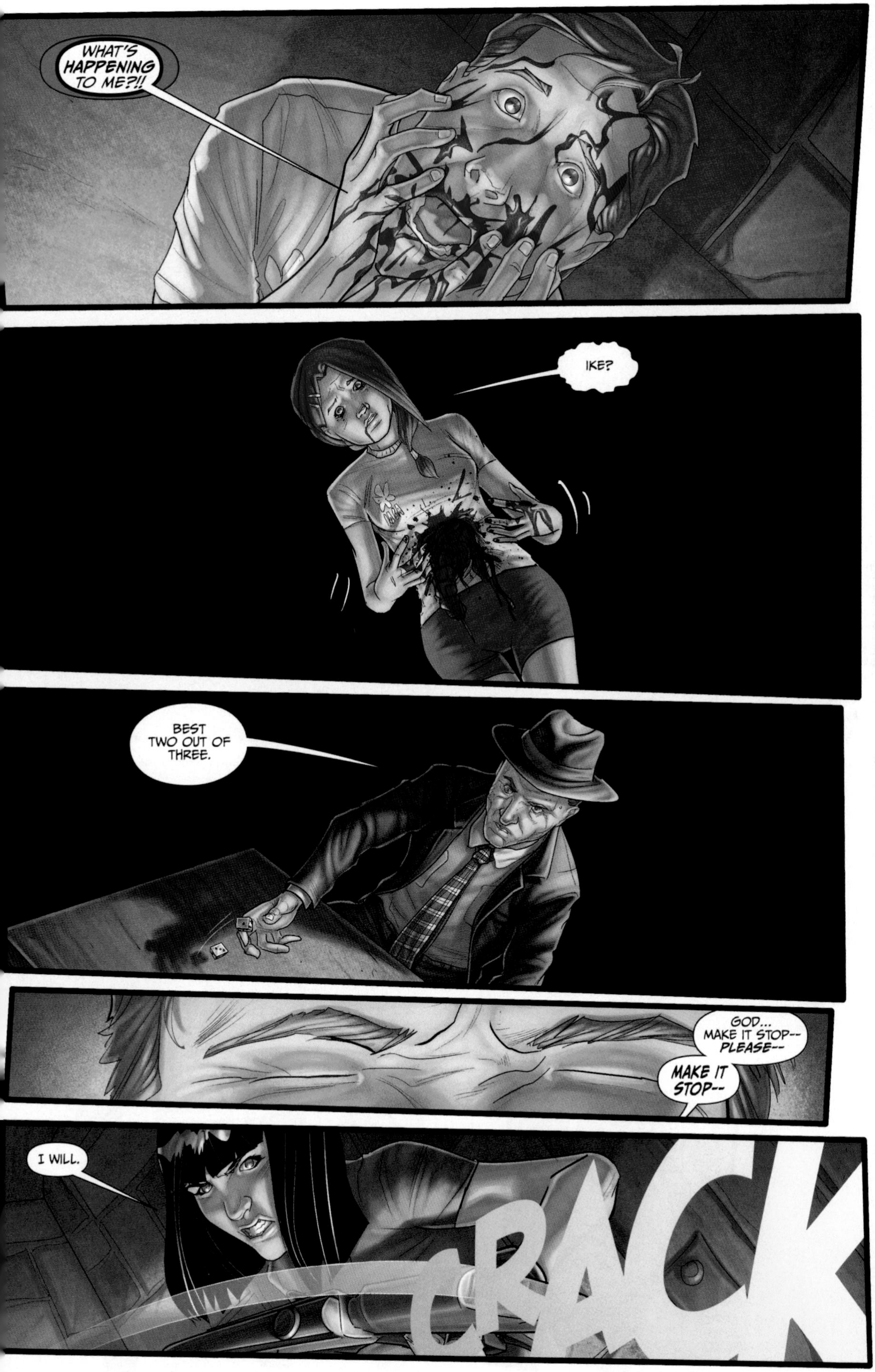
WHAT'S HAPPENING TO ME?!!
IKE?
BEST TWO OUT OF THREE.
GOD... MAKE IT STOP-- PLEASE--
MAKE IT STOP--
I WILL.
CRACK

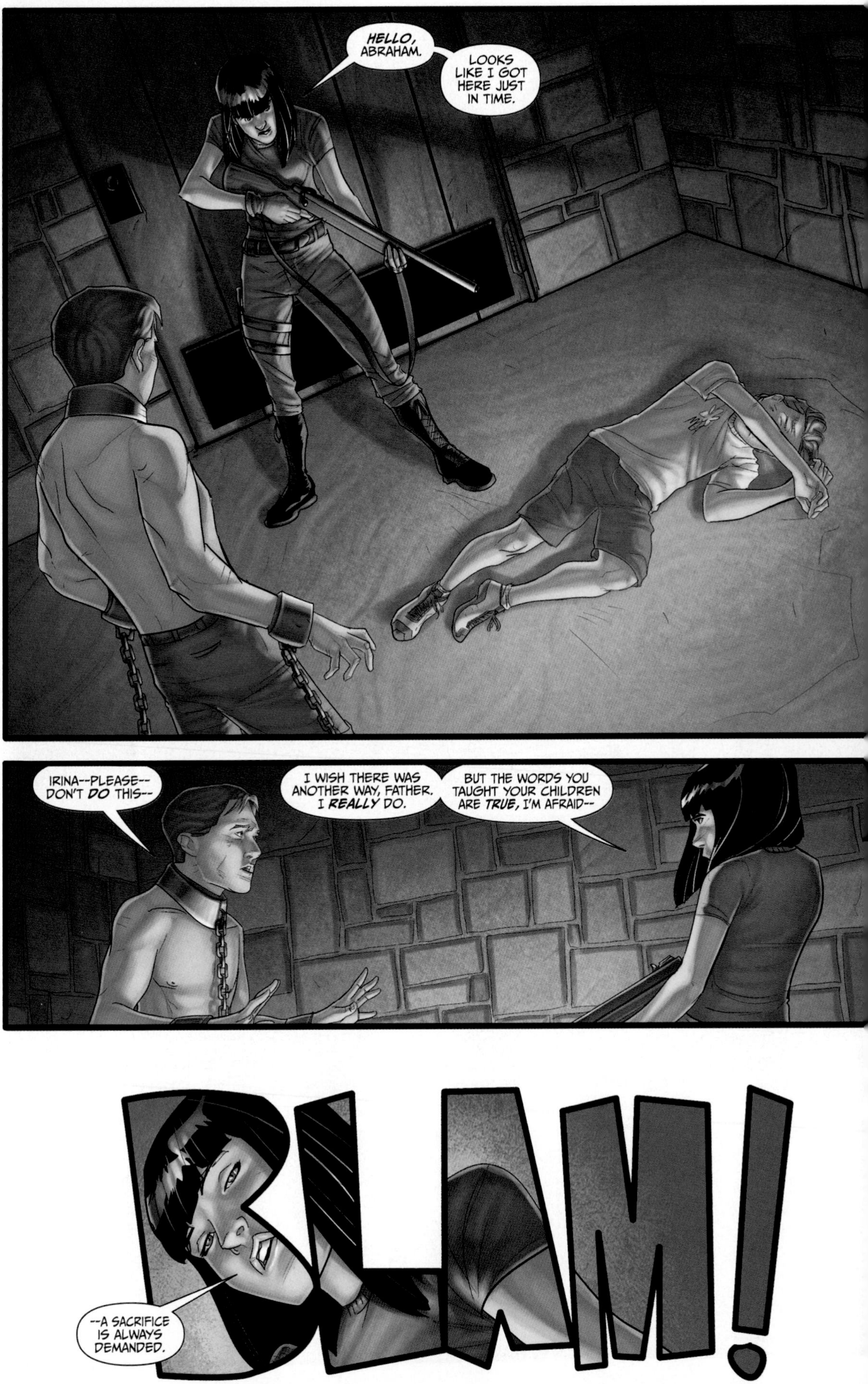
HELLO, ABRAHAM.
LOOKS LIKE I GOT HERE JUST IN TIME.
IRINA--PLEASE-- DON'T DO THIS--
I WISH THERE WAS ANOTHER WAY, FATHER. I REALLY DO.
BUT THE WORDS YOU TAUGHT YOUR CHILDREN ARE TRUE, I'M AFRAID--
BLAM!
--A SACRIFICE IS ALWAYS DEMANDED.

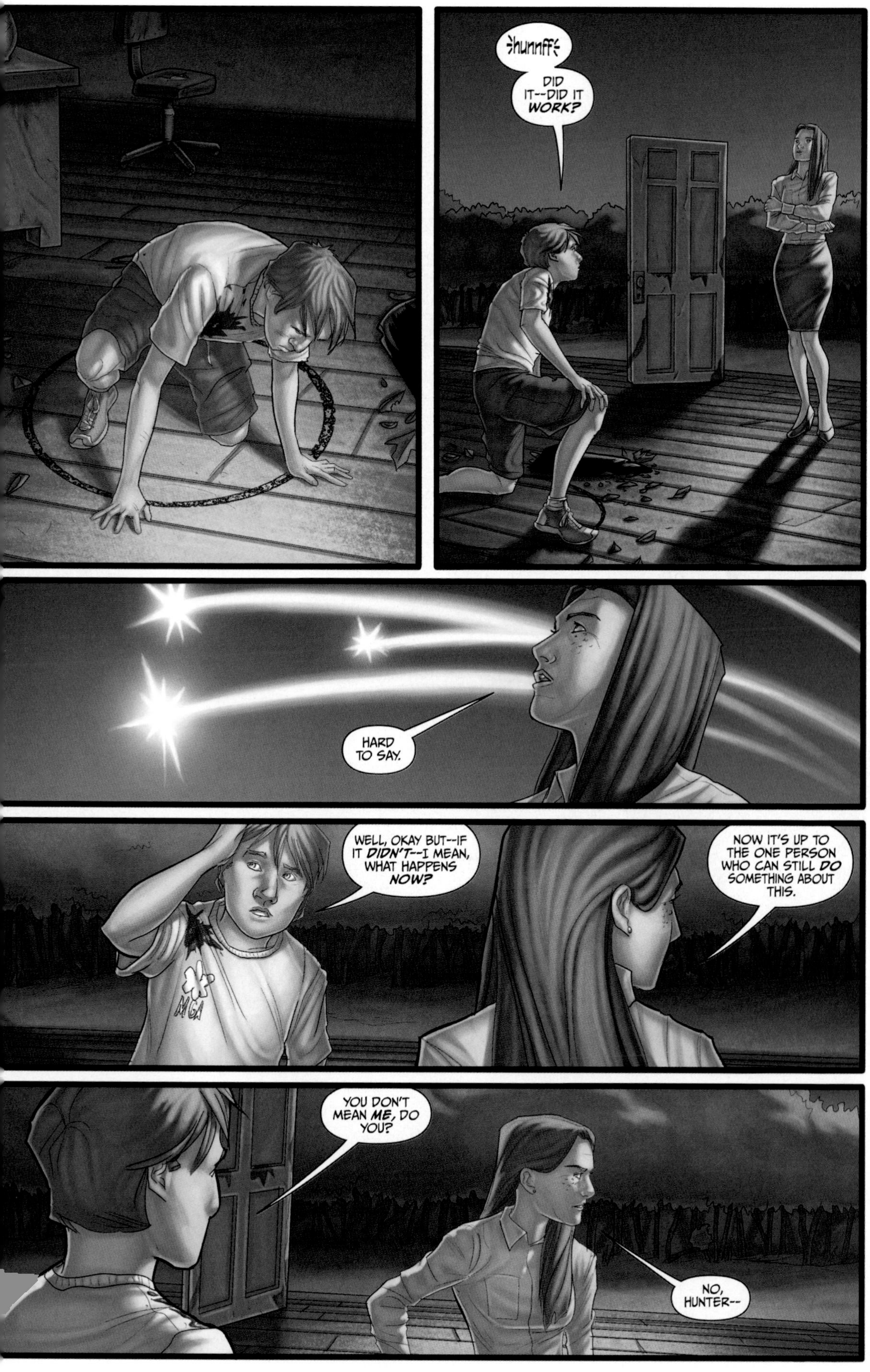
HUNNFF
DID IT--DID IT **WORK?**
HARD TO SAY.
WELL, OKAY BUT--IF IT ***DIDN'T***--I MEAN, WHAT HAPPENS ***NOW?***
NOW IT'S UP TO THE ONE PERSON WHO CAN STILL ***DO*** SOMETHING ABOUT THIS.
YOU DON'T MEAN ***ME,*** DO YOU?
NO, HUNTER--

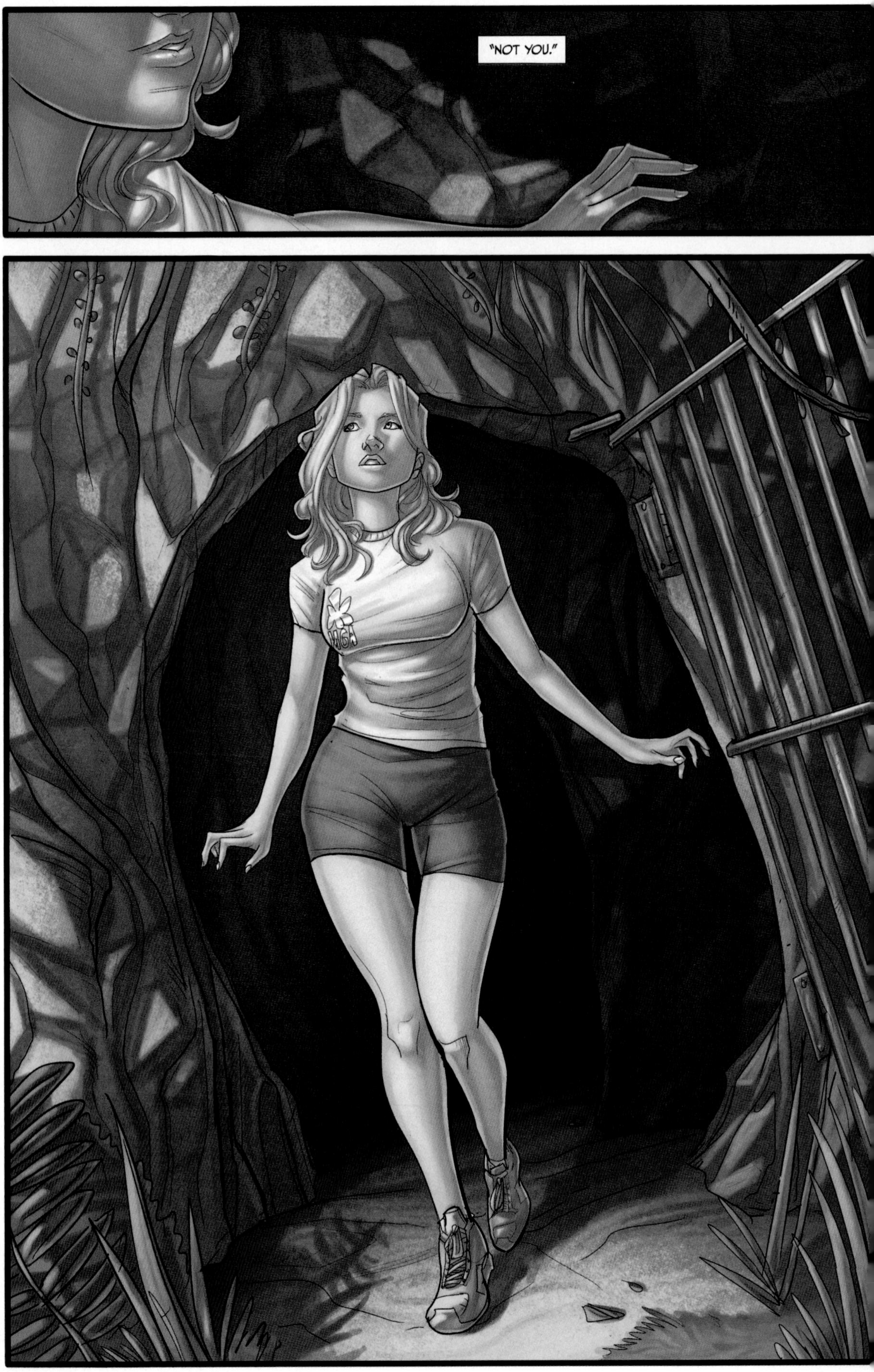
"NOT YOU."

extras

THE ART OF JOE EISMA

Distinctive character design is one of the key elements of any successful story. Morning Glories presents a real challenge with such a large ensemble cast, yet over the span of Season One, artist Joe Eisma has worked hard to ensure we easily recognize each and every cast member.

THE ORIGINAL GLORIES

hunter

ike

jade

jun

casey

zoe

AT LAST COUNT

According to Joe's own estimate (discounting non-prominent roles), he has drawn 99 distinctive characters since the inception of Morning Glories.

MEET THE TRUANTS

akiko

fortunato

ian

guillaume

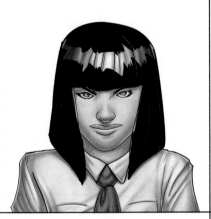

irina

vanessa